FOUNDING FRIENDSHIP

George Washington, James Madison,

and the Creation of the

American Republic

FOUNDING FRIENDSHIP

George Washington, James Madison,

and the Creation of the

American Republic

Stuart Leibiger

University Press of Virginia

Charlottesville and London

The University Press of Virginia
© 1999 by the Rector and Visitors of the University of Virginia
All rights reserved
Printed in the United States of America

First published 1999

∞The paper used in this publication meets the minimum requirements
of the American National Standard for Information Sciences—Permanence
of Paper for Printed Library Materials, ANSI Z39.48-1984.

Library of Congress Cataloging-in-Publication Data

Leibiger, Stuart Eric.
Founding friendship : George Washington, James Madison, and the
creation of the American republic / Stuart Leibiger
    p.   cm.
Includes bibliographical references and index.
ISBN 0-8139-1882-0 (cloth : alk. paper)
1. Washington, George, 1732–1799—Friends and associates.
2. Madison, James, 1751–1836—Friends and associates.
3. United States—Politics and government—1783–1789
4. United States—Politics and governments—1775–1783.   I. Title.
E312.29.L45   1999
973.4'1'0922—dc21   99-19854
                                                    CIP

Frontispiece: *The Resignation of General Washington, at Annapolis, Maryland,
23 Dec. 1783,* by John Trumbull, 1824. As president, Madison approved Trumbull's
decision to include the resignation as one of four subjects to commemorate the
Revolution. Trumbull took the license of inserting Madison in the painting
(far back wall, just to the right of the left doorway). (Courtesy of
the U.S. Capitol Historical Society)

For my father

Gustave A. Leibiger

1930–1998

Select the most deserving only for your friendships, and before this becomes intimate, weigh their dispositions and character *well*. True friendship is a plant of slow growth; to be sincere, there must be a congeniality of temper and pursuits.

—George Washington, 28 November 1796

CONTENTS

ILLUSTRATIONS

ACKNOWLEDGMENTS

THIS BOOK, many years in the making, could not have been possible without seemingly endless hours of assistance from countless individuals. While it would be difficult for me to remember, let alone recognize, the many people who contributed in one way or another over the years, I would like to thank those who helped the most. Professor W. W. Abbot of *The Papers of George Washington* reassured me that the Washington-Madison collaboration was a topic worth pursuing. Professor Don Higginbotham of the University of North Carolina at Chapel Hill directed the dissertation upon which this book is based with patience, enthusiasm, and encouragement. The following scholars, who read and commented upon the entire manuscript, offered helpful suggestions, caught numerous factual errors, and steered me away from dubious interpretations: Kenneth R. Bowling, Peter A. Coclanis, Drew R. McCoy, Donald R. Mathews, John M. Murrin, John K. Nelson, the late Eugene R. Sheridan, and Harry Watson.

The professionalism of the staff at the University Press of Virginia, especially Dick Holway and Ellie Goodman, made it easy for me to choose a publisher. Dick patiently answered questions and solved problems for me for nearly four years. James Rees of Mount Vernon and my colleagues in the History Department at La Salle University provided letters of support for my various grant applications. I would like to thank my students at La Salle University (especially those in my fall 1997 Revolutionary America class) who read and discussed drafts of various chapters. The staffs of numerous libraries and museums, too, cheerfully fulfilled my many needs and requests. Gervasio Ramirez showed me how to produce camera-ready line art. Nor would this book have been possible without the financial support of the History Department and Graduate School at the University of North Carolina, the Virginia Historical Society, and the Leaves and Grants Committee at La Salle University.

My parents, Gisela W. Leibiger and the late Gustave A. Leibiger, deserve recognition for their steady love, encouragement, and support over the years, as do my siblings, Carol, Marion, and Steven, and their families. I owe a special, heartfelt debt of gratitude to Jennifer Mager for coming into my life at a critical personal juncture. Without her love and companionship this book might not have seen the light of day.

Finally, I would like to thank those who, upon learning what my book was about, exclaimed, "I never knew that George Washington and James Madison were close friends." Such reactions renewed my drive to see this project through. All too often, when contemporary Americans mention Washington and Madison in the same sentence, the context leaves something to be desired. Take, for example, the following ESPN press release in February 1992: "In honor of President's Day, ESPN will televise the basketball game between George Washington and James Madison. These teams will probably present a better matchup than the two presidents would have. Washington was 6-2 (quite tall for that time) and Madison was the shortest president at 5-2."

FOUNDING FRIENDSHIP

George Washington, James Madison,

and the Creation of the

American Republic

INTRODUCTION

T HE COLLABORATION between James Madison and Thomas Jefferson has attracted considerable attention from historians, becoming the subject of a monograph, a volume of published lectures, and a three-volume edition of the entire correspondence between the two men.[1] Others have argued that either the Thomas Jefferson–John Adams or the James Madison–Alexander Hamilton collaboration played the primary role in the founding.[2] I contend, however, that the George Washington–James Madison collaboration, which has received little notice, was the most important and revealing pairing of all, outweighing all other permutations during the all-important 1785–90 period.[3]

Madison's relationship with Washington did not last even one-fourth as long as his friendship with Jefferson, but it was more indispensable to the constitutional revolution of 1787–88 and the federal government established under it. The relationship flourished because each possessed something the other needed. Washington relied heavily on Madison's advice, pen, and legislative skill. Madison, in turn, found Washington's prestige essential for achieving his goals for the new nation, especially a stronger federal government. Although in the early 1790s the Washington-Madison collaboration became eclipsed by two new relationships (the Madison-Jefferson and the Washington-Hamilton pairings), it remains the founding's central team overall.

Washington and Madison shared parallel careers marked by telling points of convergence and divergence. Both men retired to Virginia from Continental service in 1783, both attended the 1787 Federal Convention, both assumed public office under the new Constitution in 1789, and both retired to Virginia again in 1797. The rise of the friendship between these two crucially important Virginians during the mid-1780s provides a case study in the emergence of the Federalist persuasion in reaction to the political, social, and economic problems of

Revolutionary and Confederation America. Their gradual estrangement during Washington's second term as president (1793–97) illuminates the growth of the Republican counterpersuasion in response to the advance of Hamiltonianism. I demonstrate that during the 1780s and into the 1790s, the two men did not differ as widely as most other Federalists and Republicans. On a scale running from liberty, localism, and states' rights on the left to order, cosmopolitanism, and consolidation on the right, Madison falls slightly to the left of center and Washington a bit to the right of it. The extremities are occupied by Jefferson and the more radical Republicans on the left and by Hamilton and the High Federalists on the right.

During the 1780s Washington and Madison struggled to conceptualize a form of government that would be responsive to the will of the majority without violating the rights of minorities. Refusing to sacrifice either of these objectives, they came to favor a powerful and extremely republican federal government. Both wanted to curb majority tyranny in the states by shifting power to an energetic yet balanced and republican federal government. After 1789 they began moving in opposite directions. Madison began to see the Revolution's fruits threatened from a new and unexpected source. Fearing the takeover of the central government by a corrupt northern mercantile minority determined to transform the federal government of limited powers into a consolidated national government of unlimited powers, he turned to the states to stave off what he perceived to be encroaching despotism. Rather than reversing his nationalism (which, as Lance Banning has shown, always had its limits), Madison remained consistent to his highest goal—republicanism.[4] Washington, who did not share this conspiratorial outlook and for whom nationalism and republicanism never conflicted, continued to see the states as the potential source of oppression.

The title *Founding Friendship* has two meanings. In addition to studying a collaboration that helped found the Republic, I examine what it takes to found a friendship. I rely on kinship universes and other techniques of family historians to explore the relations between these two members of the Chesapeake elite. My methodology is based on the assumption that the correspondence between two individuals alters in recognizable ways as their friendship develops. By studying the letters of Washington and Madison I can infer when their friendship began and ended and how it changed over time. Examining seemingly formulaic portions of their correspondence, such as letter openings and closings, has yielded some new discoveries. For example, I have found that Washington always addressed letters to remote acquaintances "Sir," letters to familiar acquaintances

"Dear Sir," but reserved "My Dear Sir" for intimate friends. Moreover, only to intimates did he end his letters with the complimentary closing "affectionately." Madison practiced similar habits. I also have studied the frequency and duration of Madison's visits to Mount Vernon, correlating them with changes in letter salutations. By analyzing clues that most historians have ignored (the older printed editions of the two men's writings did not even transcribe letter closings fully), I have determined when the friendship became effective (November 1784) and when it became intimate (October 1785).

The Washington-Madison collaboration began as a marriage of convenience but eventually grew into a genuine companionship. By working together, these two men, who on the surface at least had little in common, discovered that in addition to similar political objectives they shared an abiding interest in agriculture and science. This study shows that although the founding might not have succeeded without the relationship, the relationship was itself a product of the founding. Without a common cause to bring them together, these men would never have become friends. Once they became companions, each influenced the thinking, behavior, and achievements of the other in profound ways. Their collaboration, in turn, helped shape the early American Republic.

With the exception of many Madison scholars who have acknowledged its existence, the Washington-Madison collaboration has been neglected by historians. Lance Banning in *The Sacred Fire of Liberty: James Madison and the Founding of the Federal Republic* points out that in 1785 Madison was "working closely now with Washington" to secure river improvement legislation in Virginia, and that in 1789 "Madison was Washington's most influential confidant at the beginning of the new administration, a principal advisor on appointments, presidential protocol, and the interpretation of the Constitution." Most other Madison studies also briefly comment on the close collaboration between the two men in 1789, but instead of exploring when, how, and why they became friends, scholars simply take their intimacy in 1789 for granted.[5] Nor is sufficient attention paid to the termination of the relationship, or how Madison's friendship with Washington differed from those of other Republican leaders like Jefferson. By neglecting to address the following important questions, writers fail to probe the nature of the collaboration. What did each man get out of the relationship? Were they equal partners, or was one dominant? To whom was the friendship more important? Did each man perceive their interaction in the same way? What can we learn about these men by studying their friendship? And most important, what impact did the relationship have on the events of the 1780s and 1790s and vice versa? In large measure the inadequacies of the scholarship on the Washington-Madison collaboration have arisen because it has always been approached exclusively from Madison's perspective. This book, for the first time, focuses on the collaboration itself.

GEORGE WASHINGTON was born in 1732 in Westmoreland County, Virginia, the oldest child of Augustine Washington and his second wife, Mary Ball Washington, both members of the lower-middle gentry. Following Augustine's death, Washington spent his teenage years shuttling between Fredericksburg, where his mother resided, and Mount Vernon, his older half-brother Lawrence's Potomac estate. Receiving a few years of formal schooling and some instruction from relatives, he acquired a rudimentary knowledge of history and literature and more substantial skills in mathematics, surveying, and draftsmanship. Coming into contact with Lawrence's in-laws, the rich and well-connected Fairfaxes, whetted his appetite for the good life.[6]

In 1749 appointment as Culpeper County's surveyor lured Washington west, where he began acquiring land. When his half-brother Lawrence contracted tuberculosis, Washington accompanied him to Barbados in search of a cure. In 1752 Lawrence died, shortly after returning to Mount Vernon. The following year, when Virginia's acting governor Robert Dinwiddie sought an emissary to warn the French out of the Ohio country, Washington volunteered for the assignment. After the enemy refused to comply with his message to leave the region, Washington led a force of Virginians to secure the contested territory. Encountering a small French detachment, Washington, now a lieutenant colonel, on 29 May 1754 launched a controversial attack that initiated the Seven Years' War. After displaying conspicuous bravery during General Edward Braddock's 1755 defeat, Washington scraped together the colony's remaining forces and tried to defend the frontier against marauding Indians. Admiring the Royal Army, he vainly sought a commission as a regular officer.

At the close of the decade, Washington exchanged military for domestic life, marrying wealthy widow Martha Dandridge Custis. Along with the inheritance of Mount Vernon a few years after Lawrence's death, the marriage propelled him into the Chesapeake's upper echelons. Assuming a country squire's role, he busied himself with plantation management, agricultural experiments, socializing, and amassing thousands of acres of western land. By the 1770s he had become visible in the House of Burgesses, where he opposed British attempts to tax the colonies. After attending the first two Continental Congresses, he became the

Continental army's commander in chief, an appointment that owed as much to his southern domicile as to his military reputation.

George Washington was a complex man. Six feet three inches tall, with a large and athletic frame, he cut a commanding and majestic figure. His strong facial features, including high cheekbones, a large nose, and piercing blue-gray eyes, produced a pleasing effect, but his ill-fitting dentures made him reluctant to smile. Washington reached decisions deliberately but carried them out aggressively. He was generous, respectful, hospitable, and polite but demanding, unforgiving, and sometimes displayed a volatile temper. He loved domesticity and husbandry but exhibited political skill, financial shrewdness, and material ac-

George Washington, by Ellen or James Sharples, c. 1796–1823.
(Courtesy of the Independence National Historical Park)

quisitiveness. He often veiled his personal opinions and feelings behind an in-
scrutable veneer. James Madison contrasted his public and private personality:
"Washington was not fluent or ready in conversation, and was inclined to be tac-
iturn in general society. In the company of two or three intimate friends, however, he was talkative, and when a little excited was sometimes fluent and even
eloquent. The story so often repeated of his never laughing . . . is wholly untrue;
no man seemed more to enjoy gay conversation, though he took little part in it
himself. He was particularly pleased with the jokes, good humor, and hilarity of
his companions." Washington possessed a strong sense of duty and honor, prized
his personal reputation, and carefully cultivated his image. According to W. W.
Abbot, he demonstrated "an uncommon awareness of self: his strong sense that
what he decided and what he did, and how others perceived his decisions and
deeds, always mattered."[7]

In 1751, the year nineteen-year-old George Washington sailed to Barbados with
Lawrence, James Madison was born in Port Conway, Virginia. He grew up at
Montpelier, the family estate in Orange County, the oldest of ten children in a
gentry family of average wealth. At age eleven Madison began studying languages
and the classics at Donald Robertson's academy in King and Queen County. In
1769 he entered the College of New Jersey in Princeton, where he applied himself so unremittingly that his health deteriorated. After completing his degree
twelve months early, he stayed an extra year under President John Witherspoon's
tutelage. While at Princeton, Madison imbibed Whiggish principles and a commitment to personal liberty, especially freedom of speech and conscience.[8]

Upon returning to Virginia, Madison tutored his siblings and brooded over
his future and his frail health (some historians conjecture that he suffered from
epilepsy) until America's resistance to Great Britain embarked him on a political career that lasted most of his life. In 1776, while serving in the Virginia convention that adopted George Mason's Declaration of Rights, Madison suggested
substituting the word *entitlement* for *toleration* in the article protecting freedom
of worship, a change that converted religious liberty from a privilege to "a *natural and absolute* right." The following year, after he lost his bid for the general
assembly because he refused to treat the voters, the legislature elected him to the
council of state under Governor Patrick Henry.[9]

Madison's contemporary Edward Coles provided a penetrating analysis of his
appearance and personality:

> In height he was about five feet six inches, of a small and delicate form, of rather
> a tawny complexion, bespeaking a sedentary and studious man; his hair was
> originally of a dark brown colour; his eyes were bluish . . . his form, features,

and manner were not commanding, but his conversation exceedingly so, and few men possessed so rich a flow of language, or so great a fund of amusing anecdotes, which were made the more interesting from their being well timed and well told. His ordinary manner was simple, modest, bland, & unostentatious, retiring from the throng and cautiously refraining from doing or saying anything to make conspicuous—This made him appear a little reserved and formal. . . . [He was] the most virtuous, calm, and amiable of men; possessed of one of the purest hearts, and best tempers with which man was ever blessed. Nothing could excite or ruffle him. Under all circumstances he was collected, and ever mindful of what was due from him to others, and cautious not to wound the feelings of any one.[10]

James Madison, by James Sharples, c. 1796–97.
(Courtesy of the Independence National Historical Park)

WASHINGTON AND MADISON did not meet until 1781, but their relationship began earlier. Through his voluminous correspondence with civilian authorities, Commander in Chief Washington played a key role in the political education Madison received as a member of the Virginia Council of State (1777–79) and the Continental and Confederation Congresses (1780–83). Although their formal, preconcerted collaboration did not begin until 1784, Washington and Madison nevertheless indirectly cooperated in quelling military unrest at Newburgh, New York, and in trying to obtain revenue power for Congress. This episode reveals that Washington and Madison were much more moderate in their nationalism than Alexander Hamilton and Robert Morris. After the war their cooperation inspired Virginia and Maryland to charter the Potomac and James River companies. This joint effort graduated the friendship from effective to intimate status, helped launch the canal era, and started the chain of events resulting in the 1787 Constitutional Convention. By no means did they chart the road to Philadelphia in 1784, but they pushed internal improvements at the state level in the belief that doing so would promote continental political reform.

By clearing away obstacles to his participation, Madison helped convince a cautious but not entirely reluctant Washington to attend the Philadelphia Convention. The collaborators, along with the other members of Virginia's delegation, produced the Virginia Plan, which committed the convention not only to strengthening the federal government but to changing its very structure. Aside from the Virginia Plan, the collaboration did not contribute indispensably to the convention's success. Among the Virginians, however, their alliance played an immense role, resulting in the delegation's support for the Constitution. During ratification the younger Virginian secretly provided his friend with copies of the *Federalist* papers and other propaganda to distribute throughout the Chesapeake. Washington persuaded Madison to attend the Virginia ratification convention, where he emerged as the Constitution's ablest defender, while Madison, in turn, helped Washington manage his acceptance of the presidency. As with his decision to attend the Federal Convention, Washington's collaboration with Madison sheds light on his willingness to become president, suggesting that shortly after the Constitution became ratified, Washington accepted his return to public life as inescapable.

During 1789 and 1790 Madison was Washington's most influential adviser, providing guidance on policy, appointments, etiquette, and especially on precedent-setting issues. His counsel proved crucial during the federal government's initial months, before the cabinet's creation, when Madison acted in effect as Washington's prime minister. The collaboration contributed immeasurably to the adoption of the Bill of Rights, the Compromise of 1790 (which located the national capital on the Potomac River), and the planning of Washington, D.C. His friendship with Madison even occasionally altered Washington's thinking, for example by transforming him into more of a votary of personal liberty, especially freedom of conscience. Although Madison did not give day-to-day advice after 1790, he continued to help manage precedent-setting issues. In 1792 he wrote a farewell address (which Washington turned to four years later), but his influence diminished shortly thereafter. Discovering the extent of Madison's partisan opposition to Alexander Hamilton's economic program helped convince the president to serve another term. When Jefferson retired as secretary of state in 1793, Madison's refusal to succeed him deprived the administration of a Republican voice to match Hamilton's. Without it, Washington failed to maintain his nonpartisan course, instead becoming increasingly Federalist. Yet the collaborators remained on excellent personal terms, as evidenced by the Washingtons' encouragement of Madison's 1794 marriage to Dolley Payne Todd. Ultimately, however, ideological differences between Washington and Madison (which had been subsumed under their collaboration) made their continued partnership all but impossible. A dispute over the Democratic Societies' responsibility for the Whiskey Rebellion caused Washington to doubt Madison's personal loyalty and motives. When the Jay Treaty dispute confirmed these suspicions, the president ended the friendship. After both retired to Virginia in 1797, the two men never communicated again.

Studying the collaboration between Washington and Madison not only illuminates the American founding, it also helps us better to understand each man. This book supports the recent claims of Lance Banning and Drew McCoy that the 1780s provide the key to Madison's political career. Neither a strong nationalist of the Hamiltonian variety nor a political consolidationist, Madison always favored a federal system firmly grounded in popular self-government. An accurate understanding of the Madison of the 1780s makes it clear that he did not retreat from nationalism to states' rights in the 1790s. This misrepresentation, pinned on Madison by contemporary Federalist enemies, has been accepted by subsequent historians and has become virtual gospel among early Americanists. Along with Banning's work, this book shows that Madison's highest goal, to which he remained consistent throughout his career, was republicanism.[11]

Similarly, studying Washington's collaboration with Madison sheds light on Washington's career. As with Madison, a contemporary Federalist misinterpretation of Washington was picked up by later generations, becoming entrenched in the historical record. This traditional view depicts Washington as having been more of a Hamiltonian nationalist in the 1780s and more of a High Federalist in the 1790s than he actually was, at least until late in the decade. In general, Hamilton's influence over Washington has been exaggerated, as a result of projecting backwards the influence he possessed in Washington's second term.[12] Beside our distorted image of Washington's political philosophy has been an equally inaccurate and damaging picture of his style of political leadership and an underestimation of his contributions to constitutionalism, areas recently addressed by Glenn Phelps. Far from being a majestic figurehead presiding over powerful appointees who took the lead in decision making, Washington, guided by his own strong constitutional vision, always maintained control of his administration. He may have collected advice extensively, reached decisions deliberately, and employed ghostwriters regularly, but he always remained in charge, governed thoughtfully, and often cloaked his instrumentality. Washington, in short, was our first "hidden-hand president."[13]

The following pages, then, argue that Washington and Madison have been in many ways misunderstood, and that a close examination of their collaboration provides a new lens through which to bring them into sharper focus. Their friendship, moreover, was the most indispensable collaboration in the creation of the American Republic.

1

WINNING INDEPENDENCE

As george washington entered Philadelphia on 30 August 1781, crowds received him "with shouts and acclamations," noted a member of the military entourage. After the local cavalry escorted the commander in chief into town, ships fired salutes of welcome. "In the evening the city was illuminated," recorded the *Pennsylvania Packet,* "and his Excellency walked through some of the principal streets, attended by a numerous concourse of people, eagerly pressing to see their beloved General." Among the celebrants was Congressman James Madison of Virginia. Washington spent nearly a week in the city before resuming his journey from New York to Yorktown, where he hoped to defeat a British force under Charles, Lord Cornwallis. Washington and Madison first met during this brief stay.[1]

All we know about their first encounter is that on his arrival, Washington "went up to the State House, and paid his respects to Congress." The two men came together again on 3 and 4 September, when Washington joined the delegates to review the troops marching south. Both attended the fancy dinner given by the French minister, the chevalier de La Luzerne, on the fourth. They probably crossed paths a few more times, because the army established headquarters at Robert Morris's home, a block down Market Street from Mrs. Mary House's boardinghouse where Madison resided. The congressman may have been present either at Washington's visit to the City Tavern or at a large dinner at Morris's, both on 30 August.[2]

In a sense, the Washington-Madison relationship began much earlier than 1781. Long before the two men ever saw each other, they had interacted indirectly and formed impressions of one another. By the time Madison first glimpsed Washington, a negative impression formed in 1775 had given way to admiration. After serving two years on the Virginia Council of State and eighteen months in the Continental Congress, Madison had gained an appreciation of the day-to-day trials Washington faced and the tenacity, sound judgment, and respect for civilian authority with which he invariably dealt with them. As important as what he learned about Washington was what Madison learned from him. The older Virginian played a large role in the political education Madison received while sitting on the council and in Congress. Washington, though not very familiar with Madison when the two first met, already had recognized him as a rising, competent, and dedicated public servant on whom he could count as an ally.

MADISON's earliest surviving reference to Washington, written after the 1775 Powder Magazine incident, is hardly favorable. On the night of 20/21 April, Virginia's governor John Murray, earl of Dunmore, seized the colony's gunpowder supply in Williamsburg. When an angry mob demanded the powder's return, Dunmore assured them that the powder had been taken as a precaution against an anticipated slave rebellion and promised to restore it once tempers cooled. Although the mob disbanded at the urging of House of Burgesses Speaker Peyton Randolph, Williamsburg remained tense for days. Throughout the colony the seizure provoked outrage. Only a soothing letter from Randolph dissuaded thousands of militiamen assembled at Fredericksburg from marching on the capital. Rather than risk a confrontation with Dunmore by trying to take back the powder, Randolph preferred to let the Continental Congress suggest a response. One member of Virginia's delegation to Philadelphia disagreed. As Randolph, George Washington, Richard Henry Lee, and Benjamin Harrison departed for Philadelphia, Patrick Henry took matters into his own hands. He summoned the Hanover County militia and, spurred by news of Lexington and Concord, led it toward Williamsburg. When Carter Braxton and Thomas Nelson, Jr., two unofficial emissaries for the royal governor, intercepted the force outside the capital with payment for the powder, Henry called off the march. As the Hanover men returned home, they met militiamen from Orange County, including twenty-four-year-old James Madison, also coming to Williamsburg to rescue the powder.[3]

After returning home, Madison, a member of the Orange committee of safety, drafted an address praising Henry's behavior. Privately he contrasted Henry's exploits to the weakness of "Peyton Randolph, Edm. Pendleton, Richd. H. Lee, and George Washington Esqrs": "I expect his [Henry's] conduct as contrary to the opinion of the other delegats will be disapproved of by them, but it [has] gained him great honor in the most spirited parts of the Country. . . . The Gentlemen below whose property will be exposed in case of a civil war in this Colony were extremely alarmed lest Government should be provoked to make reprisals. Indeed some of them discovered a pusilanimity little comporting with their professions or the name of Virginian." As far as Washington is concerned, Madison's accusation of cowardice is too harsh. Upon hearing of the powder's seizure, Washington went to Alexandria to ready the militia to march on Williamsburg, but when the troops at Fredericksburg disbanded, he gave up on a military response and departed for Philadelphia. Unlike Randolph, who feared a showdown with the governor, Washington can be charged with nothing worse than leaving his state before obtaining redress from Dunmore. Madison's statement not only illustrates his enthusiasm for the Revolution but also reveals the piedmont gentry's resentment of their firmly established conservative tidewater colleagues. Not knowing much about the particular men involved, he based his condemnation upon his image of the colony's eastern elite. Although Madison began his political career with a low opinion of Washington's Revolutionary ardor, his respective attitudes toward Washington and Henry soon reversed.[4]

Upon being appointed the Continental army's commander in chief in June 1775, Washington emerged as a hero overnight. As the one Revolutionary symbol all Americans shared in common, he became the focus of public acclaim even before he took charge of the troops. Long accustomed to worshiping the king of England, the rebels quickly shifted their veneration to Washington, often employing the same rituals once reserved for George III, such as birthday celebrations. The Virginian's reluctant assumption of command, his humility, and his careful use of power made hero worship seem consistent with a republican revolution against a tyrannical monarch. An ebullient rebel, Madison participated in this emotional surge, quickly forgetting his reservations.[5]

When Madison joined Governor Patrick Henry's council of state in 1778, he came to appreciate Washington's abilities firsthand. Reacting to fears of monarchy, Virginia's 1776 constitution had created a weak executive, consisting of the governor and the council of state. The governor, chosen yearly by the assembly, could serve no more than three consecutive terms and lacked veto power. He could act only with the consent of a majority of his eight-member council (or "board"), also picked by the legislature. Although the executive was nearly impotent in theory, the demands of war gave it serious powers and responsibilities, particularly during legislative recess. Council membership, moreover, was an honor rarely conferred on a twenty-six-year-old such as Madison. His colleagues were considerably older and hailed for the most part from established tidewater families.[6]

Madison took the oath as councillor to the state's first governor on 14 January 1778. That same day Henry placed before his advisers a letter from Francis Lightfoot Lee, one of Virginia's delegates in Philadelphia, "representing the alarming accounts of the Distresses of the American Army for the Want of Provisions, insomuch that it is hinted to Congress, by General Washington, that the Troops, unless an immediate supply is sent, must either '*Starve Dissolve or Disperse.*'" The troops' deplorable condition opened the eyes of the idealistic Madison. In response, the governor in council dispatched four state agents to purchase and transport to camp 10,000 pounds of meat and 2,000 bushels of salt.[7]

The army's predicament resulted from wartime shortages and Congress's failure to raise sufficient revenues, which left the Continental commissary unable to supply adequate food. In February, Washington pleaded directly with the governor for supplies. There existed "little less than a famine in camp," he insisted, and "unless the most vigorous and effectual measures are at once, every where adapted . . . we shall not be able to make another campaign." The commander realized that the request "does not naturally fall within the circle of your attention," but with the commissary faltering, he hoped "that the full force of that zeal . . . you have manifested upon every other occasion, will now operate for our relief." Taking "the most vigorous and proper measures the Executive power could devise," Henry and the council directed Continental and state agents "to push some pork up the Bay for the grand Army."[8]

The events of Madison's first months on the board set the tone for his entire tenure. From January 1778 to the end of Henry's third term as governor in May 1779, Madison perused many more letters from Washington to the executive, most appealing for recruits, food, or equipment. Well before Madison took his seat, Washington and Henry had, through a steady correspondence, established an efficient working relationship. This close communication, continuing through Madison's stay on the council, thoroughly exposed him to wartime administration and the value of civilian-military cooperation. In accord with Virginia's constitution and his own inclinations, Henry engaged in no official acts without his board's approval, commonly writing official correspondence in the first person plural. The body reached decisions by consensus after informal debate, with Henry guiding the agenda. Usually five or fewer advisers were present. Because Madison attended more often than his colleagues, more work and responsibility fell on his shoulders. To meet Continental needs the executive issued a steady stream of warrants on the state treasury to reimburse agents who had purchased supplies and delivered them to camp. After paying for the materials, the executive settled accounts with Congress. With the commissary's failure, Washington relied more and more on this procedure, causing Henry to complain about "the great load of Continental business thrown on me."[9]

Henry and the council met the state's quota of Continental troops as best they could, but apathy and hardship prevented their success. By 1778, as the *rage militaire* with which Americans began the war evaporated, potential recruits concerned themselves more with their suffering families than with fighting the British. As Virginia fell short of its quota, Henry kept the militia ready to aid Washington. Other federal concerns included caring for British prisoners held in Charlottesville, encouraging Virginia's troops to reenlist, and getting new regiments to camp. Washington and Henry exchanged information about enemy movements and about officers' deaths, promotions, resignations, and punishments. The executive prodded the state legislature to raise taxes and, at Washington's request, convinced it to approve a liberal enlistment bounty. By issuing proclamations and publishing Washington's letters and addresses, the executive kept the public conscious of the army's situation and encouraged sacrifices for the cause.[10]

When Thomas Jefferson succeeded Henry as governor on 1 June 1779, he and Washington quickly established the same close communication and cooperation that had characterized the previous administration, thanks largely to continuity within the council. Like his predecessor, Jefferson used "we" in speaking of the executive and always accepted the board's judgment. But the same old problems of raising men, money, and supplies and of balancing state and Continental needs grew more daunting.[11]

Although Virginia never met its Continental requisitions for money or men, it provided vital succor to the army during 1778–79. As a member of the state's overburdened executive, Madison deserves much of the credit for its contributions. But Madison gained as much as he gave. As Ralph Ketcham puts it, "In taking his seat on the Council of State in the seemingly provincial town of Williamsburg, Madison in fact found himself entangled almost immediately with most of the major, persisting problems of the revolution. His day-to-day work there gave him a practical grasp of these issues a mere observer, or even a legislator, would not likely attain." If the council was Madison's classroom, then the commander in chief was his preceptor, one whose words, experiences, and problems provided many valuable lessons in wartime politics, administration, and civilian-military relations. Washington's letters exposed the inefficiency of having a deliberative body manage the war at the continental level and taught Madison that the challenge of winning was more financial and administrative than military. Most important, he learned firsthand the value of effective communication and cooperation between political and military leaders. As he observed with dismay Virginians' reluctance to endure hardship, he realized the wisdom of Washington's requests for adequate pay for the troops. Perceiving that popular virtue was inadequate for the sacrifices necessary to win independence and that Continental authorities needed to resort to self-interest to inspire men to bear the war's burdens profoundly shaped Madison's thinking.[12]

In addition to learning from Washington, Councillor Madison learned about him through the daily experience of reading the commander's correspondence, grappling with the problems it raised, and empathizing with his struggle to keep an army together against the most powerful nation in the world. After two years on the council, Madison recognized the general as a tenacious and patriotic officer who treated his troops sternly but caringly and meted out punishments fairly. He knew that the commander in chief was a superb administrator who tirelessly cultivated good relations with civilian authorities at both the national and state levels. Finally, Madison perceived Washington's obsession with his own reputation; his ambition was not only to be a disinterested public servant but to be recognized publicly as such. Of course, he did not fully understand so impenetrable an individual. In many respects, moreover, Madison came to know the public image that Washington carefully projected rather than the true man.[13]

Madison, believing that the fates of Washington and the Revolution were inseparably linked, joined his colleagues in looking after the commander's wellbeing. In April 1778 the council learned "that his Excellency General Washington has been unsupplied for some time past with many articles of Living which Custom & the great fatigues to which he is constantly exposed must make necessary to the preservation of his health." Immediately the executive directed "the Commissary of Stores to procure a Stock of good rum, wine, Sugar, & such other Articles as his Excellency may think needful & send them on to head Quarters." Washington thanked "the Governor and Council for their agreeable present. . . . when it arrives . . . it will find us in a humour to do it all manner of justice."[14]

Madison's service on the council ended when the Virginia assembly elected him to the Continental Congress on 14 December 1779, in response to a plea from Washington for representatives of higher caliber. Not only had the Continental commissary and financial matters degenerated, so too had political leadership, as America's best talents had found it less costly, less frustrating, and more convenient to serve at the state level. Washington complained that the nation's destiny rested in the hands of petty men who engaged in "party disputes and personal quarrels" while financing the war was "postponed from day to day, from week to week as if our affairs wore the most promising aspect." Virginians Richard Henry Lee, Thomas Jefferson, and George Wythe had given way to the likes of Meriwether Smith, Cyrus Griffin, and William Fleming, who often resisted nationalistic measures. Soon only one delegate from the Old Dominion remained in Philadelphia, causing the state to forfeit its vote.[15]

This deplorable situation prompted Washington to appeal to House of Delegates Speaker Benjamin Harrison to send Virginia's "ablest and best Men to Congress." "Where is Mason, Wythe, Jefferson, Nicholas, Pendleton, Nelson, and another I could name [Harrison]," he wondered. The commander used an Enlightenment metaphor to explain the fallacy of having qualified people holding state office when the public interest required them in Congress: "Our political system may, be compared to the mechanism of a Clock . . . it answers no good purpose to keep the smaller Wheels in order if the greater one which is the support and prime mover of the whole is neglected." With the war's critical juncture at hand, Washington begged the assembly to "send an extra Member or two for at least a certain limited time till the great business of the Nation is put upon a more respectable and happy establishmt." The legislature responded by electing Madison, along with John Walker, James Henry, and Joseph Jones, to Congress.[16]

Washington knew little or nothing about Madison at the time of his election (he may never have heard of him). Nevertheless, the commander looked favorably on him based solely on his inclusion with the other continentalists that the Old Dominion sent to Congress, all of whom he knew personally. In particular, having been elected alongside Joseph Jones boosted Madison's stock. As close friends and fellow burgesses, Washington and Jones had helped bring the Revolution to Virginia. After Washington left the colony in 1775, he and Jones carried on a steady private correspondence. Jones also enjoyed a strong bond with Madison, because both had served on the committee that in 1776 drew up Virginia's Declaration of Rights, and later, as fellow congressmen, they would board together. A companion of both Washington and Madison, Jones would play a vital role in getting them to know one another.[17]

Although favorably predisposed to Madison, Washington did not at first realize how well the appointment answered his plea. The general not only wanted able men sent to Congress, he also hoped that those chosen would "go into a thorough investigation of the causes that have produced so many disagreeable effects in the Army and Country." Madison tackled exactly such a course of study before departing for Philadelphia. In his autobiography he wrote that "to prepare himself" for Congress, he analyzed "the state of the Continental affairs, and particularly that of the finances which, owing to the depreciation of the paper currency, was truly deplorable." Madison concluded that inflation depended more on the lack of public confidence in the government than on the money supply. To stave off depreciation, he reasoned, the delegates need not print less currency but must avoid constantly postponing the date of redemption, which caused the people to lose faith in eventual repayment. If Congress stuck to its reimbursement schedule, it could then issue new paper in greater quantities without causing inflation.[18]

This challenge to dogma reveals how much Madison's thinking had matured during his two years on the council of state. He better understood the need to balance state concerns with those of the Union as a whole. Madison's continentalism, blossoming during the 1780s, stemmed largely from his public service at the state level during the 1770s. Most Americans who gained that viewpoint, in contrast, did so primarily through their experiences in national affairs. George Washington, whose correspondence forced him to view events from a broad vantage point, deserves much of the credit for Madison's wide focus. The commander had unknowingly cultivated a valuable ally who would provide him considerable support in Congress. Indeed, the young Virginian was just the sort of man he had urged his state to send north. Once the new delegate arrived in Philadelphia, their cooperation would begin.[19]

THE Washington-Madison relationship did not formally commence until 1784, but the two men started collaborating indirectly when Madison entered Congress in March 1780. From 1780 to 1783 they worked for virtually the same goals—to win American independence and unite the states under a permanent, effective federal government—and although they did not knowingly coordinate their actions, each man's activities nevertheless complemented those of the other. Madison lived up to Washington's hopes for Virginia's new delegates by consistently supporting the measures necessary to win the war, especially congressional revenue and adequate payment for military service. During these years Madison's admiration and affection for Washington grew immensely, as he observed from a new perspective the latter's careful obedience to civilian government. Over the same period Washington, in turn, eased Madison's job. While guarding against an actual mutiny against civil authority, he supported Madison's efforts to obtain federal income. Both men thought more and more alike during these years, culminating in their mutual obsession with reforming the Confederation and in their shared belief in the evils of disunion. Even among continentalists, the similarities in their thinking stand out. Although they did not become close during these years, they got acquainted and began to correspond.

Arriving in Philadelphia, a dismayed Madison found that Congress possessed no money, no credit, and little talent. In 1779, after inflation had left Continental currency worthless, that body stopped printing paper money. The following year it passed the task of provisioning and paying the army to the states. Already too heavily burdened for further taxation, the states speeded up their own printing presses, resulting in further inflation. The Continental army, meanwhile, continued to suffer. From headquarters at Morristown, where the troops starved and shivered through a winter reminiscent of Valley Forge, Washington discerned the same centrifugal trend that Madison saw in Philadelphia. To Jones he wrote, "I see one head gradually changing into thirteen. I see one Army branching into thirteen; and, instead of looking up to Congress as the supreme controuling power of the united States, are considering themselves as dependent on their respective States. In a word, I see the powers of Congress declining too fast for the consequence and respect which is due to them as the grand representative body of America, and I am fearful of the consequences." The commander urged Congress to assume powers "competent to the great purposes of War."[20]

Madison, who read Washington's letter to Jones, agreed with its diagnosis and worked to implement its advice. A hard worker who eagerly took on committee assignments, Madison proved a valuable ally in the quest to reclaim powers Congress had surrendered to the states. Unlike most congressmen, he attended legislative sessions regularly, and instead of going home for good after a few months, he stayed in Congress for three-and-one-half years. Thanks to low attendance and high turnover, he quickly emerged as a leader despite being the youngest delegate present.[21]

Madison's arrival in Philadelphia coincided with a nationalist resurgence in Congress—brought on by financial and military crises—that lasted until war's end. As Lance Banning has shown, Madison was by no means one of these nationalists, "not, at least, in several of the senses commonly suggested by that term." Specifically, Madison limited his nationalism in three ways. First, he upheld the interests of Virginia, particularly concerning western lands and Mississippi River navigation rights. Second, Madison saw the doctrine of implied powers as a threat to republicanism, regarding constitutional amendments a safer way to expand federal authority. Third and perhaps most significant, he did not wish to see the Confederation government manipulate the war debt to promote economic development or bring America's political economy into line with Britain's. Madison was at most a conditional nationalist, or what Banning terms a "Virginia continentalist." Although moderate in his nationalism, Madison nevertheless aligned himself with the pro–Benjamin Franklin, pro–Robert Morris forces in opposition to the localist Lee-Adams faction. The former group, recognizing the potential of an energetic central government, attempted to strengthen Congress and invigorate the army. The Lee-Adams contingent, in contrast, fearing that centralized power would inevitably degenerate into tyranny, resisted empowering Congress or Washington.[22]

Although limiting his nationalism, Madison lived up to Washington's expectations for the new delegates. To increase efficiency, he supported replacing executive committees with individual secretaries of war, foreign affairs, and finance. Madison argued (in vain) that under the Articles, a majority of the delegations present could carry a vote, which would prevent absent states from impeding important business. Madison favored bolstering Washington's powers and strengthening his army through military reforms, including longer enlistment terms. In 1780, when a congressional committee suggested giving the commander dictatorial powers, the young Virginian poked fun at colleagues who defeated the idea. Later that year he advocated pensions for veterans after he read the commander's "judicious & valuable" endorsement of the proposal. When the opposition proved insurmountable, Madison helped arrange a compromise substituting a lump sum payment equaling five years' full pay.[23]

The younger Virginian served as Congress's self-appointed caretaker of Washington's reputation. Instead of blaming him for not sending more troops south when the British invaded the Old Dominion in 1781, Madison wrote to Jefferson and others insisting that the commander in chief was doing all he could. As part of the Yorktown surrender terms, Washington allowed certain captured Loyalist merchants in Virginia to export tobacco to New York. When the Lee-Adams delegates attacked this arrangement as an example of wartime profiteering and trading with the enemy, Madison, although opposed to coddling Tories, rushed to Washington's defense. He urged friends in Virginia to support the commander, explaining that "there are several reasons which make me regret much this variance between Congress & Virga. of which a material one is that a great Personage will be touched by it since it originates in his Act."[24]

Outside of Congress, Madison aided Washington by relaying information. In an age of painfully slow and time-consuming communications, the commander in chief could not possibly keep every state government up-to-date on the war.

Madison eased the situation as far as Virginia was concerned by sending excerpts from Washington's correspondence with Congress to Jefferson and his successor as governor, Benjamin Harrison. The intelligence Madison forwarded usually dealt with enemy movements, officers' promotions, prisoners' treatment and exchange, and the troops' condition. Being well-informed enabled state officials to understand and meet the army's needs more effectively. As a representative of Virginia, a large and influential state that saw heavy fighting, Madison was in a unique position to aid Washington. Undoubtedly a dose of local pride and a strong desire to advance his personal career lay behind Madison's faithful backing. But because the general did not yet know Madison well, his support probably often went unnoticed at headquarters.[25]

Madison the congressman demonstrated the same concern for Washington's wellness that he had as councillor. In 1780, as a member of the Admiralty Board, Madison often shipped portions of captured ship cargoes to camp. In May he sent "about a dozen Boxes Lemons." That same month the commander thanked the board for two pipes of wine. "As for our illustrious general . . . the rich Madeira should flow in copious streams," Madison explained. The young Virginian's growing affection for Washington also can be seen in his emotional response to Benedict Arnold's treason in September 1780. Not only had Arnold betrayed his country, he had also attempted, Madison believed, to hand over "our Great General Washington" as "Peace offering to the Enemy." He described Arnold's machinations as the "Blackest Circumstances of treason and Perfidity that ever enterd the heart of any, wretch, but his own." In the wake of Arnold's betrayal, Washington more than ever came to symbolize, for Madison and other Americans, the cause's beleaguered virtue.[26]

The congressman's willingness to accept the general's opinions as his own also indicates his admiration. He avidly read Washington's letters to Jones and the president of Congress and appears to have adopted many of their opinions. When the Pennsylvania Line rebelled early in 1781, Madison unquestioningly accepted Washington's advocacy of concessions, not punishment. But when New Jersey troops marched on Trenton a few weeks later, the commander subdued the malcontents by force. Again the younger Virginian followed the general's lead, this time adopting a stern attitude toward disaffection.[27]

The Asgill incident, too, demonstrates Madison's willingness to accept Washington's advice and to defend his interests. In 1782, when the British failed to punish Richard Lippincott, a Loyalist officer who had murdered an American prisoner, Washington ordered that a randomly selected captive, Captain Charles Asgill, die in retaliation. Madison endorsed the decision. The cessation of hostilities, French pressure, an emotional appeal from Asgill's mother, and hopes that the enemy would improve its behavior, however, convinced Washington to throw the matter into Congress's lap, suggesting that Asgill be spared. Madison helped to devise a face-saving resolution making it clear that Washington had neither caved in to the French nor had his bluff called by the British.[28]

Although the congressman frequently took cues from Washington, their thinking usually paralleled naturally, as with their attitudes toward the French and British. Judging French assistance indispensable to military victory, neither dreaded, as did the Lee-Adams forces, that the United States would succumb to foreign influence. Even as they discounted fears of French duplicity, however, both suspected British intentions. They worried that the enemy would circulate peace rumors to weaken American war preparations, and when the armistice finally came, they argued in vain against releasing prisoners prematurely. Their fears were well founded. Once the British regained their POWs, they dragged their feet in implementing the peace treaty.[29]

Perhaps Madison's greatest service to Washington was his 18 May 1781 motion allowing the army to impress supplies, which initiated the chain of events leading to Cornwallis's surrender at Yorktown. As British forces terrorized Virginia during the spring of 1781, Washington could send only a token detachment under Lafayette. He would have liked to send more men south, but his troops lacked the supplies and food necessary for the journey. Because the Articles of Confederation did not explicitly authorize him to impress supplies, the commander had no choice but to await requisitions from the states. At this critical juncture Madison momentarily set aside his personal qualms about broad constitutional interpretation, convincing his colleagues that the power to make war implied the power to impress. Washington took advantage of this unusual display of congressional vigor by ordering Anthony Wayne's soldiers, languishing in Pennsylvania, to Virginia. Once in the Old Dominion, Wayne and Lafayette pursued Cornwallis toward tidewater, setting the stage for Yorktown.[30]

Late in November 1781 Madison noted that " our illustrious General" had just arrived in Philadelphia, "returning to his position on the North river. We shall probably . . . have his company here for some days at least, where he will be able to give Congress very seasonable aid in settling the military establishment for the next year, about which there is some diversity of opinion." Madison anticipated that Washington's presence would reinforce his quest for vigorous prosecution of the war. His thinking matched the commander's, whose "greatest Fear is that Congress viewing this stroke [Yorktown] in too important a point of Light, may think our Work too nearly closed, and will fall into a State of Langour and Relaxation." When the delegates received Washington on 28 November, Madison witnessed firsthand a ceremonial exhibition of the commander's obedience to the civilian government. At Congress's request the general remained in Philadelphia until March 1782 to plan the coming campaign and to "enjoy a respite from the fatigues of war." During this interval Washington and Madison finally got to know one another, and their association passed from "unfamiliar" (or "peripheral") to "noneffective." In the former stage two individuals know about one another but do not personally know each other. In the latter state they have occasional contact but do not directly assist or serve each other.[31]

Although Madison did not sit on the military preparations committee, the two men worked together at other meetings, such as those concerned with clothing the troops. They also met socially at Philadelphia's plays and other events, as well as at Mrs. Mary House's boardinghouse, home to the Virginia delegates. Washington, who resided nearby at the Chew mansion on Third Street, noted that his time "was unusually (for me) divided between parties of pleasure and parties of business." Perhaps the younger Virginian went to the Southwark Theatre on 2 January to see Pierre Augustin Caron de Beaumarchais's *Eugenie* and David Garrick's *The Lying Valet,* both performed in the commander's honor. The evening closed with "a brilliant illumination" celebrating "WASHINGTON—*the pride of his country and the terror of Britain.*" No doubt the crowds and events impressed Madison, who admired the diffidence with which Washington received acclamation, because it revealed a man who respected power rather than one who lusted for it.[32]

That winter Madison took advantage of Washington's intimacy with Lafayette to help the American cause. The Frenchman had returned to France to plead for more troops, ships, and money. Hoping to intensify these efforts, Madison decided to massage Lafayette's ego by urging the Virginia assembly to "pay some handsome compliments to the Marquis for his judicious & zealous services." The legislature accordingly resolved to present Lafayette with a bust of himself. For the tribute to have an impact, Madison needed to get word of it to France without making his attempted flattery transparent. He turned to Washington, who knew the marquis well enough to notify him unobtrusively. The commander happily complied, although he remarked, "I am not a judge of Etiquette upon these occasions, but it really does seem odd to me to present a man with his own likeness." Perhaps Virginia's accolades spurred Lafayette to success: he obtained a six-million-livre loan.[33]

As a congressman Madison enjoyed a better vantage point from which to assist and observe Washington than he had in Virginia. By looking after the commander's interests, he made the most of the opportunity, thereby living up to Washington's notion of the model delegate. By 1783 his three years of experience in Congress not only had made him a leader but also had prepared him to help the commander diffuse a potential mutiny at Newburgh, New York.

WASHINGTON and Madison continued collaborating indirectly in 1783 when they resisted the Newburgh conspiracy and supported Congress's revenue plan. Although their cooperation came about by coincidence rather than by premeditation, they could not have coordinated their efforts better had they tried. These two episodes show that Washington and Madison stand out among continentalists for their strong commitment to republicanism. Their indirect, or informal, collaboration laid the foundation for the formal, preconcerted collaboration that emerged after 1783.

The nationalists of the 1780s can be divided into two groups: the moderates (or democratic nationalists) like Washington and Madison and the extremists (or economic nationalists) like Alexander Hamilton, Robert Morris, Gouverneur Morris, and many public creditors and army officers. Although moderates wanted to invigorate the Confederation, their highest priority was to win the war as quickly as possible. If the fighting ended before the creation of an efficient central government, they were willing to take the chance that reform would come afterwards. Extremists, in contrast, believed that the Confederation had to be restructured during the war or never. Once peace returned and the threat of defeat no longer loomed, localism would reassert itself, dooming hopes for a powerful national government. For the intransigents, political reform and military victory carried equal weight. They also wanted a regime similar to Britain's, one that promoted economic development by means of a funded debt, a national bank, and investment incentives. Moderates Washington and Madison did not share this vision.[34]

The differences between moderates and radicals became obvious during the winter and spring of 1783, when military and financial crises came to a head. Congress's attempt to persuade the states to grant a 5 percent impost died late in 1782 when Virginia repealed its ratification and joined Rhode Island in opposition. Early the next year a delegation of army officers met with a congressional committee and demanded back pay and the pension promised them in 1780. They warned that if their demands were not met, a mutiny might occur. In response, a subcommittee that featured Madison recommended a settlement of soldiers' accounts and the commutation of pensions into a lump sum payment. To generate the requisite funds, the committee called for the establishment of a congressional revenue.[35]

The ultranationalists were not satisfied with the report. They had been shocked at the impost's demise because it derailed their centralization plan in its initial phase. With peace imminent, moreover, they realized that time ran against them. Once the war ended, the localist-dominated states would never grant an independent revenue or any other powers. Believing it essential to scare Congress and the states into strengthening the Confederation before the war ended, Hamilton and the Morrises resolved to create a crisis within the army. They secretly encouraged Horatio Gates and other Continental officers to plan a coup against the civilian government and promised support from the public creditors. To increase the discontent, Robert Morris told the headquarters delegation that politicians in Philadelphia were dragging their feet. The participating officers were pawns of the extremists, who wanted to generate the psychological impact of a coup but not the reality. While the Morrises encouraged treason, Hamilton, no longer an officer but now a delegate from New York, simultaneously urged Washington to look out for the uprising and, once it commenced, to take charge of it. Hamilton and the Morrises hoped that such a revolt, if moderated and controlled by Washington, would jolt Congress and the states into granting the Confederation an independent income.[36]

Washington knew nothing and Madison little of the Morris group's secret actions. Had they understood what was going on, they would have sympathized with the immediate goal of obtaining a congressional income but rejected the larger objective of centralized fiscalism. Moreover, they agreed that the army's just grievances had to be met, but not at the risk of a coup that might subvert the Revolution's principles. In grappling with the problem of raising funds to pay the troops, Madison, unlike the ultranationalists, operated within the legislative process. He knew that unless it paid its bills, Congress would die. And if the Confederation crumbled, the Revolution's fruits would be lost; either the army would mutiny and establish a dictatorship, or the states would divide against one another. To protect themselves, individual states would ally with foreign powers, and America would again fall under Europe's corrupt influence. On 28 January 1783, in one of his most important speeches, the Virginian called for adequate federal revenues.[37]

A month later Madison met nationalist congressmen at Thomas Fitzsimons's home. According to Madison, Hamilton confirmed "that the army had secretly determined not to lay down their arms until due provision . . . should be afforded on the subject of their pay." Washington was losing control of the troops for failing to endorse the proceedings, the New Yorker continued. His "unpopularity was daily increasing & industriously promoted by many leading characters." Hamilton had urged Washington to take charge of the discontented "in order that they might be moderated & directed to proper objects, & exclude some other leader who might foment & misguide their councils." He did not, however, divulge his own role in fomenting the uprising. Madison carefully recorded Hamilton's characterization of Washington: "Mr. Hamilton said that he knew Genl. Washington intimately & perfectly, that his extreme reserve, mixed sometimes with a degree of asperity of temper both of which were said to have increased of late, had contributed to the decline of his popularity; but that his virtue his patriotism & his firmness would it might be depended upon never yield to any dishonorable or disloyal plans into which he might be called; that he would sooner suffer himself to be cut into pieces."[38]

Hamilton's revelations moved Madison deeply. Privately he noted, "The influence of General [Washington] is rapidly decreasing in the army insomuch that it is even in contemplation to substitute some less scrupulous guardian of their interests." Equating Washington's fate with the Revolution's, Madison continued, "It depends much in my opinion on the measures which may be pursued by Congress & the several States within the ensuing period of 6 months whether prosperity & tranquility, or confusion and disunion are to be the fruits of the Revolution." His 28 January speech calling for a congressional revenue notwithstanding, Madison and fellow moderate nationalists Fitzsimons, Nathaniel Gorham, Richard Peters, and Daniel Carroll resisted as unattainable Robert Morris's and Hamilton's demands for another impost. He also opposed flirting with a coup to strengthen the Confederation, because he understood that even if Congress succumbed to military bullying, the states would not. Instead, Madison carefully prepared a Report on Public Credit more palatable to the states and submitted it to Congress on 6 March.[39]

Madison's plan provided for a twenty-five-year impost couched in terms less objectionable than in 1781: collectors would be appointed by the states, while Congress would continue to requisition $1.5 million annually. War-ravaged states would receive "abatements" on their requisitions, and the Confederation would assume each state's entire war debt. Madison would have preferred a more nationalistic arrangement—one that did not rely on requisitions at all—but he was pragmatic enough to design a ratifiable program. As Jones explained to Wash-

ington, "Although it was the wish of many to settle the plan upon clear principles of finance, yet such were the prejudices of some States and of some individuals, and such their jealousies, we were obliged to take a middle course . . . or
hazard ultimately the loss of the measure." Hamilton and the Morrises opposed
Madison's endeavors to sweeten the impost with requisitions, time limits, and
state enforcement. That a plan lacking these incentives had no chance of voluntary approval did not trouble them, because they hoped to scare Congress and
the states into acquiescence. Madison understood, as Hamilton did not, that if
the army pressured the delegates into passing an impost, the states would be all
the more determined to block it.[40]

While Congress debated Madison's report, attention shifted to Newburgh,
New York, where the army's discontent boiled. When the officers received reports
of legislative inactivity in Philadelphia, Gates set his plan in motion. An anonymous circular called the officers to meet on 11 March. Major John Armstrong, Jr.,
anonymously issued a second circular dwelling on the army's sufferings and mis-
treatment and suggesting that unless Congress paid it, the army should refuse
to lay down arms. In an obvious reference to Washington, Armstrong urged the
abandonment of any leader who counseled moderation.[41]

After Jones warned that the intrigue had originated in Philadelphia, not at
camp, Washington politely but sternly told Hamilton that he would not flirt with
a coup, regardless of the need for a national revenue. Like Madison, Washington believed in staying within the political process, preferring to take the chance
that Congress and the states would grant the army its due once peace returned.
Realizing that he could not keep the officers from meeting, Washington called
his own gathering on the fifteenth and used the intervening days to lobby for
moderation. Afraid of losing the initiative, Armstrong's forces accepted the time
change. At the meeting Washington delivered a brief prepared address, conced-
ing that the officers' complaints were just but condemning the anonymous attacks on Congress as being subversive and founded on passion rather than reason.
He urged the officers not to defy the civilian authorities and promised to lobby
in their behalf. Appealing for forbearance and patriotism, Washington assured
the men that the quickest and safest way to obtain redress was to trust the government. For corroboration, he read aloud a letter from Jones affirming Congress's commitment to the army. Emotion reinforced logic when Washington
donned his spectacles, after vainly struggling to decipher Jones's writing without them, remarking, "I have grown gray in your service and now find myself
growing blind." That poignant moment underscored how much their leader had

quietly sacrificed for the cause. After Washington departed, his supporters, led by Henry Knox, took charge of the meeting and rammed through resolutions condemning the anonymous addresses and affirming loyalty to the commander and Congress. Convention barred Gates, who presided, from speaking.[42]

Throughout the crisis the attention of the delegates was riveted on Newburgh, and Washington kept them up-to-date. "The steps taken by the Genl. to avert the gathering storm & his professions of inflexible adherence to his duty to Congress & to his country, excited the most affectionate sentiments towards him," Madison noted. "The conduct of Washington does equal honor to his prudence and to his virtue." In the moment of truth, the commander remained faithful to the Revolution. Instead of initiating a military tradition of attempted coups, the general solidified a tradition of civilian control of the military. Years later Madison commented, "I have always believed that if General Washington had yielded to a usurping ambition, he would have found an insuperable obstacle in the incorruptibility of a sufficient portion of those under his command, and that the exalted praise due to him & them, was derived not from a forbearance to effect a revolution within their power, but from a love of liberty and of country which . . . no facility of success could have seduced. I am not less sure that General Washington would have spurned a sceptre if within his grasp, than I am that it was out of his reach, if he had secretly sighed for it."[43]

Despite success at Newburgh, Madison and Washington recognized that the crisis was only half over. Indeed, Congress needed money now more than ever, because if the officers' just demands were not soon met, the commander would lose hold of the army. To Joseph Jones, Washington pleaded, "Do not, My dear Sir, suffer this appearance of tranquility to relax your endeavors to bring the requests of the Army to an issue. Believe me, the Officers are too much pressed by their present wants, and rendered too sore by the recollection of the past sufferings to be touched much longer upon the string of forbearance. . . . The well wishers . . . of their Country, will exert themselves to . . . give every satisfaction that justice requires, and the means which Congress possess, will enable them to do." Jones showed the message to Madison, who considered it so important that he preserved a copy. When Congress immediately approved five years' full pay for officers in lieu of a pension and promised to settle accounts, Madison determined to do more. He explained that "the manner . . . in which he [Washington] found it necessary, and indeed felt it to be his duty, to espouse their [the army's] interests enforces in the highest degree the establishment of adequate and certain revenues." Washington had provided just the sense of urgency Madison needed to push his revenue plan through Congress.[44]

Before finally approving his report on 18 April, the legislature struck out two provisions that Madison believed necessary to win state approval: Congress refused to assume each state's war debt or to grant abatements to states suffering heavy fighting. Despite these disappointments, the young Virginian fought for ratification. Appointed to a committee to prepare a circular encouraging acceptance of the revenue plan, Madison took on the assignment himself. The Address to the States, adopted by every delegation on 26 April 1783, emphasized the virtues of a plan which Madison privately realized to be imperfect. He carefully summarized the provisions, stressing their superiority over the alternatives. He explained that requisitions alone could not provide the needed revenue and pointed out that the impost would hardly interfere with state sovereignty. Only a reliable federal income could preserve the Confederation and render the "fruits of the Revolution" secure. The United States could not prove the viability of republican government without paying its debts. In hopes of bringing Washington's prestige to bear upon the state legislatures as they took up his revenue plan, Madison appended to his address a series of documents pertaining to the abortive coup. He included the commander's counterproclamations, his Newburgh speech, and his letters to Congress chronicling the entire episode. By broadcasting the events at Newburgh, Madison's address boosted Washington's reputation even as it sought to manipulate that reputation to carry the revenue plan into effect.[45]

The address provided Washington with the opportunity to deliver a message of his own to the states, his circular to the governors, which enthusiastically urged that the revenue plan be ratified. The circular is recognized as one of his most important writings, but few realize that it was inspired by and intended to supplement Madison's Address to the States. Washington praised the address, although he may not have realized who wrote the anonymous document. "Congress have, in their late Address," he asserted, "explained their Ideas so fully, and have enforced the obligations the States are under, to render compleat justice to all the Public Creditors, with so much dignity and energy, that in my opinion, no real friend to the honor and Independency of America, can hesitate a single moment . . . complying with the just and honorable measure proposed; if their Arguments do not produce conviction, I know of nothing that will have greater influence."

A comparison of Washington's circular with Madison's address reveals remarkably similar ideas about the critical state of American affairs, even among men who "thought continentally." In particular, both agreed that the war's sacrifices would have been in vain if the Confederation was not preserved and invigorated. Without a strong Union, the states might break apart into regional confederacies, each of which would seek foreign alliances and raise military forces to protect itself. Standing armies, good republicans knew, led inexorably to tyranny. America would lose its hard-won liberty, and the rest of civilization would lose an example of successful republican government. As Washington put it,

> The eyes of the whole World are turned upon them, this is the moment to establish or ruin their national Character forever, this is the favorable moment to give such a tone to our Federal Government, as will enable it to answer the ends of its institution, or this may be the ill-fated moment for relaxing the powers of the Union, annihilating the cement of the Confederation, and exposing us to become the sport of European politics, which may play one State against another . . . to serve their own interested purposes. For, according to the system of Policy the States shall adopt at this moment, they will stand or fall, and by their confirmation or lapse, it is yet to be decided, whether the Revolution must ultimately be considered as a blessing or a curse . . . not to the present age alone, for with our fate will the destiny of unborn Millions be involved.

Perhaps most significant, Washington and Madison agreed that national reform needed to be achieved within the Revolution's republican framework. Unlike the Morris circle, they saw that Congress and the states had to accept change willingly, not through coercion or chicanery.[46]

Despite their collaboration on the 1783 revenue plan, important differences divided Washington and Madison. The general believed that national reform must give Congress "such Powers as are adequate to . . . all the general purposes of the Confederation" but not "having to do with the particular policy of any State, further than it concerns the Union at large." He did not specify the exact powers he had in mind, if, indeed, he could answer that difficult question. Although the younger Virginian, too, wanted to strengthen Congress, he never matched Washington's blanket statement of the need for centralized power. Before 1784 he favored a federal revenue and nothing more, not even congressional control of commerce. Indeed, Madison wanted no more reform than was necessary to protect republicanism and preserve the Union. Another significant difference is that Washington favored "a Convention of the People" to give Congress all the powers it needed in one fell swoop, whereas Madison preferred gradually amending the Articles. He would adhere to this position until 1787, when the failure of step-by-step change finally convinced him to support the idea of a general convention.[47]

In the weeks following the Newburgh crisis, Washington sorted out what had happened. He told Hamilton that he opposed using the army "as mere Puppets to establish Continental funds" and warned that the army was "a dangerous instrument to play with." Just as the commander knew that Hamilton and the

Morrises were behind a scheme that nearly ended in disaster, he also knew that Jones and Madison had resisted in Congress the same forces he had opposed at Newburgh. The episode tightened the bond between the moderates, leaving them wary of the ultranationalists.[48]

From Newburgh and Philadelphia, Washington and Madison anxiously followed the revenue plan's fate. They watched Virginia with special interest because they wished their "country" to lead the states just as they hoped the United States would guide the world. Despite receiving a shot in the arm from Washington's circular, the proposal did not win the assembly's approval until late 1784. Ultimately, the 1783 revenue plan went the way of the 1781 impost because the New England states, ever suspicious of military pensions, refused to ratify it. With the preliminary peace's arrival in April 1783, the urgency generated at Newburgh quickly dissipated.[49]

Determined to receive their pay, the Third Pennsylvania marched on Philadelphia and surrounded the State House in June 1783. When Pennsylvania declined to defend the delegates, they adjourned to Princeton. With Congress usually unable to muster a quorum at his alma mater, Madison spent much of his time in Philadelphia. Late in July, when Washington moved his headquarters close to Congress so that he could provide advice on the peacetime military establishment, Madison boarded the stage for Princeton, arriving in time for the commander's official reception on the twenty-sixth.[50]

As a member of the committee to plan America's defenses, Madison must have met with Washington fairly often. The men also met socially, as at Princeton's September commencement, which honored the commander. After the ceremony President John Witherspoon, Madison's old mentor, asked the general to sit for a portrait by Charles Willson Peale. Perhaps Witherspoon embarrassed Madison with anecdotes from the young Virginian's college days, as was his wont. Even though Washington was residing at Rocky Hill, five miles outside town, Madison probably enjoyed his company frequently. One headquarters guest remembered dining "day after day with the general and Mrs. Washington, and members of congress." Because Madison roomed with Washington's close friend Joseph Jones, he probably had more opportunities to visit Rocky Hill than most delegates. During one of these gatherings, the trio contemplated the best place to locate a national capital permanently. Perhaps they also discussed improving and linking America's eastern and western rivers, a subject that had long fascinated the commander.[51]

With independence won at last (the final peace treaty arrived late in 1783), the two Virginians retired. After resigning his commission to Congress at Annapolis on 23 December, the victorious general headed to Mount Vernon. Madison, whose three-and-one-half years in Congress closed at Princeton, had returned to Orange a month earlier. To be sure, Madison regretted not witnessing the resignation ceremony, a dramatic display of virtue reminiscent of Cincinnatus. Years later President Madison and artist John Trumbull chose four subjects for paintings commemorating the Revolution. After selecting the signing of the Declaration of Independence and the surrenders at Saratoga and Yorktown, Trumbull suggested Washington's resignation for the fourth picture. According to the artist, "After a momentary silent reflection, the president said, 'I believe you are right; it was a glorious action.'" Madison pronounced Washington's resignation "a spectacle too peculiarly interesting, whether as a contrast to the military usurpations so conspicuous in history, or as a lesson and example to leaders of victorious armies who aspire to true glory." Trumbull took the license of inserting Madison (and Martha Washington) in the picture, which now hangs in the United States Capitol.[52]

Washington's and Madison's collaboration during the Revolutionary War, albeit unpremeditated, played no small role in its victorious conclusion. Because neither viewed the Revolution as complete, however, they did not stay preoccupied with private affairs for long. Once they rejoined the quest for political reform, their friendship ripened and their formal relationship began.

2

IMPROVING RIVERS
AND FRIENDSHIPS

Thanks to the ties established late in the war, the two Virginians did not drift apart after retiring in 1783. Once Washington discovered that Madison made an excellent lieutenant in the general assembly, their friendship grew rapidly.

By early 1781, even before the two men met, Madison occasionally added his regards to other delegates' letters to Washington. But they did not begin their own correspondence until April 1783, when James McHenry, who desired a foreign service job, informed Washington that "Mr. Maddison from your State has weight in Congress and could promote" the appointment. Washington wrote to Madison, but like McHenry, he misspelled the young Virginian's name. His apology "for the freedom of this recommendation" and the fact that he addressed the letter "Sir" also indicate a noneffective relationship. When writing letters, Washington carefully used salutations to designate the level of his intimacy with his correspondent. He invariably opened letters to strangers and distant acquaintances with "Sir," letters to more familiar associates with "Dear Sir," but reserved "My Dear Sir" for close friends. Madison replied that he planned to retire before Congress made overseas appointments, but if they were taken up beforehand, he would honor Washington's request. He, too, addressed his letter "Sir."[1]

After spending the winter at Montpelier, Madison entered the Virginia General Assembly in May 1784. By trying to get his state to pay its pre-Revolutionary debts to the British, to meet its requisitions, and to strengthen Congress, he did as much in Richmond to protect the Union as he had in Philadelphia. Membership in the legislature also provided an opportunity to cement a valuable friendship with Washington. In June, Madison opened a letter from Mount Vernon that asked: "Can nothing be done in our Assembly for poor [Thomas] Paine? . . . He is poor! he is chagreened! and almost, if not altogether, in despair of relief." Washington wanted the legislature to reward Paine's services to the patriot cause. Eager for Virginia to lead rather than follow, he pointed out that New York had already provided for Paine. By now Washington was familiar enough with Madison to apologize for requesting the favor, and he opened his letter with "Dear Sir," the salutation he used with friends but not intimates, instead of "Sir." Yet the tone remains businesslike, and Madison was not Washington's sole contact; Patrick Henry and Richard Henry Lee received similar notices.[2]

Madison immediately took up the cause. Knowing that Paine had made enemies in Virginia by attacking the state's western land claims, Madison sought a modest gift. Paine's foes, however, doubled the testimonial, causing the legislature to throw out the entire proposal. Trying to salvage something before the session ended, Madison got another committee appointed, became its chairman, and wrote a new bill that failed by one vote. Madison sent a full report to Mount Vernon, although he characteristically wrote in the passive voice, deemphasizing his own valiant efforts. Whether Washington learned his true role is unclear, but his young friend's responsiveness pleased him. Madison, who agreed that Paine deserved a reward and that Virginia should set an example for other states, also acted out of eagerness to serve a man he admired and hoped to impress.[3]

In June the House appointed Madison to a committee to thank Washington "for his unremitted zeal and services in the cause of liberty." The committee praised Washington's wisdom, firmness, dignity, moderation, and equanimity, as well as "the exemplary respect which . . . you have shewn the rights of civil authority." The legislature resolved, upon the recommendation of Madison's committee, that the executive procure "a statue of General Washington, to be of the finest marble and best workmanship." Commissioning a likeness was a common eighteenth-century means of expressing admiration; a statue or painting would inspire emulation of the subject's virtues. Madison wrote the inscription for the pedestal: "The General Assembly of the Commonwealth of Virginia, have caused this statue to be erected as a monument of affection and gratitude to George Washington, who, uniting the endowments of the hero, the virtues of the patriot, and exerting both in establishing the liberties of his country, has rendered his name dear to his fellow-citizens, and given to the world an immortal example of true glory." A few months later the great French sculptor Jean Antoine

Houdon agreed to perform the work. Madison would be present when Houdon visited Mount Vernon to begin his masterpiece.[4]

Happy with Madison's efforts on Paine's behalf, Washington enlisted the young Virginian in his next public service project: an attempt to link East and West through Potomac River improvements. From October 1784 to January 1785 the two men almost single-handedly secured state legislation chartering the Potomac and James River companies. This effort was significant for three reasons. First, it brought Washington and Madison into sustained, direct contact for the first time on a joint project that succeeded so well they continued to collaborate. Second, in launching the river improvement companies, these two men initiated the chain of events that produced the 1787 Philadelphia Convention. Third, the corporations themselves became significant milestones in the history of internal improvements in Virginia and the United States.

Washington, who hatched his Potomac plans without any help from Madison, hoped to open the river to navigation as far upstream as possible by removing obstructions from the riverbed and building canals around the various falls. Roads would connect the highest point of navigation with rivers running into the Ohio. These tributaries and the Ohio itself, in turn, could be improved, a process, Washington believed, that could be extended as far as the Great Lakes. If successful, the project would open the entire Northwest to market agriculture, the fruits of which would flow to the Chesapeake. The lucrative Great Lakes fur trade would follow the same path.

Far-fetched though the idea of improving rivers to their headwaters and connecting them by mountain roads seems, Washington considered it "no Utopean Scheme." He calculated the distance from Detroit to Alexandria to be about seven hundred miles, considerably less than to New Orleans, New York, Quebec, or Montreal, the other possible destinations. Philadelphia offered a roughly equidistant alternative outlet for western produce, but that path entailed considerable overland travel. Only twenty miles of the James and Potomac routes could not be covered by water. Thus Washington waxed enthusiastic about the Potomac as the nearest and most convenient channel to the West. He insisted that it could compete with much larger rivers because barges drawing only a foot of water but carrying twenty tons of cargo would be used. Finally, among the competitors for the western trade, Virginia seemed to enjoy the most advantageous position to seize the initiative. The Spanish, instead of opening the Mississippi to woo the West into secession, had foolishly closed the river. Meanwhile, hostile Indians, the British occupation of the Northwest posts, and seasonal snow and ice thwarted the New Yorkers.[5]

An Enlightenment figure, Washington believed that natural wonders could not reach their fulfillment until man had captured and channeled them for utilitarian purposes. But a variety of more concrete private, regional, and national motives also influenced Washington. He owned over 40,000 acres in what is today southwestern Pennsylvania, West Virginia, Ohio, and Kentucky, which he had obtained in the early 1770s as compensation for his military service during the Seven Years' War and by purchasing other officers' claims. Much of it consisted of rich bottomland bordering the Ohio and its tributaries, the Great and Little Kanawha rivers. Washington had failed to lease these lands because their isolation prohibited commercial agriculture. Establishing a convenient water route to the Atlantic would transform relatively unsought-after tracts into the country's most desirable new farmland. Opening the Potomac, in short, promised Washington almost incalculable personal profits. His faltering finances could sorely use such windfalls.[6]

Personal motives were by no means Washington's only, or even primary, objective. Virginia and Maryland also would reap enormous benefits if the Northwest's agricultural output could be channeled into the region. The Chesapeake then would develop huge ports for exporting crops and importing European manufactures. Clearing the Potomac's branches also would bring large portions of both states' backcountry into the market. The most valuable benefit Washington envisioned, however, would not be personal, regional, financial, or commercial but political. He expected foreign immigrants with no special attachment to either the United States or republicanism to settle the frontier. "The Western settlers," Washington insisted, "stand as it were upon a pivot—the touch of a feather, would turn them any way." Unless the states furnished a trade route, pioneers would gravitate either toward Spain, which controlled the Mississippi, or to Britain, which dominated the Great Lakes–St. Lawrence channel. If the West fell under the influence of a foreign power, Washington feared, America would become like Europe, divided into hostile countries and constantly beset by wars and intrigues. "The consequences to the Union [of opening Virginia's rivers] . . . are immense—& more so in a political, than in a Commercial point," Washington wrote. "For unless we can connect the New [western] States, which are rising to our view . . . with those on the Atlantic by interest . . . they will be quite a distinct People; and ultimately may be very troublesome neighbours to us." In the meantime Washington hoped the Mississippi River would remain closed. He considered Spain misguided for shutting the waterway, because it bought time for the United States to establish rival trading patterns with the frontier.[7]

Washington saw an additional political benefit in opening the Potomac, one that scholars have overlooked. If one or two states cooperated on farsighted measures, they could set an example for other states to emulate, a process that would help achieve continental political reform. "The want of energy in the federal government; the pulling of one State, & parts of States against another . . . have sunk our national character much below par; & have brought our politics and credit to the brink of a precipice," wrote Washington. "Liberality, justice & unanimity in these States, wch do not appear to have drank so deep of the cup of folly, may yet retrieve our affairs." Again and again Washington insisted that Americans must "*feel* before they can *see*." That is, they had to experience the difficulties brought about by an impotent federal government before they would understand the need to strengthen it. By the same token, if a few states demonstrated the benefits of cooperation, others would wish to participate, surmounting the biggest obstacle toward reform. Washington's desire for river improvements was not the first step in a premeditated plan leading to the 1787 Philadelphia Convention, but he anticipated that river improvements could help strengthen the Union and that they should be pursued for that reason.[8]

Since 1754 Washington had thought it feasible to open the Potomac and connect it with the western waters by portage roads. A number of London merchants and prominent Northern Neck Virginians founded the Ohio Company in 1747 and two years later obtained a grant of 200,000 acres. To facilitate Indian trade and to encourage western settlement, the company hired Christopher Gist to open the first route to the Ohio River. Gist's trail went overland from Alexandria to the Potomac's Great Falls, then by water to Wills Creek, where the company built Fort Cumberland. From there, Gist blazed paths to the Monongahela and Youghiohogeny rivers, tributaries of the Ohio. As a young surveyor working for the Ohio Company, Washington became familiar with these routes. In 1753 the twenty-one-year-old traversed this land again as Virginia's emissary to the French, and a year later he marched from Cumberland against the enemy. He joined Edward Braddock's 1755 expedition, which improved the road into a military supply route. Convinced that the Potomac offered the best avenue west, he became incensed in 1758 when General John Forbes, Braddock's successor, launched his campaign from Philadelphia.[9]

The disruption of trade caused by the French and Indian War sent the Ohio Company into permanent decline, but the Potomac remained alive in Washington's mind. In 1769 he and Richard Henry Lee tried to persuade their colony to clear "the River Potomac from the great Falls . . . to Fort Cumberland," but legislative parsimony and regional jealousy forced them to give up on public funding. In 1770 Maryland's Thomas Johnson interested Washington in getting their states jointly to charter a private improvement corporation. That same year, as an agent for Virginia military officers with western land claims, Washington studied the Ohio between the Monongahela and Kanawha rivers. Two years later he convinced the House of Burgesses to allow a private company to open the Potomac. Johnson pushed a similar law in Maryland, but pressure from Baltimore merchants, who feared losing their overland trade, killed the proposal. When an ambitious entrepreneur named John Ballendine tried to go ahead without Maryland's support, Washington enthusiastically backed him. Although he believed the plan to be "in a tolerable train" in 1775, the Revolution sidetracked it.[10]

Washington's prewar efforts were not totally in vain, however, because they taught him the political realities he would face after the war. First, no improvement bill would pass the assembly that did not include the James River, the state's other western waterway. Second, Washington knew the legislature would do no more than charter a private company, which would have to assume full risk for the venture. Third, Maryland's cooperation would be necessary (that state's charter granted full jurisdiction over the river), but the Baltimore merchants would mount stiff opposition. Prior knowledge of these stumbling blocks played no small role in Washington's ultimate success in lobbying for a Potomac company.[11]

During the Revolutionary War, Washington seized every opportunity to investigate alternate avenues to the frontier, including Forbes's route from Philadelphia and the path later taken by the Erie Canal. This study further convinced him that the Potomac offered the shortest and most accessible way west. After the war Thomas Jefferson reignited Washington's enthusiasm for improving Virginia's rivers. "Nature . . . has declared in favour of the Potowmac," Jefferson assured him early in 1784, "and through that channel offers to pour into our lap the whole commerce of the Western world." But unless Virginia set to work, the Hudson, which New Yorkers already were trying to improve, would win out. Jefferson knew that getting a Potomac bill through the Virginia legislature would be so difficult that only Washington's support could bring success. The general assembly would never approve the scheme, no matter how worthwhile, Washington responded, because it would not recognize the project's long-term benefits.[12]

Despite his tepid response, Washington's interest had revived. In September 1784 he began a five-week trip to inspect his western lands. "One object of my journey," he explained in his diary, was "to obtain information of the nearest and best communication between the Eastern & Western Waters; & to facilitate as much as in me lay the Inland Navigation of the Potomack." Washington carefully explored the wilderness between Fort Cumberland and the Cheat and

Youghiogheny rivers and quizzed local inhabitants to determine the navigational potential of the various waterways and the best portage routes between them. Taking a more southerly path home, Washington investigated whether the James and Ohio rivers could be linked. The strenuous and dangerous 680-mile trip reinforced Washington's belief that "the more the Navigation of the Potomack is investigated, & duely considered, the greater the advantages arising from them appear."[13]

Jefferson also wrote to Madison urging Potomac improvements, adding that Washington had the navigation "of the Patowmac much at heart. The superintendance of it would be a noble amusement in his retirement & leave a monument of him as long as the waters should flow. I am of opinion he would accept of the direction as long as the money should be . . . emploied on the Patowmac, & the popularity of his name would carry it thro' the assembly." Unimpressed, Madison responded that "the commercial genius of this State is too much in its infancy . . . to rival" the northern states. But because Jefferson thought Washington willing to participate, Madison suggested that each state appoint commissioners to work out a solution to the river jurisdiction problem. Shortly thereafter Jefferson departed for Europe, where he would soon succeed Benjamin Franklin as minister to France. With Jefferson gone, the Potomac enterprise fell to Washington and Madison.[14]

Madison's ideas about western commerce differed greatly from those of Washington and Jefferson. Whereas the latter men were confident that the Potomac would become the primary trade route, Madison doubted that the river could be made navigable. Instead, he believed the Mississippi would remain the frontier's primary outlet, and that the United States would therefore have to open that river. He did not worry (as Washington did) that if Spain granted access, the United States would lose its hold on the West. Nor did he think that the Spanish closure of the Mississippi would quickly result in the opening of alternate trade routes (such as the Potomac) that would bind East and West together. If the Mississippi remained closed, the West, eager for access to the market, might well be lured into secession, Madison feared.[15]

Madison also apprehended that with the Mississippi shut, the West would be limited to subsistence farming for a long time, regardless of what happened with the Potomac. Instead of migrating to the frontier and becoming independent yeomen, Americans would pile up in cities as a propertyless proletariat, causing the seaboard to experience accelerated economic development incompatible with the survival of republicanism. Only an agricultural republic would ensure that Americans maintained the economic independence and commonality of interests he considered vital for successful popular self-government. Washington, in contrast, did not fear any dramatic economic development in the East while the Mississippi remained closed. He believed that when the West grew sufficiently populous, it would gain access to the river whether Spain liked it or not. Madison shuddered when Washington spoke of the river's closing as a blessing in disguise, arguing instead that the United States should secure its natural trading outlet rather than direct commerce "into artificial channels."[16]

For one who worried that the Potomac could divert attention from the Mississippi, Madison would exert considerable energy to realize Washington's dream. Powerful reasons impelled him to fight for Potomac navigation. Sharing Washington's Enlightenment mind-set about the need to improve nature's gifts, he conceded that opening the Potomac might prove feasible. Madison realized that with Washington's backing, satisfactory legislation would be more likely. A successful effort, he believed, would "double the value of half the lands within the Commonwealth, will extend its commerces, link with its interests those of the Western States, and lessen the emigration of its Citizens." Moreover, merely attempting the project might mollify the West, where secession sentiment already stirred. Most important, Madison, too, thought Potomac navigation would foster cooperation among the states and perhaps even a stronger Union. Finally, he sensed an opportunity to cultivate a gratifying and potentially useful friendship with Washington. For a variety of reasons, then, Madison pushed river improvements despite believing in the Mississippi's superiority. In June 1784 Madison sponsored a resolution appointing a Potomac River commission and inviting Maryland to do the same. Aside from this measure, he "found no opportunity of broaching a scheme for opening the Navigation of the Potowmac under the auspices of Genl. Washington." It would require a push from Mount Vernon to get the project started.[17]

After returning from his western explorations, Washington wrote to Richard Henry Lee, president of Congress, urging that the Ohio and its tributaries be surveyed. But he directed his efforts primarily toward the Old Dominion even though his main objective was continental in scope because he believed that individual states needed to initiate national reform. Washington thus sent Virginia governor Benjamin Harrison a lengthy letter calling for the establishment of a company to open either the James or Potomac River. If both waterways were opened, all the Ohio Valley's trade west of the Little Kanawha would end up in Richmond, while all the trade east of it (as far north as Lake Erie) would come to Alexandria. Washington warned that unless Virginia made it profitable for the

West to stay with the states, Britain or Spain would woo it into secession. The governor submitted the letter to the assembly.[18]

Next, Washington went to Richmond, purportedly to meet the marquis de Lafayette but really to lobby for river improvement companies. When he arrived, Madison, Joseph Jones, and three other delegates waited on him with a message from the assembly declaring that its members "not only retain the most lasting impressions of the transcendent services rendered in his late public character, but have, since his return to private life, experienced proofs, that no change of situation can turn his thoughts from the welfare of his country." Madison probably wrote this address, designed to smooth the way for Washington's efforts. When Richmond's mayor praised Washington's generalship, the guest of honor looked forward, not backward: "That this growing city . . . may improve such of the advantages as bountiful nature has bestowed, and that it may soon be ranked among the first in the union, for population, commerce and wealth, is my sincere and fervent wish." The visit touched off a week of public celebration in Virginia's capital, featuring gun salutes, processions, illuminations, dinners, and an "elegant ball" at the Capitol attended by Washington, the general assembly, "and a large concourse of ladies and gentlemen."[19]

During the next week the distinguished guest shared "several conversations" with Madison and Jones over "inland navigation; and the benefits which would . . . be derived from a commercial intercourse with the Western territory." Madison later recalled that "the conversation of the Genl. during a visit paid to Richmond in the course of the Session, still further impressed the magnitude of the object on sundry members," including himself. It was probably during these informal gatherings that the Washington-Madison association graduated from noneffective to effective status. An effective friendship is characterized by regular if not frequent contact and the mutual rendering of favors.[20]

In coming to Richmond, Washington made a shrewd and probably decisive move in the Potomac and James River companies' genesis, because it lined up support among businessmen, town officials, and legislators. Once again Washington's ability to enthrall the public struck Madison, dispelling any doubts he may have had as to whether his friend's support could secure satisfactory river improvement statutes. Carefully exploited by Madison's legislative skill, that influence would soon win concrete results in the assembly. After Washington and Lafayette left for Mount Vernon, Madison became the Potomac project's floor leader when Jones, whom Washington knew much better than Madison, accepted an executive council seat. Jones's departure cleared the way for the Washington-

Madison relationship to grow. Instead of trying to replace Jones, Washington wisely relied exclusively on Madison to obtain the enactments he wished.[21]

From Mount Vernon, Madison received a sample Potomac River bill prepared at a meeting in Alexandria. Washington's cover letter affirmed the "practicability and importance" of opening the Potomac and requested that a public company be chartered. Unless the legislature provided "efficient funds" to avoid a "limping conduct," however, the project "had better be placed in the hands" of a private company. Leaving the specifics to Madison, Washington remarked, "Your own judgment in this business will be the best guide." When the younger Virginian presented the papers on 4 December, the assembly appointed a committee to prepare a bill.[22]

The fact that Maryland would have to concur in the legislation complicated the task. Washington used Lafayette's departure from Mount Vernon for New York as an excuse for a trip to Annapolis, where the Revolutionary heroes' arrival had almost as great an impact as it had in Richmond. After conversing with assemblymen, Washington concluded that although the state would not fund the improvements (thanks to Baltimore's opposition), it would charter a private company. Back home in early December, Washington reminded Madison that because capital was not abundant in either state, the "prospect of great gain" would be necessary to entice investment. To coordinate matters between the two states, Washington advised Madison to persuade the Virginia assembly to appoint a committee to meet with Marylanders. Washington suggested placing three items on the meeting's agenda. First, the commissioners should draft identical Potomac bills to be introduced in each legislature. Second, they should obtain permission for Chesapeake-bound commerce to cross Pennsylvania's backcountry. (The Monongahela traversed that state before joining the Ohio, as did the best portage route to the Youghiohogeny.) Third, the conference should recommend that Virginia and Maryland build roads connecting the eastern and western waters. To spur his lieutenant, Washington reiterated the "*political advantages which would flow from a close connection with the Western Territory,*" concluding that the present moment was "important, favorable, and critical" for action.[23]

Madison dutifully set aside his own draft legislation and then got the assembly to name Washington, Horatio Gates, and Thomas Blackburn to join Marylanders in pursuing the three-pronged agenda. Realizing that his friend was the most qualified individual to carry out the negotiations and that his presence would guarantee Maryland's enthusiastic participation, Madison shrewdly pushed for his inclusion on the commission. Although claiming to be surprised at the assignment, Washington nevertheless sacrificed Christmas at Mount Vernon to take his Potomac campaign back to Annapolis, where he met with a ten-man delegation appointed by the state legislature. Washington, the lone Virginian present, presided over the conference. The committee report called for the chartering of a private company to improve the Potomac, in which both states were advised to purchase shares. The commission urged the states to build a road connecting Fort Cumberland to the Cheat or Monongehela rivers and advised them to seek permission to build a route through Pennsylvania to the Yougiohogeny. Thanks to Washington's intensive lobbying, the Maryland legislature hastily approved these proposals despite opposition from the Baltimore interests. Since 1772 western Maryland had grown influential enough to pursue convenient trade routes without interference from the eastern section of the state. Washington's immense prestige proved equally hard to resist.[24]

An express rider delivered the committee report and bill to Richmond so that Madison could secure passage of identical legislation before the assembly adjourned. Although Washington's official letter stated that the documents met "our entire approbation," his private communication confessed otherwise. Haste to pass the bill and get it to Richmond before adjournment had resulted in poor drafting and many inaccuracies. Nevertheless, Washington pressured Madison to secure its adoption verbatim, because with the session nearly over, "to alter the Act now . . . will not do." Playing on a sentiment that he knew his friend shared, Washington wished that Virginia's "public spirit" might match Maryland's. "It is now near 12 at night," Washington concluded, "and I am writing with an Aching head, having been constantly employed in this business" for a week "without any assistance from my Colleagues—Genl. Gates having been Sick the whole time, & Colo. Blackburn not attending." He confessed being "ashamed to send such" a scrawled and rambling letter. But he trusted Madison enough not to worry about making a bad impression or about the letter falling into the wrong hands and embarrassing him. As Washington put it, in "letters of friendship . . . allowances are expected, & made."[25]

Madison gave the Maryland bill to the governor, who forwarded it to the assembly, which appointed a three-man committee, including Madison, to examine it. Next he withdrew a James River bill that he had introduced earlier in the session so that he and William Grayson could introduce updated James and Potomac River bills based on Maryland's example. "The only danger of miscarriage arises from the impatience of the members to depart, & the bare competency of the present numbers," Madison reported to Washington. "By great efforts only they have been detained thus long." The hard work finally paid off when both bills became law on 4 and 5 January 1785, just before the session ended. Chartering a private company proved to be a less objectionable method of funding improvements than selling bonds because the project's considerable financial risk would fall not on the state but on private investors. Madison proudly sent copies of the finished legislation to Mount Vernon.[26]

The "act for opening and extending the navigation of Powtomack river" chartered a private "Potowmack Company" to clear the North Branch of the Potomac as far upstream as possible. The corporation received a permanent right to collect tolls on river traffic, exemption from taxes, and the ownership of all canal works. The Potomac Company was capitalized at $222,222 2/9, divided into five hundred shares of $444 4/9 each. The states of Virginia and Maryland each agreed to buy fifty shares. The "act for clearing and improving the navigation of James river" varied only in details. Because the James had few obstacles to remove, the company was capitalized at only $100,000, of which Virginia promised to purchase one hundred shares.[27]

In addition, Madison secured a resolution (patterned after Maryland's) appropriating money for public roads from the highest navigable points on the Potomac and James rivers to waters running into the Ohio. It also invited Pennsylvania to join the talks over Potomac jurisdiction that would take place at Mount Vernon that spring. In addition, Madison drafted two river improvement laws that deserve mention. The first granted James Rumsey a patent to manufacture mechanical boats, and the second awarded company shares to Washington for his wartime service.[28]

James Rumsey, a tavern keeper and tinker from Bath, Virginia, had previously requested a patent from the assembly for a mechanical boat he claimed could travel up to forty miles per day against a ten-mile-per-hour current. As the rushing water turned a paddle, two huge spoked wheels walked along the riverbed, moving the vessel upstream. "The apparent extravagance of his pretensions," Madison explained, "brought a ridicule upon them, and nothing was done." Undeterred, Rumsey demonstrated a model of his invention when Washington visited Bath on his way west in September 1784. Duly impressed, Washington provided Rumsey a written endorsement describing the contraption as "one of those circumstances which have combined to render the present epocha favorable above all others for securing . . . a large portion of the produce of the Western Settlements." According to Madison, this recommendation "opened the ears of the Assembly," convincing it to approve his bill granting Rumsey the exclusive right to manufacture his mechanical boats in Virginia for ten years. Thus Washington's influence transformed skepticism into belief. Irving Brant suggests that the farsighted Madison secured a patent for Rumsey's device to establish a precedent to protect authors' and inventors' rights without subjecting the public to unreasonable monopolies. Although Madison may have had such motives in mind, a simpler explanation of his action is that Washington's opinion had the same impact on him that it did on other delegates. Indeed, it caused Madison to take Rumsey's invention so seriously that he suggested using a similar mechanism to propel hot-air balloons. He also sponsored the bill as a personal favor to his friend.[29]

The second noteworthy act Madison wrote rewarded Washington with fifty shares in the Potomac River Company and one hundred in the James River Company as a testimonial from the state. In expressing Virginia's gratitude for his public service, the bill ranked the general's role in river improvements alongside his wartime achievements. Assemblyman William Grayson explained to Washington that Madison sponsored the measure to forestall other delegates from introducing legislation granting the retired commander an even more generous financial gift. Caught between the assembly's desire to reward Washington and his likely refusal to accept, Madison had suggested conveying river company shares as a compromise. He figured his act compensated Washington in a manner he could accept and would allow him to continue his instrumental association with the Potomac project despite his shortage of cash for investment. Madison understood his friend better than his legislative colleagues, but even he underestimated Washington's scrupulous fidelity to his 1775 pledge not to profit from public service.[30]

In less than two months, Washington and Madison got an entire package through two legislatures, an impressive record that would have been impossible without hard work and careful cooperation. The former's prestige and energy, a catalyst in both assemblies, complemented the latter's parliamentary skill. Chartering the Potomac and James River companies solidified their friendship, as each man came away from the experience deeply impressed with the other's abilities and what they had been able to achieve together. Their accomplishment also set in motion events leading to the 1787 Constitutional Convention. Finally, the corporations had great historical significance in their own right, launching Virginia, Maryland, and other states on an internal improvements craze and providing later projects with many valuable lessons.[31]

After briskly selling most of its shares to prominent Chesapeake gentry, the Potomac Company organized itself in May 1785. Washington became president, a post he held until he became chief executive of the United States in 1789. Over the next four years, he carried out—free of charge—his duties with an energy and exuberance that few people today realize he possessed. Nothing quelled his unbounded optimism about the Potomac's navigability, as Mount Vernon visitors attested. One guest recalled that Washington's "conversation had reference to the interior country, and to the opening of the navigation of the Potomac. . . . Hearing little else for two days from the persuasive tongue of this great man, I confess completely infected me with canal mania, and enkindled all my enthusiasm."[32]

In addition to conducting shareholder meetings and preparing annual reports, Washington (assisted by four directors) hired managers to supervise the work, secured time extensions to complete construction, and harassed delinquent subscribers into paying installments on their shares. Because America possessed no engineer with suitable experience and endeavors to procure a European failed, the company hired James Rumsey, who knew the river well, to oversee operations. By February 1786 Rumsey acquired over a hundred laborers (including many slaves) and began removing rocks and other obstructions as far upstream as Fort Cumberland. Whenever possible, Washington personally encouraged the work, which went on despite insufficient funds, unskilled and unruly help, engineering problems, and seasonal droughts and freshets. When wet weather raised the river level too high, efforts shifted to the five canals around the Potomac's various falls, ranging from Harpers Ferry downstream almost to Georgetown. The canals, about twenty-five feet wide and six feet deep, built on both banks, varied in length from fifty yards to two miles. By far the most ambitious project was the canal around Great Falls, built in Virginia and finished only in 1802. This ¾-mile canal included five locks to raise and lower boats around the seventy-six-foot falls. Two of them, blasted into a cliff of solid rock, constituted a remarkable engineering achievement. Before the completion of this last link, cargoes were carried around the falls by wagon or slid along inclined planes.[33]

Even before its first president left the company in 1789, however, construction slowed to a crawl. Rumsey resigned, overmatched by technical difficulties. His successors, a series of untrained and inexperienced overseers whose costly trial-and-error methods overburdened the corporation's finances, met the same fate. With shareholders defaulting on their subscriptions, the company had to negotiate loans and increase its capitalization. In 1822 a joint investigation by Virginia and Maryland found the corporation deeply in debt and unable to fulfill its obligation to keep the river navigable or to reach the Ohio. In 1828 the Potomac Company lost its charter to the Chesapeake and Ohio Canal Company, jointly established by Virginia, Maryland, Pennsylvania, the United States government, and the District of Columbia. The new venture abandoned river improvements in favor of a continuous still-water canal paralleling the river in Maryland. Like its predecessor, the C&O Canal Company failed to reach the Ohio, and it was ultimately driven out of business by the Baltimore and Ohio Railroad. Thus Washington's dream of a Potomac water channel to the West never materialized. A succession of later projects, however, including the Cumberland Road, the National Road, and two B&O branches, vindicated his belief in the Potomac route. That this avenue opened too late to compete with the Erie Canal illustrates the wisdom of Washington's warning that Virginia and Maryland might lose western trade to the North. The Erie also justified Washington's faith in a water route to the West.[34]

Although it got off to a slower start, the James River Company in the end enjoyed more success than the Potomac River Company. After selling its shares, the company organized itself in August 1785 and elected Washington president. Distance from Richmond and preoccupation with Potomac affairs forced Washington to decline an active role, but he retained the nominal presidency until 1795. By the mid-1790s the corporation had completed a seven-mile canal system around the falls of the James at Westham, just above Richmond. Over the next decade it removed river obstacles all the way to Crow's Ferry, Botetourt County, 220 miles above the capital. Early in the nineteenth century, it finally earned profits and soon emerged as one of the most successful internal improvements of its day. As the company made money, however, it came under attack for taking better care of its stockholders than the public. By 1820 so much pressure had built up against private ownership that the state purchased the company and operated it as a public enterprise. The James River Company (1785–1820), like its Potomac counterpart, never realized Washington's dream of connecting the Chesapeake with the Ohio. The state-owned successor, however, the James River and Kanawha Company, finally achieved that goal.[35]

The James and Potomac River companies are of great significance in American history. Within Virginia, Madison's and Washington's legislation established "a river improvements program from which the state was unable to divorce itself for more than eighty years." To projects outside the state, the companies bequeathed many organizational, managerial, and technological lessons, thereby helping to initiate a canal boom throughout the country. River improvements linked those who lived along the Potomac and James to the market, permanently changing their lives. The companies also helped bind East and West, as Washington originally envisioned, as eleven states joined the Union during the heyday of the canal companies, doubling the country's size. Even though the Potomac never became a highway to the West, the expectation that it would do so helped solidify frontier allegiance. River improvements and the hopes they engendered became a major argument for placing the United States capital on the Potomac.

Most important, by bringing states together to discuss commerce and by setting an example of successful cooperation, they fostered continental political reform. John Seelye concludes that "Washington emerges supreme at the end of the eighteenth century as the Man of Improvements." But without Madison's collaboration Washington's dream would never have been put to a practical test. Although neither man played a direct role in either company after the 1780s, their collaboration initiated these pioneering ventures.[36]

The project brought the men into steady, close cooperation for the first time. Madison, already deeply impressed with Washington's Revolutionary achievements, expressed renewed admiration: "The earnestness with which he [Washington] espouses the undertaking [river improvements] is hardly to be described, and shews that a mind like his, capable of great views & which has long been occupied with them, cannot bear a vacancy; and surely he could not have chosen an occupation more worthy of succeeding to that of establishing the political rights of his Country, than the patronage of works for the extensive & lasting improvement of its natural advantages." Madison eagerly enhanced his friendship with such an influential and admirable man. Washington benefited more directly: he had found someone he could trust to get things done in the assembly.[37]

Despite their legislative triumph, Washington and Madison had not yet advanced beyond effective friendship. The latter failed to perceive that the bill granting shares would deeply embarrass Washington. Moreover, both men continued to open and close their rather businesslike letters with words indicating nothing more than ordinary friendship. From late 1784 to late 1785, Madison and Washington remained on effective terms, not yet familiar enough to correspond about matters unrelated to river improvements. Madison did not mention other measures he sought at the 1784 assembly, such as British debt payment and state constitutional revision. The same held true the following year, when he worked to pass the revised legal code prepared by Thomas Jefferson, Edmund Pendleton, and George Wythe, including the Statute for Religious Freedom. Not fully knowing Washington's attitude toward these goals, Madison did not seek assistance in accomplishing them. Perhaps he pushed Potomac navigation, about which he himself had doubts, partly to gain an ally for his other objectives.

Madison's 1784 fight against religious assessments exemplifies his failure to seek Washington's aid in a matter he considered vitally important. Although Virginia's 1776 constitution weakened the state's established Anglican church, it did not outlaw a tax "to support teachers of the Christian religion." Many Virginians, including Patrick Henry and Richard Henry Lee, called for such a levy to stave off a perceived decline in morality. Madison, long an advocate of the total separation of church and state and complete religious freedom, considered the proposal tyrannical. Unable to defeat the assessment measure in 1784, Madison succeeded in postponing a final vote to the following year and took advantage of the legislative hiatus to rally the public. In June 1785 he anonymously wrote a "Memorial and Remonstrance against Religious Assessments," which George Nicholas and George Mason circulated throughout the piedmont and tidewater. The petition declared that freedom of religion, as a matter of "reason and conviction," was a natural right that no majority could abridge. Madison concealed his authorship to avoid alienating legislators who backed the assessment but whose support he needed on other measures.[38]

Mason sent a copy of the memorial to Washington, explaining that it had been "confided to me by a particular Friend, whose Name I am not at Liberty to mention." Ironically, the remonstrance arrived at Mount Vernon in October, less than two weeks before Madison first visited there. Did Madison see his essay lying on a table, or did his host discuss it with him? Washington assured Mason he would study the petition, adding that he opposed the assessment because it would be divisive. Pragmatic considerations aside, Washington by no means shared Madison's and Mason's views: "Altho' no mans Sentiments are more opposed to *any kind* of restraint upon relegous principles than mine are; yet I must confess, that I am not amongst the number of those who are so much alarmed at the thoughts of making People pay towards the support of that which they profess, if of the denominations of Christians; or declare themselves Jews, Mahomitans or otherwise, & thereby obtain proper relief." Washington, whose notion of freedom of conscience had not yet risen to the level of Madison's and Mason's, was not bothered by lingering remnants of a religious establishment funded by the state. By the time he became president of the United States, however, his ideas on religious freedom virtually matched Madison's, a result that probably owed much to their friendship. Although Washington never signed the Memorial and Remonstrance, the 1785 assembly passed Jefferson's Statute for Religious Freedom instead of the assessment.[39]

In March 1785 commissioners from Virginia and Maryland met at Mount Vernon to settle jurisdiction over the Potomac River and its portage routes. Madison and Edmund Randolph did not attend this conference, because Governor Patrick Henry neglected to inform Virginia's delegates of the meeting time and place. Madison did not even find out about the gathering until June. Virginia's other representatives, George Mason and Alexander Henderson, learned about it only when the Marylanders, after arriving in Alexandria, came looking for them. Pennsylvania was entirely absent, because Henry also neglected to notify that state. At Washington's invitation the delegates gathered at Mount Vernon.

Although Mason and Henderson had not been sent the assembly's resolutions regulating the discussion, they decided to negotiate rather "than to disappoint the Maryd. Commissioners; who appeard to have brought with them the most amicable Dispositions." In so doing, they unknowingly violated the instructions, which required three Virginia delegates to be present before official business could even commence. Unaware that they were not authorized to deliberate over Chesapeake Bay and the Pocomoke River, they also made agreements respecting those waters. The Mount Vernon Compact provided that "the River Potomack shall be considered as a common High Way, for the purpose of Navigation and Commerce to the Citizens of Virginia and Maryland and of the United States and to all other Persons in amity with the said States trading to or from Virginia or Maryland." The compact recommended that Virginia and Maryland coordinate their law enforcement and defense measures and make their currencies uniform. What turned out to be the most significant provision—it led to the Annapolis and Philadelphia conventions—called on the states to meet annually to discuss commerce. Finally, the commissioners requested Pennsylvania's permission to build a road to the Ohio River.[40]

When sickness prevented Mason from attending the 1785 assembly, Madison got the Mount Vernon Compact ratified, but he failed to convince Virginia to submit the settlement to Congress for approval. Had he done so, he would have upheld Congress's authority to review agreements between states—as specified in the Articles of Confederation—and won a battle at the state level in the war for federal control of commerce. By missing the conference, Madison lost an opportunity to visit Washington's Potomac plantation. He made it there in September 1785, however, when he stopped for three days en route to Philadelphia and New York, and he spent another three days there on his way back in October. "I called at Mount Vernon & had the pleasure of finding the Genl. in perfect health," Madison wrote. "He had just returned from a trip up the Potowmac. He grows more & more sanguine, as he examines further into the practicability of opening its navigation." Although Madison had traveled north the year before, these were his first visits to the estate. Although unexpected guests were common at Mount Vernon, Madison probably would not have come without encouragement. Perhaps the previous fall in Richmond, Washington had urged him to drop by.[41]

After they discussed the Potomac Company's progress, the conversation turned to continental affairs and whether cooperation between Virginia and Maryland would lead to a strengthening of the Articles of Confederation. Years later Madison told Edward Coles about his 1785 talks with Washington. "I remember hearing Mr. Madison speak of what passed during a visit he made to Mt. Vernon, about the time of the embarrassments experienced from conflicting commercial regulations of Va. & Maryland; & his having said he had long conversations with Genl: Washington on the subject," wrote Coles. "In these conversations reference was made, not only to this but to other difficulties growing out of the articles of Confederation, of which Mr. Madison . . . urge[d] that advantage should be taken of the occasion & the opportune report of the Alexandria Commissions, to urge on the Legislatures the adoption of measures of relief to a greater extent than was generally contemplated: In fine to remedy this, as well as other grievances, the Country was subjected to, under articles of Confederation—in which views & wishes, I understood Mr. Madison to say, Genl: Washington concurred." Before departing, Madison left behind some pamphlets on foreign affairs. The host in turn gave his guest Noah Webster's *Sketches of American Policy,* a pamphlet calling for a strong general government.[42]

Madison's October 1785 Mount Vernon visit corresponded with that of the sculptor Jean Antoine Houdon. While in France, Thomas Jefferson had arranged to have Houdon, whom he judged "the first statuary in the world," undertake the likeness of Washington that the Virginia assembly had requested. According to tradition, Madison watched as the artist took Washington's measurements. He may even have been present when Houdon cast his famous life mask, although the evidence suggests that it was made before his arrival. Washington, never one to enjoy sitting for artists, must have been at ease in his friend's presence to allow him to witness the proceedings. Perhaps the bilingual Madison acted as English-French interpreter.[43]

Houdon depicted Washington as an eighteenth-century Cincinnatus exchanging his military cloak and sword for a walking stick and plow. One wonders whether the artist discussed any of this symbolism with Madison; after all, who could have provided better insight into Washington's relationship with civilian government than Madison? When the finished statue finally arrived in America in 1796, it was placed in the Virginia State Capitol in Richmond, where it stands today. By then disgust with the Washington administration's policies prevented it from receiving a formal dedication ceremony. Not until 1814 was Madison's inscription finally chiseled onto the pedestal.[44]

George Washington, by Jean Antoine Houdon, 1785–88. Madison served on the
Virginia General Assembly committee that proposed procuring a statue of
Washington, wrote the inscription for the statue's pedestal, and was present at Mount
Vernon at the same time as Houdon. (Courtesy of The Library of Virginia)

Madison's visits to Mount Vernon in September and October 1785 mark the end of their effective friendship and the beginning of their intimacy. Afterwards, Washington opened his letters with "My Dear Sir," instead of the "Dear Sir" with which he had addressed Madison since 1784. This switch is significant because he carefully reserved that salutation for intimates. Moreover, Washington also added the word *affectionately*, another expression used only with his closest companions, to the closings of his letters. In the eighteenth century male friends could express their intimacy in such a fashion because fear of being accused of homosexuality had not yet established itself in American masculine culture. Madison, in contrast to Washington, continued to end his replies with expressions of "esteem" and "respect" but did not yet reciprocate use of the word *affectionately*. It is not surprising that Washington, nineteen years older and a figure of immense renown, initiated this change in the friendship, and that Madison hesitated to respond in kind.[45]

A week after Madison left Mount Vernon, Washington requested that "if any thing should occur that is interesting, & your leizure will permit it, I should be glad to hear from you on the subject." Madison took the cue. Unlike their previous correspondence, their letters began to range beyond matters of immediate concern, and they nearly doubled in length. Potomac improvements, for example, consumed no more than a fourth of any given communication, while state, continental, and occasionally personal affairs took up the rest. Madison's correspondence with Washington now resembled those carried on with his other intimates, James Monroe and Thomas Jefferson.[46]

The relationship's complete development is summarized visually in chart 1, which shows Madison's changing status in Washington's friendship universe. Before September 1781, Madison was an unfamiliar or peripheral acquaintance; Washington knew who he was, but nothing more. After they met in September 1781, Madison became a noneffective friend, a stage characterized by infrequent contact (two or three times a year) and knowledge of one another's activities, but no direct involvement in each other's lives. During Washington's 1784 visit to Richmond, the two men graduated to effective friendship, marked by regular contact (six or seven times a year) and direct mutual aid. Once they became intimate in October 1785, contact and mutual aid became frequent (at least once every six weeks). It should be noted that the diagram for Madison's friendship universe would be slightly different from Washington's. Because Madison did not immediately reciprocate signals of intimacy, the date for Washington's entrance to Madison's intimate circle would not be October 1785 but November 1786.[47]

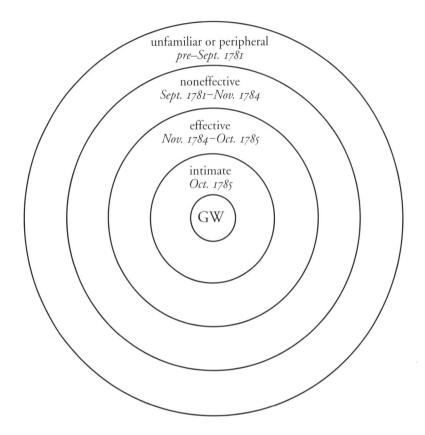

Chart 1. Madison's changing status in Washington's friendship universe

Over the next few years, Madison returned to Mount Vernon more than half a dozen times. In addition to discussing vital national affairs, the collaborators shared a variety of personal interests. In 1787 Washington told Madison about a request he had received from Russia's empress for authentic Indian documents to help her prove, by a comparison of languages, that the New World's natives were related to early inhabitants of northeastern Russia. As scientific patrons, both men took an interest in the project, and before long Madison sent his friend "a sample of the Cherokee & Choctaw dialects."[48]

Nothing illustrates the growing friendship better, however, than the interest Washington took in Madison's land speculation partnership with Henry (Light-Horse Harry) Lee. The venture originated in 1788 with Lee's purchase of 500 Virginia acres adjacent to the Great Falls Canal site, where he hoped to establish a town to be named Matildaville after his wife. Because the canal was still years from completion, produce arriving from the vast hinterland being opened by the Potomac improvements had to shift from water to land conveyances there. Manufactured goods, in turn, would be loaded on the empty barges for the voyage upstream. The overexuberant Lee expected to make Matildaville a lucrative transshipment center by erecting warehouses. Lee invited Madison to join the investment and, to convince him of the offer's worth, offered Washington's testimony: "No man more highly estimates it [the land] than General washington who is one of the best judges of property & is intimately acquainted with the place." Wary of Lee's enthusiasm, Madison sought direct confirmation from Mount Vernon. Not surprisingly, given his zeal for Potomac improvements, Washington praised the offer, but he did warn that profits from the speculation "cannot be immediate."[49]

After receiving Washington's assurances, Madison joined Lee. To help attract foreign investment for development, Lee and Madison turned to their mutual friend. While Madison prepared promotional literature (which drew heavily on information from Mount Vernon), Lee approached Washington for a written endorsement. To lend credibility to their overtures, Lee boldly requested a letter "to Mr Jefferson stating . . . the situation of the navigation of the potomac & the aptitude of the spot for water works & manufactory of all kinds." Washington assisted his friends without hesitation. Writing to Jefferson, he casually raised the subject of Potomac navigation and then praised the particular site's commercial and industrial potential. Washington left the letter unsealed for Lee's inspection, noting that he had been as discreet as possible. His willingness to use his influence to support a private speculation in which he had no direct personal stake demonstrates his loyalty both to Potomac navigation and to his two close friends. The episode also reveals that Washington, Madison, and Lee linked personal friendships to the nation's destiny: whatever benefited one, benefited the other. They would prosper personally while uniting America and making it self-sufficient. This attitude led neither to breach of law nor to the use of public office for personal gain. Their speculations were private ventures and were not based on privileged information or abuse of the people's trust. Like so many of Lee's dreams, this one quickly dissipated when Jefferson failed to persuade Europeans to invest. After Madison wisely dropped out of the partnership in 1791, Lee optimistically carried on alone until he almost went bankrupt a few years later. By the early nineteenth century, Matildaville with its six structures was a ghost town.[50]

DURING Madison's 1785 visits to Mount Vernon, Washington asked for advice on how to decline the Potomac and James River stock the assembly had voted him. The act moved him deeply, especially Madison's preamble, which expressed thanks not only for his public service during the Revolution but also for his advocacy of river improvements afterward. Nevertheless, Washington feared that accepting the present would damage his carefully cultivated public image. To understand this view, it is important to remember, first, that he expected the shares to earn immense returns quickly. Washington worried that accepting the shares would break his 1775 pledge to serve his country with no remuneration besides reimbursal of his expenses. Second, he wished to avoid the appearance of supporting Potomac navigation for personal gain, because he wanted the project to win popular approval. Third, Washington knew that accepting the shares would make him hesitant to push important public measures in the future. Looking ahead toward continental reform, he hoped to preserve his influence by keeping his motives above question.

Finally, Washington may have sensed an opportunity to boost his popularity by refusing the shares. He had, after all, built his reputation by returning power to the people, as he did when he resigned his commission in 1783. Refusing financial largesse would have the same impact. But how, he asked Madison, could he decline the shares without offending the assembly or appearing to make an "ostentatious display of disinterestedness or public virtue"? Madison, too, realized that by declining the shares Washington had "a fine opportunity at once of testifying his disinterested purposes, of shewing his respect for the Assembly, and of rendering a service to his Country." Madison recommended that the act granting shares be amended so that the profits from Washington's shares would be donated to charity.[51]

After leaving Mount Vernon, Madison drafted for Washington a letter (now lost) declining the shares. Presumably he performed this service by request, because to do so without invitation would have been uncharacteristically presumptuous. It made sense, moreover, for Washington to consult a skillful legislator for help in writing such a delicate message. Although he asked others for advice, including William Grayson, Benjamin Harrison, Thomas Jefferson, and Governor Patrick Henry, he turned to Madison alone for a sample letter. Washington thanked Madison warmly for providing the draft that formed the basis for his official response to the governor. For the first time he had sought not only Madison's advice but also his pen. The younger Virginian proved so able a ghostwriter that Washington would resort to him again, particularly in his first few months as president of the United States.[52]

Washington's letter to the governor thanked the assembly for the gift but hoped it would understand that he could not accept it without breaking his pledge not to profit from public service. He followed Madison's advice, first, by declining the proceeds rather than the shares themselves (so the navigation companies would still benefit) and, second, by asking that all dividends go to charity. To Madison he explained, "Both your requests are complied with—the first, by congeniality of sentiment; the second because I would fulfil your desire." By asking how his demurral was received in Richmond, Washington in effect pleaded with his friend to take charge of the affair. The assembly appointed Madison to a committee to prepare appropriate legislation. Madison's bill, which passed easily, praised Washington's decision as a "fresh and endearing proof of his title to the gratitude of his country" and specified that the proceeds from the shares go to charities of his choice. Madison thus helped convert an embarrassing situation into a public relations success.[53]

Washington, hoping to use the profits to establish a school for the poor on each river, asked Madison's advice about where to donate the proceeds. "Genl. W . . . has been pleased to ask my ideas with regard to the most proper objects," Madison proudly informed Jefferson. Madison, in turn, requested Jefferson's thoughts "on the case which . . . no less concerns the good of the common wealth than the character of its most illustrious citizen." With an eye to enhancing Washington's public image, Madison suggested dividing the money between "some institution which would please the [phil]osophical world and some other which may be of [a] popular cast." Ultimately, Washington's will designated that the Potomac River Company proceeds go toward establishing a national university and the James River Company profits go to Liberty Hall Academy, the predecessor of Washington and Lee University. In the end, however, the former company earned nothing; the latter raised only a modest sum.[54]

With the river improvement companies established and the problem of the gift shares resolved, the Washington-Madison correspondence petered out. In June 1786, when Madison journeyed north on personal business, he traveled not by Mount Vernon but via Harpers Ferry, where he enthusiastically inspected the Potomac works. Washington, meanwhile, occupied himself with farming, correspondence, visitors, and river improvements. Despite this communication lag, they remained intimate friends. By year's end, as both began to worry that the Union was approaching a crisis, they quickly turned to one another for advice and assistance in meeting the emergency.[55]

3

FRAMING AND RATIFYING
THE CONSTITUTION

WITHOUT THE Washington-Madison collaboration, the 1787 Federal Convention might not have taken place. As a Virginia legislator Madison placed Washington at the head of the state's prestigious delegation to Philadelphia, and as a Confederation congressman he helped remove many obstacles to Washington's involvement. Perhaps most important, he pressured his friend to attend. Washington played a more passive but equally crucial role in the convention's genesis, acquiescing in Madison's promotional use of his name, which convinced the other states to send their best men equipped with broad authority to negotiate. His name bestowed the legitimacy and popular approval vital to the convention's success. The conclave's favorable prospects, in turn, virtually assured Washington's own participation.

MADISON played a leading role in getting the 1787 convention called. At the May 1784 Virginia General Assembly session, he chaired a committee that proposed empowering Congress to prohibit trade with any country refusing concessions to the United States. Although passed by the legislature, nothing came of it. During the 1785 session Madison tried again. The northern states, losing their trade battle with Britain, seemed willing to grant the national government direction of overseas commerce. Most southerners opposed the measure, worrying that trade restrictions might leave them dependent on a northern shipping monopoly. Madison, hoping that if Virginia overcame this fear, the rest of the region would follow, suggested authorizing Congress to regulate trade and levy a 5 percent impost for twenty-five years. When, after much sectional rhetoric, the assembly limited the proposal to thirteen years, Madison joined in tabling it. On the session's last day, John Tyler salvaged something for the reformers. Building on the Mount Vernon Compact's call for interstate talks, Tyler won appointment of delegates (including Madison) to a conference to consider giving Congress control of commerce. To allay southern fears that northern commercial interests would dominate the proceedings, the convention was to meet in Annapolis in September 1786.[1]

To Washington, Madison explained that the Annapolis call "seems naturally to grow out of the proposed appointment of Commssrs for Virga. & Maryd, concerted at Mount Vernon for keeping up harmony in the commercial regulations of the two States. Maryd has ratified the Report, but has invited into the plan Delaware and Penna. who will naturally pay the same compliment to their neighbours &c. &c." Thus the Mount Vernon Conference led directly to the Annapolis and Philadelphia conventions. Although Madison supported Tyler, he did not initially condone the strategy, apprehending that a convention—where opponents of reform might obstruct the proceedings—would weaken Congress without achieving anything positive. At first he hoped Tyler's resolution would fail, whereupon he would reintroduce a bill giving Congress control of commerce. His initial lack of enthusiasm for the Annapolis Convention, then, in no way indicates reservations about ends, only means.[2]

With his own efforts having failed, Madison now willingly risked a convention. Before long, new states would join the nation, making ratification increasingly difficult, while further delay might encourage the European powers to try to divide and conquer the states. But Madison warned that too much should not be essayed at Annapolis. As much as he wanted vigorous action, he realized that "rigor . . . if pushed too far may hazard every thing." If the delegates merely demonstrated their good intentions, then the states might sponsor a subsequent convention. He hoped that a follow-up meeting would give Congress control over taxation and commerce, but he doubted even a second convention could achieve that much. The important thing was getting the reform process moving in the right direction, however slowly.[3]

In the spring and summer of 1786, another obstacle emerged. Secretary of Foreign Affairs John Jay, negotiating with Spanish minister Diego de Gardoqui, asked Congress for permission to waive Mississippi River navigation rights in return for the removal of restrictions on American trade with the Spanish Empire. Sectional debate raged until August, when seven northern states voted in favor of

Jay's request. The measure failed only because the Articles of Confederation required that nine states approve crucial matters including treaties. A steadfast defender of America's natural and legal right to the Mississippi, Madison was appalled by the northern majority's willingness to ignore the southern minority's interests. Although confident that Jay would never succeed in giving up the rights to the river, he feared that the attempt to do so would arouse sectional jealousies crippling to the Annapolis Convention. The country's regions would become too suspicious of each other for the mutual trust and concessions needed to invigorate the Confederation.[4]

Washington considered strengthening the national government essential and believed that all "discerning" Americans agreed with him. He viewed the need for congressional control of commerce as "so selfevident that I confess I am at a loss to discover wherein lyes . . . the objection to the measure." The bulk of the citizenry, however, did not yet recognize this need. Not before they had suffered the consequences of misguided policies would the masses understand the necessity: "It is one of the evils of democratical governments that the people, not always seeing & frequently misled, must often feel before they can act right—but then evils of this nature seldom fail to work their own cure. It is to be lamented nevertheless that the remedies are so slow, & that those, who may wish to apply them seasonably are not attended to." For the "discerning" to try to bring about change before the people were ready would only lead to violent "convulsions," ultimately terminating in tyranny. As long as things remained peaceful, Washington willingly let the process run its course. His optimism varied with his correspondent—he tended to be more pessimistic in writing to Americans than to foreigners—but he believed waiting on events to be the safest policy. While it would not hurt for the "discerning part" to prod the people in the right direction, forcing change prematurely would be a serious mistake. As far as his personal involvement in public affairs was concerned, Washington maintained that "it is not my business to embark again on a sea of troubles."[5]

In September, Madison attended the Annapolis Convention. Meeting at a time of confusion and sectional distrust generated by Jay's negotiations with Gardoqui, the gathering had no chance of giving Congress power over commerce. The northern states, believing that the South was not serious about reform, did not bother to send delegates. For their part, southerners suspected northerners of favoring the Confederation's dissolution. Topping matters off, the host state, afraid of weakening Congress, absented itself, leaving only Virginia, North Carolina, and the mid-Atlantic states in attendance. Rather than adjourn without doing anything constructive, the delegates called another convention to meet in

Philadelphia in May 1787 to examine all of the Confederation's defects and take measures to render it "adequate to the exigencies of the Union."[6]

When Madison stopped at Mount Vernon for three days on his way home, continental affairs crowded out other topics of conversation. With important events impending, the men agreed to renew their correspondence, which had flagged since the previous winter. Thereafter the younger Virginian began to add the word *affectionately* to the closings of his letters. It had taken an additional year and a third visit, but Madison finally reciprocated Washington's expressions of intimacy. From Mount Vernon, Madison traveled to Richmond for the 1786 assembly, where he drafted legislation sending delegates to the Federal Convention. After it passed overwhelmingly, Governor Edmund Randolph sent copies to his fellow state executives. Next, Madison faced the volatile Mississippi issue. In hopes of reducing localist sentiment, especially among westerners, he needed to assuage fears that Congress would surrender the river. Accordingly, he introduced resolutions affirming America's navigation rights, warning against the sacrifice of one region's interests for the benefit of another, and forbidding Virginia's delegates to abandon the Mississippi. The overwhelming passage of Madison's resolutions calmed opposition to political reform.[7]

Madison happily reported to Washington that his bill to send delegates to Philadelphia met no opposition. In order to enhance the convention's chances of success, he believed it necessary to appoint the most eminent Virginians as delegates and to publicize their names nationally. That way, all the legislatures would send able men entrusted with liberal authority to energize the government. Consequently, Madison intended to nominate Washington even though he had no idea whether his friend would attend: "It has been thought advisable to give this subject [the forthcoming convention] a very solemn dress, and all the weight which could be derived from a single State. This idea will also be pursued in the selection of characters to represent Virga. in the federal Convention. You will infer our earnestness on this point from the liberty which will be used of placing your name at the head of them. How far this liberty may correspond with the ideas by which you ought to be governed will be best decided where it must ultimately be decided." Perhaps Madison thought the best way to obtain Washington's participation was to present the appointment as a fait accompli, as he had done during the Potomac Company campaign.[8]

The younger Virginian kept his friend posted on the assembly's other business as well, including the Revised Code of Laws, tax bills, and his own election to Congress. From representative David Stuart, his relative and neighbor, Washington received favorable reports on his friend's legislative skills: "I have no doubt but Mr Maddison's virtues and abilities make it necessary that he should be in Congress; but from what I already foresee, I shall dread the consequences of another Assembly without him."[9]

Although relieved to find the assembly well disposed to the convention, Washington warned Madison that special circumstances prevented him from attending. He explained that the Society of the Cincinnati would meet in Philadelphia at the same time as the convention. Because poor health and pressing personal business already had caused him to decline that invitation, he did not feel free to visit the city on other business. Washington had a more weighty reason for missing the Cincinnati's conference but did not yet reveal it.[10]

The Society of the Cincinnati was a fraternal organization of American and French army officers who had served together during the Revolutionary War. Its goals of maintaining old friendships and caring for deceased comrades' widows and orphans were harmless enough, but the group's hereditary membership, national conventions, and wearing of medals embroiled it in controversy. Many believed that the society intended to replace America's republican institutions with aristocracy. Washington, the society's president, understanding these fears, tried to eliminate hereditary membership at the 1784 meeting. The national conference approved his reforms, but many state societies refused to go along. In disgust, Washington excused himself from the 1787 gathering, pleading sickness and pressing private affairs so as not to offend officers who had remained loyal to him during the war's darkest hours.[11]

Ignoring Washington's decision not to attend the convention, Madison nominated him anyway. In December 1786 the legislature selected Washington to head Virginia's representation, which also included Patrick Henry, Edmund Randolph, John Blair, George Mason, George Wythe, and Madison. The younger Virginian explained that "it was the opinion of every judicious friend whom I consulted that your name could not be spared from the Deputation." The convention was so important that Washington would be excused for going to Philadelphia despite his earlier declaration that he had no time for the Cincinnati. But even if he chose not to, Madison continued, his name needed to remain atop the delegation for its effect. The belief that the retired general would participate indicated Virginia's "earnestness" and would secure the appointment and attendance of "the most select characters from every part of the Confederacy."[12]

In response, Washington confided his real reason for not wanting to be in Philadelphia. After summarizing his attempts to reform the Cincinnati, he suggested removing his name from the delegation. But because Madison "had the whole matter fully before" him in Richmond, Washington left the final decision up to him. Washington also wrote to Governor Randolph, formally declining the appointment and explaining that he ought not to stand in someone else's way given the probability of his nonattendance. Had Washington realized that his friend would not withdraw his name, or was he masterfully cultivating the appearance of not wanting to participate even as he kept open that very possibility? Madison and Randolph refused to replace Washington, reiterating that whether Washington actually attended the convention or not, the impression that he would do so was vital to its success. Moreover, leaving his name in would allow "your acceptance hereafter, in case the gathering clouds should become so dark and menacing as to supercede every consideration, but that of our national existence or safety." David Stuart warned Washington that his involvement "appeared to be so much the wish of the House that Mr. Maddison conceived. it might probably frustrate the whole scheme" if he did not go to Philadelphia.[13]

In February 1787, after sitting out three years, Madison returned to the Confederation Congress. He left Richmond in such a hurry that he paused only briefly in Orange and neglected to visit his close friend and fellow land speculator James Monroe in Fredericksburg. Despite his haste, Madison spent a night in late January at Mount Vernon, where he tried to persuade Washington to go to the convention. He appears to have left Virginia believing his friend would attend, because he stopped pressuring him after he got to New York. Also, once Washington finally decided to participate, he did not inform the younger Virginian; if Madison already knew his intentions, there would have been no reason to notify him. Just how explicit an assurance Washington gave is anyone's guess; he probably agreed to go if the gathering promised a full turnout. If Madison received (or thought he received) such confirmation, he did not tell anyone. To Jefferson he explained, "Genl. Washington has prudently authorized no expectations of his attendance, but has not either precluded himself absolutely from stepping into that field if the crisis should demand it." Nevertheless, this statement contains an undercurrent of confidence that although Washington had made no promises, he would do the right thing.[14]

Regardless of what Madison heard or imagined at Mount Vernon, Washington had not yet made up his mind. During the visit the older Virginian probably listed four reasons besides the Cincinnati against going. Most likely Washington discussed these factors with Madison in person, because he did not convey them by mail, as he did to Henry Knox, Edmund Randolph, and David Humphreys, his other advisers. Madison's subsequent correspondence certainly indicates an understanding of these reservations. Washington's first argument against going to Philadelphia was his desire to honor his 1783 retirement pledge. Were he to attend, it would "be considered as inconsistent with my public declaration delivered in a solemn manner at an interesting aera [of] my life, never more to intermeddle in public matters." Washington was especially sensitive in this regard because his 1783 Circular to the States had coupled his return to private life with a call for a stronger federal government. To come out of retirement for the purpose of invigorating the Confederation, he worried, would leave him especially vulnerable to charges of insincerity.[15]

Second, Washington hesitated to become involved in a chain of events inexorably drawing him from the domestic bliss he had so recently regained. He pointed out that participating in the convention would "sweep me back into the tide of public affairs, when retirement and ease is so essentially necessary for, and is so much desired by me." Third, Washington wanted to make sure that he did not go to an abortive convention. He knew that his influence, however immense, would dissipate quickly if used too often or spent unwisely. For the maximum impact he had to bring his influence to bear at the right moment. "I very much fear that all the States will not appear in Convention," Washington explained, "and that some of them will come fettered so as to impede rather than accelerate the great ends of their calling which, under the peculiar circumstances of my case, would place me in a disagreeable Situation which no other Member present would stand in." Fourth, the issue of constitutional legitimacy bothered Washington. The Articles of Confederation specified that amendments must originate in Congress and be approved by all thirteen states. Instead, the Philadelphia Convention had been called by the Annapolis gathering, itself extralegal. To partake in an out-of-doors proceeding, Washington feared, would make him an overthrower of republicanism. If the convention failed, he might go down in history not as a Cincinnatus but as a would-be Caesar. Congress could help validate the Philadelphia convocation by approving the Annapolis call, but even so it would remain technically illicit.[16]

It also should be emphasized that Washington's qualms about the Cincinnati were real. He characteristically worried about how his actions would be received, especially by those whose opinion he respected. He feared that to attend the conclave after having refused to meet the Cincinnati "might be considered disrespectful to a worthy set of men for whose attachment and support on many trying occasions, I shall ever feel the highest gratitude & affection." Of course if he participated in the convention, he could then not very easily avoid continuing his embarrassing association with a controversial organization. Thus Washington faced an agonizingly difficult choice. If he went and the convention failed, his carefully cultivated reputation would be shattered. But if he stayed home and the

Republic he had helped to create crumbled, would he not deserve blame? As Garry Wills puts it, "In this major gamble of his life, no one had more to lose than he, and no one was more honest with himself about the probable stakes of a meeting in Philadelphia." The most judicious assessment of Washington's behavior and Madison's response to it is that Washington recognized that the forces pulling him to Philadelphia outweighed those repelling him. But to leave his options open, he suspended a final decision until the convention showed signs of promise.[17]

Madison understood that he could guarantee Washington's participation only by removing the obstacles to it. From New York, Madison pledged to keep Washington posted on congressional events during the winter of 1787, provided that his friend not trouble himself with "regular answers or acknowledgments." Readily agreeing to the bargain, Washington banteringly replied with a metaphor casting himself in the role of those he thought were threatening the individual property rights the Revolution supposedly protected: Washington insisted that his paltry letters would be like paying off a debt "in depreciated paper." But "being *that* or *nothing*, you cannot refuse. You will receive the nominal value, & that you know quiets the conscience, and makes all things easy—with the debto[rs]." Madison had plenty of news to report. The Congress to which he returned was weaker and more contemptible than ever. Not only had state funds virtually ceased coming in, so too had representatives, often leaving less than a quorum of seven states present. Madison had his hands full convincing this body to sanction the Philadelphia Convention and making sure the Mississippi issue did not ruin the climate for reform. He knew that unless he achieved these goals, Washington would stay home. On the other hand, Madison understood that if Congress lent legitimacy to an otherwise extralegal gathering, hesitant states would send delegates, which would bring Washington around. But most delegates refused to endorse the conclave, fearing that for Congress to push its own empowerment might damage the reform movement and dreading to kill the Confederation before creating anything to replace it. Only after Madison helped arrange for New York's legislature to request federal sanction did Congress give its blessing. As Madison expected, the move helped convince Washington to participate.[18]

Next, Madison attempted to neutralize the Mississippi River issue by moving that the talks be shifted to Spain, with Thomas Jefferson to proceed to Madrid to carry them out. When the northern states blocked his motion, Madison pointed out that Jay had no authority to abandon Mississippi navigation rights, because Article IX required the approval of nine states for treaty-related matters, but only seven states had voted to surrender the river. Although the motion again failed, it showed how much opposition there was to relinquishing the river, effectively settling an issue that would have disrupted the Federal Convention.[19]

Before leaving Richmond for New York, Madison had arranged for the governor to continue efforts to bring his collaborator to Philadelphia. Early in March, Randolph reported, "Genl. Washington will be pressed again and again; but I fear ineffectually." In spite of what he may have said (or what Madison inferred) in February about attending the convention, Washington described going through a "long struggle," lasting from December 1786 through March 1787, before finally deciding. Until late 1786 he was willing to take the chance that in time the people would recognize the need for a stronger government. That fall, however, a crisis erupted in Massachusetts that changed his thinking. Indebted farmers led by Daniel Shays, suffering from an agricultural depression and a shortage of specie, violently resisted farm foreclosures. Massachusetts forcibly suppressed the uprising, but what if state authorities had been overwhelmed? Would Congress have been able to restore order?[20]

Washington received exaggerated reports about the insurgents' strength and ambitions from Henry Knox, who insisted that the Shaysite "creed is, 'That the property of the United States has been protected from the confiscations of Britain by the joint exertions of all, and therefore ought to be the common property of all.'" These reports jolted Washington. Could the predictions of America's enemies be coming true? Was man truly incapable of governing himself? Could "the brightest morn that ever dawned upon any Country" have clouded so quickly? "If three years ago any person had told me at this day, I should see such a formidable rebellion against the laws & constitutions of our own making," he confessed, "I should have thought him a bedlamite—a fit subject for a mad house." While shocked by the lawlessness, Washington found the reaction to it among New England's political leadership equally troubling. The rebellion seemed to have instigated a loss of faith in popular self-government that historians have termed "a crisis of republican convictions." To Madison, Washington insisted that the people would not tolerate any attempt at a counterrevolution against republicanism: "I am fully of opinion that those who lean to a Monarchical governmt. have . . . not consulted the public mind. . . . I also am clear, that even admitting the utility;—nay necessity of the form—the period is not yet arrived for adopting the change without shaking the Peace of this Country to its foundation."[21]

Shays's Rebellion changed Washington's attitude toward reform. Whereas before he had been content to wait until the people saw the need for a stronger national government, he now worried that time was running out. With the

Confederation already crumbling and influential men losing faith in representative democracy, the government had to be remade immediately, even if the citizenry was not quite ready to accept it. "My opinion is, that this Country have yet to *feel,* and *see* a little more" before it would be ready for reform, Washington commented. Nevertheless, "I would try what the wisdom of the proposed Convention will suggest. . . . It may be the last peaceable mode of" saving republicanism "without a greater lapse of time than the exigency of our Affairs will admit." Necessary though he perceived the convention to be, Washington doubted its success. "Yet I would wish to see *any thing* and every thing essayed to prevent the effusion of blood, and to avert the humiliating, & contemptible figure we are about to make in the Annals of Mankind," he wrote.[22]

Although Washington knew that trusted leaders like him had to help resolve the crisis, his obsession with not breaking his retirement pledge had left him reluctant to go to Philadelphia. But by March 1787 he apprehended that he would look worse if he did not attend than if he went. Would he be charged with deserting his country in its moment of need? Would he be accused of favoring tyranny by refusing to lift a finger to prevent it? He wondered "whether my non-attendance in this Convention will not be considered as a dereliction to republicanism—nay more—whether other motives may not (however injuriously) be ascribed to me for not exerting myself on this occasion in support of it."[23]

Yet the impact of Shays's Rebellion on Washington's decision must not be exaggerated. It was not only the uprising that brought him around but the convention's chances of drawing a full turnout, which did not become clear till March 1787. Writing to David Humphreys late in 1786, Washington summarized his exchange of requests and refusals with "my particular friend Madison." He then asked a series of questions: How would the Cincinnati react if he went to Philadelphia? What did the northern states think of the convention? And most important, should he attend? Early the following March, still not knowing what to do, Washington again appealed to Humphreys for advice, and to Knox as well. To John Jay, Washington grumbled that "my name is in the delegation to this Convention; but it was put there contrary to my desire, and remains contrary to my request." As late as the fifteenth, he insisted he would not attend. In mid-March, Madison alleviated his concerns about an abortive convention by reporting that at most three states (Connecticut, Rhode Island, and Maryland) would fail to send delegates.[24]

Congressional sanction finally convinced Washington to attend, because it lent legitimacy to the gathering and removed lingering doubts about the meeting's success. Shortly before Congress acted, Madison hinted that the matter would be resolved favorably. Surprisingly, however, he did not report the final outcome directly to his friend, instead notifying Randolph, who sent word to Mount Vernon. Washington only found out about it on 24 March, over a month after the fact. Four days later he decided to go, placing three conditions on his involvement. First, his health would have to cooperate. "I have, of late, been so much afflicted with a rheumatic complaint in my shoulder that at times I am hardly able to raise my hand to my head, or turn myself in bed," he explained. Second, he would only go if Randolph had not appointed someone in his place. Third, he would not attend unless there was "a *decided* representation in *prospect*," particularly from Virginia. Washington emphasized that in going, he sacrificed his own judgment to that of his friends, who "with a degree of sollicitude which is unusual, seem to wish for my attendance on this occasion." That he did not notify Madison of his decision in a letter written three days later supports the conclusion that he had already given a qualified commitment.[25]

The governor notified Madison that "there is every reason to believe, that Genl. Washington will be present at the convention," confidently adding, "I trust that the rheumatism, with which he is afflicted severely, will be speedily baffled." Madison's tepid response to the good news indicates that he had been expecting it all along. He warned Randolph that Washington should postpone his final decision until it became clear whether the convention would elicit high attendance. He should do this even if it meant his late arrival in Philadelphia and Benjamin Franklin's being named convention president instead. If Washington ever received the advice, he ignored it. He had made up his mind. Washington's participation was indispensable to the convention's success because it guaranteed a large turnout of dedicated men and added legitimacy. The mere presence of that "great and good man," the Cincinnatus who had accepted the sword reluctantly and surrendered it eagerly, helped persuade the public of the reform movement's justness and sincerity. The fact that he had agonized over whether to attend encouraged the people to trust his decision all the more.[26]

Using the collaboration as a lens through which to view the decision to attend the convention shows that by late January 1787 Washington leaned toward participation if certain conditions (high attendance and congressional sanction) were met. A large part of the decision, in short, involved evaluating the fulfillment of these conditions. In 1804 Madison admitted having "pressed" Washington to go to Philadelphia. His suggestion, however, that the exhortations of others had "contributed more than mine to his final determination" is too self-effacing. In particular, he should have taken more credit for his actions, as opposed to his words. Putting his collaborator's name on the list of delegates and leaving it there promoted the convention. A full turnout, in turn, influenced Washington more than all the cajoling of Madison and others. For his actions alone, the younger Virginian deserves the lion's share of the praise for bringing Washington around. Alexander Hamilton, in contrast, did not exchange a single letter with Washington between September 1786 and May 1787, while David Humphreys strongly urged him to stay away from Philadelphia. Madison's use of Washington's name to promote the Federal Convention (even before he knew whether his friend would attend) is the first instance in which he used his intimacy with his collaborator to further his own goals for the nation's destiny. Dearly wishing to see a stronger general government adopted, he manipulated Washington's popularity to help achieve it. Of course the older Virginian shared Madison's goal and acquiesced in the use of his name, albeit with considerable anguish over his reputation.[27]

As with Washington, Shays's Rebellion also convinced Madison that the Confederation faced both lawlessness arising among its lower sorts and "a propensity towards monarchy" among its elites, a dual threat that left but two alternatives: either loyal Revolutionaries would save republicanism by reforming the Confederation, or the states would break apart, leading inexorably to despotism. "I hope the danger," Madison prayed, "will rouse all the real friends to the Revolution to exert themselves in favor of such an organization of the Confederacy, as will perpetuate the Union, and redeem the honor of the Republican name." Yet Madison, too, doubted the convention would succeed, even though it promised to be "very full and respectable." "The nearer the crisis approaches, the more I tremble for the issue," he wrote. "The necessity of gaining the concurrence of the Convention in some system that will answer the purpose, the subsequent approbation of Congress, and the final sanction of the States, presents a series of chances, which would inspire despair in any case where the alternative was less formidable."[28]

The collaborators' thinking also corresponded in that both envisioned national change originating at the state level. The most farsighted states would articulate the Confederation's problems and cooperate to solve them. They would appoint prestigious delegations and entrust them with full powers to find solutions. These measures would energize a latent reform impulse within other states, encouraging them to join in. Virginia, of course, would lead the way. After expressing "pleasure" that the 1786 assembly acted with "wisdom, justice, & liberality," Washington continued, "it is much to be wished that so good an example from so respectable a State will be attended with the most salutary consequences to the Union."[29]

When Madison arrived in Philadelphia on 5 May 1787, he took quarters at Mrs. Mary House's lodgings. To facilitate preconvention meetings he reserved rooms for Washington, Randolph, Mason, Wythe, Blair, and James McClurg (Patrick Henry's replacement) at the same establishment. "Genl. Washington," Madison wrote, arrived on 13 May "amidst the acclamations of the people, as well as more sober marks of the affection and veneration which continues to be felt for his character." The city's distinguished guest accepted an invitation to lodge in Robert Morris's home despite having turned down the same offer earlier. Although this development frustrated Madison's plan to keep the Virginians closely quartered, he took quiet satisfaction in what had been accomplished so far. Delegates from every state but Rhode Island would come to Philadelphia, most favoring thorough reform, and perhaps most important, Washington himself was present. For these achievements the collaboration deserves considerable credit.[30]

LONG BEFORE arriving in Philadelphia, the collaborators began thinking about how to make the federal government "adequate to the exigencies of the Union." They exchanged their ideas by mail and contemplated and critiqued each other's suggestions. Having finally decided to participate, the older Virginian initiated this dialogue, writing to Madison that he wanted not a mild revision, consisting of a few amendments to the Confederation, but "a thorough reform of the present system." In Washington's view the federal government needed strengthening vis-à-vis the states for it to achieve critical national objectives. These included removing the British from the Northwest, paying the national debt, securing advantageous commercial treaties, protecting American shipping, opening the Mississippi River, and maintaining domestic tranquillity. "The primary cause of all our disorders," he pronounced, "lies in the different State Governments. . . . The local views of each State and separate interests by which they are too much govern'd . . . must render the situation of this great Country weak, inefficient and disgraceful." Washington also believed that the rights of minorities within states, especially those relating to property, needed better protection. The present general government, Washington wrote, "has been found too feeble, and inadequate to give that security which our liberties and property render absolutely essantial, and which the fulfilment of public faith loudly requires." The problem sprang from the state governments' very structure. Reacting against the "tyranny" of George III, the state constitutions vested virtually all authority in the popularly elected lower legislative houses. With the governors, judiciaries, and upper houses unable to match the lower chambers, majority tyranny could not be stopped.[31]

To fix these problems, Washington wished to see the federal government strengthened sufficiently to act effectively in all areas that collectively concerned the states, especially taxation and commerce. With the central government's empowerment would come a commensurate weakening of the states. To keep it from "frittering" away its new powers, Congress would have to be authorized to coerce individual states. "But the kind of coercion . . . indeed will require thought." Not only did the general government need more powers, some of them would have to be shifted to less popular branches. "Having the Legislative, Executive & Judiciary departments concentered, is exceptionable," he insisted, because it robbed the government of "secrecy" and "dispatch." For Washington, effective republican government depended on strengthening, stabilizing, and balancing the general government at the states' expense to solve continental problems and end majority tyranny in the states. Washington prayed "that the Convention may adopt no temporising expedient, but probe the defects of the Constitution to the bottom, and provide radical cures" to save popular self-government. Rumors that some Americans already had given up on republicanism alarmed him: "I am told that even respectable characters speak of a monarchical form of government without horror. . . . But how irrevocable & tremendous! What a triumph for the advocates of despotism to find that we are incapable of governing ourselves, and that systems founded on . . . equal liberty are merely ideal & falacious!"[32]

Washington's prescription for sweeping change surely emboldened Madison's reform agenda, which was based on years of practical experience and months of study. In Congress, Madison had seen firsthand the general government's inability to raise money, to provide for defense, and to negotiate and enforce treaties. In Virginia he had observed the same problems from the opposite perspective, as the legislature, jealous of its authority and distrustful of other states, refused to address Congress's needs. The Confederation's failure to protect continental interests, Madison believed, had driven Virginia and the other states not only to dispute with one another over commerce but also to threaten minority property rights within their borders. Madison supplemented personal experience by studying the history of "Ancient and Modern Confederacies," which convinced him that confederacies lacked the centralized authority necessary to keep them from fragmenting. In April 1787 he wrote his essay on the "Vices of the Political System of the United States," which focused on abuses within the states. Foreshadowing his *Federalist* No. 10, "Vices" argued that a large republic could protect minority rights more effectively than a small republic because it would be harder for a self-interested faction to achieve a majority.[33]

Encouraged by his friend, Madison, too, came out for thorough reform, even if it jeopardized ratification. Better to fix the government once and for all and hope for approval than to adopt halfway measures out of fear that an effective prescription would be rejected. He believed that in shifting power from the states to the general government, the convention needed to seek "some middle ground, which may at once support a due supremacy of the national authority, and not exclude the local authorities wherever they can be subordinately useful." To best achieve this mix, "the national Government should be armed with positive and compleat authority in all cases which require uniformity," particularly commerce and taxation.

Not surprisingly, Madison offered a more specific blueprint than Washington. In reply to his friend's query about ending state abuses, Madison proposed giving the central government "a negative *in all cases whatsoever* on the legislative acts of the States." Far from seeing it as a way to consolidate power nationally, Madison viewed the veto as a way to keep the states from chipping away at any new powers the general government might receive and from interfering with each other. The veto would also eliminate state laws violating minority rights because the general government would be immune to the localized factions that occasionally controlled states. Structurally, Madison, like Washington, favored separate executive, legislative, and judicial departments, whose powers would be carefully checked and balanced. The bicameral legislature's upper house would consist of fewer members serving longer terms than the lower chamber. Being well insulated from popular passions, this house would make appointments and veto state laws. In a major departure from the Articles of Confederation, Madison hoped to base representation in both houses on population. Finally, he hoped to see the "new System" ratified by the people, not by the state legislatures, so as to legitimize the convention's work and establish it as the supreme law of the land.

In general, then, Washington and Madison increasingly aimed not at a revised Confederation but a new national government acting directly on the people, able to tax, control commerce, and enforce its decrees and featuring separate, well-balanced executive, legislative, and judicial branches. Although the states would be significantly weakened, they would still govern internal affairs. Both men believed a government so conceived could be made effective within a republican framework. Recognizing these similarities, Madison expressed pleasure that Washington's "views of the reform which ought to be pursued by the Convention, give a sanction to those which I have entertained." Washington studied his collaborator's proposals carefully, took notes on them, and even hand copied Madison's lengthy "Notes on Ancient and Modern Confederacies." His enthusiastic backing would help Madison sell his plan to the rest of the state delegation.[34]

THE Washington-Madison collaboration's major contribution to the 1787 Federal Convention was the Virginia Plan, a blueprint that quickly committed the meeting to replacing a confederation of states with a government based on the people. Although the collaboration did not, after the plan's adoption, contribute indispensably to the convention's success, it played an important role within the Virginia delegation. Together, Washington and Madison offset Edmund Randolph's and George Mason's resistance to a vigorous central government equipped with strong executive and legislative branches. They ensured the delegation's support for the finished Constitution, which Mason and Randolph opposed. The four months Washington and Madison spent together in Philadelphia enhanced their intimacy and strengthened their respect for each other's abilities. As close allies in a daily struggle for compromise among diverse and jarring interests, they came to appreciate how similarly they interpreted the American Revolution. Throughout the summer the men stood out among the delegates in their commitment to create a powerful and extremely republican government. In short, both men were what Lance Banning calls "democratic nationalists," equally committed to preserving popular self-government and protecting private property rights, fully determined to find a republican solution to the shortcomings of republican government.[35]

To the collaborators' disgust, few delegates reached the Quaker city by 14 May, the scheduled commencement date. While they waited for dilatory colleagues, they put their time to good use. "On the arrival of the Virginia Deputies at Philada it occurred to them that from the early and prominent part taken by that State in bringing about the Convention some initiative step might be expected from them. The Resolutions introduced by Governor Randolph were the result of a Consultation on the subject; with an understanding that they left all the Deputies entirely open to the lights of discussion, and free to concur in any alterations or modifications which their reflections and judgments might approve."[36]

Although credit for the Virginia Plan (as the proposal became known) belongs to the entire delegation, the ideas hardly differ from those Madison had sent to Mount Vernon. Arriving with well-thought-out proposals that Washington already backed facilitated the acceptance of Madison's blueprint. By assuming that merely increasing Congress's powers would not overcome inherent structural flaws, the Virginia Plan took the first step in replacing the Confederation with a muscular and balanced federal regime based on the people, where individual states would no longer thwart the central government, trespass on other states' sovereignty, or violate minority rights within their borders.[37]

When the conclave finally convened on 25 May 1787, the delegates unanimously elected Washington president. Madison noted that his friend "in a very emphatic manner . . . thanked the Convention for the honor they had conferred on him, reminded them of the novelty of the . . . business in which he was to act, lamented his want of better qualifications, and claimed the indulgence of the House towards the involuntary errors which his inexperience might occasion." This speech was among the first of many that Madison, who perceived the convention's historical significance, carefully recorded. "In pursuance of the task I had assumed I chose a seat in front of the presiding member" to take shorthand notes on what was said, Madison later recalled. In the hours between sessions, while the speeches were still fresh in his memory, he wrote them out longhand, thereby leaving behind an amazingly full account. It also ensured that the collaborators would spend much of the next four months facing one another.[38]

When well-spoken Edmund Randolph presented the Virginia Plan on 29 May, the convention finally got to work. For the next two weeks, the committee of the whole debated the proposal provision by provision. Having surrendered the chair to Nathaniel Gorham of Massachusetts, Washington resumed his seat with the Virginians as an ordinary delegate. Because voting was by state, it is impossible systematically to compare Washington's balloting with Madison's, but there is no reason to believe that the two men differed on any significant issues. Only in the few instances when the Virginians split about evenly were their individual votes noted. The one recorded vote during the Virginia Plan debate shows the collaborators in agreement. On 4 June the delegates considered whether the executive should consist of more than one person. Randolph insisted that a plural executive would provide an essential check against tyranny. The Virginians split, with Madison, Washington, George Wythe, and James McClurg for a single magistrate and Randolph, George Mason, and John Blair against.[39]

By early June the convention had approved most of the Virginia Plan's specifics. After a lengthy debate the delegates agreed on popular election of the lower legislative chamber. In an important speech Madison argued that election by the state legislatures would produce inefficient rule because it would introduce to the general government the vices of the states. Although he did not join the debate (as president he felt obliged to abstain), Washington, too, supported the lower house's popular election. On the thirteenth, the committee of the whole submitted a modified Virginia Plan back to the convention. It provided for a bicameral Congress—with representation in both houses based on population—equipped with a veto over state laws conflicting with the governmental charter. The only inauspicious event during the first two weeks (from Madison's and Washington's perspective) was allowing the state assemblies to elect the upper legislative house. This decision posed two problems. First, a Senate chosen by the states would not check the abuses of either the states or the lower chamber because it would be elected by and dependent upon the same localistic bodies that produced so much unjust legislation. Second, a Senate apportioned by population and elected by the legislatures would make the upper house unwieldy (even if the smallest state possessed only one senator). Far from being a dispassionate deliberative body capable of restraining democratic excesses, a large Senate would mirror the lower house. In supporting state election of the upper house, the Virginia delegation voted against Madison. Because Washington saw the states as one of the Confederation's biggest problems, he likely sided with his friend. The only way to free the general government from localistic states would be to base it entirely on the people.[40]

Trouble started during the second week of June, when the small states, fearful of losing their influence in a government with representation based entirely on population, began to snipe at the Virginia Plan. The opposition jelled behind William Paterson, who on the fifteenth introduced the New Jersey Plan as an alternative. Instead of creating a new national government acting directly on the people, Paterson proposed strengthening the existing Confederation. The New Jersey Plan called for the retention of a unicameral legislature with the states each possessing one vote, to which would be added executive and judiciary branches. Viewing the Confederation as inherently flawed, the collaborators saw the New Jersey Plan as a grave threat. Because the state legislatures impeded Congress and caused many injustices, their direct agency in the central government had to be eliminated by adopting a strictly national regime. Besides, the large states would never invest significant new powers in a government lacking proportional representation.[41]

Starting on 16 June, the committee of the whole debated the New Jersey Plan. After James Wilson, Edmund Randolph, and Alexander Hamilton questioned the viability of confederations, Madison delivered the coup de grâce. Under that form of government, he argued, Congress would steadily lose power to the states. Nor could a confederation protect minority rights within the states. Ominously he reminded the small states that they would be safer in a government based entirely on population than they would be without any general government at all. After Madison demolished the New Jersey Plan, the committee immediately rejected it. But Paterson's followers refused to give in. On 20 June, with Washington back in the chair, the delegates debated the Virginia Plan as reported by the committee of the whole. Over the following days the small states made clear that they would settle for nothing less than state equality in the Senate. Unable to agree on a solution, the convention on 2 July passed the thorny representation issue to a committee. The resulting compromise based representation in the lower house on population; in the upper house each state would have two senators.[42]

The settlement angered the collaborators because they could not understand why the Senate should enable the small states, representing a popular minority, to impede the majority. Allowing the states an equal voice would only make the Senate a carbon copy of the gridlocked Confederation Congress. "The State of the Councils," Washington despondently wrote on 10 July, was "in a worse train than ever. In a word, I *almost* dispair of seeing a favourable issue to the proceedings of the Convention, and do therefore repent having had any agency in the business." He blamed the small-state delegates: "The men who oppose a strong and energetic government are, in my opinion, narrow minded politicians, or are under the influence of local views." Only a national government could fix America's problems, yet these men opposed curbing the states. "The crisis is equally important and alarming," Washington concluded.[43]

When, after considerable wrangling, the convention accepted the compromise on 16 July, Randolph moved to adjourn so that the large-state men could contemplate their next move. At a meeting the following morning, Madison pleaded in vain for the large states to hold their ground, even if Paterson's supporters went home. When the caucus failed to agree on a course of action, the small-state victory was secure. As a large-state man, Washington presumably attended this gathering and witnessed Madison's stubbornness at its worst. This obstinacy probably did not bother him, however, because Washington's earlier declarations about the importance of thorough reform suggests that he, too, remained intransigent. Some have argued that Washington supported compromise, but little evidence supports this view. On the contrary, delegate Luther Martin of Maryland insisted, "During this *struggle* to prevent the *large* States from having *all power* in their hands, which had nearly terminated in a dissolution of the convention, it did not appear to me, that . . . Mr. *Washington* . . . was disposed to favor the claims of the *smaller States,* against the *undue superiority* attempted by the large States." The only evidence that Washington worked for compromise appears in an 1825 statement, attributed to delegate Jonathan Dayton, that he sanctioned conciliation with facial expressions. Washington's mere presence, of course, had a powerful moderating effect, but whether he actually pushed mutual concessions is another matter. His own statement that he "was ready to have embraced any tolerable compromise that was competent to save us from impending ruin" does not reveal whether he supported the Great Compromise, because we do not know whether he considered the solution "tolerable."[44]

Later the same day Madison's and Washington's hopes received another blow when the convention struck out Congress's power to veto state laws in favor of making the Constitution the supreme law of the land. To commiserate with his colleague after two bitter defeats, Washington dined that afternoon at Madison's boardinghouse. It is of course fortunate that the collaborators failed to obtain the congressional veto, because its adoption would have killed off all hope of ratification by the states. As Lance Banning argues, the veto was not intended to achieve consolidation of power in the general government but as a defensive measure to protect the federal government from state encroachments. The delegates, wisely seeing the veto's liabilities, voted it down.[45]

Although dissatisfied, neither collaborator gave up on the convention, a decision that reflects a change of heart of sorts. Before the Great Compromise's adoption, they intended to hold out for the perfect government. Now both settled for the best constitution they could get because they realized the alternative would be disunion and despotism. Once an element of state influence, or federalism, had been injected into what they had hoped would be a strictly national government, Madison and Washington reoriented their thinking about how the government's branches should be balanced. Because a group of small states, representing a popular minority, could use the Senate to thwart the majority, the collaborators believed it necessary further to check Congress vis-à-vis the executive and judiciary. One of the rare ballots for which a breakdown of the Virginians survives provides an illustration. On 12 September, Washington and Madison voted to require three-fourths rather than two-thirds of Congress to overturn a presidential veto. They carried the Old Dominion, but they were outvoted six states to four. Although they hoped to bolster the executive and judicial branches, the collaborators still favored a strong legislature. On 21 August they showed how far they would go by twice voting to allow Congress to tax exports. They supported the measure because they did not want to restrict control over commerce or taxation, even if the power might be turned against the South.[46]

On 12 September the committee of style reported a draft constitution for final revision. After last-minute changes the states unanimously approved it on the fifteenth. Virginia's vote was quite close, with Washington, Madison, and Blair edging out Mason and Randolph, who thought the convention's work would lead to tyranny. Shortly before final approval, the disgruntled Virginians moved that the state ratifying conventions be allowed to propose amendments to be considered by a second general convention. All twelve states voted against the motion. Again the Virginia delegation split, with Washington, Madison, and Blair once more defeating Mason and Randolph.[47]

On 17 September, when the convention assembled to sign the completed Constitution, Gorham urged a reduction in the number of constituents each congressman would represent from 40,000 to 30,000. Madison recorded Washington's reaction:

> He said that although his situation had hitherto restrained him from offering his sentiments on questions depending in the House, and it might be thought, ought now to impose silence on him, yet he could not forbear expressing his wish that the alteration proposed might take place. It was much to be desired that the objections to the plan recommended might be as few as possible. The smallness of the proportion of Representatives had been considered by many members of the Convention an insufficient security for the rights & interests of the people. He acknowledged that it had always appeared to himself among the exceptionable parts of the plan, and as late as the present moment was for admitting amendments, he thought this of so much consequence that it would give him much satisfaction to see it adopted.

The convention accepted this republican-minded change unanimously without further debate. With the final alteration in place, all the delegates except Mason, Randolph, and Elbridge Gerry of Massachusetts endorsed the Constitution. Before the convention adjourned sine die, it gave custody of its journal to its president, who allowed Madison to use it to revise and correct his convention notes. Washington retained the volume until his relationship with Madison soured. During the 1796 Jay Treaty fight, he deposited it in the State Department in an effort to embarrass Madison and the Republicans.[48]

Almost all of the delegates shared certain attitudes toward their task. Most sought a stronger central government equipped with separate executive, legislative, and judicial branches and capable of governing effectively in matters affecting the states collectively. They hoped to curb abuses within the states, especially attacks on minority rights, but in strengthening the government, the conventioneers wanted it to remain republican. Within these broad parameters the delegates ranged considerably. Madison and Washington, of course, stood with nationalists like Gouverneur Morris, Robert Morris, Alexander Hamilton, Rufus King, and the Pinckneys in favoring a powerful, strictly national government.

Like the Morris-Hamilton-King-Pinckney group, they favored a constitution strong enough to coerce the states or veto state laws. But the collaborators differed from most nationalists in the depth of their commitment to self-government. In fact, what distinguishes them from their colleagues is their faith in building a powerful yet extremely republican framework. Among the delegates James Wilson most closely matched their dual attachment to an energetic and popular central government. Neither Washington nor Madison doubted (as Hamilton openly did) that republicanism was the best political system devised by man.[49]

Madison consistently argued that the solution for republicanism's shortcomings was republicanism itself. By creating a large republic with separate, balanced branches representing different constituencies, rule by the people could be made effective, stable, and just. From the convention's beginning, he eloquently defended popular election of the House of Representatives "as a clear principle of free Govt." On 10 July, Madison suggested doubling the lower chamber's size so that it would better mirror the public. After the Great Compromise's acceptance, he argued that letting the people choose the executive would make it more independent than would legislative election. Madison also opposed property qualifications for voting, favored a short naturalization period, and advocated Congress's periodic reapportionment. He summed up his attitude when he told the convention that "he conceived it to be of great importance that a stable & firm Govt. organized in the republican form should be held out to the people." Washington also sought a powerful and republican constitution. Significantly, the only time he spoke during the entire convention (when he urged reducing the size of congressional districts), it was to make the government not more energetic but more republican.[50]

That the collaborators consistently voted together indicates how closely their thinking corresponded. On only six occasions were the Virginians' individual votes recorded. Of these half-dozen times, they balloted alike every time but one. In their quest for a strong executive, they favored a single chief magistrate, a three-fourths vote to override a veto, and election by the people. To strengthen Congress's control over commerce, they twice voted to allow a tax on exports. In only one recorded instance did the collaborators vote against each other: Washington favored and Madison opposed allowing the House of Representatives to originate appropriations bills. The younger Virginian considered the occurrence so unusual that he asterisked into his notes an explanation of his friend's behavior: Washington had previously sided with Madison but "gave up his judgment he said because it was not of very material weight with him & was made an essential point with others who if disappointed, might be less cordial in other points of real weight."[51]

A comparison of Virginia's votes with the speeches of its delegates reveals that Washington and Madison balloted alike on at least four other issues. On 15 September, for example, Randolph and Mason defended a second convention, but the delegation as a whole rejected the measure. Because the only other Virginians present were Madison, Washington, and Blair, all three must have united in opposition. All told, the two men voted together eight out of the ten times that their individual votes can be determined. At first, a mere ten votes out of the hundreds taken seem weak grounds for concluding that Washington and Madison consistently voted alike. However, it must be remembered that the only ballots in which individual votes were recorded or can otherwise be pinpointed were the most divisive and therefore the most controversial ones. If the two men voted together on 80 percent of the convention's most controversial motions, it seems safe to conclude that they rarely disagreed with one another, especially over fundamental principles.[52]

Contemporary writings corroborate that Washington and Madison voted together. After McClurg went home late in July, Madison pleaded with him to return to Philadelphia. McClurg declined, pointing out "my vote could only *operate* to produce a division, & so destroy the vote of the State." Because Mason, Randolph, and Blair typically voted in unison, McClurg could only have meant that if he returned, the delegation would split Washington-Madison-McClurg versus Mason-Randolph-Blair, and the state's vote would be lost. Thus McClurg took for granted that the collaborators voted alike. Of course, Madison did not approve McClurg's reasoning; from his and Washington's perspective, tie votes were better than defeats.[53]

Not long after McClurg's departure, rumors circulated in Richmond that Madison and Washington balloted against the state's other delegates. "It is *whispered* here," Joseph Jones informed Madison, that "there is great disagreemt. among the Gent. of our Delegation—that the General and yourself on a very important question were together." According to Jones, "The question in dispute . . . respected either the defect in constituting the convention, as not proceeding immediately from the people, or the referring the proceedings of the Body, to the people for ultimate decision and confirmation." Jones assured that the story sprang "from the fountainhead." If the Virginia delegation split over the gathering's legitimacy or the method of ratifying the Constitution, the convention records do not show it. Silence hardly rules out its occurrence, however, because individual votes were rarely recorded. On the contrary, the rumor seems very plausible, especially considering that McClurg returned to Richmond to sit alongside Jones on the council of state. Anything McClurg told Jones certainly sprang "from the fountainhead."[54]

Generally, the collaborators opposed the same men within the delegation. The Virginians divided infrequently, but when they did, Washington and Madison almost always countered Mason and Randolph. The collaborators were more inclined to empower the central government than their foes and were more willing to strengthen the executive and judiciary within that government. Thus Washington and Madison formed a crucial bulwark without which Virginia's delegation would not have approved the Constitution. Had the state delegations not acted unanimously, the reforms probably never would have won acceptance. Had Virginia—probably the most influential state—rejected the Constitution at Philadelphia, the new government might not have gotten off the ground.[55]

Contemporaries and historians disagree over the separate roles Washington and Madison played during the convention. Some believe that the former exercised considerable hidden-hand leadership in working out compromises, while others insist that he took a hands-off approach. Some emphasize the latter's leadership in debate, while others focus on his intransigence over the representation question. What seems clear is that after the Virginia Plan's adoption, the collaboration probably did not indispensably contribute to the convention's success (with the exception of its role within the Virginia delegation). The convention had an important impact on the collaboration, however. Four months of daily contact strengthened the intimacy that had grown over the preceding years.[56]

The convention met from 25 May to 17 September, usually about five hours a day, six days a week. The delegates took only one lengthy recess, from 26 July to 6 August. Despite this rigorous schedule, neither man missed even a portion of a session. As a result, each was able to observe the other's performance in a deliberative assembly for the first time. Washington had heard of Madison's abilities; now he witnessed them firsthand. From among America's finest intellects, Madison emerged as perhaps the most knowledgeable and hardest-working delegate, whose study of ancient and modern confederacies left him better prepared than his colleagues. His charisma may have been weak, but his dispassion, logic, and consistency were unmatched. "Mr. Maddison is a character who has long been in public life; and what is very remarkable every Person seems to acknowledge his greatness," wrote Georgia delegate William Pierce.

> He blends together the profound politician, with the Scholar. In the management of every great question he evidently took the lead in the Convention, and tho' he cannot be called an Orator, he is a most agreeable, eloquent, and con-

vincing Speaker. From a spirit of industry and application which he possesses in a most eminent degree, he always comes forward the best informed Man of any point in debate. The affairs of the United States, he perhaps, has the most correct knowledge of, of any Man in the Union. He has been twice a Member of Congress, and was always thought one of the ablest Members that ever sat in that Council. Mr. Maddison is about 37 years of age, a Gentleman of great modesty,—with a remarkable sweet temper. He is easy and unreserved among his acquaintance, and has a most agreeable style of conversation.

Convention secretary William Jackson agreed with Pierce. In 1819 he recalled that "by far the most efficient member of the Convention was Mr. Madison."[57]

Madison's performance, easily the most impressive of his career to date, also profoundly impressed Washington, who regarded highly his friend's approach to debate. Washington's advice on how to address a legislative body, given to a young member of Virginia's legislature only a few months after the convention, reads like a description of Madison: "If you mean to be a respectable member, and to entitle yourself to the Ear of the House" speak "on important matters—and then make yourself thoroughly acquainted with the subject. Never be agitated by *more than* a decent *warmth,* & offer your sentiments with modest diffidence—opinions thus given, are listened to with more attention than when delivered in a dictatorial stile. The latter, if attended to at all, altho they may *force* conviction, is sure to convey disgust also." The fact that Washington consistently agreed with Madison's arguments made them all the more convincing.[58]

The convention reinforced Madison's impressions of Washington. Doubtless he would have seconded William Pierce's characterization: "Like Gustavus Vasa, he may be said to be the deliverer of his Country;—like Peter the great he appears as the politician and the States-man; and like Cincinnatus he returned to his farm perfectly contented with being only a plain Citizen, after enjoying the highest honor of the Confederacy,—and now only seeks for the approbation of his Country-men by being virtuous and useful." America's love for Washington had not diminished since his retirement.[59]

The four months the collaborators spent in Philadelphia offered frequent opportunities to socialize and, quite likely, to forget the convention briefly. They could not spend as much time recreating together as they would have liked, because busy schedules consumed their time. Washington complained that the convention, personal business, and social obligations left "scarcely a moment" to spare, while Madison kept busy transcribing his notes into polished prose. Even when together, the two were rarely alone. The surviving records reveal only a handful of the many social events both attended, such as on 16 May, when Benjamin Franklin hosted the two dozen delegates present. A week later Madison and a few others joined Washington for a trip across the Schuylkill River to visit two noted horticulturists. First, the sightseers observed extensive agricultural experiments at Belmont, the home of Pennsylvania assemblyman Richard Peters. In addition to demonstrating a new harrow, Peters may have regaled his guests with some of his off-color poems. Next they toured William Hamilton's Bush Hill, renowned for fine landscape gardening and rare plants. Washington and Madison regularly discussed the year's harvest and exchanged information about a drought in Virginia's Northern Neck. Often the delegates met after hours for meals or other events, as on 4 July, when they adjourned early to hear an Independence Day oration. From time to time the conventioneers messed together at the Indian Queen or City taverns. Twice Washington ate at Mrs. House's, where Madison stayed. After one of these dinners, the men visited the gardens, greenhouses, and nature trails at Gray's Ferry. Finally, after the Constitution's 17 September signing, Washington recorded that "the Members adjourned to the City Tavern, dined together and took a cordial leave of each other."[60]

The Virginia Plan—the Washington-Madison collaboration's main contribution to the 1787 Federal Convention—meant that instead of reforming the Confederation, the assemblage designed a partly national, partly federal government capable of resolving America's political problems. After the Virginia Plan's adoption, the Washington-Madison friendship did not play a vital role in the convention's success, but it did offset Mason's and Randolph's influence within the Virginia delegation. That the two men consistently voted alike indicates a remarkable congruity in their thinking. Among the delegates they stand out for their dual commitment to a powerful and republican central government. Consistently cooperating drew Washington and Madison closer, thereby setting the stage for their collaboration during the ratification campaign.

"A GREATER Drama is now acting on this Theatre than has heretofore been brought on the American Stage, or any other in the World," wrote Washington about ratification. "We exhibit at present the novel & astonishing Spectacle of a whole People deliberating calmly on what form of government will be most conducive to their happiness." Throughout this "drama" Washington and Madison worked together to ensure a denouement favorable to the Constitution. If the collaborators recognized imperfections in the convention's handiwork, they favored its unconditional acceptance because they saw the alternative as disunion. Their identical views provided a firm foundation for their cooperation during ratification. Between September 1787 and August 1788, they inspired one another to impressive exertions for the cause. Together they mapped strategy and exchanged information that helped achieve Federalist victory in Virginia and the nation. During ratification the collaboration became publicly recognized for the first time.[61]

At the Federal Convention, Madison sought to strengthen the central government's control over the states and to check the House of Representatives. These objectives reflect his belief that all-powerful legislatures (such as the states had created in 1776) could pass shortsighted and even tyrannical legislation because they blindly obeyed the majority, often ignoring constitutions and violating minority rights. By shifting power to the continental level, Madison reasoned, the common good would prevail over factional interests because self-interested groups would find it harder to dominate a large republic than a single state. Moreover, he believed that the federal government's big electoral districts guaranteed the election of broad-minded men over locally oriented candidates. Within the federal government the executive, judiciary, and Senate needed strengthening against the House of Representatives to prevent despotic or myopic legislation in case a national faction emerged.

Although generally successful, Madison failed to achieve important specifics. To keep the states from encroaching upon the central government, to protect the states from one another, and especially to guard state minorities, he had hoped to allow Congress to veto state legislation. To his displeasure the convention instead made the Constitution the land's supreme law and prohibited states from certain activities, such as coining money and impairing contracts. Madison also hoped to base Senate representation on population and to have the House—rather than the state legislatures—elect senators. This policy would ensure the election of farsighted men over factional candidates and demagogues. He failed as well to obtain a joint executive-judicial council to review prospective federal laws. Madison preferred this method over judicial review because it provided a remedy before unjust legislation took effect. He also feared that neither the executive nor the judiciary was individually powerful enough to nullify a law passed by a popularly elected legislature. Together, these disappointments convinced Madison that the Constitution would "neither effectually answer its national object nor prevent the local mischiefs which every where excite disgusts agst the state governments."[62]

Madison nevertheless applauded the proposed framework, especially the division of powers between the levels of government. Keeping local issues local, he explained in *Federalist* No. 14, would allow the "practicable sphere" of the Republic to be large. Direct taxation and control of commerce, however, had been properly lodged with Congress. Perhaps Madison would have preferred a general government based solely on the people rather than a federal government based on the people and the states, but he now saw the benefits in the Constitution's partly federal, partly national composition. His *Federalist* No. 62, for example, noted that federalism doubly checked unfair acts, because "no law or resolution can now be passed without the concurrence first of a majority of the people, and then of a majority of the states." Madison favored the Constitution's strong executive and judicial branches (although he wished they were stronger), especially the way they checked and balanced the legislature. As for Congress, he hoped six-year Senate terms would provide experience and continuity, enabling that body to thwart sudden popular impulses from the House. Most important, Madison rejoiced that such a stable and energetic government possessed a firm republican foundation.[63]

Because Washington had not arrived in Philadelphia committed to many specifics, his satisfaction with the Constitution matched or exceeded Madison's. Certain that the proposed government's strengths outweighed its weaknesses and unwilling to jeopardize ratification, Washington focused on the Constitution's assets. Because "the general Government is not invested with more Powers than are indispensably necessary to perform [the] functions of a good Government," he believed, "no objections ought to be made against the quantity of Power delegated to it." Because those powers were balanced among the government's branches and levels, tyranny was impossible "so long as there shall remain any virtue in the body of the People." Washington thought national control of taxation and commerce would enable the United States to defend itself, to secure trade concessions, to protect property, and to encourage economic growth and prosperity. Madison testified "that no member of the Convention appeared to sign the Instrument with more cordiality than he [Washington] did, nor to be more anxious for its ratification. I have indeed the most thorough conviction from the best evidence, that he never wavered in the part he took in giving it his sanction and support."[64]

Although they may have questioned some of the Constitution's details, both collaborators agreed that nothing better could have been achieved. "It appears to me," Washington wrote, "little short of a miracle, that the Delegates from so many different States . . . should unite in forming a system of national Government, so little liable to well founded objections." Considering that the convention had to balance the interests of the large and small states, the North and South, federal and state powers, and republicanism with energy and efficiency,

Madison concluded, "it is impossible to consider the degree of concord which ultimately prevailed as less than a miracle." Rather than dreaming of the ideal, Washington asked, "Is the Constitution . . . preferable to the government (if it can be called one) under which we now live?" He answered affirmatively. In *Federalist* No. 38, Madison agreed: "It is a matter both of wonder and regret, that those who raise so many objections against the new constitution, should never call to mind the defects of that which is to be exchanged for it. It is not necessary that the former should be perfect; it is sufficient that the latter is more imperfect."[65]

These Virginians saw disunion as the alternative to ratification. Without strong central authority, the states would break into regional confederacies and begin fighting among themselves, which would inevitably result in despotism. The men even used the same metaphor—a foundering ship—to describe America's republican experiment. To his collaborator Madison characterized reform as an "anchor against the fluctuations which threaten shipwreck to our liberty." Looking back after ratification (and perhaps borrowing his symbolism from Madison), Washington explained, "The great danger . . . was that every thing might be thrown into the last stage of Confusion before any government whatsoever could have been established; and that we should have suffered a political shipwreck."[66]

Understandably, then, the collaborators opposed anything that might jeopardize ratification, particularly any attempt to amend the new document prematurely. Having seen one convention nearly fail, they held no illusions about the success of another. If Antifederalists from a single state could not agree on the Constitution's defects, Washington wondered, "what prospect is there of a coalescence . . . when the different views, and jarring interests of so wide and extended an Empire are to be brought forward and combated?" Both men categorized Americans into three groups. The largest, which included themselves, favored "adopting without attempting Amendments." The next largest wished to ratify but first wanted amendments. The smallest, hostile to the Constitution, hoped to exploit the first two groups' differences to prevent adoption. Under these circumstances the Union's true friends needed to unite behind unconditional ratification.[67]

The collaborators represent the Federalist mentality. For them a weak confederacy posed a greater threat to liberty than an energetic federal government. Lacking this faith, Antifederalists preferred an ineffective government rather than risking the loss of their liberty to a powerful government. Washington had not "been able to discover the propriety of preventing men from doing good, because there is a possibility of their doing evil." Unlike the Antifederalists, these men did not view the Constitution as a radical departure from the Articles of Confederation. As Madison put it, "The powers vested in the proposed government, are not so much an augmentation of the powers in the general government, as a change rendered necessary, for the purpose of giving efficacy to those which were vested in it before." Instead of envisioning the shift of authority from the state to the federal level, they saw it as being transferred from many smaller constituencies to a single large one. "The power under the Constitution will always be with the people," Washington emphasized. They also understood, as the Antifederalists could not, that the Federal Convention had created a partly national, partly federal mixture rather than a consolidated central government. Indeed, they believed that the balance of power still favored the states, and that the greatest threat to American liberty was not minority but majority tyranny.[68]

Interpreting ratification as a clear-cut choice between freedom and tyranny, the collaborators judged the Constitution's opponents as being too ignorant and shortsighted to understand the nation's true interests. Pennsylvania Antifederalists needed "only to be seen to be disregarded," Washington derided, while Madison noted that in most states "men of intelligence, patriotism, property, and independent circumstances" overwhelmingly supported the Constitution. But in Virginia—where the elites divided evenly—the collaborators ascribed the gentry's Antifederalism to egotism or worse. Their attitude toward George Mason is a case in point. Shortly after the convention Mason wrote a pamphlet complaining that the federal government's powers had been poorly checked and balanced. The House of Representatives was too weak; the Senate was too powerful, and its responsibilities were unduly blended with the president's. Mason wished to see the executive restrained by a council of state, the South protected against unfair commercial laws, and personal liberty guarded with a bill of rights. The pamphlet concluded that unconditional ratification would quickly result in aristocracy or monarchy.[69]

Washington forwarded a copy of Mason's handiwork to Madison, describing it as an attempt "to alarm the people" and suggesting that "sinister and self important motives governed Antifederalist leaders." Madison, too, questioned the author's intentions and arguments, suggesting that Mason entertained "a vain opinion . . . that he has influence enough to dictate a constitution to Virginia, and through her to the rest of the union." Both were frustrated with Mason's course partly out of state pride. After Virginia had led the reform movement, they did not want it to end up like Rhode Island, which they scorned for obstructionism. Washington and Madison explained away rank-and-file Antifederalists as having been misled by demagogues like Mason. "Every art that could inflame the passions or touch the interests of men have been essayed," Washington complained. "The ignorant have been told, that should the proposed Government obtain, their lands would be taken from them and their property disposed of."[70]

If they shared attitudes toward ratification, the collaborators' roles during the contest differed. From Philadelphia, Madison returned to New York, where he publicly defended the Constitution in Congress, wrote partisan essays, and acted as a Federalist clearinghouse. Washington, in contrast, remained above the fray, not wandering "six miles beyond the limits of my own farms" for the next half year. As certain first president should the Constitution be ratified, Washington felt obliged to appear disinterested, a position that did not hurt the cause because his position was widely known. Anything he said would only have opened his motives to question. His isolation from the Federalists' campaign was more apparent than real, however. Despite protesting that "there is not perhaps a man in Virginia less qualified than I am, to say from his own knowledge & observation, what will be the fate of the Constitution," no one followed the issue more closely. He mined so many newspapers, correspondents, and visitors for the latest information that Mount Vernon secretary David Humphreys described him as "the focus of political Intelligence for the New World." In addition to staying informed, he campaigned actively but invisibly. Accompanying "the weight of Genl. Washington's name," Madison shrewdly noted, would be "some exertion of his influence."[71]

Washington helped sell the new government in the newspapers. Antifederalists had hardly begun their attacks before he complained, "The opponents of the Constitution are indefatigable in fabricating and circulating papers, reports, &c. to its prejudice, whilst the friends [who] *generally* content themselves with the goodness of the cause and the necessity for its adoption suppose it wants no other support." Washington suggested that able defenses "by good pens" should be published "in the Gazettes." In New York, Alexander Hamilton began a series of newspaper essays known collectively as the *Federalist.* Madison and John Jay joined the task, an ambitious study of virtually every aspect of the new government. Between November 1787 and May 1788, Madison's twenty-nine pieces exposed the Confederation's weaknesses and defended the Constitution's republican nature. "I inclose herewith the 7 first numbers of the federalist, a paper addressed to the people of this State," he wrote to Mount Vernon from New York in November. "They relate entirely to the importance of the Union. If the whole plan should be executed, it will present to the public a full discussion of the merits of the proposed Constitution in all its relations." Madison suggested that the Old Dominion needed the material as much as New York. "If you concur with me, perhaps the papers may be put into the hand of some of your confidential correspondents at Richmond who would have them reprinted there."[72]

Madison revealed his own involvement: "I will not conceal *from you* that I am likely to have such *a degree* of connection with the publication here, as to afford a restraint of delicacy from interesting myself directly in the republication elsewhere." Aside from Washington, Madison confessed his role only to Edmund Randolph, saying nothing about it to Joseph Jones, James Monroe, or even his own father. Nor did he inform his intimate friend Thomas Jefferson until after ratification. In October 1787 Hamilton mailed his first essay to Washington, but he did not confess his authorship to him until the following August. Instead, Madison hinted of Hamilton's involvement to Washington, stating, "You will recognize one of the pens concerned in the task." Presumably Washington understood this reference, but if he did not, Madison surely revealed his coadjutors during his March 1788 visit to Mount Vernon. Although Publius's identity became a matter of great curiosity, Washington hid Madison's role. Writing to Henry Knox in February, he either discreetly tested the essays' anonymity or sought to verify the identity of Madison's literary allies, asking, "Pray, if it is not a secret, who is the author, or authors, of Publius?"[73]

Washington forwarded the papers to Fairfax County representative David Stuart, advising, "If there is a Printer in Richmond who is really well disposed to support the New Constitution he would do well to give them a place in his Paper." He swore Stuart to secrecy: "Altho' I am acquainted with some of the writers . . . I am not at liberty to disclose their names, nor would I have it known that they are sent by *me* to *you* for promulgation." Stuart passed the essays to Augustine Davis, who printed them in the *Virginia Independent Chronicle* in December 1787. Madison continued to send *Federalist* essays to Washington, who forwarded them to Stuart for publication. When the weekly paper fell behind the torrent of ratification material, Davis left the *Federalist* to be published in book form.[74]

Washington assured Madison the essays would "have a good effect." To other correspondents he praised the authors' "great ability." To Hamilton, Washington declared, "I have read every performance which has been printed on one side and the other of the great question . . . and, without an unmeaning compliment, I will say, that I have seen no other so well calculated (in my judgment) to produce conviction on an unbiased Mind, as the *Production* of your *triumvirate*." Washington presciently judged the *Federalist* one of the greatest works on government ever written: "When the transient circumstances and fugitive performances which have attended this Crisis shall have disappeared, That Work will merit the Notice of Posterity; because in it are candidly and ably discussed the principles of freedom and the topics of government, which will always be interesting to mankind so long as they shall be connected in Civil Society." To Madison, Washington expressed approval by requesting a "neatly bound" edition for his library. If Washington read the essays closely enough to perceive the authors' philosophical differences, he kept it to himself.[75]

Aware that access to information from around the country would give the Federalists an advantage over their foes, the collaborators corresponded regularly about ratification prospects, exchanging intelligence and passing it to local allies. From New York, Madison reported late in September that he and his allies had failed to win Congress's backing for the Constitution. Instead, they settled for the document's unanimous transmission to the states, which the Federalists hoped would be interpreted as an endorsement. Madison's letters detailed ratification prospects in the states and often enclosed newspapers bearing important headlines. By early 1788 he sent word that Pennsylvania, Delaware, New Jersey, Georgia, and Connecticut had easily ratified, but Massachusetts would be a close contest. During January and February the younger Virginian deluged Mount Vernon with correspondence about the Boston convention, including hand-copied extracts of dispatches from delegate Rufus King. In mid-February, Madison reported that once the Federalists had agreed to recommend amendments, the Bay State narrowly ratified. Madison's information enabled Washington to stay informed without abandoning his detached image.[76]

While the outcome in Massachusetts remained in doubt, Madison delicately suggested that Washington write to someone in the state. "An explicit communication of your good wishes for the plan," he advised, "would be attended with valuable effects. I barely drop the idea." Unwilling to descend into the fray, Washington pleaded that he had "no regular correspindt. in Massachusetts." Becoming worried about the Bay State, however, Washington wrote to conventioneer Benjamin Lincoln, declaring "it is . . . to be hoped that your final decision will be agreeable to the wishes of good men and favorable to the Constitution." By the time he sent the message, Massachusetts had already decided.[77]

Washington's letters to Madison also contained critical information, especially about Virginia's 1787 assembly. From Mount Vernon, Madison learned that Federalists had prevented an implicit endorsement of amendments from being added to the call for a ratifying convention but had failed to stop the allocation of funds for a second general convention. As the Massachusetts convention got under way, Rufus King reminded Madison "that information from the southern States relative to the proposed Constitution will be of importance to us at Boston while engaged on that subject." Madison dutifully responded that "the Genl. thinks that . . . a large majority in Virga. are in favor of the Constitution." Thus the intelligence from Mount Vernon, relayed by Madison, assisted the Federalist cause in the northern states.[78]

Washington performed a final, crucial behind-the-scenes service—he overcame Madison's reluctance to judge the Constitution he had helped write. Given his friend's forensic skill and firsthand knowledge of the Federal Convention, Washington considered it crucial that he participate in Virginia's ratification convention. "I hope you will make it convenient to attend; explanations will be wanting—none can give them with more precision and accuracy than yourself," the general declared. Mount Vernon secretary Tobias Lear echoed his employer's sentiments, declaring Madison "the only man in this State who can effectually combat the influence of Mason & Henery," and that should he "be left out, not only this state but the whole continent will sustain a considerable loss." Observing other delegates sitting in state conventions, the younger Virginian no longer felt obligated to disqualify himself. With Washington foremost in mind, he added that "sundry very respectable friends" had influenced his decision. Madison agreed to participate even though he dreaded embroiling himself in public debates with Antifederalist friends and hated campaigning. Heartened, Washington classified his collaborator among Virginia's "first characters" and offered some fatherly advice: "The consciousness of having discharged that duty which we owe to our Country, is superior to all other considerations, and will place smaller matters in a secondary point of view." Coming from a man who had adhered to this admonition countless times, these words carried weight. Madison assumed his responsibility without further complaint.[79]

Madison did not leave New York for Orange until the last minute so that he could finish his final *Federalist* essay. Promising himself "the pleasure of taking Mount Vernon in the way," he arrived on 18 March and, despite his haste, stayed to the twentieth. On the nineteenth Washington's diary reads, "Remained at home all day"—an unusual entry for one who rarely broke his routine for company—so that the two men could discuss ratification. Lear and Humphreys noted that even without important guests, "The Constitution and its circumstances have been almost the sole topics of conversation" at Mount Vernon. The collaborators evaluated possible convention strategies and may even have decided to try in Virginia the recommendatory amendment technique that had worked so well in Massachusetts. The Massachusetts convention probably changed their opinion that any talk of constitutional changes would play into Antifederalist hands. Instead of helping its foes destroy the Constitution, recommendatory amendments provided a way to unite the Union's friends. The Boston convention also demonstrated that a deliberate evaluation more effectively subdued the opposition than Pennsylvania's peremptory approach. Convinced of the Constitution's merits, the collaborators wanted Virginia's ratification debate to be dispassionate and thorough.[80]

After leaving Mount Vernon, Madison visited Baptist minister John Leland near Fredericksburg. Leland's followers opposed the Constitution because they feared it did not sufficiently protect religious freedom. Madison changed the minister's mind, perhaps promising—if elected—to support recommendatory amendments guaranteeing liberty of conscience. He arrived in Orange on the twenty-third, just in time to deliver a campaign speech (probably promising recommendatory amendments) that helped secure a four-to-one victory. That Madison actually spoke of recommendatory amendments with Washington and Leland or in his stump speech cannot be proved. Only two weeks after stopping at Mount Vernon, however, he unequivocally advised Virginia's Federalists to emulate Massachusetts, a position presumably hammered out with Washington.[81]

In Orange, Madison received warning that Maryland and South Carolina Antifederalists planned to get their conventions to adjourn without ratifying, as New Hampshire had done. Madison immediately alerted South Carolinian Charles Pinckney and Marylanders James McHenry and Daniel Carroll that adjournments would be as devastating as rejections. Not knowing Carroll's whereabouts, Madison asked Washington to forward the letter, which he shrewdly left open for inspection. If he hoped that his missive to Carroll would alarm Washington into dashing off supplementary notes, then his plan worked perfectly. Because his friend had written to Massachusetts reluctantly, Madison may have used this more subtle approach to spur him to action. Washington cautioned conventioneers Thomas Johnson and James McHenry that "an adjournment . . . of your Convention . . . will be tantamount to the rejection of the Constitution." At Maryland's April convention, Johnson circulated the letter to "strengthen the Friends of the new Constitution and expedite it's Adoption." Maryland ratified by a lopsided majority.[82]

However detached Washington wished to remain, ratification teamed him and his collaborator in a public debate that focused as much on personalities as on political science. Madison guessed that choosing a government was so intellectually challenging that most Americans would decide for or against the document based on their leaders' opinions. Conversation naturally focused on who favored and who opposed ratification—and on which side would prevail. From France, Jefferson wrote that while George Mason, Patrick Henry, Benjamin Harrison, Thomas Nelson, Richard Henry Lee, and Arthur Lee opposed ratification, "Genl.

Washington will be for it, but it is not in his character to exert himself much in the case. Madison will be it's main pillar." Newspapers across the country followed the contest between Virginia's elite. The *Connecticut Courant* insisted that it was not George Mason who spoke the state's true sentiments but "a Washington, a Blair, a Maddison and a [Henry] Lee." Similarly, "The New Litany," published in the *Virginia Herald,* pleaded that the Lord "keep and strengthen in the true knowledge of thy ways, thy servants WASHINGTON, RANDOLPH, and MADISON." The *Philadelphia Independent Gazetteer* depicted Madison as Washington's protégé and ally when it named him Virginia's "young Washington for patriotism." Nor could Washington and Madison keep their own emotions out of the struggle. By presenting ratification as a contest between individuals as well as political systems, newspapers made the contest a personal one. Thus the press not only publicized their collaboration, it also helped develop it, as the polarization among the gentry drew the two men together. As Washington put it, "It is a natural circumstance for us, to feel a predilection for" those "whose ordinary pursuits and political principles are consonant to our own." Tension climaxed when the rival leaders (minus Washington) faced off in Richmond.[83]

During the Virginia ratification convention, which met from 2 to 27 June 1788, Madison defended the new government, usually in response to Patrick Henry's effusive oratory. As Washington had anticipated, only Madison could answer Antifederalist claims that the Constitution would jeopardize the Revolution's republican fruits and Virginia's sectional interests. The Federalists followed Massachusetts's recommendatory amendment example: to prevent those who wanted changes in the Constitution from joining the intransigent Antifederalists, the Federalists agreed to suggest revisions. The plan worked well: on 25 June the convention rejected conditional amendments by a vote of 88-80 and then ratified the Constitution 89-79.[84]

Throughout the convention Madison mailed brief progress reports every three to five days to the anxious Washington. His earliest communications told of an "auspicious opening" in Richmond, as Antifederalists played into Federalist hands by calling for the Constitution's clause-by-clause examination. Equally encouraging, Governor Randolph came out for unconditional ratification, while opposition leaders Mason and Henry appeared "awkward" and "lame." During the convention's second week, Madison's letters turned pessimistic. Antifederalists resorted to "private discussion & intrigue" to win converts and began coordinating resistance with friends in New York and Pennsylvania. With "the business . . . in the most ticklish state that can be imagined," Madison fell victim to a "bilious indisposition" that kept him away from the debates. By 18 June the Federalists maintained a slight edge, but Madison remained "extremely feeble," barely able to attend the convention or to write. A week later Madison sent the news Washington waited to hear: the Old Dominion had ratified! Referring to Mason and Henry, the younger Virginian gloated, "*Two* of the leaders however betray the effect of the disappointment, so far as it is marked in their countenances." His final dispatch listed the recommendatory amendments and warned that Henry remained unreconciled to the outcome."[85]

Washington's spirits rose and sank with these letters. "I cannot avoid hoping, and believing, to use the fashionable phraze, that Virginia will make the ninth column in the federal Temple," he noted early in June. Madison, he boasted, would "obviate the objections of Mr. Henry and Colo. Mason." In mid-June he became worried, noting that "affairs in the Convention, for some time past, have not worn so good an aspect as we could have wished." But Washington remained optimistic. After hearing the final results, he went to Alexandria's public celebration, where news of New Hampshire's ratification enlivened the festivities. Now enough states had approved to set the new government in motion.[86]

Characteristically, Madison's letters downplayed his own crucial role. But Washington learned of his impressive performance from his nephew, who reported that Madison spoke "with such force of reasoning, and a display of such irresistible truths, that the opposition seemed to have quitted the field." Washington read similar praise in the many newspapers he received. The *Pennsylvania Mercury* printed a letter from Richmond reporting that "Mr. Henry's declamatory powers" were "vastly overpowered by the deep reasoning of our glorious little Madison." The *Massachusetts Centinel* published a letter from Petersburg that waxed poetic:

> *Maddison* among the rest,
> Pouring from his narrow chest,
> More than Greek or Roman sense,
> Boundless tides of eloquence.[87]

In debate Madison twice referred to Washington's support for ratification. In hopes of dealing the Constitution a lethal blow, Patrick Henry quoted a Thomas Jefferson letter that suggested the best way to secure a bill of rights would be for four states to refuse to ratify until the other nine adopted amendments. Henry pointed out that because New Hampshire would soon become the ninth state to ratify, Virginia, New York, North Carolina, and Rhode Island needed to reject. To neutralize Henry, Madison alluded to Washington's position: "The honorable member [Henry] in order to influence our decision, has mentioned the opinion of a citizen who is an ornament to this state. . . . Is it come to this then, that we are not to follow our own reason?—Is it proper to introduce the opinions of respectable men not within these walls? If the opinion of an important character were to weigh on this occasion, could we not adduce a character equally great on our side?" Washington's influence was so pervasive that Madison did not need to speak his name. After this exchange Henry did not cite Jefferson again.

Although he lambasted Henry for injecting personalities into the debate, Madison could not resist doing the same. To bolster his case that the Articles of Confederation provided too weak and inefficient a government, Madison referred to Washington's 1783 Circular to the States: "At the conclusion of the war, that man who had the most extensive acquaintance with the nature of the country; who well understood its interests, and who had given the most unequivocal and most brilliant proofs of his attachment to its welfare—When he laid down his arms, wherewith he had so nobly and successfully defended his country, publicly testified his disapprobation of the present system, and suggested that some alteration was necessary to render it adequate to the security of our happiness." Unconvincingly, Madison protested that he "did not introduce that great name to bias any Gentleman here. Much as I admire and revere the man, I consider these members as not to be actuated by the influence of any man; but I introduced him as a respectable witness to prove that the Articles of the Confederation were inadequate, and that we must resort to something else." Madison could wield Washington's influence with more authority than any other delegate, because their collaboration had been publicized during the ratification debate. If he brandished his friend's name during the formal debates, he probably made freer use of it out of doors. After the convention James Monroe commended this tactic when he wrote that Washington's "influence carried this government."[88]

When Washington learned that Madison had fallen sick, he became as concerned with his friend's health as with ratification. Worried that the younger Virginian would rush from Richmond to New York to resume his congressional duties, Washington admonished, "Relaxation must have become indispensably necessary for your health, and for that reason I presume to advise you to take a little respite from business." Hoping that Madison would unwind at Mount Vernon, he suggested "that part of the time might be spent under this Roof on your Journey thither. Moderate exercise, and books occasionally, with the mind unbent, will be your best restoratives. With much truth I can assure you that no one will be happier in your company than your sincere & Affecte. Servt." Not very often did so demanding a man urge someone to take a break, especially with the country's fate at stake. But Washington apprehended that frenetic labors might exact too heavy a toll on one whose friendship he cherished and whose abilities he needed.[89]

Madison arrived at Mount Vernon on 4 July and stayed to the seventh. As usual, Washington "remained at home all day with Mr. Madison." For a while at least, the two men concerned themselves with trivial matters, as the guest showed the gold pocket watch that Jefferson sent from Paris, which his host liked so much that he asked Gouverneur Morris to purchase him one just like it there. But however much Madison needed rest, neither he nor Washington could resist pondering issues that lay ahead: When and where should the new regime be born? What amendments should pass? How could the West's loyalty be cemented? And most important, should Washington accept the presidency?[90]

Three weeks after leaving Virginia, Madison notified Washington that New York had approved the Constitution. With the accession of that critical state, it would only be a matter of time before holdouts North Carolina and Rhode Island followed suit. In July a relieved Washington mused that "we may, with a kind of grateful & pious exultation, trace the finger of Providence through those dark & misterious events, which first induced the States to appoint a general Convention & then led them one after another . . . into an adoption of the system . . . thereby, in all human probability, laying a lasting foundation for tranquility and happiness; when we had but too much reason to fear that confusion and misery were coming rapidly upon us." Washington might have added that his collaboration with Madison had helped secure the Constitution's adoption. The information the two men relayed and distributed, the strategies that they formulated, and the efforts they encouraged one another to make contributed to the Federalist triumph. The collaboration played an especially crucial role in Virginia. Without their backing, the state might not have ratified, an outcome that would have inspired similar results in New York. Failure in two powerful states might have led to a second constitutional convention; perhaps it would have killed the reform movement altogether.[91]

4

WASHINGTON'S
"PRIME MINISTER"

Because ratification by ten states did not end the Antifederalist threat, the collaborators did not relax their cooperation during the first federal elections. Considering Madison's parliamentary skills indispensable to the new legislature, Washington insisted that he stand for the Senate. After losing that contest, Madison won a place in the House of Representatives. For Washington the big question was not whether he would win the presidency, or even whether he would serve, but how best to assume the office. Madison advised him on his acceptance and then assisted in drafting a suitable inaugural address. While collaborating with Washington in the fall of 1788 and 1789, Madison befriended the entire Mount Vernon family.

In August 1788 Madison sent Washington disturbing news from New York: in return for that state's ratification, Federalists permitted Governor George Clinton to issue a circular to the states suggesting that the First Congress call a second convention. Madison would rather have seen the Constitution voted down, while Washington pronounced New York's acceptance more damaging than North Carolina's rejection. Clinton's letter raised the stakes in the first federal elections: Antifederalists would now try to win seats in the national legislature, where they could weaken the federal government. To stop them, Washington urged the election of Federalists to Congress.[1]

Correctly fearing that Virginia's legislature, led by Patrick Henry, would support New York's call for a second convention, Washington became despondent.

"I heartily wish Mr. Madison was in our Assembly," he pined, "as I think . . . it is of unspeakable importance Virginia should set out in her federal measures under right auspices." At Henry Lee's suggestion Washington even urged Madison to enter the Virginia legislature to combat Patrick Henry, but Madison choose to stay in New York. Meanwhile in Richmond the delegates prepared to elect United States senators. A career parliamentarian, Madison wanted to serve in the House rather than the Senate to avoid the charge that he had supported the Constitution for personal advancement, and because his tight budget could not support a senator's lifestyle. He also knew he had little chance of being chosen by an Antifederalist-dominated assembly. Madison instructed Congressman Edward Carrington, who in October journeyed from New York to Richmond to attend the legislature, to notify state Federalists of his decision. At Mount Vernon the envoy found Washington concerned the delegates would name two Antifederalists unless the Federalists ran a candidate "very well established in the confidence of the people." When Madison learned that Washington insisted that he "be brought forward upon this occasion," he yielded. If those "who are entitled to peculiar respect" considered his candidacy essential, he would "not hesitate to comply."[2]

Assemblyman Charles Lee warned Washington that "Mr Henry has publickly said that no person who wishes the constitution to be amended should vote for Mr Madison to be in the senate, and there is much reason to fear he will not be elected." On 9 November 1788 the legislature chose two Antifederal senators: Richard Henry Lee received 98 votes; William Grayson, 86; and Madison, 77. Accepting in stride an outcome he considered inevitable, Madison expressed surprise "that in the present temper . . . of the Assembly, my name should have been honored with so great a vote as it received." In contrast, Washington angrily faulted the delegates for ignoring the people's Federalist sympathies. To Madison, he complained, "The Edicts of Mr. H—— are enregistered with less opposition by the Majority . . . than those of the Grand Monarch are in the Parliaments of France." The outburst failed to mask guilt over having forced a very public defeat upon his friend.[3]

Flushed with victory, Henry's followers tried to deny Madison a seat in the House of Representatives by placing Orange County in a strongly Antifederal district. To keep him from switching districts, the legislature added the unique requirement that candidates run where they resided. Henry even persuaded war hero James Monroe, an outspoken advocate of amendments, to oppose him. "Sorry indeed should I be," Washington asserted, "if Mr Madison meets the same fate in . . . Orange . . . as he has done in the Assembly—and to me it seems not at all improbable." Washington fretted about Madison's election because he knew that should he become president, he would need reliable legislative contacts and because he felt responsible that Antifederalists had avenged themselves at Madison's expense. Unable to strike at Washington, Henry aimed at the closest target.[4]

To others, the election mattered little. Alexander Hamilton declared that if Madison lost, "I could console myself . . . from a desire to see you in one of the Executive departments." Henry Lee went further: "I profess myself pleased with your exclusion from the senate & I wish it may so happen in the lower house." In that case, "you will be left qualified to take part in the administration, which is the place proper for you. I had a full & confidential conversation with our Sachem on all these points." That Washington wanted his friend to lose is improbable, because the election was a referendum on his collaborator's conduct, but despite his exaggeration, Lee was correct that Madison's talents would not go to waste. Mount Vernon secretary David Humphreys insisted that defeat "may be the means of having" Madison "better employed as Minister for the Home-Department." Talking about appointments years later, Madison himself declared "that there was nothing that General Washington would not have given him if he chose it, as they were very well together."[5]

Throughout November and December 1788, Virginians warned that Madison would not win in February 1789 unless he personally refuted rumors that he opposed amendments. Although he hated electioneering, he left Philadelphia (where he was visiting) for his piedmont district, stopping at Mount Vernon from 19 December to Christmas Day. During this longer than usual stay, he became better acquainted with Washington's domestic relations. Residing with George and Martha Washington were George Augustine Washington (Washington's nephew) and his wife Fanny Bassett Washington (Martha's niece). Two of Martha's grandchildren, Nelly and George Washington Parke Custis, also lived at the Mansion House. Secretaries Tobias Lear and David Humphreys rounded out the household. After this visit Madison often added "respectful compliments to Mrs. Washington & the others of your family" to his letters. By 1788 Madison's correspondents occasionally even addressed his mail to the Potomac estate, knowing that Washington would know where to forward it. Gouverneur Morris kept his letters from Philadelphia to Mount Vernon brief because "Maddison . . . will I am perswaded give you fuller Information than I can of the several occurrences worth Notice."[6]

By January, Madison was home explaining to prominent neighbors that with the Constitution safely approved, he now favored a bill of rights. He wanted Congress, not a second convention, to propose changes because he believed it the

West front of Mount Vernon, attributed to Edward Savage, 1792. Madison
visited Washington's plantation a total of ten times from 1785 to 1791. During his
stays, lasting up to a week, the collaborators discussed important state affairs, such
as Washington's decision to attend the Federal Convention and to accept
the presidency. (Courtesy of The Mount Vernon Ladies' Association)

quickest, easiest, and safest mode. Pragmatically seizing a politically advantageous
issue from his foes, Madison championed amendments to ensure the election of
Federalists who could add them to the national charter without weakening it. He
also advocated a declaration of freedoms on abstract grounds. Aware that "parchment barriers" could not prevent tyranny, he nevertheless had decided that rights-
related amendments would improve the Constitution. They would reduce unjust
legislation by making popular majorities aware of individuals' rights and would
provide a useful weapon against encroaching tyranny. Though distasteful, his canvassing helped Madison win election to the House of Representatives by a margin of 1,308 to 972. Pleased with the returns, Washington offered congratulations
on such "a respectable majority."[7]

As early as August 1788, shortly after enough states had ratified to ensure the
Constitution's implementation, Washington received letters urging him to accept
the presidency after his inevitable election. Alexander Hamilton, the most persistent advocate, hoped he would "comply with what will no doubt be the general call of your country." Others, including Benjamin Lincoln, Thomas Johnson,

and Gouverneur Morris, echoed these themes. "Perplexed & distressed" by the issue, Washington futilely hoped his countrymen would elect someone else, thereby sparing him an agonizing decision. Not only did he and his wife treasure life at Mount Vernon, he also thought breaking his 1783 retirement pledge would invite charges of deceit and ambition damaging both to his reputation and the new government. Washington finally accepted the inescapability of his election, an unrelenting theme in the newspapers and each day's mail. If the new government's success depended on his participation, then he would answer the call, regardless of his own reputation or private preference.[8]

As with Washington's decision to attend the Federal Convention, his collaboration with Madison sheds light on his acceptance of the presidency, suggesting that almost from the outset, Washington knew he would have to return to public life. Among the general's close correspondents, only Madison never wrote urging Washington to become chief executive. Instead of fretting over his friend's intentions, Madison remained quietly confident. For example, he added no caveats to his statement to Jefferson "that Genl. Washington will be called to the Presidency." Similarly, Washington's letters to Madison do not mention the vicissitudes of his decision. The obvious explanation is that the two men discussed Washington's future during Madison's July 1788 visit to Mount Vernon. The face-to-face consultation on this momentous issue that Madison later recollected could only have occurred during the summer 1788 meeting. Obviously Madison came away confident that Washington would answer the nation's call.[9]

David Humphreys's *Life of General Washington* suggests an alternative but less plausible interpretation. In June 1788, when Baltimore's merchants sailed the miniature ship *Federalist* to Mount Vernon as a gift, Washington privately worried that acknowledging the present would commit him to become chief executive. According to Humphreys, the general then initiated "the first conversation . . . ever held with any person on the question of his accepting or refusing the Office of the President. . . . For several months afterwards they scarcely failed one day of conversing on the same subject." The Mount Vernon secretary labored to change what he perceived to be Washington's strong inclination against reentering public life, arguing that a refusal "would give such a shock to the friends of the government, & such an advantage to its opponents, that it might possibly produce its entire subversion." Humphreys intimated that presiding over the new government would be more glorious than onerous; nothing more than honesty and common sense would ensure lasting national prosperity. After listening patiently, claimed Humphreys, Washington postponed his decision. But Humphreys probably exaggerated Washington's reluctance to become president, perhaps out of misunderstanding, perhaps to magnify his own importance in changing Washington's mind, or perhaps to help perpetuate the Cincinnatus myth.[10]

Having confided in Humphreys, Washington certainly would have done so a month later with the more experienced and better informed Madison, which would account for their letters' silence. Madison's failure relentlessly to pursue the matter by mail suggests that Humphreys's *Life* overplayed Washington's diffidence, or at the very least, that Madison interpreted Washington's declarations more rhetorically than did Humphreys. Given Madison's experience under similar circumstances in 1787, he rested assured about Washington's decision even though he lacked an unconditional affirmative.[11]

Nevertheless, while at Mount Vernon, Madison, too, tried to influence the issue, suggesting that only Washington was sufficiently loved and trusted to win over the Antifederalists. He also warned that his friend's reputation would suffer if he helped to bring down the Confederation but not to implement its replacement. In 1792 Madison "well recollected the embarrassments under which his [Washington's] mind labored in deciding the question, on which he had consulted me, whether it could be his duty to accept" the presidency "after having taken a final leave of public life." Madison remembered the advice he had given: "I . . . entertained & intimated a wish that his acceptance, which appeared to be indispensable, might be known hereafter to have been in no degree the effect of any motive which strangers to his character might suppose, but of the severe sacrifice which his friends knew, he made of his inclinations as a man, to his obligations as a citizen. . . . I . . . suggested as the most unequivocal tho' not the only proof of his real motives, a voluntary return to private life as soon as the state of the Government would permit, trusting that if any premature casualty should unhappily cut off the possibility of this proof, the evidence known to his friends would in some way or other be saved from oblivion and do justice to his character." Madison thus promised to guard Washington's reputation should he die in office.[12]

Madison also probably relied on Humphreys's argument that the first president would likely preside over a prosperous nation, a sentiment he knew Washington shared. That same July, Washington wrote, "There are few who rejoice more fervently in the expectation that the beams of prosperity will break in upon" the new nation. Would not such optimism have tempted him to preside over a serene epoch? By late 1788 Washington finally accepted the inevitability of becoming president, commenting "if the sacrifice has been great, the occasion was still greater." It had been a hard reality to face; Washington may have seen clear skies for the nation, but he expected the chief executive to face clouds. Privately, Washington dreaded that his "movements to the Chair of Government will be accompanied with feelings not unlike those of a culprit who is going to the place of his execution: so unwilling am I, in the evening of a life nearly consumed in public cares, to quit a peaceful abode for an Ocean of difficulties, without that competency of political skill—abilities & inclination which is necessary to manage the helm." While Washington is guilty of false modesty here, it is true that he believed that advancing age and insufficient schooling would be liabilities for him as president.[13]

Madison, more concerned over the vice presidency than the presidency, hoped to prevent a rival candidate from obtaining too many electoral votes. If the second-place finisher followed close behind, it might impair the executive's prestige and effectiveness. Warning that the place would go to a New Englander, Madison asked whether his friend preferred John Hancock or John Adams. Refusing to commit himself, Washington promised to work with anyone. When the Federalists settled on Adams, Madison made sure that Alexander Hamilton had arranged for some electors to throw away votes. Privately he feared that Adams "would not be a very cordial second to the general."[14]

Early in January 1789, after the soon-to-be president had begun preparing his inaugural address, he turned to Madison for help. "Is there any safe, and tolerably expeditious mode by which letters from the Post Office in Fredericksburgh are conveyed to you?" Washington asked. "I want to write a private & confidential letter to you, shortly, but am not inclined to trust to an uncertain conveyance, so as to hazard the loss or inspection of it." Washington sent the secret missive, now lost, late in January. So private was it, that he did not keep a transcript. Later Madison wrote that the letter, "being peculiarly confidential was . . . left . . . at Mt. Vernon on my way to N. York [that February]. The return tho not asked nor probably expected, was suggested by a motive of delicacy . . . nor was any copy of my answer to the communication retained." Historian Jared Sparks, who saw this missing document in the nineteenth century, noted that it related "to the message to the first Congress." According to Sparks, it also mentioned a draft address that had been prepared by someone whom Washington described only as "a gentleman under this roof." The author was David Humphreys.[15]

In mid-February, Washington sent Humphreys's draft to Montpelier. Afraid that he might not be home when Madison passed by on his way to the First Congress, he asked the younger Virginian to await his return before proceeding to New York. Washington added that in his absence, "I have not the smallest objection to your conversing freely with Colo. H——— on all matters respecting this business." If Madison did not know it already, this sentence revealed the manuscript's author. Humphreys's text, consuming a whopping seventy-three pages, assessed the Confederation's weaknesses and the Constitution's strengths, didactically recommended specific legislation and amendments, and defended the breaking of Washington's 1783 retirement pledge. Although not content with the proposed address, the general took it seriously enough to copy it and probably revised it. The draft's contents will never be fully known, however, because Sparks cut apart the only surviving text and distributed the fragments as samples of Washington's autograph. If Madison made written comments on the proposed inaugural, they are now lost, but years later he agreed with Sparks that Humphreys's work was "certainly an extraordinary production for a message to Congress, and it is happy that Washington took counsel of his own understanding and of his friends before he made use of this document." Madison added that "nothing but an extreme delicacy towards the author of the draft, who no doubt, was Colonel Humphreys, can account for the respect shown to so strange a production."16

When Madison arrived at Mount Vernon on 22 February, the two men scrapped Humphreys's text in favor of a shorter speech drawn up by Madison and edited by Washington. This conclusion is warranted by the relationship between the two men, by the correspondence that preceded his visit, by Madison's presence at Mount Vernon, and by his success with a previous drafting assignment. Whether he prepared this new address at Mount Vernon or had it waiting in New York is not known. In any case, he probably did not come to Mount Vernon with an address already written (unless the general's missing letter authorized him to do so), because he would have waited for a request rather than to presume himself a ghostwriter.17

The final inaugural address explained that Washington accepted the presidency out of duty despite feelings of "incapacity as well as disinclination." It asked for continued blessings from the Almighty, admonished Congress to avoid "local prejudices" and "party animosities," and requested that instead of a salary, Washington receive reimbursement for his expenses (as he had as commander in chief). The four-page address, taking about twelve minutes to deliver, retained only one item from Humphreys's legislative agenda: it requested constitutional changes to protect the people's liberty and to win Antifederal support without weakening vital national powers. Convincing Washington to support amendments—the first move in Madison's congressional campaign for a bill of rights—had not been a hard sell. As early as July 1788, Wasington agreed that the Constitution should undergo changes.18

The conversations at Mount Vernon looked beyond the inaugural address to issues that would confront the president, including making appointments, creating executive departments, initiating executive-legislative communication, generating federal revenue, locating the national capital, and cementing the West to the new government. To reduce the risk of losing that region to England or Spain, the federal government would have to prevent Indian conflict and to open the Mississippi River. Washington showed letters from frontiersmen warning of British intrigue, and Madison shared information from Kentucky friends. Because Madison would take up his congressional duties before Washington even received official notification of his election, the collaborators needed to reach an understanding on these matters. Had they waited until Washington arrived in New York, it would have been too late to influence Congress's initial activities.[19]

Convening on 6 April 1789, Congress counted electoral ballots and declared Washington president. That morning Madison warned his friend that a messenger, Charles Thomson, the longtime secretary of the Continental and Confederation Congresses, would set out for Virginia to notify him as soon as the official tabulations were completed. Having made up his mind to accept the presidency, Washington wrote asking Madison, with whom he had already discussed the matter at Mount Vernon, "to engage Lodgings for me previous to my arrival." Believing it inappropriate for the president to impose himself on a private family, Washington insisted on having either a rented house or a tavern suite. If placed in a house, he preferred one small enough to excuse the immediate entertaining of guests. Aware that his initial living arrangements would set a precedent and would be scrutinized as a measure of the government's republicanism, he wanted to be modest and deliberate. Although not a member of Congress's presidential reception committee, Madison surely made these desires known to it. In accordance with the committee's recommendation, the legislature obtained the president of Congress's former house to serve as Washington's abode. Perhaps Madison stopped by to make sure that the arrangements would meet Washington's approval. Preparations to receive the executive "are making . . . in a very splendid style," he wrote.[20]

On 16 April, only two days after receiving the official notification, Washington, accompanied only by Thomson and Humphreys, began his journey north. He proceeded through Alexandria, Baltimore, Wilmington, Philadelphia, Trenton, Princeton, and New Brunswick, where he met cheering crowds, public addresses, dinners, military escorts, booming cannon, tolling bells, fireworks, and illuminations. A week after leaving home, the presidential party reached Elizabeth, New Jersey, where a congressional committee and an elaborate festooned fifty-foot barge waited to ferry it to the capital. Madison likely remained in Manhattan, attended the House of Representatives, and then joined the throng eagerly awaiting Washington at water's edge. A vast assemblage of cheering New Yorkers greeted the president-elect as he docked near Wall Street and climbed steps carpeted in crimson. While state and local officials greeted their guest, the city's church bells chimed. Madison surely joined the "old and faithful" companions who (according to Elias Boudinot) met Washington "and who now joined the universal Chorus welcoming their great deliverer." A procession then escorted the president-elect to his new home, as citizens shouted and waved handkerchiefs, hats, and flags from decorated buildings. Madison did not record his impressions of the triumphal arrival, but he, like those who described these events, must have been struck with the immense enthusiasm and goodwill that Washington brought to the new government.[21]

On 24 April, Madison and the rest of the House of Representatives formally waited on Washington. Later the same day, when the congressman returned to the presidential mansion as part of a committee to arrange the swearing-in, Washington cheerfully agreed to whatever arrangements were thought best for the 30 April ceremony. As the city's homes and taverns overflowed with spectators eager to witness the festivities, the two men polished Washington's address. At noon on Inauguration Day, a military procession escorted Washington to Federal Hall, where Wall Street meets Broad and Nassau. Formerly Old City Hall, the renamed structure had been handsomely renovated to accommodate Congress. Washington alighted, passed between ranks of soldiers, entered the building, and climbed stairs to the Senate chamber where Congress received him "in the most respectful manner." After a "solemn silence," Madison watched Vice President-elect Adams lead Washington from the Senate chamber across an open gallery to a bunting-covered balcony under a recessed portico. While Washington bowed to the roaring crowd, Congress followed into the gallery to watch, as the day's program prescribed. After Chancellor Robert R. Livingston administered the oath and then, following the familiar royal convention, shouted, "Long live George Washington, President of the United States," the assemblage below "sent forth such a shout as seemed to rend the skies."[22]

Well before the tumult subsided, Washington returned indoors and delivered the inaugural Madison had helped him prepare. Congress listened, according to Lear, "with eager and marked attention." To Pennsylvania senator William Maclay, the president appeared nervous and awkward. "This great Man was agitated and embarrassed more than ever he was by the leveled Cannon or pointed Musket," Maclay wrote. "He trembled, and several times could scarce make out

Federal Hall: The Seat of Congress, by Amos Doolittle, 1790. Washington delivers the inaugural address, ghostwritten by Madison, 29 April 1789, as Madison and the rest of Congress watch from behind. (Courtesy of the Winterthur Museum)

to read, tho' it must be supposed he had often read it before." Massachusetts representative Fisher Ames instead interpreted Washington's discomposure as awe at the responsibility he was assuming: "It was a very touching scene, and quite of the solemn kind. His aspect grave, almost to sadness; his modesty, actually shaking; his voice deep, a little tremulous, and so low as to call for close attention; [Washington's demeanor] added to the series of objects presented to the mind, and overwhelming it, produced emotions of the most affecting kind among the members." Because the inauguration marked the fruition of years of collaborative effort, Madison must also have felt the deep emotions Washington manifested during the address.[23]

Maclay noted that the message received "merited applause." Spanish minister Gardoqui pronounced it "eloquent and appropriate," while the comte de Moustier, the French minister, described it as "a very pathetic speech on the political situation, and on the position in which he [Washington] personally found himself." Rudolph Van Dorsten, secretary of the Netherlands' legation, wrote that "by this address this admirable man made himself all the more beloved." The president must have been relieved that he had accepted Madison's advice to be brief. The Washington-Madison inaugural got the administration off to an infinitely better start than the seventy-three-page Washington-Humphreys version would have produced.[24]

After the address the procession re-formed outside Federal Hall (with the House preceding and the Senate following the president) and made its way to St. Paul's Church on Broadway for a special service. The day closed with a massive celebration, featuring fireworks and illuminations, followed a week later by an inaugural ball in the City Assembly Rooms, attended by a who's who of those in New York at the time, including Madison. When the rest of the First Family arrived late in May, the scenes that had greeted Washington were reenacted, albeit on a smaller scale.[25]

The fledgling federal government benefited from the outpouring of goodwill over the inauguration. Madison, who rejoiced to see America's love for Washington transferred to the new government, did not yet join Benjamin Rush and a few others in worrying that the pomp and circumstance lavished on the president threatened republicanism. Washington, who understood the value of his popularity, viewed support for and loyalty to himself, his administration, and the federal government as one and the same. "The numerous congratulations which I have received . . . since my appointment to my present station, are truly grateful," he wrote, "as they hold forth the strongest assurances of support to the Government." Madison would have been well advised to take note of this attitude.

As long as he and Washington agreed on policy, their collaboration would thrive. But Washington, who functioned by seeking candid opinions from his advisers, expected his counselors to close ranks behind him once he reached a decision. Any public disagreement could shatter their friendship, because Washington would take it personally.[26]

THE FIRST federal elections produced a Federalist-dominated Congress, guaranteeing against a second convention. They also placed Madison in the House of Representatives and Washington in the executive's chair. With the new government started, the Washington-Madison collaboration's finest moment had arrived. The First Congress of the United States (April 1789–March 1791) has been described as a second federal convention because it breathed life into the Constitution, giving meaning to passages unavoidably or purposely left vague by the framers. This task fell primarily to the legislature because the executive departments and the judiciary took months to create. But the president, too, played a large role in fleshing out the new framework. During the first session of this critical Congress (April–September 1789), the collaboration had its greatest impact on the early American Republic and deserves much of the credit for the federal government's successful start. Madison not only became Washington's closest adviser but a virtual prime minister as well, linking the executive and legislature and helping the president exercise "hidden-hand leadership."[27]

Washington relied heavily on Madison, his closest political confidant, for advice during Congress's opening session. He could not obtain counsel from administration officials because the executive departments did not yet exist. Not until August and September 1789 did Henry Knox and Alexander Hamilton take over the treasury and war departments, respectively. And Thomas Jefferson did not come aboard as secretary of state until March 1790. True, Confederation officials such as Knox and John Jay temporarily retained old posts, but their status was ambiguous. For six of the most difficult months of the American presidency, Washington and John Adams, in short, constituted the entire executive branch. During this trying period, when every move set important precedents, Washington regularly sought Madison's advice about relations with Congress, etiquette, appointments, and policy. The new chief understood the significance of his initial actions. "In our progress towards political happiness my situation is new; and . . . I walk on untrodden ground," he mused. "There is scarce any part of my conduct wch. may not be hereafter drawn into precedent." Diffident about making proper judgments on his own and anxious "that every new arrangement should be made in the best possible manner," the president consulted Madison whenever he faced precedent-setting situations. Usually they involved interactions with Congress.[28]

The collaborators played a large role in initiating executive-legislative communications. The day after the swearing-in, the House appointed Madison chairman of a committee to prepare an address congratulating Washington on his unanimous election and pledging cooperation. After the lower chamber unanimously accepted Madison's draft, Washington asked his friend to write a response: "Notwithstanding the conviction I am under of the labour which is imposed upon you by *Public* Individuals as well as public bodies," he apologized, "yet, as you have began, so I would wish you to finish, the good work in a short reply to the . . . House . . . that there may be an accordance in this business." The assignment was not too trifling for the president to perform alone but too weighty: "As the first of every thing, *in our situation* will serve to establish a Precedent, it is devoutly wished on my part, that these precedents may be fixed on true principles." A few days later Washington requested an answer to the Senate as well. Madison's dialogue with himself (he wrote the inaugural, the House's rejoinder, and the president's replies to both chambers) reflects his dual role as a legislator and adviser. The exchange of addresses opened efficient communications between the two branches and solidified the president's role in shaping Congress's agenda.[29]

This exchange of an executive address and a legislative congratulation drew heavily on British precedent. At the beginning of each session of Parliament, the prime minister and cabinet drafted both the king's message and Parliament's reply. One wonders how consciously the collaborators borrowed from the British model, or to what extent they saw Madison as filling the prime minister's role. Although as a congressman deeply involved in formulating administration policy, Madison in effect played just such a role, he probably would have been uncomfortable with the analogy. Madison was, after all, a strict constructionist acting under a Constitution that forbade elected officials in one branch from holding other federal offices. Moreover, Madison himself would soon accuse Hamilton of being the corrupt minister, carrying out a conspiracy behind the president's popularity to introduce a British-style monarchy to America. No doubt the collaborators saw Madison's role as a temporary one, whose irregularity was justified by the special circumstance of needing to launch the ship of state on a duly republican course.

The governmental charter provides little guidance in routine executive-legislative communications, merely stating that the president "shall from time to time give to the Congress Information of the State of the Union, and recommend to their Consideration such Measures as he shall judge necessary and expedient." In August 1789 Washington asked Madison how to handle his initial dispatch to Congress. "Would an Oral or written communication be best?" the chief wanted to know, and "what mode is to be adopted to effect it?" Perhaps to spare his overburdened companion, Washington did not ask Madison to prepare a draft but sent one of his own for editing. In contrast to Washington's other advisers (Hamilton, John Jay, and Adams), who offered written suggestions, Madison gave spoken recommendations. Although little trace of his advice survives, these personal consultations indicate Madison's unique presidential access. Ultimately, War Secretary Knox carried the finished message to Congress, where a clerk read it, unlike the annual messages, which the president delivered in person. An experienced parliamentarian, Madison helped guide the president's initial relations with Congress, producing a strong and independent executive.[30]

Although a representative, Madison gave opinions on Washington's formative interactions with the Senate. The Constitution states that the president "shall have Power, by and with the Advice and Consent of the Senate, to make Treaties, provided two thirds of the Senators present concur." The document also requires that the executive make appointments with the upper house's "Advice and Consent." These specifications left a lot of leeway. Should the chief magistrate communicate verbally or in writing? If in person, where should meetings take place? Should he seek counsel or simply submit his decisions for approval or rejection? To a Senate committee the president expressed his preference for oral communication of diplomatic matters (so he could receive suggestions) and written notification of nominations (so his presence would not influence confirmation). The committee, in contrast, preferred that all contact be by word of mouth. When asked his opinion, Madison recommended that Washington hold his ground in the name of executive independence. In his next audience with the committee, Washington convinced it that "not only the *time*, but the *place* and manner of consultation should be with the President." Having won full discretion, Washington evolved his own practices. Nominations he always made by letter. Initially, he met the Senate face-to-face over foreign affairs, but finding that body too cumbersome, he began submitting diplomatic matters in writing, either in the form of questions or finished treaties. Subsequent executives followed these precedents.[31]

Another constitutional gray area involved recognizing foreign nations. Should the legislature specify when and where to send ministers and consuls, leaving the executive merely to fill the openings it created? Or ought the president himself choose which countries to recognize and then nominate accordingly? When the

House took up a bill to compensate diplomats, it debated whether the president needed to obtain the Senate's sanction before disbursing to specific members of the foreign service funds appropriated by Congress. Washington summoned his friend to a meeting at the executive mansion to ask whether such a requirement did not invade the executive's power to choose the location and level of overseas diplomats. Madison replied that the senators "have no Constitutional right to interfere . . . their powers extending no farther than to an approbation or disapprobation of the person nominated by the President all the rest being Executive and vested in the President by the Constitution." Washington subsequently pressured a few senators to approve a bill granting the president adequate control over the diplomatic service. Bolstered by Madison, Washington thus further fixed executive control over foreign policy.[32]

Almost immediately, the new chief faced problems of etiquette. Were he to gratify the curiosity of all casual visitors, he would never get any work done. But how to restrict the flow of guests? Not two weeks after taking office, Washington asked Madison's aid in finding a "true medium" between seclusion and accessibility. Washington's specific questions are now lost, but they probably matched those submitted to Adams. Should the president receive unscheduled guests? Should he make unannounced visits? Should he extend dinner invitations on a revolving basis? Should he entertain the general public? Madison's answers, given in person, cannot be recovered, but surely he favored less "State and Pomp" than Adams and more accessibility than Hamilton, who urged the president to close his door to congressmen. By late May 1789 Washington settled his social arrangements. Gentlemen could pay their respects to the president at Tuesday afternoon levees. On Thursdays about a dozen congressmen, government officials, foreign ministers, and their wives dined with the chief executive. The First Lady hosted teas (or "drawing rooms") for mixed company on Friday evenings, attended informally by her husband. Otherwise, Washington received no unplanned visits, accepted no invitations, and returned no calls.[33]

The levees were formal affairs. Washington wore gloves, a hair bag, and a dress sword and "received his visitor with a dignified bow," with his hands "so disposed of as to indicate, that the salutation was not to be accompanied with shaking hands. This ceremony never occurred in these visits, even with his most near friends, that no distinction might be made," wrote a guest. The first levee did not come off as either collaborator envisioned. Years afterwards Jared Sparks recorded Madison's reminiscences: "When Washington came into the room the folding-doors were suddenly thrown open, and Humphreys preceded him, and just as he entered, cried out in a loud and pompous voice,—'The President of the United

States.'—The effect was the more ludicrous, as not more than five or six gentlemen had assembled. Washington gave Humphreys a look, which Mr. Madison said he could more easily remember than describe."[34]

Madison received invitations to the Thursday dinners about once every six weeks, no more or less than other congressmen. William Maclay described the atmosphere at these meals as being stiff and dry: "It was the most solemn dinner ever I eat at, not an health drank scarce a Word said. untill the Cloath was taken away. then the President filling a Glass of Wine with great formality drank the health of ever individual by name round the Table. every body imitated him charged glasses and such a buz of health sir and health madam, & thank You sir and thank You Madam. never had I heard before." Madison dutifully attended these functions, but he did not care for them. Such ceremonies had little appeal for a shy and retiring man, who, after all, enjoyed private access to the president. Nor did Washington relish these events. But unlike Maclay, Madison, who was not immediately troubled by the court surrounding Washington, recognized the need for these occasions. True, in the spring of 1790, Madison told Thomas Jefferson "that the satellites & sycophants which surrounded him [Washington] had wound up the ceremonials of the government to a pitch of stateliness which nothing but his personal character could have supported, & which no character after him could ever maintain." But by then Madison's growing opposition to Alexander Hamilton's financial program had colored his views.[35]

A "rage for office" (as one seeker put it) swept the country in the months surrounding the inauguration, as friends and strangers alike sought appointment as clerks, postmasters, revenue officials, and even federal justices. Having refused to assign any jobs before being sworn in, the new president faced an overwhelming chore. Far from having a cabinet to assist him, he needed help choosing the department heads themselves. Madison became Washington's closest adviser in the difficult task of choosing high-ranking federal officials, not to mention lower federal officeholders in Virginia and Kentucky. Doling out offices posed Washington's most unpleasant and "delicate" problem because several candidates often came away empty-handed for every successful one. This disagreeable matter required painstaking deliberation because Americans watched the distribution of offices carefully. The president understood that appointments were more important in representative governments than in other kinds of regimes because "it is the nature of Republicans, who are nearly in a state of equality, to be extremely jealous as to the disposal of all honorary or lucrative appointments." Were relatives and cronies to receive the choicest places, a storm powerful enough to sink the Constitution might rise. Besides, the nation needed competent officials at its inception more than at any other time. The president developed firm guidelines to see him through this morass. When numerous suitable applicants presented themselves, considerations besides merit, including domicile, incumbency, recommendations, support for the Constitution, past public service, and personal circumstances came into play. "In comparing the candidates for office," wrote Madison, Washington was also "particularly inquisitive as to their standing with the public and the opinion entertained of them by men of public weight." More than anyone else, Madison helped implement this rigorous procedure.[36]

Despite extensive congressional duties, Madison remained at the executive's beck and call to discuss applicants and recommendations, for which the president occasionally apologized. "I am very troublesome, but you must excuse me," he wrote in September. "Ascribe it to friendship and confidence, and you will do justice to my motives. Remember the Attorney and Marshall for Kentucky, and forget not to give their Christian names." The president's highest appointments received Madison's blessing, including the selection of Alexander Hamilton, Henry Knox, Thomas Jefferson, and Edmund Randolph to head the treasury, war, state, and legal departments, respectively. Madison helped find "the first characters of the Union" to fill the federal judiciary. Concerning his chief justice nominee, Washington wrote, "I have had some conversation with Mr. [John] Jay respecting his views to Office, which I will communicate to you at our first interview—and this, if *perfectly* convenient and agreeable to you, may be this afternoon," Washington requested in August 1789.[37]

When neither collaborator knew the right man for a job, Madison searched for someone appropriate. In February 1790 Washington's secretary, Tobias Lear, instructed Madison "to consult . . . Gentlemen from Virginia . . . upon a suitable person" for Louisville's port collector, "and let the President know the result of your consultations this evening." Sure enough, Madison found a candidate that day. Madison also mediated between the president and his nominees, pressuring some to accept their appointments, while sounding out others' willingness to join the administration. These measures helped prevent rejections, which Washington feared would "bring the Government into discredit." To keep feelings from being hurt, Madison explained or justified decisions to some disappointed applicants. He told Edmund Pendleton, whose walking was impaired, that he had been nominated a district rather than Supreme Court justice to spare him extensive travel; but if Pendleton preferred the higher office, he could have it.[38]

Having personally met many of the applicants for higher office during his career, Madison provided valuable counsel. He gave unreserved character appraisals, as his verbal assessment of Gouverneur Morris, which Washington recorded in his diary, illustrates: "Mr. Morris is a man of superior talents—but . . . his imagination sometimes runs a head of his judgment—that his Manners before he is known—and where known are oftentimes disgusting—and from that, and immoral & loose expressions had created opinions of himself that were not favourable to him and which he did not merit." Equally useful, Madison understood appointment politics: he knew that some individuals possessed too much influence to be ignored. "High as the existing Presidt. stands," he remarked, "I question whether it would be very safe for him even not to reinstate J——y [John Jay]—or K——x [Henry Knox] &c." In a quandary, Washington asked him what to do with Arthur Lee, an applicant more formidable than qualified.[39]

Whether Arthur Lee sought Madison's backing cannot be determined, but he did understand that the congressman could catch Washington's attention. In September 1789 Lee urged Tench Coxe to apply for the soon-to-be-vacated office of postmaster general and added, "If you gain Mr. Madison's interest with the President, I think you will succeed." Coxe immediately wrote a lengthy letter asking Madison to intercede on his behalf, explaining that "I could not I think bring myself to make a formal Application in my own name directly to the President." Whether Madison took up Coxe's cause is unclear, but the position went to Samuel Osgood, who possessed superior credentials.[40]

Like Coxe, other office seekers recognized Madison's insider status and placed their fortunes in his hands. Edmund Randolph believed that men of "real merit" ought not to stoop to writing letters of application to the president. Instead, Randolph turned to Madison, a strategy that resulted in his appointment as attorney general. Hoping to become federal marshal for Virginia, Edward Carrington asked Washington for a job but specified to Madison the exact post he wished. Seeking an overseas assignment, Charles Pinckney sought Madison's backing: "Knowing your intimacy with the President & the deserved confidence he has in you, it is my wish you would mention this to him." Droves of obscure people looked to Madison for preferment, as evidenced by the many letters addressed to him that today reside among Washington's papers. Not knowing many of these applicants personally, Madison often did not push them but simply forwarded the papers to Tobias Lear.[41]

Some appointees asked Madison to convey delicate matters to Washington even after assuming office. When Attorney General Randolph returned to Virginia in 1790 to fetch his family, he found his wife carrying "a dead fetus . . . more than seven months old." He requested Madison to explain his resulting absence to the president. "I would write to him," Randolph excused, "but the subject does not become an official letter, to be filed away in the public archives." Nor did a private note "seem adviseable." As his domestic complication dragged on, Randolph reluctantly tendered his resignation through Madison, who replied that retirement was not necessary. Fortunately, Betsy Randolph recovered, allowing her relieved husband to return to New York.[42]

No congressmen was as privy to the nomination procedure as Madison, whose private correspondence reveals advance knowledge of appointments. Madison knew Hamilton's and Knox's destinations three months before their names went to the Senate. Other contemporaries, including senators, representatives, and administration officials, in contrast, noted that while the president welcomed recommendations, he cloaked his decisions. Madison valued the pull that enabled him to incur successful candidates' gratitude, to shape the administration, and to solidify his influence within it. Washington's habit of consulting Madison over appointments rankled William Maclay, who regarded it as an infringement on the Senate's prerogatives. Senator Ralph Izard of South Carolina grumbled that Madison "was deep in this business" of distributing patronage.[43]

Thomas Jefferson's selection as secretary of state demonstrates Madison's multiple roles. Not only did he counsel the nominator and the nominee, he also served as their go-between. Much of the credit for persuading the brilliant but reluctant Jefferson to join the administration belongs to Madison. In May 1789, when Washington wondered whether the minister to France wanted a domestic job, Madison conveyed the overture to Paris. Before a demurral arrived from Europe, Jefferson already had been confirmed as secretary of state. Madison had lobbied for the nomination, pointing out that it would please the West. Washington, who considered the State Department the most important office at his disposal, clearly expected Jefferson to take on the new assignment.[44]

The nominee, meanwhile, left Paris for a visit to America. Fearful that he would turn down the appointment prematurely, Madison frantically urged Jefferson not to decide until they talked. "I wish on a public account to see you as soon as possible after you become informed of the new destination provided for you," he wrote. "It is of infinite importance that you should not disappoint the public wish on this subject. . . . The President is anxious for your acceptance of the trust." Anticipating that Jefferson would land at a northern port, Madison stayed behind a month after Congress adjourned before finally returning to Orange. To Madison's surprise, Jefferson docked at Norfolk in November and proceeded to Charlottesville.[45]

Only after Christmas did Washington's envoy finally meet his elusive friend at Monticello. Jefferson expressed concern that supervising both foreign and domestic affairs would overburden one man and questioned the wisdom of quitting his ministry with commercial treaties within grasp. Were the secretary's duties too onerous, Madison rebutted, they could be divided between two departments, while commercial treaties could be pursued at home as well as abroad. Madison emphasized that the president sorely wished Jefferson to join the administration, but official dignity prevented him from pleading. He stepped up the pressure by persuading local residents to thank Jefferson for past and future public service.[46]

Upon returning to New York, Madison convinced Washington that one more presidential letter would bring the nominee around. Madison dashed off two supporting notes warning that "a universal anxiety is expressed for your acceptance" before Jefferson finally gave in. But no sooner had he consented than the need to arrange his daughter's dowry and wedding threatened further delay, a circumstance Jefferson asked Madison to explain to the president. Recognizing that the general's temper had not yet reached its limit, Madison showed him Jefferson's letter. Although pleased with the answer, the president regretted that it came so unwillingly. Having himself sacrificed private to public life, he expected the same from others.[47]

Merrill Peterson writes, "Only the President's esteem for Jefferson can explain his extraordinary patience to obtain him as secretary of state; only Jefferson's loyalty to Washington can finally explain his submission to the halter." Madison's persistent mediation provided a third essential ingredient. Jefferson had serious doubts about serving, but he also played hard to get. Though the president needed Jefferson, he refused to diminish executive prestige by begging. By unofficially conveying the requisite supplications, Madison enabled the executive to obtain an acceptance without groveling. If Jefferson had turned Washington down, would Madison have become secretary of state? Gouverneur Morris, who wrote that Washington "never had a very high opinion of" Jefferson, "but he was attach'd to" Madison "unmeasurably," certainly thought so.[48]

In the absence of department heads, Washington, during his first few months in office, individually carried a great burden of routine policy making. As he did with precedents, etiquette, appointments, and relations with Congress, Madison gave day-to-day advice. For example, in July 1789 the president asked how he ought to respond to Spanish minister Gardoqui's impending return to Europe. In September he inquired about sending an unofficial agent to the British to discuss implementing the 1783 Peace. Although he usually asked Madison about diplomatic matters, the president also occasionally requested advice on fiscal and military affairs. When preparing his first annual message, for instance, he asked about establishing a militia.[49]

Madison raised subjects—often by letting the executive read portions of his mail—he thought deserved attention. Washington abstracted in his diary one letter from George Nicholas to Madison describing Kentucky's public temper. The president needed friends to be his eyes and ears because many constituents were too shy to criticize his conduct to his face. Madison undoubtedly received instructions similar to those Washington gave his relative and Virginia neighbor David Stuart: "Your communications—without any reserve—will be exceedingly grateful & pleasing to me. While the eyes of America—perhaps of the world— are turned to this Government . . . I should like to be informed through so good a medium, of the public opinion of both men & measures; and of none more than myself—not so much of what may be thought the commendable parts, if any, of my conduct, as of those wch are conceived to be blemishes."[50]

Washington depended on his collaborator for more than informal counsel. He also relied on him in exercising "hidden-hand leadership" (acting behind-the-scenes "to diffuse conflicts rather than to bring them to a head"). The best example of such governance is the defeat of executive titles. In accord with the recommendation of a joint committee that included Madison, the House simply addressed its messages to "the President of the United States," but the Senate refused to go along. Hoping to give the executive the appellation "His Highness, the President of the United States of America, and Protector of Their Liberties," John Adams, supported by Richard Henry Lee, convinced his colleagues to demand a conference committee. Adams was not a monarchist; he simply believed a popularly elected executive needed such trappings to obtain respect. But the House committee, chaired by Madison, would not budge. To Congress, Madison suggested that pretentious designations, like "splendid tinsel," would only "disgrace the manly shoulders of our Chief." Washington heartily agreed. "It is to be lamented," he privately complained, that Adams "and *some others,* have stirred a question which has given rise to so much animadversion; and which I confess, has given me much uneasiness, lest it should be supposed by some . . . that the object they had in view was not displeasing to me—whereas the truth is—the question was moved . . . contrary to my opinion; for I foresaw and predicted the reception it has met with, and the use that would be made of it by the adversaries of the government.[51]

The logjam finally broke when the Senate, fearful of appearing aristocratic, gave in. William Maclay, the Senate's leading opponent of titles, recognized that Washington had orchestrated this result but was not sure how. "Through the whole of this base business I have endeavored to mark the conduct of General Washington," Maclay wrote. "I think it Scarce possible but he Must have dropped

Something, On a Subject Which has excited so much Warmth." Maclay did not know that Madison had visited the executive mansion and received instructions to hold out against fancy styles. According to Adams,

> Madison visited Washington to know his sentiments. . . . I know not all that passed between Washington and Madison, because I was not present; but this I believe to be the truth from information I ought to credit. Washington was far from expressing any disapprobation of a title, so far that he thought a decent title to the office to be useful and proper; but he wanted no title himself, and was convinced from what he heard in conversation, and read in the public papers, that if the title of Highness was given it would excite such a popular clamor that Congress would either be obliged to rescind it, or it would produce such a prejudice against the national government as would do more harm than good. Mr. Madison! Am I right in this? I appeal to you. If you contradict me, I will give it up.

With the president's backing Madison convinced the House conferees not to compromise, thereby forcing the Senate to back down.[52]

In theory, neither collaborator opposed titles. Madison told Congress that he did not conceive them "to be so pregnant with danger as some gentlemen apprehend. . . . a President . . . cloathed with all the powers given in the constitution would not be a dangerous person to the liberties of America, if you were to load him with all the titles of Europe or Asia." Wisely, however, he and Washington avoided an issue that would have antagonized Antifederalists. "This I hope will shew to the friends of Republicanism that our new Government was not meant to substitute either Monarchy or Aristocracy, and that the genius of the people is as yet averse to both," wrote Madison. Thanks to his friend, the executive covertly diffused a touchy problem without alienating or embarrassing the Senate. "Had the [Senate's] project succeeded," Madison explained, "it would have subjected the president to a severe dilemma and given a deep wound to our infant government." Once again, their republican sensibilities separated the collaborators from other advocates of a strong executive branch.[53]

Having resolved the titles controversy, the collaborators turned their attention to opening foreign ports to American shipping. Washington sympathized with his friend's vain attempt to enact commercial discrimination during Congress's first session, supplying hidden-hand assistance if not a public endorsement. During the debates over tonnage fees, Madison vigorously supported levying heavier duties on those nations lacking commercial treaties with the United States, reasoning that the British would never make concessions if treated the same as countries with agreements. When his opponents defended free trade and warned against inviting British counterrestrictions that could jeopardize vital federal revenues, Madison rejoined that free trade could only be achieved once Britain removed its artificial barriers. He did not fear retaliation, believing that Britain needed America's foodstuffs and markets more than America needed its manufactures. The House's tonnage bill included discrimination, but the Senate struck it from the final act.[54]

Siding with his collaborator in this dispute, Washington privately commented that "the opposition of the Senate to the discrimination in the Tonnage Bill, was . . . adverse to my ideas of justice & policy." Keeping silent publicly, the president provided Madison confidential letters chronicling Britain's attempts to entice the American West into secession. The documents were powerful weapons; by being shown to congressmen, they could arouse enough anger against the British to secure discrimination. A cover sheet advised, "As you are upon business which requires every information of the State of the Union and knowledge of our relative situation with G. Britain I give you the perusal of them." Washington's hidden-hand effort failed when Madison's opponents, promising even more vigorous and effective measures than discrimination, carried the day. Persuaded these promises were sincere, the president signed the tonnage bill. Madison suspected that the assurances were a ruse to defeat his proposals and probably told his friend as much.[55]

When Washington asked his friend to prepare his second annual message in December 1790, Madison included a plea to break the British hold on American commerce through "encouragements to our own navigation." Early in 1791, after Washington informed Congress of the failure to open trade negotiations with the ministry, a committee that included Madison reported a commercial discrimination bill. In debate the Virginian presented his plan as a vital element of the president's foreign policy: "We should arm our executive magistrate, that he may be able to negociate with effect." Otherwise, "we send him into the field of negociation without any kind of armor, offensive or defensive." Once again, all efforts failed. Congress referred the matter to the secretary of state, who would not submit his Report on Commerce until December 1793.[56]

Madison's quest for amendments enjoyed greater success than his effort for commercial discrimination. Now acknowledging the validity of the Antifederalist case that personal liberty needed additional safeguards, Madison, during the spring of 1789, studied the two hundred or so changes recommended by the ratifying conventions and drafted amendments protecting personal rights, especially freedom of conscience, speech, and the press. Seeking to boost the Constitution's republican credentials, Madison proposed adding to the document a Lockean statement affirming that all power derives from the people, that government exists "for the benefit of the people," and that the people have the right "to reform or change their government, whenever it be found adverse or inadequate to the purposes of its institution." These declarations would in effect have incorporated the principles of the Declaration of Independence into the Constitution. Another proposal would have prevented states from violating "the equal rights of conscience, or the freedom of the press, or the trial by jury in criminal cases." The restriction on state laws, which Madison considered the most valuable amendment on the whole list, was designed to protect individual liberties from infringement by the states. The Federalist-dominated Congress, impatient with what it considered Madison's time-consuming efforts to placate Antifederalists, deleted both the Lockean principles and the state restriction before sending the amendments to the states for approval.[57]

Indeed, growing weary of waging a "nauseous" battle against colleagues who did not share his belief that amendments would improve the Constitution and fearful that none of his proposals would make it through the First Congress, Madison asked Washington to back his specific proposals. The sympathetic president, who usually refrained from influencing the legislative process, supplied a letter stating that the changes, if approved, would both mollify Antifederalists and strengthen the Constitution. "Upon the whole," Washington asserted, "they have my wishes for a favorable reception in both houses." Even after showing this presidential endorsement to his colleagues, Madison barely got any amendments approved. Without Washington's help, Madison's crusade for what has become a constitutional cornerstone would have been hopeless.[58]

The collaboration's contribution to personal liberty went beyond the Bill of Rights. Both men also deserve credit for the president's replies to sectarian addresses, which breathed life into the soon-to-be-ratified First Amendment. In answering Jews, Catholics, Quakers, and other denominations, Washington promoted religious freedom by publicly acknowledging each sect's Revolutionary contributions and by welcoming their immigrant brethren to America. Most important, he declared freedom of conscience to be a right rather than a privilege. For Washington, these pronouncements represent a forward stride from 1785, when he declined to support Madison's "Memorial and Remonstrance against Religious Assessments." Paul F. Boller, Jr., suggests that by 1789 Washington's ecclesiastical ideas had become "so Jeffersonian in spirit that one cannot help wondering whether his association with Jefferson had something to do with the clear-cut enunciation of his views on religious liberty that he made while he was President." The problem with this interpretation is that some of Washington's best articulations of the separation of church and state predate Jefferson's arrival in New York. During the previous five years (while Jefferson was in France), the two men had not corresponded about religion. Madison was as concerned with rights as Jefferson and had maintained close contact with Washington since 1785. It is more likely that Madison influenced the executive, especially considering the numerous discussions of amendments the two men had shared.[59]

Their conversations about religious freedom were not theological; the utilitarian president lacked patience for esoteric speculations. In fact, Madison did "not suppose that Washington had ever attended to the arguments for Christianity, and for the different systems of religion." Rather, they acted to protect personal liberty and to preserve social stability, hoping a bill of rights would educate the people about inalienable rights, thereby making majority tyranny less likely. There is no evidence that the younger Virginian drafted or edited any of the religious messages; his impact was more subtle and indirect: he helped shape Washington's overall thinking about rights, which then found expression through the president's own pen. By urging Virginia's Baptists to address the president, however, Madison created opportunities for his friend to promote religious freedom.[60]

Abstract reasons aside, Madison wanted amendments to lure North Carolina into the Union. Governor Samuel Johnston, recognizing Madison's support of amendments and his special relationship with the president, asked him to deliver an address to Washington, explaining that his state had "no Agent or any person in a publick Character . . . in New York." The dispatch congratulated the chief magistrate on his election and forecast the Constitution's approval in North Carolina upon the adoption of rights-related amendments. Madison forwarded the document, and when a presidential illness prevented a prompt reply, he made sure Johnston understood the delay. Once Washington was well enough to prepare a response (alluding to forthcoming amendments and countenancing ratification), Madison forwarded it to Johnston, suggesting that it be published throughout the state. Johnston thanked Madison for interceding, assured him that "every one is very much pleased with the President's answer to our Address," and requested that it be published in New York as well as his own state. North Carolina's November 1789 ratification owed much to Washington's encouragement and Madison's Bill of Rights. The same month Madison notified Washington that amendments had quelled Antifederalist disapproval of the Constitution: "The great bulk of the late opponents are entirely at rest. . . . One of the principal leaders of the Baptists lately sent me word that the amendments had entirely satisfied the disaffected of his Sect."[61]

In spite of its hidden-hand nature, the Washington-Madison collaboration drew attention; some individuals even jealously overestimated it. For example, when Madison defended the executive's exclusive power to remove subordinates, William Maclay accused him of "urging the Doctrine . . . to pay his Court, to the President, whom I am told he already affects to Govern." Although he surely discussed the issue with the president, constitutional factors motivated Madison more than personal ones. Madison, like Washington, believed in maintaining the strength and independence of the executive against legislative encroachments. In fact, the congressman warned his colleagues not to be blinded by the president's greatness. "We ought in this and every other case to adhere to the constitution, so far as it will serve as a guide to us," Madison admonished, adding "we ought not to be swayed in our decisions by the splendor of the character of the present chief magistrate."[62]

In October 1789, shortly after Congress adjourned, the president requested last-minute advice before Madison departed for Virginia: would a tour of the northern states keep him close to the people and generate support for the government? He noted that "Mr. Madison . . . saw no impropriety in my proposed trip to the Eastward." Thus Madison ended the session as he began it, serving as Washington's right-hand man, as a prime minister, as a vehicle for hidden-hand leadership, and as a counselor on relations with the legislature, etiquette, appointments, and policy. In return for advice that helped establish the strength, independence, and dignity of the presidency, Madison received assistance in his fights for commercial discrimination and amendments. As the first session closed, Congressman William Loughton Smith of South Carolina evaluated the relationship: "Mr. Madison is a great friend to a strong government—his great abilities will always give him much weight with the administration—I believe he now is much in the confidence of the President & he will hereafter stand a chance of being President himself; in the mean time, he will be a leading man in the Cabinet Council." As they said their good-byes, neither man suspected that their collaboration would soon come under siege, or that their mutual trust could ever be shaken.[63]

5

FRIENDSHIP TESTED

The collaborators had never been and were never again as close as during the First Congress's first session in 1789. As the executive departments took shape and precedents became fixed, Washington inevitably needed Madison's guidance less often. At the same time that these circumstances distanced them, Treasury Secretary Hamilton's proposals for funding the federal debt, assuming the state debt, and creating a national bank posed a more direct and serious threat to the friendship. Although it tested the collaboration, Hamilton's financial program did not destroy or even severely damage it. On the contrary, the crisis over funding and assumption produced one of its greatest achievements: the Compromise of 1790. And even though Washington and Madison could not reconcile their differences over a national bank, they emerged from that disagreement without questioning each other's motives. Nevertheless, Hamilton's growing influence drove Madison to steps that would soon undermine his relationship with the president.

As the executive branch found its feet, Madison no longer acted as a prime minister and his role as Washington's right-hand man waned. Two reasons, neither reflecting diminished friendship, account for this unavoidable development. First, as precedent-setting situations (which Washington regularly brought to Madison's attention) became rare, the president could go about business without advice. Second, with the executive departments' creation, the president less frequently needed Madison's help with appointments, speeches, or policy. Instead, he turned to advisers within his own governmental branch. After Madison ghostwrote the annual message for the last time in December 1790, the cabinet assumed responsibility for preparing addresses and responses. Washington, who always regretted the extraconstitutional burden placed on Madison, eagerly shifted the work to constitutionally appointed subordinates, while Madison, his hands full with Congress, happily relinquished this responsibility. Although it was not the result of an estrangement, the collaborators nevertheless saw less of each other after the cabinet's appointment, as each of these busy men went his own way. With Washington usually at Philadelphia when Madison traveled to and from Congress, moreover, their Mount Vernon meetings became rare.[1]

The decline in Madison's role as counselor should not be exaggerated. When difficult or precedent-setting situations arose, Washington still called on his right-hand man. Madison's invariable chairmanship of the House committee to answer the annual messages testifies to his standing, as does an August 1791 letter from Jefferson urging his return to Philadelphia from a New York vacation: "All your acquaintances are perpetually asking if you are arrived. It has been the first question from the President every time I have seen him for this fortnight. If you had arrived before dinner to-day, I had a strong charge to carry you there." The department heads sometimes turned to Madison for advice on day-to-day matters, often at the president's urging. Jefferson frequently assured Washington that Madison approved his recommendations, and even Hamilton sought Madison's guidance until ideological differences intervened.[2]

If the cabinet subtly undermined the Washington-Madison friendship, Hamilton's financial program posed a more direct and ominous threat. Having established a reliable federal revenue during its opening session, Congress faced the federal debt at its second meeting, a problem Hamilton addressed in his Report on Public Credit, submitted in January 1790. Hamilton's top priority was to achieve economic and political stability (what economists call "stabilization") in a nation not yet recovered from wartime dislocations. He proposed federal policies designed to reduce market fluctuations, elevate government stock prices, and enlist the support of the wealthy. An ardent nationalist and an admirer of Britain's political economy, Hamilton sought not only to restore public credit but also to promote a powerful federal government dedicated to economic development. As long as America remained an agricultural nation, it would never live up to Hamilton's notions of grandeur. Lacking economic diversity and self-sufficiency, a country of farmers relied too heavily on foreign markets. This situation left America particularly vulnerable in wartime, unable to produce weapons and susceptible to ship seizures. By following Britain's footsteps, Hamilton hoped to transform the country into an economic superpower. Introducing industry would provide cheap manufactures and domestic agricultural markets, not to mention increased productivity and higher standards of living. Because Hamilton's desire to industrialize America occasionally conflicted with his stabilization goal, however, he sometimes sacrificed it to his higher priority.[3]

Hamilton's report rejected scaling down the nation's $54 million debt, claiming that public credit required payment at par. Nearly half of the $42 million domestic debt consisted of government certificates originally issued to farmers and soldiers in return for supplies and service during the war. Since 1783, much of this paper had changed hands at a fraction of its face value, ending up in investors' pockets. As rumors of the treasury secretary's forthcoming proposals spread, those in the know combed the countryside buying up certificates from unsuspecting holders. Although Hamilton deplored speculation, he knew that it would create a powerful class loyal to the new regime and would generate the capital concentrations necessary to drive economic development.[4]

In theory, Madison opposed funding programs because he believed that they created interests that clashed with the public good. Nevertheless, he supported the idea as a necessary evil, recognizing that public credit could not otherwise be secured. Madison's misgivings about funding reflect his "Country" mentality, a term that emerged in early eighteenth-century England to describe the opposition to Prime Minister Robert Walpole. The Country interest borrowed heavily from the English Civil War's Commonwealthmen, who argued that power destroyed liberty. Its adherents accused Walpole of using patronage power to buy parliamentary support for his policies, charging that this corruption would not only impoverish the nation, it would also imbalance the constitution, resulting in tyranny. These same fears of despotic conspiracies shaped America's response to British policy in the 1760s and 1770s, resulting in the Revolution. In 1790 Madison worried that through funding, Hamilton might reintroduce the wretched system from which the United States had just broken free.[5]

Unlike Hamilton, who thought the government should promote industry, Madison wanted policies encouraging agriculture. For the Virginian, rural nations possessed strength because they consisted of virtuous, politically and economically independent yeomen. As countries developed, they aged and became decrepid. Industrialized Britain already exhibited decay, because its many factory workers could protect neither their political rights (they lacked the freehold requirements necessary to vote) nor their economic independence (they depended on their employers and on whims of the economy). "The class of citizens who provide at once their own food and their own raiment," wrote Madison, "may be viewed as the most truly independent and happy. They are more: they are the best basis of public liberty, and the strongest bulwark of public safety. It follows, that the greater proportion of this class to the whole society, the more free, the more independent, and the more happy must be the society itself." The Country ideology resonated with Virginia planters like Madison, who often experienced the world of commerce negatively. Their crops rarely covered their imports, leaving them indebted to British consignment merchants. Instead of blaming their plight on falling prices or their own extravagance, Virginians blamed the mercantile community.[6]

Hamilton, in contrast, grew up in the West Indies under the tutelage of merchants. Seeing fiscalism not as a destructive force but a constructive tool, Hamilton rejected the Country mentality in favor of the "Court" ideology. Also originating during Walpole's time, the Court party consisted of government insiders. Sharing the same political culture of liberty, power, and virtue, the Court party nevertheless failed to perceive corruption in funded debts. Instead they saw sound management of Britain's affairs: trading patronage for votes brought order out of chaos.[7]

Given his Country mentality, it is not surprising that Madison challenged aspects of the Report on Public Credit, even though he grudgingly accepted funding. He objected to Hamilton's proposal to pay only the current owners of certificates. Instead, the Virginian suggested "discriminating" between the original and present creditors by paying the latter the highest market value of their securities and restoring to the former the difference between the highest market value and the face value. His plan would reduce the degree to which sharpers could profit from the hardship and ignorance of veterans and other certificate holders. Spreading the debt among the original recipients also helped ensure its reinvestment in agriculture instead of industry or speculation. As usual, Madison used the president's name to influence Congress, pointing out that more than public credit hung in the balance—so did the honor of the nation's first citizen. Washington's 1783 pledge that the country would do the soldiers justice, Madison reminded, had helped end the war peacefully. Now it was up to Congress to fulfill the promise.[8]

Renewing charges first leveled during the amendment debate that fear of his constituents and desire for popularity motivated Madison, critics asked how the claims of thousands of original holders could ever be verified. Besides, not to pay in full investors who had demonstrated faith in the government amounted to breach of contract and threatened national credit. These objections proved telling: the House easily defeated discrimination by a vote of 36-13. Although he kept clear of the debate, the president agreed with Madison's opponents that discrimination would be unfair to current holders and exceedingly difficult if not impossible to implement. "Mr. Madison, on the question of discrimination, was actuated, I am persuaded, by the purest motives; & and most heartfelt conviction," he confided, "but the Subject was delicate, & perhaps had better not have been stirred."[9]

Madison's and Washington's respective constituencies partially account for their disagreement over discrimination. The former had to defend the interests of piedmont Virginians, few of whom held public securities in 1790. The latter, on the other hand, acting for all Americans, knew that were he to support discrimination, he would open himself to accusations of regional prejudice. Ever sensitive to appearances, Washington took care to avoid even a shadow of sectional partiality. Yet the collaborators differed over discrimination for a more fundamental reason than either practicality or constituencies. Unlike Madison, the president accepted Hamilton's goals of winning over investors and boosting development. But why would Washington support a measure calculated to promote industry over agriculture? After all, he shared a rural background with his fellow Virginian. He was happiest when farming Mount Vernon and had railed against the consignment merchants who sold his tobacco. In 1786 Washington described husbandry as "an object of infinite importance to the country; I consider it to be the proper source of American wealth & happiness." Madison certainly saw himself and Washington as kindred spirits, poles apart from Hamilton. Years later he remarked that the treasury secretary should not "be classed with those country gentlemen, like Washington, Jefferson, and himself, whose foundations were in the mother earth, and who held stocks, scrip, and such ephemeral and delusive things, in great disesteem."[10]

Despite his Jeffersonian musings, Washington was not as pastoral as other Virginians. On the contrary, he accepted financial capitalism and industry and often thought more like a modern businessman than a farmer. True, he envisioned America's future industry more in terms of household and plantation manufacture than of factories. But unlike the Jeffersonians, he did not dread large-scale industry, and he never would have agreed that the nation's factories ought forever to remain in Europe. Washington took great pride in early American industrial enterprises, such as the Hartford Woolen Manufactory, whose cloth he wore to his inauguration. He saw the North's economy as prosperous and egalitarian; the South's as stratified and stagnant. Because Washington thought development would bolster rather than undermine America, providing diversity and self-sufficiency, fear of economic development simply could not, by itself, convince him to support discrimination. Like other eighteenth-century Americans, he deplored corruption and debt, but he saw in Hamilton's policies secure public credit and strong federal government. Washington thus adhered more to the Court than the Country persuasion, yet his enthusiasm for development did not match Hamilton's. The president did not fear industry, but he did not join the treasury secretary in favoring federal bounties to encourage it. Ideologically, Washington stood between Madison and Hamilton.[11]

Madison accepted discrimination's defeat with unusual grace because he believed that he had supported a just cause, and that America's rural majority backed him. Unruffled by the president's unenthusiastic response, he wrongly suspected that the chief favored discrimination in theory if not in practice. Years later Madison remarked that "when the plan was proposed for paying the whole amount of the bills to the present holders, and thus deprive of their just claims the soldiers," Washington "could not easily be reconciled to it." Knowing that his friend's commitment to agriculture did not match his own would have troubled Madison.[12]

The Report on Public Credit recommended that Congress assume most of each state's outstanding Revolutionary War debt. Hamilton wanted to take on this additional $21 million burden because it would transform state creditors into federal creditors, helping to cement the Union. If Madison accepted funding as a necessary evil, then he considered assumption an unnecessary evil. Why increase the federal deficit by a third, he asked, when public credit did not require it? The country's debt could be reduced more quickly and efficiently if the states and the federal government retired their respective shares concurrently. Madison believed that assumption treated unfairly those states, mostly southern, that had already paid much of what they owed. To make assumption palatable to Virginia, an honest settlement of accounts between the several states and the federal government would have to accompany it. Aside from agreeing that assumption must treat all states equitably, Washington again did not share Madison's position. Because all Americans had benefited equally from independence, the president thought states that had seen less fighting and incurred fewer obligations should share their neighbors' costs. Like Hamilton, the president agreed that assumption would strengthen the federal government in a direct, tangible way and saw it as a symbol of the triumph of unionism over localism.[13]

Contrasting opinions over what threatened republicanism underlay the collaborators' disagreement over assumption. During the 1780s Washington and Madison both feared majority tyranny within the states. Their solution had been shifting power from the state to the federal level, where popular despotism would be less likely, and better balancing the federal government's branches to keep its legislature in check. With the launching of Hamilton's program, the Country-oriented Madison began to see the Revolution's fruits threatened from a new and unexpected source. He now feared the central government's takeover by a corrupt northern mercantile minority dedicated to a political economy inimical to republicanism. In response, Madison turned to the states to stave off this new despotism. If he is at all guilty of retreating from his quest for a strong federal government, it is because he remained consistent to a higher goal—republicanism. For Washington, in contrast, the federal government's purview never threatened republicanism. Unlike Madison, the president's Court mentality kept him from envisioning despotism stemming from Hamilton's agenda. Instead, Washington continued to see the states as the potential source of oppression. One way to understand the disagreement between Washington and Madison (and the breakup, after 1789, of the coalition that supported a stronger federal government) is to think of the Constitution as an umbrella that sheltered men of similar but not identical philosophies. Rather than being an end in itself, that document served as a means to different ends for different men. Madison wanted an agricultural republic that practiced strict construction, while Hamiltonians wanted a financial-industrial republic dedicated to loose construction. Shortly after the Federalists began implementing the Constitution in 1789, these discordances emerged. Madison's disagreements with Hamilton may have been unpleasant, but they did not come as a huge surprise: their conflicting views had previously exhibited themselves. His differences with Washington (whose sympathy for Hamiltonianism was moderate at best), on the other hand, were novel and probably shocked both men.

Unlike some of his supporters, Madison never declared assumption unconstitutional, but he found Hamilton's justification for the measure disturbing: "It has been asserted that it would be politic to assume the state debts, because it would add strength to the national government. There is no man more anxious for the success of the government than I am, and no one who will join more heartily in curing its defects; but I wish these defects to be remedied by additional constitutional powers, if they should be found necessary. This is the only proper, effectual, and permanent remedy." Madison thus saw in Hamiltonianism implications that could prove lethal to the governmental charter. To Madison, Hamilton seemed to be taking the Constitution of limited and enumerated powers that the people had ratified and turning it into a constitution of unlimited and implied powers that Hamilton had all along craved. Antifederalist warnings that the federal government would turn into a consolidation, in short, seemed to be coming true. Madison's view that constitutions can only evolve for the worse is representative of the Country mentality. Washington, in contrast, thought assumption could expand national powers without imbalancing the Constitution because he viewed that document as capable of growth and improvement. At the 1787 Federal Convention, the collaborators stood apart in their commitment to a powerful yet extremely republican government. In 1790 Madison began placing greater emphasis on republicanism than power, which he began to see as a threat. Washington, on the other hand, continued giving equal priority to power and republicanism.[14]

Northerners, who deemed assumption vital to their states' solvency and to the nation's prosperity, threatened to kill the funding bill and perhaps sever the Union unless it passed. Southerners, meanwhile, grew increasingly annoyed over their inability to locate the national capital on the Potomac River. That waterway flowed across the midpoint of the eastern seaboard, they insisted, and the center of population edged toward it with each passing year. To Madison it seemed only a Potomac capital could cement all sections and prevent the West's secession. Centrally seating the government, Madison believed, would provide a much-needed symbolic gesture to the South and West that the federal government would not be dominated by northerners pursuing their own sectional interests. Madison himself considered whether an adjournment of Congress was the only way to handle the deadlock. The collaborators saw in this explosive sectional atmosphere the potential for a compromise of constitutional proportions.[15]

From January to June 1790, while the House debated Hamilton's funding and assumption proposals, congressional delegations engaged in spirited "Jockeying and bargaining," as Maclay described it, over the federal city's location. Promoters knew that the Pennsylvanians would determine the outcome, and that the temporary and permanent capitals would be part of the settlement. When a deal between Hamilton and Robert Morris exchanging assumption for both capitals in Pennsylvania soured, Madison seized the initiative. The Virginian tentatively agreed with the Pennsylvanians to situate the government in Philadelphia for ten years before moving it to the Potomac. By June, Representative Fisher Ames noted that matters remained "perplexed and entangled" despite the exertion of "much industry and perseverance."[16]

On 19 June a distraught Hamilton encountered Jefferson outside the presidential mansion and pleaded that the nation's survival required assumption. In hopes of reaching an understanding, the secretary of state invited Madison and Hamilton to a private dinner the next evening. At their meeting Hamilton played upon Madison's loyalty to Washington, observing "that the President was the center on which all administrative questions ultimately rested, and that all of us should rally around him, and support with joint efforts measures approved by him." Before parting, the men outlined what would become the "Compromise of 1790." Madison would neither vote for assumption nor totally abandon his public opposition to it, but he agreed to secure the four House votes and one Senate vote needed to pass it. In return Hamilton agreed to persuade New Englanders not to derail Madison's agreement with the Pennsylvanians to trade a temporary capital in Philadelphia for a permanent one on the Potomac. The treasury secretary also promised to make liberal allowances to Virginia and other states in settling their Revolutionary accounts.[17]

Kenneth R. Bowling, the leading authority on the federal district's creation, concludes that Washington played a key role in cutting the deal: "Washington's exact role in the bargain is unclear, given his concern for discretion and Madison's and Jefferson's willingness to honor it. Several factors, however, indicate that the two men worked closely with the president as the bargain evolved." Contemporaries certainly perceived the collaborators at work on the compromise. Maclay insisted, "It is in fact the Interest of the President of the United States, that pushes the Potowmack, he, by Means of Jefferson Madison [Sen. Charles] Carrol & others Urges the Business. and if We [the Pennsylvanians] had not closed with these Terms a bargain would have been made, for the Temporary Residence in New York."[18]

Madison invariably receives credit for obtaining the needed assumption votes. According to Bowling, he converted Maryland senator Charles Carroll and representatives Richard Bland Lee and Alexander White of Virginia and Daniel Carroll and George Gale of Maryland, the first three representatives hailing from Potomac districts and the fourth a longtime supporter of Potomac interests in state politics. In payment for Lee's conversion, Madison promised Alexandria's inclusion in the federal city, while he won the Carrolls by pledging that all public buildings would rise in Maryland's portion of the district. These guarantees could not have been made without the blessing of the man who would execute the Residence Act. Washington's awarding of offices to Maryland representatives Gale and Carroll, whose assumption votes cost them reelection, also indicates presidential involvement.[19]

In July 1790 the deal fell into place. On the first the Senate passed Charles Carroll's bill placing the temporary capital at Philadelphia until 1800 and the permanent seat somewhere on a seventy-mile stretch of the Potomac between Williamsport, Maryland, and the Anacostia River below Georgetown, Maryland. On 9 July the House adopted the bill without amendments after Hamilton assured the New Englanders that assumption would pass. Once the Residence Act became law, the Senate, by the margin of Charles Carroll's vote, added assumption to the funding bill and sent it to the House. The representatives approved assumption for the first time on 24 July, with Madison voting nay but Lee, White, Daniel Carroll, and Gale voting aye. The Compromise of 1790 worked exactly as planned. New York, where hopes of permanently hosting the government had helped secure ratification, felt betrayed. Political cartoons, which had not surfaced even during the impassioned ratification debate, condemned the compromise's authors. Even "the Holy Name of the P——t is not much respected in the mouths of the profane," wrote a correspondent. The first cartoon ever directed at a chief executive attributed Washington's decision to sign the Residence Act to "self-gratification." New Yorkers clearly perceived his "hidden hand."[20]

Disagreements over discrimination and assumption had not prevented the Washington-Madison collaboration from playing an instrumental role in resolving the nation's first serious sectional clash under the Constitution. If anything, the compromise strengthened the collaboration, because both men demonstrated that their highest priority was the Union. Washington enthusiastically approved the conciliatory manner in which his followers had settled their differences. "The two great questions of funding the debt & fixing the seat of the government have been agitated, as was natural, with a good deal of warmth as well as ability," wrote the president. "They were more in danger of having convulsed the government itself than any other points. I hope they are now settled in as satisfactory a manner as could have been expected; and that we have a prospect of enjoying peace abroad, with tranquility at home." Washington, who seems to have been the only participant to make no concessions, with Madison's cooperation had gained a Potomac capital, one of his most cherished personal objectives. Madison, too, had reason to be pleased. With the president's help he traded assumption, an unavoidable concession, in return for a capital on the Potomac, the location he thought essential to the Republic's survival. The Compromise of 1790, an impressive example of mutual forbearance and constructive statesmanship that almost definitely saved the Union, marks the apogee of the Washington-Madison collaboration.[21]

THE FIRST CONGRESS's third session convened at Philadelphia, the government's temporary seat, in December 1790. Washington had converted Robert Morris's house into a comfortable executive mansion by the time Madison returned from Virginia. The latter, as usual, set up bachelor quarters in Mary House's boardinghouse, a block from the president's. Hamilton greeted Congress with a report outlining plans for a national bank, his financial program's second phase. Modeled after the Bank of England, the institution would be chartered by the government but privately owned and operated. Capitalized at $10 million (one-fifth coming from the treasury), the bank would collect taxes, disburse federal funds, and make loans to developers. Because public creditors could invest with debt certificates, the deficit would promote stabilization by elevating government stock prices. The institution would also facilitate economic growth by issuing a reliable currency to a society suffering chronic specie shortages.[22]

Unlike funding and assumption, the bank bill elicited Madison's unequivocal opposition. He worried that a national bank located in Philadelphia might complicate or prevent a removal to the Potomac. Hoping to lessen the danger, Madison vainly pleaded for the bank's charter to expire in 1800, Philadelphia's last year as the capital. Because airing this concern publicly would be accusing his colleagues of bad faith, Madison instead raised two other objections. First, he claimed the proposal granted special privileges to a few at the expense of many, especially southerners, who lived too far from Philadelphia to share the benefits. In typical Country fashion this argument implicitly associated banks with speculation and corruption.[23]

Madison's second complaint, introduced during the bill's third reading, concerned legality. It was unusual in the eighteenth century to object strenuously to a bill so close to passage, but Madison more than once in his career resorted to constitutional arguments at the eleventh hour. Although he admitted the lawfulness of the bank's ends (such as tax collection), he rejected the means as unconstitutional. The "necessary and proper" clause did not provide justification, he argued, because a bank was not essential for Congress to exercise its enumerated functions. The Tenth Amendment, which reserved to the states or the people powers not delegated, he insisted, reaffirmed this strict interpretation. Had the founders envisioned the creation of a bank, Madison argued, they would have explicitly said so, just as they enumerated raising armies even though Congress already possesses the broader right to declare war. Madison pointed out that the Federal Convention had considered and deliberately rejected empowering the legislature to create a bank.[24]

Though voiced at the last minute, Madison's constitutional arguments, far from forming a smoke screen for his Potomac concerns, represented real fears. Privately he wrote that to allow the governmental charter to become malleable through loose construction would "strike at the very essence of the Govt. as composed of limited & enumerated powers." For a Country advocate like Madison, strict construction protected a balanced constitution. Again, Hamilton seemed to be using implied powers to turn the Constitution of limited federal authority into one of sweeping federal authority, the very tendency toward consolidation that could drive the Antifederalists to disunion. But while Madison's argument was sincere, it also provided refuge for a man who deplored the direction of affairs. After seeing commercial retaliation stymied, he helplessly watched Hamilton seize the initiative. Funding, assumption, and a national bank promised to take America down Britain's political and economic path. Strict construction, Madison hoped, would halt the treasury program and the corruption and decay that it entailed.[25]

When the bank bill easily passed on 14 February 1791, Madison's last recourse lay in eliciting a presidential veto. Secretary of State Jefferson appended a copy of Madison's House speech to his written opinion and echoed its themes in cabinet meetings, as did Attorney General Randolph. Washington, who could not ignore his advisers' objections, agonized over whether to sign. Occupying middle ground between the economic philosophies of Hamilton and Madison, he hesitated to sanction implied powers and to unleash such a powerful engine for development. Above all, the president shared Madison's fear that a national bank located in Philadelphia could thwart a Potomac capital. After reading Jefferson's and Randolph's opinions and Madison's speech, Washington handed them to Hamilton for rebuttal. In the meantime, Madison later recalled, the president "held several free conversations with me on the Subject, in which he listened favorably as I thought to my views of it, but certainly without committing himself in any manner whatever." Madison's confidence swelled when Washington asked him to prepare a veto message; his friend had never requested a draft without using it.[26]

On 21 February 1791 Madison provided two written reasons for vetoing the bank bill, leaving the president free to choose either or both. The first asserted that Congress possessed neither enumerated nor implied powers to charter a bank; the second condemned the institution for granting special privileges incompatible with republicanism. Two days later Washington received Hamilton's lengthy defense of the bank's constitutionality, a brilliant treatise that upheld loose construction, asserted the legality of any act (unless expressly forbidden) convenient or helpful in exercising enumerated powers, and even quoted Madison's discussion of implied powers in *Federalist* No. 44. Whether Washington realized that the treasury secretary bolstered his case with his opponent's own words is anyone's guess.[27]

After waiting a full ten days, the president signed the bill. Hamilton's masterful brief certainly helped persuade him, but other factors influenced the decision. As public securities plummeted and creditors accused the president of sectional partiality, pressure mounted for him to sign, but the chief executive's obsession with the Potomac loomed above all other considerations. Even as the bank bill awaited his decision, Washington began to worry that a veto would jeopardize removal instead of guaranteeing it. How could such a reversal have occurred? Washington's 24 January proclamation of the federal district's boundaries had included Alexandria, Virginia, which lay beyond the southern boundary prescribed by the Residence Law, a decision that required congressional approval. Disgusted to see the federal district placed so far south and anxious to see the bank bill pass, northern senators ominously deferred the request. For the first time ever, Congress withheld one act to pressure the executive into signing another. To avoid a setback fatal to the Potomac, Washington approved the bank. Within hours of getting what it wanted, the Senate obligingly modified the federal district's boundaries. In a strange twist of fate, Washington's fear that Congress would repudiate the Compromise of 1790 if he vetoed the bank overcame his earlier concern that the institution would permanently bind the capital to Philadelphia.[28]

Finally, Washington's reluctance to use his veto power on a bill not clearly unconstitutional governed his behavior. "I give my Signature to many Bills with which my Judgment is at variance," he explained. "I must approve all parts of a Bill, or reject it in toto. To do the latter can only be Justified upon the clear and obvious ground of propriety." Having not yet handed down a veto when he received the bank bill, Washington rigidly adhered to this principle, preferring to reserve his first rejection for a clear-cut constitutional infringement. To veto and be overridden by Congress might permanently undermine an important executive power, a risk he could not afford. Unfortunately for Madison, the bank bill came along before the president had solidified his authority. Although Washington's decision to sign the bank bill can be read as a Hamiltonian endorsement of implied congressional powers, his reluctance to exercise his veto power can just as easily be read as a Madisonian endorsement of strict construction of executive power.[29]

Even though he had prepared a veto message, the act's passage shocked Madison less than might be expected because he understood the difficult situation the president faced. He deplored the accusations of sectionalism, complaining to Jefferson "that during the suspension of the Bank Bill in the hands of the President, its partizans . . . indulged themselves in reflections not very decent. . . . The meanest motives were charged on him, and the most insolent menaces held over him." Madison also appreciated the constitutional dilemma. Years later he explained that had Washington vetoed the bill, "it would, in my opinion, have produced a crisis. . . . ten days are allowed for the President's veto to come in. If it does not appear within that time, the bill becomes a law. I was conversing with a distinguished member of the Federal party, who observed that according to his computation the time was running out, or indeed *was run* out; when just at this moment, [Tobias] Lear came in with the President's sanction. *I am satisfied that had it been his veto, there would have been an effort to nullify it, and they would have arrayed themselves in a hostile attitude.*"[30]

Finally, Madison appreciated Washington's predicament concerning the Supplemental Residence Act, a difficulty he should have anticipated and warned against. Perhaps he thought Washington's prestige would overcome all obstacles, or that the Compromise of 1790 was so sacred that no one would impede it. Thus Madison recognized that the bank bill created a Scylla and Charybdis between which "General Washington had a most difficult course to steer." Convinced that the president had been forced to sign a bill that he opposed, Madison rationalized away any traces of betrayal he might initially have felt. Rather than feeling double-crossed, Madison resolved to work harder in the future to ensure that his friend would not shy from a veto. Instead of becoming disillusioned with Washington, Madison instead focused his hostility on Hamilton, who threatened to unseat him as the president's right-hand man. Starting with the passage of the bank bill in 1791, Madison's jealousy of Hamilton would gradually poison his relationship with Washington. But if the collaboration remained strong, their thinking continued to move in opposite directions, as evidenced by their reactions to the quick sale of bank stock in July 1791. For Washington, "the rapidity with which the subscriptions to the Bank of the United States were filled" illustrated the "confidence reposed" in the government. Madison disagreed: "The stockjobbers will become the pretorian band of the Government—at once its tool & its tyrant; bribed by its largesses, & overawing it, by clamours & combinations."[31]

Hamilton's Report on Manufactures, submitted to Congress in December 1791, outlined the financial program's third phase. The treasury secretary knew that it would take incentives to transform the wealthy into entrepreneurs. Designed to engage the federal government in promoting development, the report called for bounties to encourage investment in manufacturing enterprises. Realizing that economic diversity and self-sufficiency determined national strength, Hamilton hoped such policies would rapidly transform America into an industrial giant like Britain. Because stabilization remained Hamilton's top priority, however, he did not back any further measures to boost development, such as tariffs or reduced duties, that would have jeopardized the federal revenues on which funding and assumption depended. Madison, who hated the Report on Manufactures even more than the bank, complained that everyone would pay bounties to benefit a few northerners and that dependent factory workers would replace virtuous, independent yeomen. Even worse, in Madison's view, Hamilton's legal justification—that the general welfare clause supplemented Congress's enumerated powers —endangered the Constitution. Assumption and the bank bill had established the doctrine that if the ends are constitutional, then so are the means. This time, "if not only the *means,* but the *objects* are unlimited, the parchment had better be thrown into the fire at once," Madison warned.[32]

Although Washington again remained above the debate, this time he agreed with Madison on political and constitutional grounds. Privately he questioned whether "bounties . . . come within the powers of the general government" and doubted that it would "comport with the temper of the times to expend money for such purposes." True, the president's call for the encouragement of war industries produced Hamilton's report, but in general Washington saw the advancement of private enterprise as a state responsibility. He had looked to Virginia and Maryland to improve the Potomac, and as president, he turned specific industries' pleas for governmental assistance over to individual states. Washington's response to the Report on Manufactures is a good indication that he occupied middle ground ideologically between Hamilton and Madison.[33]

Thanks largely to a growing antifinancial mood in Philadelphia in the winter of 1792, the Report on Manufactures never came to a vote. The bursting of former Assistant Treasury Secretary William Duer's speculative bubble in United States Bank stock and the panic it precipitated caused Hamiltonian ventures to lose their appeal. After personally delivering the finishing blow in a speech against bounties, a relieved Madison could spare his copy of the Constitution from the flames. With the Report on Manufactures defeated, the younger Virginian felt that he had stemmed what had seemed an overwhelming tide. To make sure that America did not get swept away by a Hamiltonian wave, he now began organizing those who shared his principles into a "republican interest." In so doing, Madison made a huge intellectual commitment, becoming an avowed partisan in an age that condemned partisanship, thereby risking his relationship with the president.[34]

Hamilton's financial program strained the Washington-Madison friendship, exposing differences in the two men's philosophies for the first time. Whereas Washington continued to see localism as the great threat to the American Republic, Madison began to fear nationalism. More remarkable than the emerging disagreements between these two men, however, is the success with which they continued to cooperate in spite of them. Their joint efforts helped pass the Compromise of 1790, putting to rest two difficult and divisive issues that had lingered since the Revolutionary War's end. Although tested, the collaboration survived its first big challenge.

6

FOUNDING WASHINGTON, D.C.

T HE UNITED STATES CAPITAL never would have moved to the Potomac River
had it not been for the Washington-Madison collaboration. Running from
1783 until the mid-1790s, the crusade for a Potomac capital was the longest-lasting aspect of their relationship. This mutual quest shows that the collaboration
did not end in 1791 or 1792 but survived the advent of partisan politics. It also
illustrates that Madison's role during Washington's presidency was to help solve
difficult problems, leaving department heads to handle day-to-day affairs.

D ECIDING on the nature and location of the national capital posed one of the
American Revolution's most complicated issues. Along with a strong central government, continentalists like Washington and Madison wanted Congress to exercise exclusive jurisdiction over a huge federal district containing a large federal
city. Localists, who believed that distant, powerful governments lead to tyranny,
instead preferred a small, or even rotating, capital controlled by the host state.
Choosing the capital's site raised even more difficulties than establishing its character. Between 1783 and 1790 nearly fifty localities competed for a prize whose
stakes included jobs, largesse, access to information, and influence over policy.[1]
    Late in August 1783 Washington set up headquarters near Princeton, Congress's
temporary seat. Over the next two months, he and Madison first shared their mutual dream of permanently locating the national capital on the Potomac, beginning seven years of cooperation that climaxed in the Compromise of 1790. The
collaborators favored a Potomac capital mainly out of concern for the Union. Because the Potomac evenly split the Atlantic seaboard and provided, in their opin-

ion, the best access to the West, it would bind the states better than other sites. Less central a location would produce sectional animosities, especially in the West, a region that would not support a government that ignored its interests. The collaborators believed that southern and western Antifederalists would view the resolution of this issue as a sign of whether the North would dominate the federal government. Washington and Madison justified placing the capital at the nation's North-South division point, rather than at its demographic center, because they believed that the latter was rapidly moving southwest toward the Potomac. That waterway, they thought, provided the country's best natural setting for the government, offering a moderate climate, fertile soil, abundant resources, and natural defenses. "Was I to commence my career of life anew," Washington wrote, "I shd. not seek a residence . . . more than 25 miles from the margin of the Potomac." He applied the same logic to locating the federal capital.[2]

In addition to national considerations, the collaborators favored the Potomac for regional, state, local, and personal reasons. With the government nearby, southern congressmen would attend regularly, while the northern mercantile community would not unduly color legislative proceedings. A Potomac capital would benefit Virginia in particular, a state that needed its own commercial centers to keep wealth from draining to Baltimore, Philadelphia, and other cities. Locally, a Potomac capital promised Madison's and Washington's northern Virginia neighborhood great prosperity. Washington personally owned 20,000 acres of Potomac land that would rise in value if the government settled nearby, while Madison's Matildaville venture gave him a direct financial stake. But overall, they supported a Potomac capital mainly because for them, the American Revolution would not be complete without the government seated where it would cement all sections into the Union.[3]

In 1790 Senator Maclay marveled at the collaborators' eagerness to build a city in their rural idyll. But Washington accepted urbanization and large-scale commerce as inevitable. "From Trade our Citizens *will not* be restrained," he wrote. "Therefore it behoves us to place it in the most convenient channels, under proper regulation—freed, *as much as possible,* from those vices which luxury, the consequence of wealth and power, naturally introduce." Washington wanted to make commerce work to republicanism's advantage by situating the capital to promote national unity. Even Madison shared Washington's enthusiasm for a major commercial (as opposed to industrial) city in Virginia. He welcomed the national capital because he feared not capitalism and commerce per se but industrialization and the British fiscal system. Trade Madison accepted as essential to the agricultural republic; after all, industrious farmers needed to exchange surpluses for manufactures. For Madison the Potomac promised an environment in which the government could remain virtuous and healthy because it would be surrounded by sturdy yeomen instead of bankers, speculators, and factories.[4]

Madison came away from his fall 1783 talks with Washington determined to push for the government's temporary return to Philadelphia as the best means of achieving a permanent Potomac capital. That city possessed the facilities to house Congress conveniently long enough to prepare a Potomac site. If the delegates remained in cramped Princeton, however, "the necessity of a speedy removal wd. give an undue advantage to the seat happening to be in greatest readiness to receive" them. Madison failed to return Congress to its original home but nevertheless advanced his long-term goal when the delegates, in order to prevent a sectional crisis threatening to the fragile Union, voted to rotate between a northern capital on the Delaware and a southern capital on the Potomac. Until the final seats were ready, Congress would alternately sit at Annapolis and Trenton. Madison acquiesced because he knew that although this compromise would never last, it would buy time for his preferred site. After retiring from Continental service to their native state, the collaborators continued to pursue a strong federal government seated on the Potomac. At the state level they pushed river improvements, while at the federal level they supported Virginian William Grayson's efforts to block appropriations when Congress scrapped the dual residence plan in favor of a single Delaware River capital near Trenton. With Grayson's success, the issue remained dormant for the Confederation's duration.[5]

The 1787 Federal Convention avoided choosing a capital because agreeing on a site would have been difficult for delegates whose ability to compromise had already been tested. Leaving matters unsettled also facilitated ratification, for Federalists in several states could reel in supporters by dangling a nearby capital as bait. At Philadelphia, Madison foreshadowed his *Federalist* No. 10 essay by suggesting that supporters of capital sites around the country would neutralize one another, and the result would be a centrally placed government. He also proposed giving Congress power "to exercise exclusive Legislative authority at the seat of the General Government." Most delegates, including Washington, readily agreed that the national legislature should control up to a ten-mile square. During ratification Madison defended "exclusive jurisdiction" by emphasizing that the 1783 flight to Princeton proved that Congress must be able to protect itself.[6]

After Virginia ratified the Constitution in June 1788, Madison stopped at Mount Vernon en route to the Confederation Congress in New York. Knowing that body would soon choose a temporary capital for the new government, the collaborators compared New York and Philadelphia, the only two cities with adequate accommodations. Madison warned that New York boded ill for the Potomac. If initially placed at such a geographic extreme, Congress would quickly move to a more central location. A rapid departure would result in a permanent site no closer to Virginia than in New Jersey or perhaps Pennsylvania, Madison predicted, because there would not be enough time for the center of population to shift very far southwest or to forge a majority for a southern capital. But christening the Constitution at Philadelphia might buy enough time to ensure a final residence adjoining the Old Dominion. He did not fear that the capital might become mired near the Quaker City, because few outside Pennsylvania wanted it there.[7]

Washington agreed "that the longer the question respecting the permanent Seat of Congress remains unagitated, the greater certainty there will be of its fixture in a central spot." But he feared that if Congress convened at Philadelphia, the capital would stay there because the benefits of moving only a few miles to the south would not justify the expense. After weighing the arguments, however, he accepted Madison's reasoning. The pro–New York majority, which included the states north of the Hudson River (joined by the South Carolinians and Georgians, who found Manhattan easily accessible by water), turned a deaf ear to Madison's arguments for Philadelphia during a bitter ten-week fight. Rather than "strangling the Government in its birth," Madison diligently reported to Mount Vernon, the middle and southern states coalition finally gave in. Washington applauded Madison's decision not to risk aborting the new government, because both men wanted to avoid the localism that had plagued the Confederation, even if it meant sacrificing the Potomac.[8]

In February 1789 Madison and Washington decided to keep the divisive capital issue off the legislative agenda until the end of Congress's first session in order to preserve the harmony needed to pass revenue acts, approve amendments, and create judicial and executive departments. Late in the summer of 1789, Congress finally faced the explosive issue. In exchange for a permanent Susquehanna River capital, the Pennsylvanians promised the easterners that Congress would stay at New York until the new site was ready. An alarmed Madison tried to break up the deal by proposing to the Keystone State's delegation an immediate move to Philadelphia until a Potomac capital could be built. After flirting with Madison's proposal, the delegation adhered to its agreement with the pro–New York forces.[9]

Madison argued that the entire country would find the Potomac easily accessible, and that rapid southern and western population growth ensured that the waterway would soon be the country's demographic as well as its geographic center (a point his critics questioned). He retreated from his *Federalist* No. 10 argu-

ment that in a large republic competing interests automatically protect minority rights. Instead, Madison warned the eastern majority to respect other regions'
interests, adding that a large republic would more likely survive with a central
capital. Despite Madison's remarks the New York–Susquehanna bill passed easily. When Robert Morris convinced the Senate to insert Germantown, outside of
Philadelphia, as the permanent capital, Madison persuaded New York's senators
to suspend the bill to the next session. This maneuvering not only bought the Potomac time, it also spared the president a difficult decision. The chief executive
had received urgent pleas from southerners to veto the bill if it passed, confirming his belief that a Potomac site alone could preserve the Union. But however
much Washington supported that waterway, he opposed vetoing acts not clearly
unconstitutional.[10]

Having narrowly averted a Pennsylvania capital, the collaborators realized that
their delaying tactics, designed to allow southwestern population growth, had
nearly failed. With many Virginia congressmen ready to settle for any location
southwest of New York and the West restlessly awaiting a friendly gesture from
the government, they adopted a new strategy. Rather than postponing a decision,
Washington and Madison decided to bring it on at the next session and take their
chances that the Potomac would win. Even if Congress agreed on the Potomac,
a sympathetic executive would still have to see the transfer through. If matters remained unresolved when Washington retired (probably in 1793), heir apparent
John Adams could foil everything. "The presumptive successor," Madison remarked, had already given indications "which will render his administration an
ominous period for the Potomac." A favorable outcome could occur only "under
the auspices of the present Chief Magistrate." Attaining irreversible momentum
during Washington's presidency required immediate action. Madison's first step
was to visit Robert Morris in Philadelphia on his way home in October 1789 and
lay the groundwork for the Compromise of 1790 with him. Still smarting after
the eleventh-hour postponement of the Germantown bill, the senator, Madison
informed Washington, felt honor-bound to renew it at the next session. If the
northerners refused an agreement with Pennsylvania, then Morris would con-
cede the permanent capital to the South in return for a temporary seat at
Philadelphia.[11]

In the fall of 1789, Washington, Madison, Virginia senator William Grayson,
and Maryland representative Daniel Carroll launched a vigorous Potomac publicity campaign. Because the president could not visibly participate, Madison became the catalyst, stirring David Stuart and other locals to action as he passed
through Alexandria on his way home for recess. Madison targeted Washington's

friends and Potomac Company associates, no doubt using the president's name to instigate a crusade that produced broadsides, newspaper articles, and pamphlets praising the Potomac. Stuart and other Alexandrians addressed a broadside to New England town selectmen extolling the Potomac region's climate, fertility, natural resources, and defensibility. Quoting Jefferson's *Notes on Virginia* on the waterway's convenience to the West, the broadside promised that a Potomac capital would bring handsome profits to New England because the carrying trade and manufacturing markets were not monopolized locally, as was the case with Delaware and Susquehanna sites. Donald Sweig concludes that the president "was in every sense a silent participant in the broadside issued at Alexandria in December 1789. He was in full agreement with sentiments it expressed, and the purpose for which it was issued, and it is inconceivable that it would have been issued without his approval."[12]

The campaign extended to Richmond, where Madison prodded Henry Lee to convince the 1789 general assembly to promise up to ten miles square on the Potomac for the federal city. The Old Dominion also tried to involve Maryland by pledging $120,000 for public buildings, provided that state donated $72,000, a sum proportioned to its smaller population. Finally the legislature instructed the governor to remind Congress that no other potential site could boast an improvement corporation that had already begun clearing a route to the Ohio River. In fact, the company provided a focal point for the entire Potomac campaign, because the river's leading promoters, including Washington, Madison, the Carrolls, Alexander White, and many others, were closely tied to it. Eight of the ten who signed Stuart's broadside were investors.[13]

When Congress convened in January 1790, northern and southern delegations combined against the Pennsylvanians to kill the Germantown bill by establishing a rule that all bills had to originate from scratch instead of being carried over from the previous session. After abortive negotiations with Hamilton to trade assumption for temporary and permanent capitals in Pennsylvania, Morris closed the bargain he had proposed to Madison the previous October. Later, during the dinner at Jefferson's, Madison traded assumption for Hamilton's intercession with the New Englanders not to interfere. After Congress passed the necessary acts, Washington's signature completed the deal. After seven years of cooperation, the collaborators had finally secured a Potomac capital.[14]

Until July 1790 Madison publicly advocated a Potomac capital, while Washington acted behind the scenes. After the passage of the Residence Act, the collaborators' roles reversed: the president openly took charge while the congressman participated invisibly. Because Congress had waived Senate confirmation of the commission that would oversee construction, the chief executive had total control. While Madison assumed the familiar role of unofficial adviser, the participation of Secretary of State Jefferson, who handled all official correspondence with the commissioners, meant that a three-way collaboration guided the national capital's initial construction. Of America's Revolutionary statesmen, only Washington and Madison participated in three central aspects of the founding: they attended the Philadelphia Convention, held office at the national government's inception, and helped create Washington, D.C. Few, if any, men have ever had so unique an opportunity to devise political institutions.[15]

In August 1790 Washington turned once again to Madison for advice. Broadly interpreting the executive's authority to enforce the Residence Act, Madison listed four steps that Washington should take. First, the president needed to appoint the commissioners who would oversee surveying and construction. Madison suggested choosing two local Potomac boosters, and to involve the rest of the nation, he advised selecting the third commissioner from either the lower South or New England. Second, Washington should bargain with local proprietors in selecting the exact location of the ten miles square, offering to include their plots if they gave gifts of land for public buildings in return. Third, Madison pointed out that although the law required all federal structures to stand on one riverbank, the district itself could include both shores. Placing the city in Maryland but including Alexandria in the district would fulfill the promises made to Richard Bland Lee and the Carrolls to win their assumption votes. Finally, Madison suggested offering prizes for the best designs for the public buildings. Following Madison's advice closely but not slavishly, the president chose three local commissioners instead of two, none of whom Madison recommended. In choosing among longtime neighbors, the president followed his own instincts.[16]

In September, Washington directed Madison and Jefferson to join local landholders in inspecting the area from Little Falls downstream past Georgetown to the Anacostia River. To prime the proprietors for their negotiations with the chief executive, the messengers warned that a faulty beginning would play into the hands of Philadelphians not yet reconciled to a Potomac capital. They also made it clear that the funding would have to come not from Congress or states but from private land donations, which could be sold for revenue. When the two agents reported to Mount Vernon, Washington requested that they determine the attitude of his neighbor George Mason toward the federal city. The president feared that Mason, who owned the land on the Potomac opposite Georgetown north to Little Falls, might oppose Alexandria's inclusion. Washington did not feel comfortable approaching Mason directly, because the two men had been estranged since 1787, when Mason refused to sign the Constitution. The emissaries found their host, who probably suspected Washington's role in the visit, most uncommunicative but definitely favoring Georgetown as the site for the seat of government.[17]

Heeding the warning from Madison and Jefferson, a group of Potomac landholders pledged their lands on any terms the president desired. Washington, a master of real estate acquisition, now took charge of the negotiations and aggressively followed Madison's advice to play the contenders against one another. Having secretly decided to place the district at Georgetown and Alexandria, Washington nevertheless spent nearly two weeks in October 1790 touring the Potomac as far upriver as Williamsport, Maryland, in hopes of scaring landholders at the chosen site into sweetening their offers. In January 1791 the president provisionally proclaimed the district's boundaries, selecting not only the southernmost extremity allowed by Congress but including Alexandria, which lay beyond it. In return for sanctioning this move, the Senate exacted the bank bill's approval.[18]

In the spring of 1791, Washington finalized a land deal. The federal city would be divided into lots, with half going to the government for free to be sold for revenue, half remaining with the proprietors. Washington and Major Peter (Pierre) Charles L'Enfant, who was designing the city that would lie within the district, tentatively selected sites for the Capitol and President's House. After L'Enfant delivered the finished plan to Philadelphia, Jefferson informed Madison that "the President has been here, & left L'Enfant's plan, with a wish that you & I would examine it together immediately, as to certain matters, & let him know the result." In assessing the city plan, the collaborators interpreted and gave life to the Constitution they had helped write. Together Washington, Madison, and Jefferson wrote building codes and arranged the sale of government lots, which the latter two men later explained to the three commissioners in Georgetown. Madison, Jefferson, and the commissioners then gave east-west streets alphabetical names and north-south streets numerical names, designating the site of the Capitol as the coordinate system's origin. Finally, they named the district Columbia and the city Washington.[19]

On 17 October 1791 Washington, Madison, and Jefferson attended the first public land sales in Georgetown. Of ten thousand lots, only thirty-five sold (raising less than $9,000), the commissioners themselves buying four to keep them from going too cheaply. Meeting afterwards at Mount Vernon to prepare the president's 1791 annual message, the trio put the best face on the situation. The speech enthusiastically pointed out that the district's site had been fixed, the city laid out, and initial funds generated. The optimism was hardly justified. A second land sale in 1792 fared as badly as the first, and a third in 1793, at which Washington laid the Capitol's cornerstone, turned out the worst of all. By 1800 the government had sold less than 10 percent of its lots. Most potential buyers simply refused to invest large sums in a city that did not yet exist.[20]

Washington's notes to Jefferson reveal that the commissioners rubber-stamped executive decisions. Typically the president circulated the commissioners' letters past his two counselors before meeting with them to decide on a response. For example, in January 1792 Washington wrote, "The P. [president] begs that Mr. J—— & Mr. Ma—— would give the enclosed letters from the Commrs. an attentive perusal . . . before nine oclock tomorrow morning—at which hour the P—— would be glad to converse with them on the subject." After the conference Washington dispatched instructions to Georgetown. It is impossible to isolate individual contributions at these meetings, but the men clearly possessed complementary talents. Washington excelled at surveying and land acquisition, Jefferson understood city planning and architecture, and Madison knew history and constitutionalism. The congressman may also have mediated between the secretary of state and the president, perhaps reconciling Jefferson to Washington's desire for a city majestic enough to meet a rapidly growing nation's needs for centuries to come. In any case, all three recognized the need for Washington, D.C., to be ready by 1800 to accommodate the federal government.[21]

The 1791–92 conflict between Major L'Enfant and the commissioners illustrates Madison's deep involvement in federal city affairs and illuminates his collaboration with Washington. The president retained absolute control over all decisions, but he repeatedly sought his friend's counsel and relied heavily upon it. In spite of congressional duties, Madison kept abreast of Potomac events, providing indispensable advice based on the fullest and latest information.

Washington first noticed L'Enfant's engineering skills during the war. The magnificent refurbishing of Federal Hall in New York City confirmed the president's admiration, resulting in the major's appointment as the federal city's designer. Unfortunately, L'Enfant's unmanageability matched his brilliance. The planner refused to take orders from the commissioners (he was never told that they, not Washington, were his immediate superiors), insisting instead on answering directly to the president. In 1791 L'Enfant hindered the sale of lots by withholding his city plan from the public, rightly arguing that financing construction through land speculation would fail miserably. Although the commissioners should have heeded the warning, such disobedience could not be tolerated. Shortly thereafter L'Enfant again disregarded the commissioners' instructions by demolishing the foundation for a private house that partly blocked a projected square. Washington mediated between the commissioners and L'Enfant, urging the former to be more attentive and the latter to be more obedient, but to no avail.[22]

Unsure what to do next, Washington turned to Madison, who had helped Jefferson draft L'Enfant's official instructions. The congressman understood the situation through his extensive confidential correspondence with Commissioner Daniel Carroll, whom Washington had appointed to the commission after his Maryland district refused to reelect him to Congress. In February 1792 Washington invited Jefferson to discuss L'Enfant over breakfast. "If Mr. Madison can make it convenient to come with you I should be glad to see him also," the president added, and he enclosed papers for the congressman's perusal. Three days later the president invited Madison to a private consultation. After these meetings Jefferson drafted a letter giving L'Enfant a vote of confidence but demanding "subordination to the Commissioners." In response, the planner charged the commissioners with selfishness, incompetence, and vindictiveness, announcing that he would quit before acting "in Subjection to their Will and Caprice." Exasperated, Washington resolved to reach "a final decision . . . to be taken upon the best ground, and with the best advice." The president sent the offensive letter "to Mr. Madison who is better acquainted with the *whole* of this matter than any other." After meeting with Jefferson, Madison, and Attorney General Randolph, Washington decided that to endure the planner's intransigence any longer would drive the commissioners to resign, a blow that might kill the cherished enterprise. The president dispatched Tobias Lear to warn L'Enfant that he must obey the commissioners or be relieved. When Lear received a contemptuous brush-off, Washington angrily fired L'Enfant.[23]

The firing gave way to squabbling between the commissioners and the proprietors, who generally supported L'Enfant's ambitious construction schedule. Matters calmed sufficiently, however, that by late 1792 Madison's involvement with the federal city ceased, a development that had less to do with mounting partisanship than with the district's maturation. As with other matters, once legally constituted advisers took office, Madison stepped aside until a particularly difficult issue arose. For example, when in 1793 yellow fever threatened to prevent Congress from meeting in Philadelphia, Washington asked whether the Constitution allowed him to convene the legislature elsewhere, and if so, how to avoid renewing controversy over the government's seat. Madison replied that no matter how extenuating the circumstances, the executive lacked the legal authority to move Congress and warned against setting a precedent for relocating the capital. The best bet would be to announce Philadelphia's plight and to suggest a new meeting place. At the president's request Madison prepared a draft proclamation and recommended Reading or Lancaster, Pennsylvania, as the alternate sites least likely to arouse sectional discontent. The restoration of healthy conditions enabled Congress to meet in the temporary capital after all.[24]

The collaborators also worked to establish a national university in the district. For both men this dream, which promised to break down sectional barriers among the rising generation, went back at least to the 1780s. Not only would the capital provide the best classroom for students to learn republicanism, it would also save them from studying in Europe, where they might imbibe aristocratic or monarchical principles. At the Federal Convention, Madison tried to add to Article I the power to establish such an institution, but the delegates concluded that granting exclusive jurisdiction over the government's seat already conveyed adequate authority. The president's first annual address suggested a university, and the city plan approved by Washington, Madison, and Jefferson set aside land for it. In 1793, after learning the president would bequeath his Potomac Company shares to the institution, Madison helped prepare public letters to the commissioners and to Virginia's governor publicizing his intention. Despite executive prodding the university issue remained quiet until 1796, when a memorial from the commissioners led to the appointment of a committee chaired by Madison. Although the younger Virginian reported favorably on the proposal and defended it in debate, congressional stinginess doomed it. The legislature ignored a final plea in Washington's eighth annual message.[25]

However badly the collaborators wanted a national university, they did not pursue a quick-fix scheme proposed by Jefferson. In 1795 Sir Francis d'Ivernois's suggestion to transfer the University of Geneva to America captivated the former secretary of state. Besieged by French Revolutionaries, the school's only hope for survival seemed to be moving to a more tolerant environment, an idea Jefferson endorsed in a letter Madison delivered to Washington. The collaborators recognized that transferring en masse to the United States a faculty tinged with aristocracy would doom the institution. Besides, they wanted a diverse professorate from many backgrounds, American as well as European. Washington explained his views to Jefferson by mail and asked his friend to do the same. "The President touched on the subject the other day in conversation with me," Madison wrote to Monticello. "There are difficulties . . . arising from the composition of the scientific body, *wholly* out of foreign materials." Jefferson the educational reformer had overlooked obstacles that the collaborators readily spotted.[26]

After the commissioners concluded that relying on land speculation for revenue had failed, the president in December 1795 requested that Congress provide loan guarantees, offering unsold land as collateral. During the House debate Madison defended the measure only once, briefly, perhaps afraid his Federalist foes would oppose the loans if he advocated them too warmly. It would be better to let the measure come across as Washington's proposal, Madison may have reasoned. As with the bank bill in 1791, Madison's enemies linked something for the capital with something he hated: the Jay Treaty. When the House requested the papers pertaining to Jay's negotiations, a demand Madison and the Republicans supported, Federalist representatives rewarded Washington's firm refusal by approving the guarantees. Madison moaned that "the day after the message [Washington's demurral] was recd. the bill guarantying the loan for the federal City, was carried thro' the H. of Reps. by a swimming majority." He believed that the Federalists had again used the district to pressure Washington to do something he might not otherwise have done, occasioning a second bitter defeat.[27]

Despite his increasingly strained relationship with Washington, Madison continued to do what he could for the capital. Early in 1796 he offered a resolution empowering the president to commission "a survey of the main post road from Maine to Georgia," a step Representative Chauncey Goodrich of Connecticut thought Madison took to make the federal city more accessible. Although both men continued to support the Potomac capital after retiring from public office in March 1797, their collaboration had ended by then. Ironically, by 1801 the city that Washington did so much to create symbolized Republican triumph. Madison probably felt less irony than regret that his former friend did not live to see the government move to its new home. As Jefferson's secretary of state, he resumed an active role in supervising construction, and as president, Madison guarded Washington's legacy by squelching a movement to relocate the capital after the War of 1812.[28]

The Washington-Madison collaboration deserves considerable credit for the District of Columbia's successful establishment. Not only did the men play an indispensable role in achieving the Compromise of 1790, they also ensured that the settlement became a reality. By the same token, however, the two men must shoulder blame for the federal city's shortcomings. Their enthusiastic commitment to a Potomac capital made them underestimate the obstacles to creating a town by governmental fiat rather than by natural advantage and the invisible hand. Their decision to finance building through land sales failed miserably, resulting in a capital that remained overwhelmingly incomplete for nearly half a century. Some historians even blame the early American Republic's meager artistic and literary achievements on the physical removal of the nation's government from its commercial and financial centers. The collaborators are culpable on all counts. Aside from the national university, the district of course became everything they hoped for and more, but it took decades longer than they would have dreamed. Be that as it may, Washington and Madison, more than any other men, are Washington, D.C.'s fathers. Spanning nearly fifteen years, their cooperation on the federal city's founding was, chronologically speaking, the longest-lasting aspect of their collaboration. During the 1780s their mutual goal of placing the capital on the Potomac contributed to their friendship. In the 1790s it helped keep the two men close in the face of growing partisanship over administration policy.[29]

7

FOUR MORE YEARS

Nᴏᴛ ʟᴏɴɢ after his 1789 inauguration, Washington decided he would retire after one term in March 1793 because he felt obligated to fulfill his pledge to the American people to quit public office for good. He also hoped to set an example of rotating the chief magistracy, fearing that were he to serve until death, his successors might do the same, resulting in presidential elections that were pure formality. When in the spring of 1792 the time had come to decide when and how to publicize his decision, Washington again turned to his right-hand man in facing this precedent-setting situation. Months after the cabinet had evolved into a group advisory board, the president nevertheless consulted Madison over this delicate subject and appealed to him to ghostwrite his farewell address. The congressman readily agreed to the request but warned that the Republic's survival required Washington's accepting another term, a suggestion the reluctant president eventually would follow. The outcome can be understood only in the context of the political factionalism that had emerged during the previous year. Ironically, the discovery of Madison's partisan activities helped convince Washington to serve again.[1]

Wɪᴛʜɪɴ ᴀ ʏᴇᴀʀ of the bank controversy, Hamilton's supporters and foes had formed factional groupings in Congress. Although the rival interests did not amount to fully developed political organizations before the end of the 1790s, referring to them as the Republican and Federalist parties is both convenient and suitable because contemporaries spoke in those terms. In the 1780s the term *Federalists* designated supporters of the Constitution's ratification, but in the 1790s the term took on a new meaning, referring to proponents of Hamiltonianism. Madison, convinced that Hamilton aimed at a British-style monarchy, contributed as much as anyone to party growth during 1791. He saw no alternative to rallying the congressional minority and the American public to resist what he perceived to be a threat to republicanism, viewing partisanship as a temporary necessary evil to save his country's liberty. But by challenging administration policy, Madison inadvertently transformed himself into the president's enemy, because Washington, who had appointed Hamilton and approved funding, assumption, and the bank, took opposition personally. In the spring of 1792, when he asked for help with his retirement, Washington did not yet know about Madison's activities. A botanical tour with Jefferson and participation in the establishment of Philip Freneau's *National Gazette* highlighted Madison's partisan turn. The former did not hurt the collaboration, but the latter proved damaging once Washington found out about it.[2]

In May and June 1791, Madison and Jefferson toured New York's lake country, meeting along the way Robert R. Livingston and Aaron Burr and possibly other Hamiltonian opponents, such as New York's Antifederal governor George Clinton. Historians have debated whether this trip was primarily botanical or political. The most judicious conclusion is that in pursuing relaxation and intellectual stimulation, the travelers made connections and laid foundations that ultimately served partisan purposes. The trip did not harm the collaboration; after all, Jefferson held an esteemed administration position. The secretary of state kept Washington posted on their progress, listing military landmarks they visited and reporting on Madison's health. Returning to Philadelphia first, Jefferson sent back word that Washington hoped soon to reunite with Madison.[3]

If the New York vacation had no adverse effect on the collaboration, the same does not hold true for Madison's subsequent blatantly factional move. Indeed, nothing better illustrates how his developing anti-Hamiltonianism undermined his relationship with Washington than his role in establishing the *National Gazette*. By 1791 Madison had grown concerned that Philadelphia's leading newspaper, John Fenno's *Gazette of the United States,* consistently trumpeted treasury policies and high-toned government. Worried that Fenno's doctrines promoted monarchism, Madison wanted to encourage a rival organ committed to sound republicanism. He knew just the man to edit such a sheet: his old college classmate and zealous Whig Philip Freneau. To lure the sometime poet to Philadelphia, Madison persuaded Jefferson to offer him part-time work as a State Department translator. Appeals to patriotism and promises to obtain subscriptions throughout the South convinced Freneau to tackle Hamilton and Fenno in print. The *National Gazette*'s first issue appeared in October 1791.[4]

Over the next year Madison anonymously wrote eighteen increasingly partisan essays for the *National Gazette*. After proclaiming the virtues of agriculture, public vigilance, and governmental balance, he excoriated speculators, corrupters, usurpers, and monarchists. Taken as a whole, these essays recast *Federalist* No. 10. Instead of multiple factions neutralizing one another, Madison now saw only two parties, one good and one evil, locked in a death struggle, a dramatic reinterpretation that illustrates the terror that Hamiltonianism struck in him. In helping Freneau, Madison unleashed a man whose actions he could not govern. While he saw the *National Gazette* as a bulwark against tyranny, its excesses eventually embarrassed him. Politically moderate at first, Freneau by late February 1792 accused Hamilton of using the national debt to corrupt Congress and subvert republicanism. Madison welcomed these attacks, seemingly oblivious to the damage that the exposure of his connection with Freneau could inflict on his relationship with the president. Before year's end the editor targeted Washington, a course Madison did not approve. These direct presidential jabs would inflict a much more serious wound on the collaboration than the forays against Hamilton.[5]

It is impossible to pinpoint how much Washington knew about Madison's involvement with the *National Gazette*. The president habitually read the paper but appears never to have found out about Madison's written contributions. It seems that he learned of his friend's part in bringing Freneau to Philadelphia only in August 1792, when Hamilton hinted it in a newspaper attack on Jefferson. The revelation's timing is crucial. Washington discovered Madison's behavior after having obtained retirement advice but before reaching a decision. Ironically, the disclosure helped convince him to serve another term, but at the same time it weakened the collaboration because the president feared that Freneau's journalistic attacks on the government might lead in turn to disaffection, disunion, violence, and tyranny. Moreover, he took editorial accusations against the treasury secretary personally because as president he assumed responsibility for administration policy. Thus news of Madison's activities came as an unpleasant surprise because Washington viewed the *National Gazette*, not Hamilton, as the threat to republicanism.[6]

At the end of a brief Virginia vacation, Washington, Madison, and Jefferson met at Mount Vernon in October 1791 to outline the third annual message. During the visit the three statesmen learned with amazement that Congress would meet a week earlier than they had realized. As the trio hurriedly decamped for

Philadelphia, neither collaborator had any way of knowing that this visit would be Madison's last to Mount Vernon. After flourishing until the summer of 1792, their relationship would deteriorate thereafter.[7]

If Madison's connection with Freneau remained for the time being hidden from the president, his partisanship during the Second Congress's first session (October 1791–May 1792) did not. Factionalism colored most issues, with a fourth of the House consistently backing Madison, another fourth steadily supporting Hamilton, and the remainder dividing depending on the issue. The Republicans scored major victories on the Report on Manufactures and the Apportionment Bill. The Apportionment Bill, which adjusted congressional representation based on the 1790 census, gave one seat for every 30,000 people, allowing states with large remainders an extra representative. The bill, favoring the Federalist North, passed in March 1792 along the loose party-sectional lines then existing. Madison hoped the president would issue his first veto, because he thought that none of the factors that had induced Washington to sign the bank bill applied this time. He believed that by allowing some states more than one representative per 30,000 constituents, the law clearly violated the Constitution's spirit and letter.[8]

The bill produced the usual cabinet split: Jefferson and Randolph (against) versus Knox and Hamilton (for). Afraid that a veto would invite charges of southern favoritism, Washington held the bill the full ten days before asking Randolph, Madison, and Jefferson to confer. "If we three concurred in opinion that he should negative the bill, he desired to hear nothing more about it but that we would draw the instrument for him to sign," wrote the secretary of state. Once the trio prepared a rejection message, the chief executive immediately sent it to Congress. The Federalists tried to override, but the Republicans easily defeated them. "The President has exerted his power of checking the unconstitutional career of Congress," proclaimed Madison. Washington subsequently signed a replacement bill based on a 1:33,000 ratio that granted the South twenty-one of the thirty-five additional House seats. The Republicans confidently looked forward to dominating the enlarged legislature.[9]

Enraged, Hamilton accused Madison of misusing his influence with the president to serve partisan ends. Besides the Apportionment Bill, he cited a seemingly innocuous change the Virginian had made in the third annual message. The alteration favored Jefferson's desire to modify the gold and silver content in United States coins, a move Hamilton opposed. When the treasury secretary pointed out the revision's implication, Washington, admitting that he had not perceived its significance, restored the original wording. Hamilton charged that "this transaction . . . not only furnishes a proof of Mr. Madison's *intrigues,* in opposition to my measures, but charges him with an *abuse* of the President's confidence in him, by endeavoring to make him, without his knowledge, take part with one [cabinet] officer against another." This behavior proved that "Mr. Madisons true character is the reverse of that *simple, fair, candid one,* which he has assumed." If the congressman tried to sway Washington, the treasury secretary of course attempted the same thing, as both men advocated policies they believed represented the country's best interests. That Madison intentionally tricked Washington is improbable given the mutual respect between the two men.[10]

By the spring of 1792, the preceding year's events had convinced Madison that a Hamiltonian conspiracy to overthrow republicanism existed, and that creating an opposition party would provide the antidote. Espousing a party—a device contemporaries deplored as self-serving—shows how threatening he regarded Federalist policies. Madison did not blame Washington for sanctioning funding, assumption, and the bank, believing the president either had reluctantly accepted fiscal policies that he personally opposed or had approved measures without appreciating their nefarious implications. The congressman resolved to warn his friend that the Federalists hid their machinations behind his popularity. For his part Washington did not agree that corruption existed in any widespread form, that more than a few eccentrics actually favored monarchy, or that financial speculation had undermined the nation's economy or morals. Instead he saw in Hamiltonianism a sound financial policy, an energetic government, and a lasting Union. Madison's Country mentality, which the president did not share, explains his misunderstanding.[11]

While Washington regretted the differences between Madison and Hamilton, he felt certain that each man acted for the country's good. Accepting policy disagreements as inevitable, he trusted that once measures became law, everyone would submerge their differences and move on. Because Washington did not yet know about Madison's involvement with the *National Gazette,* this appraisal made sense from his perspective. He appreciated neither the personal and ideological gulf between his associates nor the intellectual barrier separating himself from Madison. During the 1780s, when both collaborators favored a stronger federal government, they never imagined that when it came time to put their ideas into practice they might disagree on how powerful it should be. Both came away from the Constitutional Convention thinking that the federal government had been left too weak vis-à-vis the states, and that within the government, the executive would prove no match for Congress. By 1791, after seeing the government in operation, Madison increasingly feared that Antifederalist warnings of federal aggrandizement were coming true, a concern Washington did not share. As this difference surfaced, each collaborator could not help thinking that he himself had remained consistent while the other had shifted ground.

By the spring of 1792, the stage was set for the attempt to retire. Still fully trusting his collaborator, Washington turned to him for help in stepping down. Madison responded that the president needed to serve again to stave off monarchism while he organized the Republicans. Although Washington did not accept this assessment, he quickly became convinced of the partisan rift's seriousness. At the same time he learned about the *National Gazette*'s origins: that his collaborator had secretly assisted an editor whose sole objective seemed to be attacking the administration! These two factors convinced the president that not accepting a second term would indeed jeopardize the Republic. Washington followed Madison's advice, but their collaboration suffered a heavy blow.

Probably at a private meeting on 19 February 1792, but definitely sometime before May, the president told his collaborator that he intended to leave office when his term ended. Caught off guard and reluctant to oppose what might (for all he knew) be a final decision, the congressman stammered that a retirement would "surprize and shock the public mind." Washington also shared his plans with Jefferson, Hamilton, Knox, and Randolph, but he discussed when and how to publicize his decision with Madison alone. On 5 May, Washington told the younger Virginian that appeals from his department heads to serve again had not altered his determination. As a result, before Madison departed for summer recess, the chief magistrate wanted advice on carrying out the decision. He still had not consulted anyone else on this matter, the president confided. That Madison, who no longer provided day-to-day counsel, received the call to help navigate the uncharted waters of presidential succession attests to the continued strength of their collaboration. When facing a precedent-setting constitutional problem, Washington again sought his right-hand man, bypassing even his cabinet. Specifically, the executive wanted to know how to publicize his intentions without presumptuously taking reelection for granted. Whom should he notify, Congress or the public? And when should he make the announcement? Would his 1792 annual message be too late?[12]

After agreeing to provide answers, Madison remonstrated against the president's leaving office. Now amply prepared, he marshaled his arguments as if before Congress, building his case around Washington's desire to fulfill his retirement pledge. He claimed that the public would view a second term as one more sacrifice for the country's good, not as lust for power. Were Washington to die in office, Madison promised, his friends would make clear that he had intended to step down as soon as the nation could carry on without him. Continuing as chief executive would solidify Washington's reputation, Madison concluded, because he was as essential in 1792 as he had been in 1789. The president replied that far from being indispensable, he lacked basic qualifications, especially in legal and constitutional matters. At age sixty, he had passed his prime, physically and mentally, could hardly withstand his duties, and craved a return to Mount Vernon. Moreover, a "spirit of party" had spread from Congress to the executive branch, dividing his cabinet. Referring to Freneau, Washington noted "that altho' the various attacks against public men & measures had not in general been pointed at him, yet in some instances it had been visible that he was the indirect object." All things considered, his personal desire comported with the public good.

Madison countered that Washington had performed better than any one else could have. After allowing his friend to raise the subject of factionalism, the younger Virginian addressed it at length, revealing his own partisan motives. Party growth, he argued, required not retirement but another term. The president could not quit until the Republic became safely insulated from two threats: one faction included a few Antifederalists "who retaining their original disaffection to the Govt. might still wish to destroy it," and the other was "in general unfriendly to republican Govt. and probably aimed at a gradual approximation of ours to a mixt monarchy." Madison thus distinguished between the Republicans, who contained a minority of Antifederalists, and the Federalists, consisting almost entirely of monarchists. If Washington served another term, it would hold the country together long enough for the Republicans to stamp out Antifederalism within their own party and build sufficient strength to defeat the Federalists in 1796.

Although he did not spell it out (presumably the president understood), Madison believed that a second term would keep the chief magistracy in neutral hands until 1796, by which time southwestern population growth, coupled with reapportionment, would give the Republicans control not only of Congress but of the presidency as well. Were Adams to become president in 1793, he might resist reapportionment, leading either to Federalist tyranny or Antifederalist disunion. (The vice president had favored the vetoed Apportionment Bill.) Madison assumed that during a second term Washington would remain a nonpartisan or perhaps even favor the Republicans. Either way, Madison's side would benefit. He never considered that his friend might ally with the Federalists.

When Washington again asked how best to publicize his retirement, the congressman reluctantly agreed to contemplate it. Four days later, on 9 May, the evening before the president departed for Mount Vernon, Madison returned to the executive mansion. He agreed that the fall 1792 message to Congress would be too late for an announcement. Instead, Madison recommended "a direct address . . . to the public in time for its proper effect on the election, which . . . might be put into such a form as would avoid every appearance of presumption or indelicacy." He still hoped Washington would reconsider, but the president reacted "in a manner that did not indicate the slightest assent to it."[13]

On 25 May, as Madison passed through Georgetown on his way to Montpelier, he met Washington returning from Mount Vernon to Philadelphia. The two men had no opportunity to talk privately, but the president handed over a letter written a few days earlier, stating that the retirement decision stood despite having been reconsidered in light of Madison's arguments. Only if Washington became convinced that stepping down "would involve the Country in serious disputes respecting the Chief Magestrate" would he change his mind. Consequently, the president asked Madison to compose a retirement announcement and asked whether a valedictory message would also be advisable. If so, how should it be promulgated? Should he include it in his retirement notification, or should he wait and issue it separately, just before his term ended? If Madison thought such an address desirable, would he use the enclosed outline to prepare a draft?

The president wanted his valedictory to explain that his advanced age and belief in rotation in office accounted for the decision. In parting, the president reminded his countrymen that the United States enjoyed almost limitless possibilities. To realize its potential, however, Americans would have to preserve the Union and the Constitution through a balance of vigilance and tolerance toward the government. He insisted that all Americans shared common interests, and that the nation's strength and independence lay in its size and diversity. Instead of fighting for regional advantage, the citizenry should compete only in sacrificing for the general good. Americans must not squander their opportunity to create the most perfect society man had ever known, one that would exemplify republicanism to the world.[14]

After considering the matter for three weeks at Montpelier, Madison advised making the retirement known in mid-September, allowing six weeks for word to spread throughout the country before presidential balloting began in November. As to the mode of communication, he recommended that publishing in the newspapers "a direct address to the people who are your only constituents" would help establish the president as the representative of the American people. A message to Congress was out of the question, since that body would not convene until after the elections had begun. He opposed issuing a circular to the states, as Washington had done in 1783, because the president was not elected by the state legislatures. Madison favored supplementing the retirement notice with a farewell address because a valedictory would call attention to the nation's first transfer of executive power and the need to choose a worthy successor. It would also give the public "salutary and operative lessons" in republicanism and gratify the people's desire to hear Washington's final reflections. Madison thought that appending the valedictory to the retirement notice would be convenient, but perhaps somewhat awkward and premature. Nevertheless, he advised combining the two for maximum impact. To give the president either option, Madison prepared retirement and departure messages that could be issued separately or jointly. The retirement notice simply stated that the need to establish the principle of rotation in office required that the incumbent not be considered a candidate in 1792. If he so chose, the president could append the valedictory to the retirement notice.

Despite trembling at the thought of a retirement, Madison faithfully rendered Washington's outline into an eloquent farewell address, refusing to allow his own partisanship to color the desired message. The congressman's explanation of how he transformed his friend's notes into a draft illuminates their collaboration: "You will readily observe that in executing it I have aimed at that plainness & modesty of language which you had in view, and which indeed are so peculiarly becoming the character and the occasion; and that I have had little more to do . . . than to follow the just and comprehensive outline which you had sketched. I flatter myself however that in every thing which has depended on me, much improvement will be made, before so interesting a paper shall have taken its last form." In ghostwriting, Madison put Washington's ideas into the prose and format he thought most appropriate but respectfully refrained from tinkering with the substance. He also understood that the executive would carefully rework everything. The finished draft, a monument to the Washington-Madison collaboration, so pleased the president that (after accepting another term) he saved it until 1796, when it became the nucleus of his Farewell Address.[15]

After returning to Philadelphia in late May 1792, Washington found waiting a letter from Jefferson dated about the time Madison had left the city. The congressman definitely knew about this note and may even have read a draft of it. In a sharply partisan vein, the document echoed Madison's argument for a second term, charging that "Monarchical federalists" in Congress had artificially augmented the national debt, burdening the citizenry with oppressive taxes to support idle speculators. Greed to share the spoils had corrupted enough legislators to give the Hamiltonians a majority in both houses of Congress, and unless the "republican federalists" reversed this trend, a British-style government would emerge. Jefferson seconded Madison's contention that Washington's reelection would hold the monarchists at bay until the Republicans could defeat them. But if a Federalist took office, the southern states might secede.[16]

Washington waited six weeks before answering the secretary of state in person on 10 July, an amazing delay considering his willingness to discuss the issue with Madison. His reply addresses Madison's arguments as well as Jefferson's. The president promised to place the country's good ahead of personal preference but feared that his retirement pledge would ring hollow if he stayed in office much longer. He also thought advancing age disqualified him. Regarding the Federalists, Washington declared that "suspicions against a particular party . . . had been carried a great deal too far. There might be *desires,* but he did not believe there were *designs* to change the form of government into a monarchy." The real danger, Washington warned, lay in "peices lately published, and particularly in Freneau's paper [that] seemed to have in view the exciting opposition to the government," which could ultimately bring ruin to America. The president added that he took attacks on Hamilton's policies personally. Jefferson verbally conveyed these remarks to Madison less than two weeks later at Montpelier. Now sure that his plea for a second term had fallen on deaf ears, the congressman fortified himself against the appearance of a farewell message come September.[17]

Yet Madison's arguments troubled Washington deeply. If his closest political confidant saw a conspiracy brewing, he felt obligated to explore the matter. To Hamilton the president rehearsed the case against the Federalists without mentioning the accusers. Had the national debt been artificially augmented to corrupt the legislature? Did a plot exist to replace republicanism with monarchy? Hamilton hotly responded with a 14,000-word point-by-point vindication. He resoundingly defended his programs as the best way to order the nation's finances, establish its credit, promote economic growth, and strengthen national attachments. Why, the treasury secretary asked, did his opponents equate a "*liberal* construction of the constitution for the public good and for the maintenance of the due energy of the national authority" with "a conspiracy to overturn the republican government of the Country[?]" He dismissed the corruption charge as "malignant & false" and assured the president that despotism could come only through Republican attempts to weaken the federal government. Perceiving whence the charges sprang, Hamilton pointed out that Madison's proposal to assume the state debts as they stood at the war's end rather than in 1790 would have made the national debt even larger.[18]

Hamilton's themes of national unity and effective government resonated with the president, reinforcing his opinion that no conspiracy existed. In one important regard, however, Washington realized that Madison and Jefferson had been right: partisanship split his administration more deeply than he had imagined. He now understood that the intense distrust between the Republican and Federalist leaders could threaten the Union were he to leave office. He knew his only hope of avoiding a second term lay in reuniting the cabinet, because he could not in good conscience bequeath a divided command.

Subsequent events drove the point home. Not content with his private letter to the president, Hamilton counterattacked in the Philadelphia newspapers. Under a variety of pseudonyms, the treasury secretary accused Jefferson of financial malfeasance while serving as minister to France, of opposing the Constitution during ratification, and of using public money to underwrite the *National Gazette.* Even though his private correspondence also rails against Madison, Hamilton publicly targeted only Jefferson because he considered Jefferson easier to smear as the Constitution's foe and more vulnerable to charges of hostility to the administration. The treasury secretary also held Jefferson responsible for what he perceived as Madison's apostasy and feared Madison's influence with the president. So great were "the powers of Mr. Madison" that Hamilton privately swore he never would have accepted his post had he known the Virginian would oppose him. The treasury secretary's public attack nevertheless struck at Madison obliquely. "It may be very true," he wrote, "That Mr. Freneau's coming to the City of Philadelphia, as a publisher of a News Paper, was at no time urged advised or influenced" by Jefferson. "And yet it may be equally a fact that it was urged advised & influenced by *a friend of* his, in concert with him." This fairly obvious reference publicized Madison's connection with the *National Gazette.*[19]

Other Federalist writers did not confine their vituperation to Jefferson. William Loughton Smith's *Politics and Views,* for example, described the congressman as the anti-administration "General." In fact, by 1792 Madison had become publicly identified not only as Hamilton's leading rival but also as the president's critic. Contemporaries already described him as "the Charles Fox of America," suggesting that he led the opposition to the administration. At a presidential birthday gala in Richmond, celebrants balanced a toast to Washington with another to Madison, "the Congressional defender of the rights and happiness of the people." No longer did Americans see the two Virginians as allies in a common cause. The public, like the president, viewed the administration as monolithic; one was either for it or against it, and Madison stood against it. If being perceived as allies during ratification strengthened the collaboration, then being perceived as foes in 1792 weakened it.[20]

Jefferson did not publicly refute Hamilton, but Madison and James Monroe did. Their pseudonymous defense of the secretary of state included the texts of letters on the Constitution that Jefferson had sent Madison from France between 1787 and 1789. While Washington could have guessed the correspondence's recipient, the younger Virginian nevertheless hoped to keep the president in the dark about his newspaper contributions. After completing their second piece, the authors had the secretary of state carry it to Philadelphia for publication. When Jefferson sent word that he had accidentally "dropped your letter with some papers of my own in the road between Mount Vernon & Alexandria," Madison panicked, wrongly concluding that his newspaper article had gotten lost. What if someone found it and showed it to Washington? "The accident . . . has caused no small anxiety," the congressman quickly replied. "The possibility of its falling into base hands at the present crisis cannot be too carefully guarded agst. I beg you to let me know its fate the moment it is in your power." Madison did not rest easy until Jefferson set him straight.[21]

Late in August 1792 an alarmed Washington tried shore up his administration by writing similar letters to Jefferson and Hamilton, pleading with each to show mutual forbearance. Internal disputes, he warned, posed a grave threat to the young Republic but one that was unnecessary, because the two secretaries differed over means rather than ends. Instead of reconciling the two men, Washington's actions deepened the fissure, as each secretary shrilly defended his own actions, making future cooperation contingent upon the other's behavior. This chain of events, which began with the resolution to retire, convinced the president of the correctness of Madison's assertion that to step down in 1793 would endanger the nation. If the administration could not cooperate, how could the country do so? After "a long and painful conflict in my own breast," Washington reluctantly faced another term.[22]

Historians commonly attribute this decision to the summer 1792 clash between Hamilton and Jefferson, which awoke the president to their deep ideological and personal differences. What has not received sufficient attention is that Madison's partisanship also jolted him. After finding that his cabinet members were at each other's throats, Washington now discovered that his collaborator—the friend to whom he took his most challenging problems—had also joined what seemed to him like madness. For both reasons, then, he concluded that he could not step down. After the Freneau accusations Madison's reputation as an administration enemy gradually caused the president to question him. True, Madison's support of Freneau was comparable to Hamilton's patronage of Fenno, but the latter defended the administration, whereas the former criticized it. Try as he might to assure himself that the younger Virginian's intentions had been pure, Washington still could not get around the fact that his collaborator had sponsored an opposition newspaper. Coming just when he was deciding whether to retire, this shocking revelation ironically helped persuade him to accept Madison's advice to serve another term, but at the same time it also undermined their collaboration. Exactly when the president made up his mind is unclear, because he never openly signified his willingness to stay in office. Mid-September 1792, the time Madison recommended that the farewell be issued, passed without a presidential proclamation. Assuming that Washington would have followed Madison's advice on timing the announcement, it seems that he had made up his mind by that deadline. As late as October the executive claimed not to have decided, but by then it was too late to back out.[23]

Madison, still in Virginia since having met Washington at Georgetown the previous May, had heard nothing from the president. The only news he had received all summer, brought by Jefferson in July, suggested that the retirement plan stood. Consequently the congressman received his mail with trepidation that September, hoping against hope it would not contain an executive bombshell. As the days slipped quietly by, he wondered whether Washington had accepted his advice after all. When October brought only yellow and red leaves to the Montpelier trees, Madison breathed a sigh of relief, realizing his collaborator would serve another term. Although the younger Virginian understood that Washington acted for nonpartisan reasons, he nonetheless thought the Republicans had scored a major triumph. At worst, reelection meant that executive power would be exercised impartially for the next four years, allowing his party to solidify its strength. At best, the Republicans would woo the president into their ranks. Madison did not anticipate that his enemies would instead win over his friend, resulting in John Adams's 1796 election. Employing similar reasoning, the Federalists, too, supported Washington, resulting in a second unanimous electoral vote. On 15 February 1793 Madison joined a congressional committee in notifying the chief magistrate of his reelection, and three weeks later he for the second time watched Washington take the oath of office and read his inaugural address.[24]

By year's end the partisan battles reverted to Congress, where the Republicans took the offensive. Late in the session—too late, Madison and his allies hoped, for Hamilton to clear his name before adjournment—they called on the treasury for a full financial accounting. Hamilton turned the tables by submitting a complete and precise report before recess. After studying the findings, Virginia representative William Branch Giles offered resolutions accusing the treasury secretary of unlawfully diverting to the domestic debt via the Bank of the United States funds designated to repay foreign loans. That none passed did not bother the Republicans because the controversy still raised preelection doubts about Hamilton.[25]

During the debate Madison hoped to drive a wedge between Washington and his department head. Again and again he emphasized that Hamilton not only had violated a legislative mandate but also had deliberately evaded explicit executive orders. "On *the very day,* on which . . . instruction issued from the President," Madison proclaimed, "the secretary commenced his arrangement for diverting part of a loan . . . to a purpose different from that specified and required by his instruction." Indeed, "the aspect here presented . . . was singular and remarkable. The subordinate officer appeared in direct opposition to the chief magistrate." Madison, presenting the incident as but one example of how Hamilton abused Washington's trust and popularity to serve corrupt ends, hoped his accusation not only would win votes but also would alert the president that Hamilton could not be trusted. Instead, Madison's course damaged his own relationship with the chief executive. The treasury secretary provided such satisfactory responses that the resolutions only made Giles's supporters look financially ignorant and grossly partisan. Yet somehow Madison came away thinking that Hamilton's self-defense had dissatisfied the president.[26]

Washington viewed dimly both his future presidency and his relationship with Madison when Congress adjourned in the spring of 1793. Instead of helping overcome factionalism, the president thought his friend had contributed to the problem. If only the younger Virginian had worked to reunite Jefferson and Hamilton rather than joining their bickering, perhaps he could have retired to his beloved plantation, now sorely needing his attention. To make matters worse, Freneau, whose connection to Madison the president finally understood, now attacked Washington directly. In January, Freneau condemned "levees, drawing rooms, stately nods instead of shaking hands, titles of office, seclusion from the people." If jabs at Hamilton had annoyed Washington, these personal assaults enraged him. Freneau's erratic behavior, over which Madison had no control, increasingly undermined the collaboration.[27]

Washington consequently distanced himself from his erstwhile right-hand man. Madison did not help prepare the 1792 annual message even though he had been invited to participate the previous spring. In February 1793 the president consulted only his cabinet about procedure for his second inaugural even though he had always taken such questions to his collaborator. Nor did the executive ask his friend to ghostwrite the second inaugural address. Perhaps he simply did not need Madison's expertise the second time around, but he had also developed doubts about the younger Virginian. Only once more, during Philadelphia's 1793 yellow fever epidemic, did Washington ask Madison's counsel on a precedent-setting matter, and he only did so then because he could not contact his cabinet.

Determined to remain a "president above party," Washington now steered a middle course in which his cabinet played a new role. Rather than forming a consensus, his advisers would demarcate opposing alternatives between which he would hew an impartial path. Only rarely would he invite Madison's assistance, because the congressman could not offer a perspective different from the secretary of state's. Instead, Washington increasingly looked to Attorney General Edmund Randolph, who had distanced himself from the factionalism, for help in navigating between Jefferson and Hamilton.[28]

Madison did not, in the spring of 1793, share Washington's pessimism either about events generally or their collaboration in particular. On the contrary, the events of the previous two years pleased him, especially the president's veto of the Apportionment Bill and his acceptance of another term. Thanks to a strong showing in the 1792–93 elections, the Republicans looked forward to dominating Congress. Madison had helped kill the Report on Manufactures, and he fooled himself into believing that the Giles resolutions had strained the treasury secretary's relations with Washington. Madison had every reason to believe that the tide that had nearly swept him away two years before had turned. He looked forward to strengthening and solidifying the Republican organization and to continued personal influence with the president. In 1797 his party would add control of the executive to its legislative dominance. If Washington had begun doubting Madison, in short, the congressman did not know it.

In retrospect, Madison's scenario seems fantastic. How could a publicly recognized opposition leader indulge in such optimistic hopes? From his perspective, however, it was not inevitable that the president would become a Federalist. Believing that he had nearly won Washington to the Republican standard, the younger Virginian from then on anticipated championing the administration, forcing Hamilton into opposition. The key would be staying right with the president. Republican measures would have to win executive approval, leaving Federalists the alternatives of acquiescing or attacking the administration. Of course Madison had no way of knowing that war between England and France would raise in America ideological disagreements more impassioned than those over financial policy. Nor did he appreciate how formidable a contestant for Washington's favor the treasury secretary would be. The very nature of Madison's relationship with the president—no longer that of a day-to-day policy adviser—would place him at a disadvantage vis-à-vis his rival.

8

"NEUTRALITY"

Aｌｔｈｏｕｇｈ Madison headed home for the 1793 recess confident about his relationship with the president, the Federalists within a year outmaneuvered
him in the contest to stay right with the chief executive. The Hamiltonians
adroitly put their own spin on the president's Neutrality Proclamation, forcing
Madison into the difficult and awkward position of opposing Federalist doctrines
while simultaneously echoing his loyalty to Washington. Although Madison handled this task fairly successfully, his belief that he was losing the struggle became
a self-fulfilling prophecy when it convinced him to decline to succeed Thomas
Jefferson as secretary of state. Without a strong Republican in the cabinet, Washington, no longer able to steer between the parties, became a Federalist partisan, an outcome that doomed the collaboration.

Mｏｒｅ ｔｈａｎ ａｎｙ ｏｔｈｅｒ ｉｓｓｕｅ, the French Revolution dominated American
politics in 1793. By that year a moderate restructuring of the Gallic government
had given way to an upheaval that threatened international stability. Before 1792
the collaborators, like most Americans, unequivocally favored the revolution,
seeing it as a by-product of American independence. They felt grateful to the
nation that had helped the United States win its freedom and applauded their
friend Lafayette's participation in the revolution's early stages. This is especially
true of Washington, who received the key to the Bastille as a gift from the young
nobleman.[1]

But below the surface the collaborators had their differences. The president
worried that the reformers "were making *more haste than good speed*" and meta-

phorically described the French as burning their mouths on liberty soup, unlike the Americans, who had waited for their dish to cool. He believed that if matters moved too swiftly, the revolution, like a pendulum, would swing from tyranny to anarchy. But for Madison, who feared that the French would not escape the clutches of despotism, let alone reach anarchy, the quicker things happened, the better. Each man's perspective mirrored his view of American politics. Madison, fearing that the Federalists aimed at monarchy, showed greater faith in the people's ability to govern themselves. Washington, worried that Republican attacks would bring down the government, thought popular participation needed to be carefully channeled and restrained. When Washington submitted France's 1791 constitution to Congress, an embarrassing clash exposed their underlying disagreements. Madison helped pass a House resolution praising the document and urging the president to congratulate the king. In response Washington, who opposed judging the constitution, angrily berated the lower chamber for "endeavoring to invade the executive."[2]

By 1793 Madison linked the French Revolution to American republicanism, maintaining that both faced the same corrupt British monarchical system. Washington, convinced by Lafayette's flight and the king's execution that the French had deviated from America's example, saw no such connection. The president feared that French fanaticism ultimately would produce a new tyranny that could threaten the United States. But unlike the High Federalists, who prayed that Britain would crush the detested revolution, Washington remained sympathetic toward France and hopeful that an efficient yet free government would prevail. Madison must have been shocked at what he regarded as Washington's lack of faith in self-government, while Washington no doubt found Madison's optimism naive. Neither man could help suspecting that the other's views extended to domestic politics.[3]

In April 1793 word arrived in Philadelphia that France and England had gone to war. When Washington asked his cabinet how to keep the United States at peace, Hamilton recommended proclaiming neutrality and nullifying the French Alliance. Jefferson countered that Congress alone could establish a neutrality policy, which followed from the power to declare war. The executive, he insisted, could only remind the country that a state of peace existed. The word *neutrality* ought to be avoided, because it suggested that the president was promulgating a new foreign policy rather than upholding a current one. Pursuing a middle course, Washington issued a proclamation (drafted by Attorney General Randolph) that omitted the word in question, even from the title. It warned Americans "to avoid all acts and proceedings" inconsistent with the "disposition" of the

United States to "pursue a conduct friendly and impartial towards the belligerent powers." By letting the French Alliance stand and by receiving the new French minister, Edmond Charles Genet, the president sided with the secretary of state.[4]

The proclamation confused Madison, who first read it in the Philadelphia newspapers that he received in Orange. Did it decide the question of war or peace (a prerogative that he, like Jefferson, believed belonged to Congress), or did it simply announce the existing state? Did it nullify the French Alliance? Madison concluded that "the proclamation was in truth a most unfortunate error" because he thought that it went against France, liberty, a valid treaty, public opinion, and the Constitution. He agreed that the United States needed to preserve peace but believed the neutrality policy favored Britain because the Royal Navy controlled the Atlantic Ocean, enabling the British to acquire American supplies and interdict French trade. The pronouncement also would dampen the people's republican ardor in the international contest against monarchism. In place of its "anglified complexion," Madison wished the administration had assumed a position more sympathetic to America's sister republic.

Blaming the proclamation on Hamilton and Knox, Madison confided to Jefferson that he was "extremely afraid that the P. may not be sufficiently aware of the snares that may be laid for his good intentions by men whose politics at bottom are very different from his own." He added: "I regret extremely the position into which the P. has been thrown. . . . It is mortifying to the real friends of the P. that his fame & his influence should have been unnecessarily made to depend in any degree on political events in a foreign quarter. . . . If France triumphs the ill-fated proclamation will be a mill-stone, which would sink any other character, and will force a struggle even on his." Lest his letters fall into the wrong hands, Madison did not sign them.[5]

Jefferson concealed these views from his superior. "The Pres. is extremely anxious to know your sentiments on the Proclamation. He has asked me several times," he informed Madison. "I tell him you are so absorbed in farming that you write me always about plows, rotations, &c." As late as August 1793, even after beginning to distance himself from Madison, Washington still sought his collaborator's opinion on difficult, precedent-setting issues. The younger Virginian would have been well advised to answer this request candidly, because the president had consulted both parties in good faith and had acted as impartially as possible. Perhaps Madison kept quiet because Jefferson convinced him that Washington listened only to Hamilton.[6]

While Madison remained reticent, Philip Freneau blasted the president for answering to "court satellites" rather than the people. From Montpelier, Madison marvelled at how the "Natl. Gazettes . . . teem with animadversions on the Proclamn." Jefferson informed him that "the President is not well. . . . He is . . . extremely affected by the attacks made & kept up on him in the public papers. I think he feels those things more than any person I ever yet met with." The two Republicans nevertheless accepted Freneau's attacks as necessary to awaken the president to the public's true sentiments. If Madison and Jefferson approved of Freneau's opening volleys, they were less enthusiastic with the more virulent assaults that appeared in June 1793 under the name "Veritas." So self-destructive were these essays that the secretary of state accused the Federalists of anonymously supplying them to Freneau in hopes of driving a wedge between Washington and the Republicans.[7]

The *National Gazette*'s charges indeed infuriated Washington, who waxed so "sore & warm" against Freneau that the secretary of state thought he was being held personally responsible for the editor's behavior. On another occasion Jefferson noted that the president became "much inflamed" over the newspapers and "got into one of those passions when he cannot command himself." Before regaining composure, Washington declared "that he had rather be on his farm than to be made *emperor of the world* and yet that they were charging him with wanting to be a king. That that *rascal Freneau* sent him 3. of his papers every day . . . that he could see in this nothing but an impudent design to insult him." If the president blamed the *National Gazette*'s campaign on Madison as much as on Jefferson, then he was by no means alone. Connecticut Federalist Timothy Dwight remarked that "Freneau . . . is regarded . . . as a mere incendiary, or rather as a despicable tool of bigger incendiaries, and his papers as a public nuisance."[8]

Sensing a golden opportunity for partisan gain, Alexander Hamilton published in the *Gazette of the United States* under the name "Pacificus" essays defending the president's proclamation. The treasury secretary's pieces reinterpreted the pronouncement to comport with the views that he had advanced in cabinet but that Washington had ruled against. He maintained that the proclamation had implemented a neutrality policy and contended that it had suspended the French treaty. Hamilton coined the title "Proclamation of Neutrality" even though the cabinet had explicitly determined to omit the word *neutrality*. Knowing that Pacificus's perversions would become gospel unless someone challenged them, Jefferson instinctively turned to Madison: "For god's sake, my dear Sir, take up your pen, select the most striking heresies, and cut him to peices in the face of the public. There is nobody else who can & will enter the lists with him."[9]

A reluctant Madison protested that he lacked time, adequate reference works, and the ability to concentrate during Virginia's oppressive June heat, objections that hid two bigger reasons for hesitating. First, Madison had no idea whether Washington agreed with Pacificus. Had the proclamation decided the question of war and peace, or did it merely recognize the existing state of affairs? "What are the ideas of the P.[?]" Madison queried Jefferson. "I could lay my course with more advantage . . . if I could . . . know how far he considers the Procln. as expressing a neutrality in the sense given to that term [by Pacificus], or how far he approves the vindication of it on that ground." And did Washington mean to abrogate the French Alliance? Without answers, Madison anticipated making false claims that Hamilton would demolish. Second, how could he challenge the treasury secretary without taking on the president as well? To save the chief executive from his most vociferous champion certainly would require creative writing.[10]

To assure Madison that Washington did not agree with Pacificus, Jefferson sent detailed reports of confidential cabinet meetings, encoding their most sensitive portions and leaving them unsigned lest they became public. "The President thought it expedient, by way of Proclamation, to remind our fellow citizens that we were in a state of peace with all the belligerent powers . . . which it was incumbent on him to preserve till the constitutional authority should otherwise declare," Jefferson explained. Consequently, there could be no doubt that Washington remained "uneasy at those [doctrines] grasped at by *Pacificus.*" Describing it as the "most grating" task he "ever experienced," Madison composed and sent five essays to Jefferson for publication. Lacking confidence in his work, he pleaded that the secretary of state correct it and at the last minute deleted certain paragraphs when he realized that Washington had used the word *neutrality* in answers to public addresses. Signed "Helvidius," Madison's pieces appeared in the *Gazette of the United States*'s August and September issues.[11]

Helvidius contrasted his own genuine loyalty to Washington with Pacificus's false devotion. "Under colour of vindicating an important public act, of a chief magistrate, who enjoys the confidence and love of his country," Pacificus had advanced principles that "strike at the vitals of its constitution, as well as its honor and true interest." As for Helvidius, "the present chief magistrate has not a fellow-citizen, who is penetrated with deeper respect for his merits, or feels a purer solicitude for his glory." Helvidius refuted Pacificus's claims that questions of war and peace belong to the president as well as to Congress. Placing the power to commence and to wage hostilities in the same hands violated the separation of powers, establishing a despotism, argued Madison, citing Article I of the Constitution and Hamilton's *Federalist* essays for corroboration.[12]

Having carefully delimited the executive's diplomatic authority, Helvidius concluded that the chief magistrate's declaration neither promulgated a neutrality policy nor abolished the French Alliance. Helvidius emphasized that the title "Proclamation of Neutrality" was not the president's. Pacificus "has called the Proclamation a Proclamation of neutrality . . . and has then proceeded in his arguments and his inferences . . . as if no question was ever to be asked, whether the term 'neutrality' be in the Proclamation." Helvidius explained that Washington had simply acknowledged the existing state of affairs. The pronouncement's "proper sense . . . remind[ed] all concerned, that as the United States were at peace ([a] state . . . only to be changed by the legislative authority . . .) the laws of peace were still obligatory and would be enforced." The Pacificus-Helvidius exchange amounted to another battle between Madison and Hamilton over implied powers and strict versus loose construction, with the presidency's very nature hanging on seemingly minor semantic disagreements. If Madison's interpretation better represented the ratifying conventions' original intent, Hamilton's position made United States foreign policy more efficient.[13]

The Helvidius essays could not have been worse-timed, because their appearance coincided with the president's clash with French minister Edmond Charles Genet. Hoping to use the new diplomat's arrival to demonstrate the strong public support of France, the Republicans clamorously welcomed Genet as he made his way from Charleston to Philadelphia in the spring of 1793. The frenzied greeting convinced the Frenchman that he could, by threatening an appeal to the people, overturn Washington's refusal to let him arm and outfit French privateers in United States ports.[14]

The Federalists took advantage of this egregious blunder to discredit France and the Republicans along with Genet. They held public meetings (a first in the process of party formation) that praised Washington and the proclamation while condemning the foreign minister and his supporters. The strategy worked so well that by August, Americans were in no mood for Helvidius's hairsplitting. Even before Madison's first piece appeared, Jefferson decided "that it will be true wisdom . . . to approve unequivocally of a state of neutrality, [and] to avoid little cavils about who should declare it." The best indication that Helvidius's foray against Pacificus failed lies in the fact that Washington's pronouncement has been known as the Neutrality Proclamation ever since Hamilton named it. Even modern editors misleadingly present Hamilton's designation as the proclamation's original title. Madison himself conceded defeat in September, when he stopped writing after five pieces even though he had planned more. Years later the Virginian regretted that the Helvidius essays exhibited "a spirit which was of no advantage either to the subject, or to the Author." In self-defense Madison noted that he had written in haste, during intense heat, and under pressure from Jefferson. To the end he maintained that he had struck "agst a publication breathing not only the intemperance of party, but giving . . . a perverted view of Presidt Washington's proclamation of neutrality, and calculated to put a dangerous gloss on the Constitution of the U. S." Perhaps inadvertently or perhaps acknowledging failure, Madison himself here referred to the "proclamation of neutrality."[15]

Washington recognized Pacificus as Hamilton, but it is unclear whether he ever learned Helvidius's identity. Nor can it be conclusively determined whether the president favored Madison's or Hamilton's construction of the proclamation, because his replies to public addresses endorsed different views at different times. To Federalist bodies Washington, like Pacificus, spoke of his pronouncement as a declaration of neutrality. He wrote to Philadelphia's merchants that "the happiness and best interests of the people of the United States, will be promoted by observing a strict neutrality in the present contest among the powers of Europe." To Republicans, however, Washington adopted a Madisonian interpretation, telling the citizens of Frederick County, Virginia, that "the proclamation declaring the actual state of things was thought right and accordingly issued" to preserve "a state of peace." Thus Washington shrewdly put either a Madisonian or Hamiltonian spin on his declaration depending on his audience's politics.[16]

Yet, in the final analysis, Washington seems to have sided with Helvidius over Pacificus despite his strong belief in implied powers. He originally followed Jefferson's advice to leave the word *neutrality* out of the proclamation. And although he frequently used that very word in addressing Federalist groups, he later apologized to his cabinet for having done so. Most important, when the department heads again debated the proclamation's meaning as they prepared the fifth annual message in November 1793 (months after the Pacificus-Helvidius exchange), Washington again sided with the Republicans. The final message described the pronouncement as "a declaration of the existing legal state of things," which it invited "Congress to correct, improve or enforce." Madison had the last word in the debate with Hamilton; Madison's House of Representatives reply described the proclamation as "a declaration of the existing legal state of things." Federalist Fisher Ames grumbled that "the President . . . sent us . . . a message rather tart. The House echo the speech." William Loughton Smith described Madison's reply as "highly approbatory of the President's Conduct." Nevertheless, the congressman felt vanquished, convinced that even though the president had been on his side, his foe had still somehow emerged victorious.[17]

Giving up on the Helvidius essays, Madison tried instead to neutralize the Federalists' public meetings, which discredited the Republicans and France by associating them with Genet's opposition to the president. By these means, Madison griped, Americans were being lured into a "connection with G. B. and . . . a gradual approximation towards her Form of Government," a strategy that worked so well because of the "general and habitual veneration for the President." The answer would be to hold Republican meetings, Madison wrote, declaring that the people "are attached to the Constitution. They are attached to the President. They are attached to the French Nation and Revolution. They are attached to peace. . . . They are averse to Monarchy. And to a political connection with . . . Great Britain. . . . Why then can not the sense of the people be collected on these points[?]"[18]

Madison and Monroe accordingly sketched resolutions that matched the Federalists' praise of Washington: "That the eminent virtues & services of our illustrious fellow Citizen G. W. P. of U. S. entitle him to the highest respect & lastg. gratitude of his Country, whose peace and liby. & safety must ever remind it of his distingd. agency in promoting the same." Resolutions condemning Genet but supporting the nation he represented won approval from public meetings in Charlottesville, Staunton, and Caroline County, Virginia. Edmund Pendleton, chairman of the Caroline meeting, mailed the petition to Washington, who gave just the response Madison had hoped to elicit: "The expressions of gratitude and affection, by the Citizens of Caroline, towards the French Nation, for their generous aid and assistance extended to us in a time of need are truly laudable." The chief executive added that "the marks of respect and affection for my person, manifested in the resolutions, demand and receive my unfeigned acknowledgements and gratitude." The Republicans made the most of these comments, publishing them as far away as Boston. By abandoning Genet and affirming loyalty to Washington, Madison's forces battled the Federalists to a draw in the neutrality fight.[19]

Late in the summer of 1793 yellow fever swept Philadelphia. Vacationing at Mount Vernon, Washington wondered what to do if the disease raged until December, when Congress would meet. Growing edgy after requesting but failing to receive advice from his department heads, who had left the capital, the president finally wrote to Orange for Madison's counsel. Unlike his first three years in office, Washington turned to his collaborator as a last resort, inquiring whether he could legally convene Congress outside the capital. If he could not, should he do nothing, or should he recommend an alternate meeting site? To what city could the legislature move without generating sectional jealousies? Washington asked for a draft proclamation, which Madison readily supplied, although it had been over a year since Madison had received such a request. For constitutional reasons and to avoid a precedent dangerous to the Potomac, Madison advised against convening Congress elsewhere. Why not simply invite the legislature to join him at a specified site, such as Lancaster or Reading, Pennsylvania. The president never used Madison's draft proclamation because the fever died out in time for the lawmakers to gather in Philadelphia as planned.[20]

The secretary of state had intended to retire when Washington's term ended in March 1793. Once the newspaper wars with Hamilton heated up, however, Jefferson agreed to stay on at least through the summer to avoid the appearance of being driven from office. After vainly pleading with the incumbent to remain, Washington decided that Madison should fill the soon-to-be vacated cabinet post. Even though he rarely relied on his collaborator for counsel now, the president hoped to employ him because Madison met three criteria for the job. First, the president needed a southerner (to balance northerners Knox and Hamilton) unsullied by speculation or any other stigma. Second, he wanted a man of exceptional ability to fill the office that he considered second in rank only to his own. Third and most important, Jefferson's replacement had to become the cabinet's Republican spokesman. To chart a middle course and to maintain his nonpartisan image, the president needed a strong voice to balance Hamilton's.[21]

Remembering Madison's 1789 desire for a congressional seat, Washington suspected that his collaborator would not accept the post, but hope and desperation nevertheless impelled him to offer it indirectly. The president casually mentioned his preferred nominee to the secretary of state, expecting the overture would be conveyed to Madison. As anticipated, Jefferson promptly notified the younger Virginian that Washington wanted him in the cabinet. But if the executive wished Jefferson to convince Madison to join the administration just as the latter had persuaded the former to do so in 1789–90, he met disappointment. Madison wrote to Jefferson that he was not interested. Whether the secretary of state ever passed this answer to Washington matters little because no reply amounted to a rejection.[22]

In 1834, when asked why he served as secretary of state under Jefferson but not Washington, Madison replied that he had turned the first president down to avoid the imputation of having favored ratification to gain political spoils, as well as to stay in Congress to resist Hamiltonianism. But he had entered Jefferson's administration because of "the part I had borne in promoting his election to the Chief Magistracy." These explanations ring hollow. Avoiding appearances of self-interest may have moved Madison in 1789 but could hardly have done so four years later. As far as the Constitution is concerned, he could have defended it as effectively in the cabinet as in Congress. Finally, Madison had played nearly as large a role in Washington's elevation to the presidency as in Jefferson's.[23]

The real reason that the Virginian chose not to become secretary of state is that he thought it would be a miserable job. He had heard the incumbent complain about being outvoted in cabinet meetings and then having to carry out policies that he opposed as if they were his own. Madison shuddered when Jefferson stated that the post had left him "worn down with labours from morning till night, & day to day, knowing them as fruitless to others as they are vexatious to myself, committed singly in desperate & eternal contest against a host who are systematically undermining the public liberty & prosperity, even the rare hours of relaxation sacrificed to the society of persons . . . of whose hatred I am conscious." Jefferson in fact exaggerated the odds that he faced, for Washington sided with him as often as with Hamilton. But Madison took the description at face value and determined to keep clear of the executive branch.[24]

Yet if Madison understood that Jefferson held an unpleasant assignment, he also recognized how influential a cabinet seat could be. When in August 1793 Jefferson spoke of retiring, Madison pleaded with him to carry on, pointing out that Washington had evinced "real anxiety" to retain him. The president needed to keep a Republican in the administration to shield himself "against certain criticisms from certain quarters." Madison urged Jefferson to "make the most of the value . . . placed on your participation in the Ex: Counsels" to exact concessions checking the Federalists. Given Madison's understanding of cabinet politics, he could blame only himself for the further alienation from his collaborator that resulted from his refusal to become secretary of state. After giving in to Madison's pleas to stay in office, the president expected continued assistance, not abandonment. Washington repeatedly told Jefferson that he rued having accepted a second term, especially now "that he was to be deserted by those on whose aid he had counted." Learning from Jefferson how the president felt did not change the younger Virginian's mind. Hamilton, in contrast, remained loyal to the president after badgering him to serve again.[25]

The long-term impact of Madison's decision was immense. Lacking a better candidate, Washington chose the mildly Republican Edmund Randolph as his new secretary of state. The former attorney general, whom Jefferson contemptuously dismissed as "the poorest Cameleon I ever saw having no colour of his own, & reflecting that nearest him," proved no match for Hamilton. Another rock-ribbed Federalist, William Bradford of Pennsylvania, became the president's new legal adviser. Without a strong Republican present, Washington could no longer identify a middle course between the two parties. Instead he rapidly became a Federalist because his counselors—Hamilton, Knox, Bradford, and Randolph—were overwhelmingly of that persuasion. Years later Madison wrote, "If any erroneous changes took place in his [Washington's] views of persons and public affairs near the close of his life as has been insinuated, they may probably be accounted for by circumstances which threw him into an exclusive communication with men of one party, who took advantage of his retired situation to make impressions unfavorable to their opponents." Thus Madison's perception that the Republicans were losing out in policy formation (when in fact they were not) became a self-fulfilling prophecy when it kept him out of the cabinet. The battle over commercial discrimination during the Third Congress's first session provides a case in point.[26]

In December 1793 Jefferson presented his long-awaited Report on Commerce, calling for commercial discrimination against Britain, which he had been preparing since 1791, when the House had referred to him Madison's proposals on the subject. In January 1794 Madison followed up the report with resolutions, aimed at Britain, calling for higher import duties and tonnage rates on countries lacking commercial treaties with the United States. Economic coercion would break down barriers, Madison contended, because America exported the food and raw materials Britain needed but imported superfluous luxuries. Even if Britain withdrew its trade, America would still benefit from his proposals as commerce diversified into more profitable channels and domestic manufactures received a boost. Federalists warned that Madison's proposals would provoke either a shooting war or a trade war with America's natural ally. Modern historians side with the Federalists, pointing out that the trade relationship between Britain and America accurately reflected the two nations' respective economic strength and that the United States enjoyed booming growth thanks to its ties with Britain.[27]

Washington's actions convinced Madison that his collaborator supported him. Early in December 1793 the president seemingly prepared the way for both Jefferson's Report and Madison's proposals with a message to Congress that compared Britain's policies unfavorably with France's. In February the younger Virginian expressed joy when the executive submitted to the legislature Minister to Great Britain Thomas Pinckney's warnings against seeking British commercial concessions through negotiation. Washington did not in fact back discrimination as unconditionally as Madison believed, because he vaguely spoke of "the pro and con of that business," apprehending that commercial war might lead to real war.[28]

In March, before Madison's resolutions came to a vote, news arrived that the British, in accordance with a November 1793 order in council, had stepped up seizures of American ships in the French West Indies. With commercial discrimination suddenly seeming an inadequate response to this violation of American neutrality, Madison convinced the House to pass a nonintercourse act that imposed drastic economic sanctions against Britain. Almost simultaneously, Washington preempted legislative efforts by nominating John Jay as envoy extraordinary to Great Britain. The president's initiative eroded just enough support to defeat the nonintercourse bill in the Senate by Vice President Adams's tie-breaking vote.[29]

Washington had felt duty bound to make one final effort at a mutual settlement with Britain before resorting to coercive measures, explaining that trade sanctions were "arrested in the Senate . . . not, as it is . . . generally believed, from a disinclination to the ulterior expediency of the measure, but from a desire to try the effect of Negotiation previous thereto." But the nomination of an envoy, coming at the new, Federalist-dominated cabinet's urging (with Randolph meekly demurring), killed Madison's proposals once and for all. There is no indication that Madison was consulted about the matter, or that he offered gratuitous advice, as did Monroe, who pleaded against Hamilton's selection as emissary. Privately, Madison thought the treasury secretary would receive the assignment.[30]

Madison complained that the president had been tricked into sabotaging his pet project by men who aimed less at British concessions than to stymie his proposals. He had confidence neither in Jay, whom he considered an Anglophile, nor in negotiation with an intransigent nation, and he believed naming the chief justice to an executive office violated the separation of powers. All in all, the mission constituted "the most powerful blow ever suffered by the popularity of the President." Madison, who thought Washington favored his resolutions, accepted the outcome as inevitable given the cabinet's makeup. If anything, he was amazed that the president had resisted naming Hamilton despite being "much pressed." Madison urged Jefferson to attack the nomination in the papers, insisting that "there is no measure of the Ex. administration perhaps that will be found more severely vulnerable." Having learned from the Helvidius episode, Jefferson declined.[31]

Trying to capitalize on their momentum and Washington's reputation, the Federalists pushed a military buildup, proposing that discretion to raise 10,000 troops rest with the president. Madison complained that "this is the 3d or 4th. effort made in the course of the Session to get a powerful military establishment, under the pretext of public danger and under the auspices of the P.'s popularity." He suspected the Federalists acted not to prepare for war but to achieve executive aggrandizement. The Virginian was pleased to see the Republicans defeat the infantry bill, but he and his allies could not derail other military and naval expenditures.[32]

Still honestly trying to steer between the parties (as well as to blunt criticism), Washington decided to balance Jay's appointment by sending a Republican to France to replace Gouverneur Morris, whose recall had been requested. Three reasons explain why the president explicitly offered the post to Madison despite having had the state portfolio turned down. First, the English crisis made the president desperate for proven talent. Second, Madison was now easily accessible in Philadelphia, not miles away in Virginia. Third, Washington wanted to give his collaborator a clear indication of his nonpartisanship. But all to no avail—fearful of becoming a Federalist pawn and dreading a sea voyage (perhaps because he may have been epileptic), the younger Virginian said no. With his quest for middle ground in shambles and unsure what other Republican to turn to, the president asked Madison whom to appoint. The congressman suggested Robert R. Livingston or James Monroe. Washington accepted this advice, and when the former declined the appointment, offered it to the latter, who accepted at Madison's urging. The new minister received instructions to assure France that Jay's negotiations did not weaken America's friendship with that republic.[33]

For Madison, neither the offer to himself nor Monroe's appointment made up for the defeat of commercial discrimination. "The influence of the Ex. on events, the use made of them, and the public confidence in the P. are an overmatch for all the efforts Republicanism can make," he moaned. "The party of that sentiment in the Senate is completely wrecked; and in the H. of Reps. in a much worse condition than at an earlier period of the Session."[34] But if the Federalists had won Washington into their ranks, Madison had only himself to blame. The president had remained remarkably nonpartisan, carefully navigating between Republican and Federalist shoals. Had Madison only realized this, he might have joined the cabinet and provided the balance that his friend needed to remain above party. Instead, Madison had allowed Jefferson to persuade him that the Federalists had already captured Washington. This belief quickly became self-fulfilling: without a Republican secretary of state, the executive inevitably shifted to the right. Jay's appointment was only the first of many reverses that Madison would now suffer. Each successive issue would produce another Federalist victory, driving the collaborators further apart. Neither man had understood how pivotal a turning point Madison's decision not to join the cabinet had been. Had Washington realized it, he would have tried harder to convince his friend to accept Jefferson's post. Had Madison understood it, he would have thought more deeply about accepting. Amazingly enough, however, their collaboration was not through yet. It would take another two years to flicker out, and it would enjoy at least one more great achievement, albeit a personal and domestic one.

9

DOMESTIC ORDER AND DISORDER

Despite their differences, Washington and Madison remained on excellent personal terms until late 1794, now rarely discussing state affairs but still communicating about nonpartisan interests such as agriculture. The president's role in the congressman's successful courtship of Dolley Payne Todd illustrates the continued warmth of their personal relations. But politically they continued to drift apart. During the Whiskey Rebellion, Madison backed Washington's use of the military even though he believed that better executive leadership might have made force unnecessary. In a subsequent dispute over the Democratic Societies' culpability, however, the president lost faith in the congressman's personal loyalty and motives. The uprising further exposed the collaborators' ideological differences, yet even this disagreement did not terminate their friendship.

Although no longer as close as they had been a few years before, the collaborators by 1794 still enjoyed a warm relationship. Madison no longer had access to administration secrets or saw the president regularly, outside of public functions. Early in the year Washington reverted to opening his letters with "Dear Sir," instead of the "My Dear Sir" he had used since 1785. Nevertheless, the Virginians' friendship still flourished, as evidenced by the fact that Washington consulted Madison about nonpartisan matters and persisted in closing his letters with the word *affectionately*.[1]

The two shared a common interest in agriculture. Washington avidly experimented with crops and crop rotations in hopes of improving American farming techniques. Madison had always found meteorology and natural history fascinating, but in the 1790s he accepted his destiny as a Virginia planter and began managing part of the Montpelier estate. That Thomas Jefferson, an accomplished naturalist, looked to both men for guidance in devising a field system attests to their wide knowledge. As the collaborators talked less about politics, they conversed more about husbandry. In 1794 Washington received a letter and pamphlets from Scottish agricultural reformer Sir John Sinclair urging the formation of a board of agriculture similar to one lately organized in London. The president asked Madison whether the plan would "meet legislative or other encouragement . . . in this Country." The younger Virginian favored a government-funded institution to disseminate information but warned that Congress did not share their advanced views.[2]

How much Washington and Madison influenced one another's thinking about slavery is unclear, but they shared similar attitudes regarding that "species of property." Both recognized the institution's incompatibility with Revolutionary ideology and saw it as a threat to the Republic's survival. They favored emancipation in theory, but fear of disunion froze them into silence and inactivity. Practical problems, including widespread racism, slaves' lack of education and skills, and the compensation of owners, also seemed overwhelming. Unlike Jefferson, Washington and Madison rejected innate black inferiority, and both must be judged humane in comparison to other owners. They often accepted economic losses for their slaves' benefit, for instance, by refusing to sell families apart and by manumitting individual servants in special cases. One can only guess whether the president divulged to Madison his developing plan to free his slaves after he and his wife died, or if he asked for advice in implementing this dream. Washington's example certainly influenced the younger Virginian, who, decades later, also took steps to emancipate his slaves after he and his spouse passed away.[3]

Like their common interest in agriculture, Washington's support of Madison's courtship of Dolley Todd illustrates the collaborators' continued friendship. In 1794 Dolley Payne Todd was a sprightly, attractive, twenty-six-year-old widow who resided with her toddler son, John Payne Todd, and her sister Anna Payne. Born in the Quaker community of Guilford, North Carolina, and raised in Virginia, Dolley Todd had lived in Philadelphia over a decade. During the 1793 yellow fever epidemic, she lost her husband of four years, John Todd, as well as an infant son. Although financially embarrassed, she nevertheless received marriage proposals within months. Having encountered Dolley Todd during his years in the city, the forty-three-year-old bachelor entered the competition in May 1794, asking Aaron Burr to introduce him formally. The day of their meeting, Dolley excitedly told a girlfriend: "Thou must come to me. Aaron Burr says that the great little Madison has asked to be brought to see me this evening." The courtship proceeded smoothly. In June a cousin wrote to Dolley that Madison "thinks so much of you in the day that he has Lost his Tongue, at Night he Dreames of you & Starts in his Sleep a Calling on you to relieve his Flame for he Burns to such an excess that he will be shortly consumed & he hopes that your Heart will be calous to every other swain but himself."[4]

Before long, the Washingtons heard about the romance. The president's nephew George Steptoe Washington had the previous year married Dolley's younger sister Lucy Payne. George Steptoe, whose education Washington supervised and funded, was the son of the president's late brother Samuel. George and Lucy made their home at Harewood, Samuel's former estate three-and-one-half miles northwest of Charles Town in Berkeley County, Virginia (now in Jefferson County, West Virginia). After her husband's death, Dolley's mother Mary Payne and her two youngest children joined them at Harewood.[5]

Because of their close connection to both Dolley and James, the Washingtons took an interest in their courtship. With the young widow's mother absent, Martha may have felt obligated to provide parental guidance. Dolley's grandniece Lucia Beverly Cutts described what happened next:

> A report soon got about of their engagement; such unwonted attentions from Mr. Madison excited comment. . . .
>
> It reached the Presidential mansion, where General and Mrs. Washington were much interested; and impatient to hear the truth, sent for Mrs. Todd, who all unconscious obeyed the summons at once.
>
> "Dolly," said Mrs. Washington, "is it true that you are engaged to James Madison?" The fair widow, taken aback, answered stammeringly, "No," she "thought not." "If it is so," Mrs. Washington continued, "do not be ashamed to confess it: rather be proud; he will make thee a good husband, and all the better for being so much older. We both approve of it; the esteem and friendship existing between Mr. Madison and my husband is very great, and we would wish thee to be happy."[6]

This secondhand account, written ninety-two years after the fact, represents at best a loose paraphrase of what transpired. Cutts probably learned of this episode either from Dolley Madison herself or from Cutts's grandmother Anna, Dolley's sister. The anecdote corresponds with Martha Washington's maternal reputation, and it fits the status of the Washington-Madison collaboration in 1794. Although no longer cooperating politically, the two men remained on excellent personal terms, and the president still held the congressman in high regard. Thus it is likely that such a meeting between Mrs. Todd and Mrs. Washington took place, and that the latter spoke with her husband's consent and encouragement.

Assuming that the Cutts memoir is reliable, the visit to the executive mansion must have had an immense impact on Dolley. To turn down her suitor after the audience with Martha Washington would be to ignore the admonition of the most prestigious couple in America! As Katherine Anthony puts it, the interview "elevate[d] the affair to a question of state." Perhaps Dolley would have accepted the proposal without cajoling. After all, she had already glowingly described her future husband as "the great little Madison." But it is also true that Dolley assented hesitantly, knowing that she would be expelled from her Quaker meeting for marrying a nonmember. Moreover, her coreligionists' opinion that remarriage would not serve her son's interest made her feel guilty. Finally, Dolley may have admired Madison, but she did not yet love him, and she appears to have experienced a case of "marriage trauma" (an "emotional reaction" many late eighteenth- and early nineteenth-century women experienced over having to "choose their bondage" in marriage) before taking her vows. Under these circumstances encouragement from as high an authority as the Washingtons may have tipped the scales in Madison's favor. Martha's mentorship may have proved especially telling, because she and George had married before falling in love.[7]

In the summer of 1794, Dolley Todd contemplated Madison's offer while visiting relatives in Hanover County, Virginia. In August she mailed a favorable response to Montpelier, and the following month the couple rendezvoused at Harewood. In the early 1770s, when Samuel Washington was still alive, George Washington frequently visited this modest, rectangular, two-story limestone mansion. The guests could not have failed to notice the resemblance between the president and his brother, whose military portrait hung in the parlor. In that same room James Madison and Dolley Todd married on 15 September 1794. The Reverend Alexander Balmain of Winchester, who a decade earlier had helped George Washington map the most convenient Potomac route to the Ohio, performed the service. The only guests present were George Steptoe Washington, his wife Lucy, and sister Harriet (the president's niece), and Dolley's mother, sisters, youngest brother, and son. After a three-week honeymoon at Harewood and at Old Hall, Madison's sister Nelly Hite's residence near Winchester, the newlyweds returned to Philadelphia.[8]

If the president gave Madison any counsel to match that given Dolley by Martha, no record of it remains. Similarly, any congratulatory messages from the First Family either were delivered verbally or have not survived. On other occasions Washington offered matrimonial advice to his friends. For example, upon

Harewood, the home of George Steptoe and Lucy Payne Washington,
northwest of Charles Town, West Virginia. James Madison and
Dolley Payne Todd married here on 15 September 1794.

hearing that the marquis de Chastellux had tied the knot, he wrote: "A wife!
. . . I can hardly refrain from smiling to find you are caught at last. . . . I am glad
of it with all my heart and soul. . . . you are well served . . . by catching that ter-
rible Contagion—domestic felicity—which time like the small pox or plague, a
man can have only once in his life: because it commonly lasts him . . . for his
whole life time." After marrying Anne Hill Carter, General Henry Lee received
the following lines from the president: "We are told, that you have exchanged the
rugged and dangerous field of Mars, for the soft and pleasurable bed of Venus,
I do in this, as I shall in every thing you may pursue like unto it good and laudable, wish you all imaginable success and happiness." Madison undoubtedly received comparable encouragement from a man who saw marriage as the key to
contentment.[9]

The congressman certainly appreciated the First Family's intentions and readily overlooked its meddling in his private life, especially at a time when he needed
reassurance of the president's goodwill. The episode reinforced his image of Washington as a great and good man, capable of rising above petty differences, and

whose errors were the fault of designing men. The chief executive may have intended his intervention as a sign of friendship in the wake of trying times. Perhaps, too, Washington agreed with Henry Lee, who joked that marriage might "soften" Madison's "political asperitys." If the interview helped convince Dolley to marry, then it was the greatest favor the president ever did for his friend, one that must have evoked eternal gratitude. It also must be classified among the collaboration's finer achievements, because Dolley proved to be a loving wife, a pillar of support, and a great political asset. Madison ever afterwards described his marriage as the most fortunate event of his life. Did this watershed in Madison's domestic life have any impact on his collaboration with Washington? Although the collaboration certainly terminated in the two years following September 1794, the outcome is coincidental rather than causal in nature. Political factors having nothing to do with Madison's marriage led to the demise of their association.[10]

Though a honeymooner, Madison could not escape national politics. As he traveled from Harewood to Old Hall and back again, attention in Virginia's western counties focused on Washington's call for militia to put down the Whiskey Rebellion in western Pennsylvania. (In fact, the two men nearly crossed paths in northern Virginia in mid-October as the president rode west to meet the troops and the congressman returned to Philadelphia.) Any goodwill generated between the collaborators by Madison's marriage quickly shattered after the uprising's suppression.[11]

The Whiskey Rebellion's origins lie in the Compromise of 1790. To generate the federal revenue required by assumption, Hamilton recommended an excise on domestically distilled liquor, a proposal Madison helped enact out of loyalty to the political bargain that would place the government on the Potomac. The congressman also thought it fair to balance heavy import duties with internal taxation, of which an excise would be the least objectionable form. Despite strong southern opposition to the bill, it passed the House and Senate. The only southerners to vote for it were Madison and the members who had switched their positions in 1790 to make the assumption of state debts and a Potomac capital possible.[12]

From Pennsylvania to Georgia, frontiersmen condemned the act, arguing that the federal government had no right to tax them after failing either to open the Mississippi River or to clear their region of hostile Indians. The excise weighed heavily on the cash-poor, semisubsistence communities that dominated trans-Appalachia. Facing prohibitive transportation costs, settlers distilled their bulky grain into whiskey and bartered it for the materials they could not manufacture at home. The inhabitants' localist mentality also led them to oppose internal taxation by a distant legislature as a sign of encroaching tyranny. Thomas Slaughter writes that in passing the excise, "the government heaped an ideologically, culturally, and economically repulsive tax on the very people least able and least willing to suffer the imposition." The unpopular measure immediately became a dead letter on the outskirts of settlement, with violent opposition springing primarily from the lower classes. Local elites tried to channel the protest in a peaceful direction, discouraging aggression in favor of petitioning for repeal, but met little success.[13]

Washington initially worried that the excise would encounter rural resistance, but after making inquiries during his 1791 southern tour, he concluded that only designing men could stir up opposition. He obtained this faulty intelligence because his route through the Carolina piedmont did not take him far enough west to reach the opposition's heart, and because interviewees were bound to tell him what they thought he wanted to hear. The president stubbornly adhered to his impressions despite growing hostility to the excise. The commercially minded and Court-oriented Washington could neither appreciate the hardships the duty wrought in a partially subsistence economy nor understand why the settlers saw tyranny in distant governments. Viewing matters from an eastern perspective, Washington thought the West ought to defray the cost of Indian campaigns. The belief that demagogues could readily lead the common folk astray came easy to him, because years of frustrating attempts to collect rents from his tenants in western Pennsylvania had convinced him that frontiersmen lacked intelligence and integrity. In fact, a decade earlier he had gone to court to eject squatters from his land in Washington County, where opposition to the excise flourished.[14]

In particular, the president blamed the Democratic Societies—voluntary political associations in an age that did not recognize the legitimacy of such activity—for inciting the ignorant rabble. Originating amid the euphoria that swept the United States after the French republic's establishment and Genet's arrival, these organizations emerged in all but two states, totaling approximately three dozen. Most members enjoyed wealth and education but tended to be political and social outsiders. Like the Republicans, these bodies admired France, hated Britain, opposed the administration, and swore that a Hamiltonian conspiracy existed to transform the Constitution into a British-style monarchy.[15]

Outside of western Pennsylvania, no evidence links the societies to the lawlessness, and even within that region many members, perhaps a majority, worked to moderate the protest. Largely because he associated them with Genet, the man who had threatened an appeal to the people, Washington nonetheless wrongly convinced himself that the societies wanted to destroy America's republican experiment: "I consider this insurrection as the first *formidable* fruit of the Democratic Societies. . . . These societies were instituted by the *artful* and *designing* members . . . primarily to sow the seeds of jealousy and distrust among the people, of the government, by destroying all confidence in the Administration of it. . . . I see, under a display of popular and fascinating guises, the most diabolical attempts to destroy the best fabric of human government and happiness, that has ever been presented for the acceptance of mankind." The president saw no reason for an interest group to establish itself permanently between the people and their elected representatives, unless, of course, it wanted to substitute its own agenda for the common good. In particular, he suspected these organizations of inciting the West to join the Spanish Empire in return for Mississippi navigation rights.[16]

Washington endeavored to eliminate the few specific excise grievances he considered justified, calling for reforms in his 1791 annual message and having Hamilton make compliance more convenient. Having taken these steps, the president expected the resistance to cease. Not understanding that frontier objections went beyond details to the excise itself, the chief executive soon concluded that far from securing submission, concessions only emboldened the law's obstructors. In September 1792 he issued a proclamation warning the insurgents to obey the law or pay the consequences.[17]

Madison, who as usual drafted the House's reply to the 1792 annual message, understood the rebellion much better than Washington. If he deplored lawlessness and supported the excise's enforcement, he also sympathized with the westerners' plight. The congressman recognized that the tax burdened backcountry communities and understood that local elites, including most Democratic Society members, favored nonviolence. Under these circumstances he thought it premature to threaten governmental repression. Instead of blaming neighborhood leaders, why not cooperate with them for a peaceful settlement? Why not restore order by building on the patriotism of the loyal rather than on fear of the disloyal? Madison's reply, which condemned illegal obstruction but urged further conciliation, did not—for the first time in four years—fully endorse the annual message. But the House, unwilling to question the president's judgment, added the following passage to the draft: "We hope, that . . . no particular part of the community may be permitted to withdraw from the general burthens of the country, by a conduct, as irreconcilable to national justice, as it is inconsistent with public decency." The insertion nullified Madison's appeal for additional concessions to the insurgents.[18]

Washington rigidly adhered to the concept of deference, whereby the people voluntarily submit to the governance of their social and economic betters. As a corollary, he believed that for the masses to defer, natural leaders needed to send them unified messages. If the elite divided among themselves, then the public might go astray. On crucial political issues such as the Constitution and the Whiskey Rebellion, he invariably faulted those members of the ruling class who disagreed with him (in this case the Democratic Societies). Washington's thinking developed during his formative political years in pre-Revolutionary Virginia, where elites resolved disputes among themselves rather than by taking them to the people.[19]

Less bound by deferential patterns of thinking and possessing more faith in popular independence and discernment, Madison was not as troubled when leaders divided over issues and appealed for public support. His Old Dominion past, too, shaped his behavior. Both men hailed from a common political culture, but Madison grew up during the Revolutionary era, which pitted Whigs against Tories in a dispute for popular approval. Yet like Washington, Madison could not fully escape these deferential assumptions, often blaming political defeats on an electorate that had been deluded by his enemies' misrepresentations and knowing that majorities could be as tyrannical as minorities. The irony of the collaborators' positions is that the Federalists would repeatedly defeat the Republicans by using Washington's name to appeal to the people.

The September 1792 proclamation failed to bring about obedience to the excise, but not for another year and a half could the president confront the problem. The neutrality crisis, the yellow fever epidemic, and the threat of war with Britain kept the executive preoccupied for months. By the summer of 1794, when Washington finally faced the rebellion, the situation had turned critical, as peaceful moderates, having been rebuffed by the government, temporarily lost control of the resistance movement to violent radicals.[20]

Once the extremists gained the ascendancy, the president acted brilliantly. Through a combination of patience and firmness, he isolated them and induced submission almost without bloodshed. Defiance of the excise spanned the frontier, but Washington focused on western Pennsylvania because proximity to the capital made it a convenient place for the government to make examples of traitors. While demonstrating the insurgents' intransigence by means of a peace commission, he summoned the militia. In calling Americans to arms against their fellow countrymen, the chief executive carefully framed the issue in terms about which all—North and South, rich and poor, Republican and Federalist—

could rally: the survival of republican government. Could the majority, acting through elected representatives, withstand a lawless minority? Once the president presented matters in this light, the militia turned out so overwhelmingly that the rebels gave up without a fight. After personally organizing the troops east of the Appalachians, the chief executive sent them westward under the command of Henry Lee and Alexander Hamilton. When the "Watermelon Army" (as one western-sympathizing satirist derisively called it) found no real resistance in the once disaffected counties, it rounded up a handful of ringleaders and headed home. Of those seized, the two found guilty of treason received presidential pardons.[21]

Madison recognized that Washington had skillfully restored order. Despite his sympathy for westerners and his preference for a nonmilitary solution, he did not second-guess the use of force. Instead, he blamed the rebels, asserting that the outcome "ought to be a lesson to every part of the Union against disobedience to the laws." He condemned the participants for enabling the Federalists to associate Republican opposition to the administration with treason and worried that like Shays's Rebellion, the Whiskey Rebellion would shift power to the central government. The creation of a standing army, Madison warned, "will be attempted in earnest during the session," but faith in Washington convinced him "that the P. will not embark in the measure."[22]

In defending the president Madison parted with some Republican leaders, such as George Nicholas, who groused that only slaves would "place such a blind reliance on any man's [Washington's] judgment or representations, as to be induced to offer their services to be the butchers of their countrymen." Nicholas thought one-hundredth of the soldiers actually raised would have been sufficient to restore order. Similarly, Thomas Jefferson wanted "to know how such an armament against people at their ploughs, will be represented, and an appeal to arms justified before that to the law had been tried & *proved* ineffectual." Jefferson chided Madison for allowing himself to be "swept away in the torrent of governmental opinions."[23]

In the midst of the crisis, Edmund Randolph notified the president "that a society under the democratic garb has arisen in South Carolina with the name *Madisonian*. It is a great grief to me, because it must place Madison under embarrassment either to seem to approve by silence what I am confident he must abhor, or to affront those who intended to evince their respect for him. I hope that he will not hesitate to adopt the latter expedient." Washington, too, wished Madison would spurn the association. "The *well* disposed people of this Country . . . will clearly see, the tendency if not the design of the leaders of these self created societies," he assured Randolph. "I should be extremely sorry therefore if Mr. M——n *from any cause whatsoever* should get entangled with them, or their politics."[24]

Considering Washington's belief that the societies had fomented the rebellion in hopes of bringing down the government, it is not surprising that he did not want his friend to get mixed up with them. The president thought that political leaders not only should steer clear of the organizations but ought to help combat them: "So generally acceptable does the law appear to be throughout the U. S. that I think it would not have met with the opposition which it has . . . if false-hoods and misrepresentations respecting it's operation and tendency had not taken place of fair and candid explanation. . . . I hope and trust that those good and enlightened characters, who have at heart the true interests of the public, will endeavor to effect by fair and just representations, what it would be extremely painful, however necessary, to carry into operation by compulsive means." Because Washington thought a united elite would have averted the rebellion, Madison's behavior toward the societies would test his motives and personal loyalty. After conveying the president's message, Randolph reported back Madison's opinion that the rebellious merited "every animadversion," an answer skirting the Democratic Societies' guilt or innocence.[25]

Although refusing to join the search for scapegoats, Madison distanced himself from the societies, ignoring their toasts, addresses, and other tributes. Despite Randolph's assurances to the contrary, Washington may mistakenly have thought that Madison had joined one or more of the despised organizations. After all, Federalist newspapers published their toasts to Madison in hopes of discrediting him, and Representative Fisher Ames believed that the Virginian had accepted honorary membership in the Philadelphia society.[26]

The Whiskey Rebellion would have produced no more controversy had Washington let well enough alone. Instead, the president tried to strike the societies dead in his 1794 annual message by attributing the uprising to the "artifice" of "self-created societies." These "combinations" of men had, for their own nefarious purposes, convinced western Pennsylvania's discontented that the government's conciliatory measures indicated weakness. To the instigators' dismay, however, the people's eagerness to defend the Constitution had demonstrated republicanism's viability. According to Federalist Representative George Thatcher of Massachusetts, the chief executive addressed Congress with uncharacteristic fervency: "Tho' he read, he made use of much more motion than has been usual for him on like occasions. He felt what he said." By attacking the government's critics, the president trampled freedom of speech and the press. James Thomas Flexner writes that "for the first time in his career," Washington "allowed himself to seem (what he desperately did not want to be) the head of a party."[27]

Shocked by the address, Madison pronounced his friend's statement "perhaps the greatest error of his political life." By threatening First Amendment freedoms, the president had assaulted "the most sacred principle of our Constitution and of Republicanism." Madison wrongly believed that the chief executive had, against his better judgment, allowed Hamilton to insert the passage into the speech. When again called to draft a reply, Madison ignored the controversial passage: "For his [Washington's] sake . . . I wish'd it might be passed over in silence by the H. of Reps." Instead, the congressman praised the handling of the insurgency and agreed that the event illustrated self-government's strength.[28]

House Federalists, unwilling to pass up what Madison described as an opportunity "to draw a party-advantage out [of] the P.'s popularity," challenged his silence on the Democratic Societies, but not before stalling long enough for the Senate to echo the president's denunciation. Pro-administration newspapers immediately published the upper chamber's reply, as well as Washington's answer, which reprobated those bodies a second time. When Representative Thomas Fitzsimons proposed inserting a condemnation of the "self-created Societies," Madison rejoined that "opinions are not the objects of legislation." Madison urged his colleagues not to allow respect for the chief executive to sway their deliberations, and—in an obvious jab at Hamilton—he questioned whether Washington even approved the foray against the societies. "Supposing the President really to entertain the opinion ascribed to him," he pleaded, "it affords no conclusive reason for the House to sacrifice its own judgment." Privately, Madison commented that "the attack made on the essential & constitutional right of the Citizen, in the blow levelled at the 'self-created Societies' . . . must be felt by every man who values liberty, whatever opinion he may have of the use or abuse of it by those institutions." After having collaborated with Washington on the campaign for the Bill of Rights, Madison, shocked to see the president trample personal liberty, could come up with no explanation other than Hamilton's evil influence. Washington's popularity threatened the Republicans just as it did the Democratic Societies. Madison's forces might win congressional elections, but as long as the president sided with the other camp, they could never control the federal government, because their forces would melt in any contest with the executive. To Madison the chief magistrate seemed to be upsetting the natural order of things by giving the Federalists the edge even though most people supported Republican principles, a dilemma that would inhibit party growth as long as Washington remained in office.[29]

As the debate over Madison's draft progressed, House Republicans realized that they would have to make a concession. Accordingly, they accepted an insertion stating that "combinations of men" had "foment[ed] the flagrant outrage, which has been committed on the laws." Compromise turned to defeat when Washington's answer to the amended address reviled the societies a third time. "The reply of the P. is claimed . . . as a final triumph" for the Federalists, and "so it will prove," Madison glumly wrote. He summarized the Federalists' strategy: "The game was, to connect the democratic Societies with the odium of the insurrection—to connect the Republicans in Congs. with those Societies—to put the P. ostensibly at the head of the other party, in opposition to both." The rapid disappearance of the censured bodies indicates that the plan worked.[30]

Madison's use of the word *ostensibly* again suggests that he believed that Hamilton had slipped the denunciation into the annual message. One wonders how Madison, who admired and respected Washington and who had worked with him so closely, could ever suspect him of being manipulated. The younger Virginian knew firsthand that the president called the shots. Clearly it was psychologically easier for Madison to impute the president's behavior to a sinister adviser than to accept that he and his friend disagreed so fundamentally, and that someone else had replaced him as Washington's right-hand man. Here Madison reacted like a typical Country thinker: it was never the king who conspired against liberty but the designing ministers surrounding him. In an anonymous pamphlet written in March 1795, Madison vented his anger against the Federalists for dragging Washington into every partisan dispute. "There are not a few ever ready to invoke the name of Washington; to garnish their heretical doctrines with his virtues, and season their unpallatable measures with his popularity," he wrote. "Those who take this liberty will not, however, be mistaken; his truest friends will be the last to sport with his influence."[31]

In one sense Madison's picture of events accorded with reality. Although Washington remained in full command, it is also true that his cabinet had become very one-sided. Not even the secretary of state warned that an attack on the societies might seem partisan. In Randolph's place either Jefferson or Madison would have moderated the president's behavior by presenting the Republican perspective. In 1793 Jefferson had stopped Washington from publishing Genet's correspondence by warning that doing so would "make the Pres. . . . the head of a party instead of the head of the nation." That the result was different in 1794 was perhaps more Madison's fault than Washington's, because by refusing to join the administration, the congressman denied the chief executive access to an alternative viewpoint.[32]

The president knew from published speeches that Madison did not share his hatred of the Democratic Societies. To the enraged chief executive, Madison's defense of First Amendment freedoms in effect aided and comforted traitors. Coming after the warning not to become entangled with the societies, Madison's actions made Washington further doubt his friend's personal devotion and commitment to the common good. The Whiskey Rebellion's repercussions carried into the New Year. When Washington designated 19 February a day of "public thanksgiving and prayer . . . for the seasonable control which has been given to a spirit of disorder in the suppression of the late insurrection," Madison privately railed against the exploitation of religion for partisan political gain. No doubt correctly guessing that Hamilton wrote the proclamation, he again accused the treasury secretary of governing the president.[33]

While their attitudes toward frontier unrest illustrate the collaborators' diverging worldviews, the difference was not as great as it may seem. Neither man understood the uprising as did Hamilton, who saw it as a sign of the government's weakness, or Jefferson, who interpreted it as proof of encroaching tyranny. Rather, Washington and Madison viewed the uprising as proof that America's republican experiment enjoyed sound health. When faced with an appeal from ballots to bullets, the citizenry promptly answered the president's call to defend majority rule. The collaborators' positions can perhaps best be understood by placing them on an ideological spectrum running from states' rights and localism on the left to consolidation and cosmopolitanism on the right. On this scale Madison falls slightly left of center, Washington a bit to the right of it. The extremities are occupied by Jefferson and the more radical Republicans on the left and by Hamilton and the High Federalists on the right. Unfortunately the controversy over the Democratic Societies obscured the considerable agreement with which Washington and Madison understood the Whiskey Rebellion.

Politics aside, the collaborators remained friendly. In March 1795 they discussed Jefferson's suggestion to bring the University of Geneva's faculty to America as the nucleus of a national university but judged it practically and theoretically unsound. A few months later the chief executive asked advice concerning John Sinclair's suggestion that Congress "reward discoveries of general benefit to society" and also presented the younger Virginian with agricultural pamphlets he had received from Sinclair. Moreover, Washington continued to close his letters with the word *affectionately* and invited the Madisons to a private family dinner in April 1795. Madison reciprocated these acts of kindness, for example, by delivering presidential mail to George Steptoe Washington at Harewood.[34]

Until the Whiskey Rebellion, the collaborators remained on warm personal terms despite their political differences, as evidenced by Washington's support for Madison's marriage to Dolley Todd. In the rebellion's aftermath, however, disagreement over the Democratic Societies' role cooled their relations. The president, who more than ever questioned his friend's allegiance and motives, experienced more of a chilling effect than Madison, who clung to the mistaken belief that Washington had fallen under Hamilton's spell. That the two men still remained cordial attests to the strength of their relationship.

10

ESTRANGEMENT AND FAREWELL

J OHN JAY'S agreement with Britain produced a head-on collision in which Madison won a battle over constitutional interpretation but Washington won the war over the treaty. The clash exposed fundamental differences between these two men about how responsive to popular pressures the government should be and the sort of political economy the nation should pursue. The contest ended their collaboration, confirming the president's loss of faith in the congressman's motives and personal loyalty. Madison, refusing to question Washington's intentions, believed that the Federalists manipulated his friend to threaten the Constitution.

SIGNED in November 1794, Jay's Treaty did not arrive in America until the following March. Shocked that Jay had obtained so little, the president and the secretary of state held the long-awaited agreement confidential until a special Senate session could convene to consider it. The British promised reparations for past seizures but gave no guarantee against future depredations. They agreed to open their West Indian ports to American ships of seventy tons or less but forbade the exportation of certain products. They consented to fulfill all outstanding obligations from the 1783 Peace, provided Americans abandoned claims for slaves carried away during the war. In return for these limited gains the United States paid dearly, accepting a disastrously wide definition of contraband, surrendering the right to sequester debts and impose commercial discrimination, and granting Britain most-favored-nation status, which virtually precluded beneficial treaties with other countries. In spite of modern assessments that Jay obtained as much as possible, Federalists and Republicans alike found the settlement a far cry from what they had anticipated.[1]

Meeting on 8 June, the Senate voted to deliberate in secret. Although unenthusiastic about the treaty, the Federalists preferred to ratify rather than to see relations with Britain deteriorate. After suspending the most offensive provision (Article 12), which limited West Indian trade, the upper house approved the pact by a bare 20-to-10 majority. When, the day after adjournment, portions of the agreement found their way into the newspapers, Washington decided to publish the complete text, but Senator Stevens Thomson Mason of Virginia handed it to the press before he acted.[2]

Even though Jay's mission stymied his attempt at commercial discrimination, Madison had changed his mind about the probable outcome while the negotiations were under way. He had concluded that even a Federalist envoy would win valuable concessions, because Britain, its hands full fighting France, needed American food and markets desperately. By the time the treaty became public, Madison, summering at Montpelier, had already received it from Senator Pierce Butler of South Carolina, who ignored the secrecy injunction. Unable to believe his eyes, Madison described the treaty as being "full of shameful concessions, of mock reciprocities, and of party artifices." If it became law, then commercial discrimination, for which he had fought so long and so hard, would be forbidden. Enactment, moreover, might provoke war with France.[3]

To fully understand Madison's abhorrence, one must look beyond specific provisions to the overall effect he thought an alliance with Britain would have on the Republic: it would reenslave America to the former mother country, gradually transforming the United States into a British twin. Instead of remaining agricultural, healthy, virtuous, and free, the nation might eventually become as industrially developed as England, a condition he associated with political tyranny and economic dependence. Why emulate a society that had replaced the production of foodstuffs, which would always have a market, with the manufacture of luxuries, ever subject to volatile overseas markets and the whims of fashion? Once Americans allied themselves to Britain, it would only be a matter of time before republicanism gave way to the corrupt British political system. Madison failed to see that the treaty was more likely to keep America in a colonial state than to expedite modernization. Nor did he adequately explain why trade with France would be less dangerous to America's political economy than trade with Britain. Madison's fantastically naive notion that undeveloped countries are more powerful than developed ones reflects his Country mentality. Madison also believed that various treaty articles (those closing the West Indies, restricting reexports, and banning commercial discrimination) exercised powers belonging to Congress as a whole and could not become legal until the lower chamber approved them. He vigilantly guarded constitutional privileges out of fear that the Federalists, having lost control of the lower chamber, would try to circumvent it by means of diplomacy.[4]

Robert R. Livingston pleaded with Madison to urge the president not to approve the treaty. The New York Republican explained that he himself had already written to the executive, but that a letter from Madison would be much more effective because the president highly esteemed his fellow Virginian. Knowing that if Washington wanted opinions he would ask for them, Madison wisely declined. Even in 1789 he had rarely offered unsolicited advice; to do so in 1795 would have been foolhardy. "With respect to the P. his situation must be a most delicate one for himself, as well as for his Country: and there never was . . . a crisis where the friends of both ought to feel more solicitude, or less reserve," Madison answered Livingston. "At the same time, I have reasons, which I think good, for doubting the propriety, & of course the utility, of uninvited communications from myself." Besides, the chief magistrate "cannot . . . be a stranger to my opinion . . . of the Treaty." The congressman confidently asserted that public opinion would discourage the executive from signing before obtaining satisfactory revisions.[5]

Unlike Madison, Washington did not worry about the socioeconomic implications of allying with Britain because his more modern, Court-oriented assumptions made him view economic development favorably. For the president the treaty decision jeopardized the Republic in a very different way. A refusal might exchange peace and prosperity for war at a time when the Republic was too young and too divided to survive it. Renewed British seizures of American merchantmen during 1795 complicated the issue, however, making a disappointing engagement even more offensive and unpopular. After canvassing Secretary of State Randolph, Washington bypassed the rest of his cabinet (Oliver Wolcott, Timothy Pickering, and William Bradford) in favor of consulting Hamilton, whose retirement to New York had not diminished his influence. The questions the former treasury secretary received reveal the soundness of Madison's instincts in not writing to the president; the chief executive already had his friend's views in mind. Is it true, Washington asked, "that as our *exports* consist chiefly of *provisions* & *raw materials,* which to the manufacturers in G. Britain, & to their Islands in the West Indies, affords employment & food; they must have had them on *our* terms . . . whilst . . . this country, offers the best mart for their fabricks; &, of course, is the principal support of their manufactures[?]" Not surprisingly, Hamilton dismissed this Madisonian argument and advised signing the treaty, arguing that the pact, although not a bad bargain itself, deserved acceptance mainly to avert a disastrous war with Britain.[6]

Having been convinced to approve the agreement, Washington followed Randolph's advice not to act until the British stopped preying on American ships. The president had hardly chosen this course when Pickering and Wolcott (who opposed using ratification as a bargaining chip) handed him a captured letter from French minister Jean Antoine Joseph Fauchet to the government in Paris. Known as "Dispatch Number 10," this document had been confiscated from a Gallic ship and delivered to London. The Foreign Office sent it to Minister George Hammond, who turned it over to Wolcott, who showed it to Pickering and Bradford. The communiqué, written during the Whiskey Rebellion, stated that Randolph had approached Fauchet with an unbelievable offer: in return for a few thousand dollars, the secretary of state seemed to have promised to settle the uprising peacefully, thereby thwarting the Federalists' attempt to gain partisan advantage against the Republicans and France. By raising the possibility of treason, Dispatch Number 10 persuaded Washington to abandon Randolph's advice in favor of Wolcott's and Pickering's. The president approved the Jay Treaty on 14 August and five days later confronted the secretary of state with the captured document. Convinced that his superior had presumed him guilty, Randolph angrily resigned and began preparing a vindication. This heady reaction removed the chief executive's doubts of his subordinate's perfidy.[7]

Madison refused to take sides in this clash between close friends. Washington never offered the congressman his version of the affair, but Randolph professed to be "happy at my emancipation from . . . a man, who has practised upon me the profound hypocricy of Tiberious, and the injustice of an assassin." Madison eagerly awaited the vindication and after reading it concluded that in trying to exonerate himself from a charge that few believed, Randolph convicted himself of indiscretion and ineptitude, an assessment with which modern historians agree. Randolph's inability to clear his name, even though the venality charge does not hold water, illustrates Washington's invincibility. Madison would soon run headlong into the same obstacle.[8]

Randolph's publication confirmed Madison's growing belief that the well-intentioned Washington had fallen victim to evil advisers. The secretary of state's departure (and Attorney General Bradford's death) led to a cabinet shuffle. Answering a presidential request for the names of potential replacements, Hamilton ruled out Nathaniel Pendleton as being "tainted with the prejudices of Mr. Jefferson & Mr. Madison," but Washington still hoped to find men the Republicans could embrace. After first choices William Paterson, Thomas Johnson, Charles Cotesworth Pinckney, and Patrick Henry turned down job offers, the president settled for whomever he could get. (Onerous and relatively unprestigious cabinet posts held little allure for such prominent men.) Wolcott remained in charge of the Treasury Department, Pickering took over Randolph's office, James McHenry replaced Pickering in the War Department, and Charles Lee became the new legal expert. All rock-ribbed Federalists, the cabinet no longer featured even mild bipartisanship. "Through what official interstice can a ray of republican truths now penetrate to the P[?]" Madison wondered. Disregarding the one-sidedness of the administration, the chief executive stubbornly maintained that he remained above party. Had he not done what he could to bring the opposition into the administration?[9]

Washington signed Jay's handiwork despite a deluge of anti-treaty petitions from around the country. The president became angry with the memorials, believing they exaggerated the pact's demerits for political gain. "The most arrant misrepresentation of facts" had convinced the citizenry "that their rights have not only been *neglected,* but absolutely *sold,*" he complained. Washington worried that France would try to exploit this artificial furor to force the government to reverse its position. The president resolved to stand firm until the delusion wore off and people realized that the accord served American interests. In reply to an anti-treaty memorial from Boston's selectmen, Washington explained that in making public policy the president and Senate would not substitute others' views for their own. All subsequent petitioners obtained the same answer (those the chief executive judged "rude" he ignored). His position reflected both approval of the treaty and his belief that his constituents should defer to his judgment rather than instruct him. The president became especially livid over public meetings held after ratification because their only objective seemed to be second-guessing him. Madison could understand neither the signing of such a detrimental engagement nor the inexplicable response to the memorials. He wondered how Washington could dismiss the citizens' interests and opinions so casually. Should not elected officials heed their constituents? Madison was deeply troubled over Washington's attitude because he believed that the Republic's very survival depended on popular vigilance toward elected officials. Indeed, he had spent the preceding four years trying to awaken the public to the need to keep the Federalists from perverting the Constitution into a monarchy.[10]

To Washington's delight Hamilton wrote, under the pen name Camillus, twenty-eight newspaper essays defending the Jay Treaty. Worried over their impact, Jefferson pleaded with Madison to answer them, but unpleasant memories of the Helvidius-Pacificus exchange dissuaded him from again entering the lists. Instead, the Virginian prepared an anonymous petition to the state assembly that blasted Washington for disregarding the popular will. It urged the legislature to block a treaty "fatal to the interests, the happiness, and perhaps finally to the liberty of the United States." Never formally submitted to the house of delegates, Madison's remonstrance appeared in the *Virginia Gazette and Petersburg Intelligencer* and other sheets around the country, contributing to the anti-treaty mood sweeping Richmond in the fall of 1795. After approving Virginia's votes against the agreement in the United States Senate, the general assembly proposed four amendments weakening that chamber's powers. The legislature distributed these recommendations to the several states and to Congress to provide a rallying point for those who wanted to stop the Jay Treaty.[11]

In the Fourth Congress, which convened in December 1795, the anti-treaty Republicans enjoyed a small majority over the pro-treaty Federalists. Madison's correspondents around the country assured him that the Republic's fate rested on his shoulders, but he knew that with thirty-nine new members present, he could expect a hard time maintaining party discipline. As always, the annual message, prepared with Hamilton's assistance, opened the session. Contrasting America's tranquillity and prosperity with the warfare raging in Europe, the speech caught an anxious Congress off guard. After promising to present the Jay Treaty once he received Britain's acceptance, the president turned to other subjects. Realizing that many Republicans would not demand a document the chief executive had pledged to submit, Madison drafted a reply that ignored the subject. For the first time ever, the other committee members (two Federalists) refused to rubber-stamp the chairman's draft response, instead adding an avowal of the public's "undiminished confidence" in the president, a declaration Madison privately condemned as "notoriously untrue." In debate the Republicans rejected the insertion, forcing the reply's submission to a larger committee. The compromise address that emerged acknowledged Washington's "zealous and faithful services" and affirmed "affectionate attachment" to him.[12]

While biding time over the treaty, Washington turned to Madison for help with the troublesome matter of George Washington Motier Lafayette, the son of his beloved former aide. After release from a European prison, the teenager (whose father remained incarcerated) came to America to place himself under the president's care. Not sure whether or how to receive young Lafayette, Washington asked Hamilton for advice. The former treasury secretary warned that taking an aristocrat into his family might offend the French government and provide the administration's enemies with ammunition. Knowing that he could shield himself from criticism if a prominent Republican sanctioned his reception of

Lafayette, Washington turned to Madison. After summarizing his predicament, he asked the younger Virginian "what you think (considering my public character) I had best do to fulfil the obligations of friendship & my own wishes without involving consequences[?]" No reply exists, but perhaps Madison helped engineer Congress's investigation of Lafayette's situation. Upon hearing the legislature's intentions, Washington asked whether the congressman, who "alone, of the house of Representatives, has ever heard me lisp a word on this subject," would make sure that the lower chamber did not embarrass him. The House subsequently conducted its inquiry in a nonpartisan manner. It had been two years since Washington requested Madison's counsel, and he only did so on this occasion because he needed something he could not get from a Federalist.[13]

Impatiently awaiting the treaty, the House grew more restive with each passing day, especially because the Federalists took advantage of the delay to rally support for the agreement. "The name of the P. is every where used with the most wonderful success . . . in subduing . . . popular objections," Madison grumbled. As the Republicans studied their options, January 1796 brought word that George III had unconditionally accepted Article 12's suspension, meaning that the agreement would not return to the Senate. Equally troubling, many state legislatures reacted to Virginia's proposed constitutional amendments with hostility. Madison now knew that the pact could only be defeated if the representatives withheld the appropriations necessary to implement it. On 22 February, House Republicans vented their frustration by voting down the traditional early adjournment that enabled the members to wish the president a happy birthday. The Federalists, Madison noted, feted the chief magistrate "with greater splendor than ever. The [treaty] crisis explains the policy."[14]

At the end of February, Washington finally delivered the settlement to Congress. The official text having not yet arrived, the president would have preferred to stall longer, but the treaty's publication in southern newspapers forced him to act. On 2 March, Edward Livingston, convinced that the House already had waited too long, called for the documents relating to Jay's negotiations. To prevent this ill-advised resolution from eliciting a presidential denial based on confidentiality, Madison tried to limit it to papers the president judged consistent with United States interests to disclose. Angering many Republicans, the amendment lost 37-47.[15]

From 8 March to 24 April, the House debated what powers, if any, it possessed over treaties. Taking the floor on 10 March, Madison pointed out a constitutional ambiguity. On the one hand, the governmental charter assigns foreign policy to the president and Senate. On the other, it awards control of commerce to Congress, an arrangement that left it unclear whether the full legislature needed to concur in trade agreements. To grant the president and Senate absolute control over all overseas engagements went too far, Madison argued, because it allowed those branches to take over the government by resorting to diplomacy in place of legislation. A safer constitutional construction would require the lower chamber to sanction those treaties that trespassed on its enumerated powers. In a government of checks and balances, why not require this safeguard, he asked. When Livingston's motion passed by a majority of nearly two-to-one, Madison guessed that Washington would hand over all of Jay's papers except sensitive ones.[16]

Hamilton counseled rejecting the House's resolution, but before his draft message arrived from New York, the president and his new cabinet had prepared an answer refusing the representatives' request. Because the Constitution vests the treaty power exclusively in the president and Senate, the House had no right to the papers, he explained. Washington based his interpretation on his personal remembrance of the 1787 Federal Convention, which had granted special powers to the upper chamber to protect the interests of the small states. Specifically, he cited a particular vote recorded in the convention journal defeating a motion that "no Treaty shall be binding on the United States which is not ratified by a Law." Washington deposited the journal, which he had retained since 1787, in the State Department for public inspection.[17]

The president's response challenged the younger Virginian's credibility as a spokesman for the Federal Convention, because Washington misleadingly presented the issue as a matter of fact, not interpretation. The message in effect said, "I was there too, and that is not what happened." "Mr. Madison is deeply implicated by the appeal of the President to the proceeding of the General Convention, and most persons think him irrecoverably disgraced, as a man void of sincerity and fairness," commented Fisher Ames. Federalists taunted Madison to settle the issue by bringing forth his notes on the convention debates, something Madison could not do, because he had lent them to Jefferson. But publishing the papers would not have resolved the nebulous question.[18]

Madison, enraged less by the rejection than by the reasoning on which it was based, described the message as "unexpected . . . improper & indelicate." Instead of withholding the documents based on national security, the chief magistrate had thrown his immense prestige behind a dubious constitutional construction and in the process had virtually branded Madison a liar. The congressman wrongly blamed Hamilton. "I have no doubt that the advice & even the message itself were contrived in New York where it was seen that if the rising force of the republicans was not crushed it must speedily crush the British party and that the only hope of success lay in forcing an open rupture with the president," he remarked. "It is to be lamented that" Washington "so easily lent himself to the stratagem." Madison also believed that the executive's eagerness to secure Federalist votes for a District of Columbia loan guarantee had inspired the refusal. Had not the House Federalists allowed the desired measure to pass the day after it received his answer?[19]

Calling for the papers produced the contest with Washington the Republicans had hoped to avoid. On 2 April the anti-treaty forces caucused to figure out how to uphold the House's powers without, as Madison put it, instigating "an overt recontre with the Executive." Their solution took the form of two resolutions, introduced by Thomas Blount, maintaining the House's right to sanction portions of treaties involving enumerated powers and maintaining that it could demand papers without specifying a reason. In a "free, but respectful" speech, Madison offered four reasons to disprove the argument that treaty power belongs exclusively to the executive and Senate. The stakes were high: at issue stood constitutional precedent, his own credibility, and his friendship with Washington. First, Madison postulated that the House had raised a different issue from that governing the Federal Convention vote cited by the executive. The representatives did not, as the president insisted, assert the right to review all parts of all treaties. Rather, they demanded a say only over those provisions involving Congress's explicitly delegated authority, such as commerce. Second, Madison questioned Washington's interpretation of the vote, suggesting that the delegates had balloted the way they did for the exact opposite reason from what the president presumed. They might have defeated the motion for Congress to sanction treaties because they considered it already implicit that the House must approve foreign pacts under certain circumstances. In short, Washington's supposed smoking gun proved nothing.[20]

Third, Madison suggested that in determining original intent, one must look not to the Federal Convention, which merely proposed the Constitution, but to the state conventions that actually ratified it. That these bodies understood the treaty power to be limited, Madison argued, could be inferred from the jealousy they had exhibited regarding Congress's powers over war, appropriations, commerce, and the like. Fourth and finally, Madison reminded the House that in 1791 he had been condemned for appealing, in a speech against a national bank, to a Federal Convention vote denying Congress the authority to grant charters. Had his colleagues changed their principles, he sarcastically asked. Years later Madison bitterly complained that in looking to the Federal Convention to determine original intent, Washington accepted from the Federalists in 1796 the very same reasoning he had rejected from Madison in 1791 over the bank bill.[21]

Thus Madison averred that Washington's message hinged on an ambiguous vote dealing with an irrelevant issue cast by a convention of secondary importance. He had a plausible case, but Washington had a better one. Including the House in treaty making would prevent the secrecy, speed, stability, and international credibility requisite to foreign policy. Consequently, neither the federal nor the state conventions probably ever intended to permit the lower chamber to nullify portions of treaties by a simple majority vote. Many Antifederalists doubtless would have liked this doctrine, but their attempts to obtain amendments weakening the president and Senate had failed. Madison assumed that after he spoke, other Republicans would reinforce and embellish his remarks, but when he finished, none of his supporters had anything to add. This outcome made the clash look as much like a contest between the two Virginians as between Federalists and Republicans. The Blount resolutions passed by twenty-two votes.[22]

Throughout the confrontation both men adopted more extreme versions of their previous opinions on the treaty power. At the Federal Convention, Madison suggested distinguishing "between different sorts of Treaties—Allowing the President & Senate to make Treaties . . . of Alliance for limited terms—and requiring the concurrence of the whole Legislature in other Treaties." Although it failed to receive support, this statement suggests that his position that the House could withhold appropriations from certain diplomatic agreements was not new. Washington saw matters differently. Earlier in his presidency he remarked that if the lower chamber judged foreign engagements, "the government would be at an end, and must *then assume another form,*" adding "that he did not like throwing too much into democratic hands." Since endeavoring in 1787 to strengthen the federal government relative to the states and to bolster the president and Senate vis-à-vis the House, the collaborators had moved in opposite directions. Worried that the executive and Senate had fallen into monarchists' hands, Madison had come to favor an enlarged role for the states and the House of Representatives as an antidote. Unbothered by the success of Hamiltonian measures but troubled by the localism of the states and the lower congressional chamber, Washington favored further insulating the federal government, especially the executive and Senate, from popular pressure. Despite their close friendship neither man understood the other's changing views. When the difference emerged, each accused the other of apostasy.[23]

With the passage of the Blount resolutions, Madison predicted that the House, having defended its prerogatives in principle, would now do so in practice by killing the Jay accord. In a lengthy speech he judged the treaty a bad bargain in itself and insisted that no extraneous reasons to implement it existed. He ridiculed Federalist warnings, suggesting that a rejection meant not war but the negotiation of a better agreement, because Britain could not afford another enemy. Amazingly, Madison suggested that Washington would not have signed the treaty had he known that his approval would not stop British seizures of American ships. After all that had happened, to claim that the president regretted his actions was truly audacious.[24]

The Federalists stalled a final vote while they rallied public support. New Englanders learned that a rejection spelled war, increased seizures, and economic recession. Westerners were told that the treaty's defeat meant that the British would retain the Northwest posts, and, worse yet, Mississippi navigation would be lost, because the Senate would reject Thomas Pinckney's settlement with Spain. But the Federalists' main theme was "to follow where Washington leads," a strategy that worked perfectly. On 18 April, Madison happily reported a balance of twenty against the treaty, but only five days later he nervously noted that the margin had slipped to eight or nine. Despite heroic efforts to hold the majority party's forces in line, the discouraging trend continued until, early in May, the House approved appropriations by three votes, a stunning Madisonian defeat that rendered the Blount resolutions meaningless. After all, what purpose did constitutional principles serve if they could not be exercised?[25]

"Poor Mr Madison" took the loss "in all its force," wrote Pierce Butler. The Virginian expressed bitterness over the defeat, blaming his Republican allies for their lack of courage and discipline. In truth, however, the Federalists' skillful use of Washington's prestige undid the opposition. "The name of the President & the alarm of war, have had a greater effect, than were apprehended," Madison diagnosed. "A crisis which ought to have been so managed as to fortify the Republican cause, has left it in a very crippled condition," resulting in disastrous spring 1796 elections and costing Madison his position as party leader. The Federalist editor Peter Porcupine (William Cobbett) chortled, "Citizen Madison was formerly reckoned as a sort of chief, but he has so sunk out of sight this campaign" as to become "no more than an aide-de-camp. . . . As a politician he is no more; he is absolutely deceased, cold, stiff, and buried in oblivion for ever and ever." Indeed, the humiliation "riveted" the Virginian's intention to retire when his term ended.[26]

Washington felt vindicated by the outcome. "No candid man . . . will believe for a moment that the *ostensible* dispute, was about papers, or that the British Treaty was a *good* one, or a *bad* one; but whether there *should be a Treaty at all* without the concurrence of the house of Representatives," he commented privately. The Republicans had attacked "the fundamental principles of the Constitution." Had he not stopped them, they would have rendered "the Treaty making Power not only a nullity, but . . . an absolute absurdity." Would anyone believe that after giving the president and Senate the authority to make treaties, the framers and ratifiers "wd. in the same breath place it in the powers of the house of Representatives to fix their Veto on them?" Like Madison, Washington, too, thought he was defending the Constitution. Had he not prevailed, Washington believed, the representatives would have emasculated the presidency, thereby undoing the revolution in the distribution of powers among the government's branches that the Constitution had wrought, resulting in majority tyranny through an unchecked legislature.[27]

On the accord's merits (as with constitutionality), Washington again probably had the stronger case, because ratification preserved the peace at a time when the nation was too young and too divided to risk a war. In practice, the pact not only turned out more favorably than anticipated, it also helped Thomas Pinckney open the Mississippi River. On the other hand, Madison's warnings largely came true: the agreement led to a serious deterioration of relations with France, an undeclared naval war, higher taxes, and repression of dissent. Although a Republican defeat, the Jay Treaty initiated a series of events resulting in Jefferson's 1800 presidential election. However much they savored victory, moreover, the Federalists were not entirely comfortable making popular appeals. Believers in deference, they knew they were creating a monster that could come back to slay them once the ever-popular Washington retired. Thereafter, the Republicans, whose ideology supported the rule of public opinion, would win control of the government by taking their case to the people.[28]

The great Supreme Court justice and Washington biographer John Marshall wrote that the Jay Treaty fight broke "the last chord of that attachment which had theretofore bound some of the active leaders of the opposition to the person of the President. Amidst all the agitations and irritations of party, a sincere respect, and real affection, for the chief magistrate, the remnant of former friendship, had still lingered in the bosoms of some who had engaged with ardour in the political contests of the day. But, if the last spark of this affection was not now extinguished, it was at least concealed under the more active passions of the moment." Although this assertion applies to other Republican leaders, it does not fit Madison. Even after the treaty's passage, he continued to admire and respect Washington, instead blaming his embarrassments on the cabinet and Hamilton.[29]

The president, in contrast, washed his hands of his friend after the treaty affair. Having pleaded that Washington serve a second term, Madison, it seemed, had accused him of usurpation, a charge the chief executive could not forgive. The doubts about the younger Virginian's personal loyalty and intentions that arose in the controversy over the Democratic Societies had been confirmed. "With respect to the motives . . . wch have not only brought the Constitution, to the brink of a precipice, but the peace happiness and prosperity of the Country, into eminent danger, I shall say nothing," the president remarked. "Charity tells us they ought to be good; but suspicions say they must be bad." Because the initiative had always rested with Washington, his attitude ended their friendship. Never again did he ask Madison's advice or invite him to family dinners. Never again would the younger Virginian visit Mount Vernon, and the only letters the two men ever again exchanged were brief perfunctory notes.[30]

IN May 1796 Washington wrote that the Jay Treaty fight had aroused "the public mind in a higher degree" than any event "since the Revolution." This statement applies to the president himself, as evidenced by the draft farewell address he prepared amid the crisis and sent to Hamilton for revisions. That Washington turned to Madison for retirement advice in 1792 but looked to the former treasury secretary in 1796 speaks volumes about the second term's impact on the collaboration. During these four years Hamilton not only replaced the congressman as the president's close adviser, he also became more influential than Madison had been at any time since 1789. Washington relied so heavily on the New Yorker because he neither possessed brilliant subordinates, as he had during the first term, nor any longer trusted Madison or other opposition members. The president also increasingly looked to Hamilton because advancing age robbed him of confidence in his own abilities.[31]

Washington copied the first half of his draft farewell almost verbatim from Madison's 1792 version. This portion thanked the country for the honor it had bestowed and urged the people to preserve the Union through a combination of vigilance and mutual forbearance. He added a brief introduction, explaining that he had intended to publish the address four years before but filed it away when friends persuaded him to accept another term. The freshly written second half, dealing with events since 1793, reflected in three ways the immense impact of the Jay Treaty fight. First, the Republicans' admiration for France evoked warnings to avoid foreign influence and to place United States interests before those of other nations. Second, the House's attempt to interfere with the treaty power elicited a plea to keep the government's branches and levels in check. Third, journalistic accusations of presidential monarchism and Anglomania produced an admonition to trust public officials instead of swallowing every slander and misrepresentation served up by the newspapers.

Washington's clash with Madison over the surrender of executive papers, like the larger Jay Treaty battle of which it was a part, also shaped his draft valedictory. The president introduced Madison's 1792 version by explaining that four years earlier he had prepared a retirement message, "but the solicitation of my confidential friends (particularly one who was privy to the draft) . . . induced me to suspend the promulgation" and accept another term. At the bottom of the page, Washington wrote "*Mr. Madison." Upon reconsidering his manuscript before sending it to Hamilton, Washington erased the parenthetical phrase, the asterisk, and Madison's name. His cover letter explained that he had "struck out the reference to a *particular character* in the first page."

To Hamilton, Washington spelled out why he quoted Madison's 1792 draft: "My reasons for it are, that it is not only a fact that such an Address *was written,* and on the point of being published, but *known also to one or two* of those characters [Madison and Jefferson] who are now stronger, & foremost in the opposition to the Government; and consequently to the person Administering of it contrary to their views." Publicizing his original intent to step down, the president believed, would persuade the public that in accepting another term, he could have had "*no* view in extending the Powers of the Executive beyond the limits prescribed by the Constitution." The revelation that Madison and Jefferson had persuaded him to stay on also would "lessen, in the public estimation the pretensions of that [Republican] Party to the patriotic zeal & watchfulness, on which they endeavor to build their own consequence at the expense of others, who have differed from them in sentiment." In short, the chief magistrate hoped to show that after begging him to stay in office, his friend accused him of usurpation. Washington took Madison's opposition to the administration personally, an attitude the younger Virginian would not have understood. Indeed, Madison would have been shocked to learn of Washington's enmity toward him because for him, resistance to government policy did not affect his personal loyalty to the president.[32]

Many historians erroneously surmise that Madison helped compose the document sent to Hamilton for revision. Flimsily based on a dinner invitation Washington sent the congressman in mid-May 1796, this supposition can easily be refuted. First, the chief executive would have had his text finished and ready to mail by the time the dinner took place. Second, Madison received a printed request to attend a weekly state dinner, not a handwritten summons to a private audience. Third, Washington by then had become so fed up that he preferred publicly humiliating Madison, not seeking his counsel. The executive mansion dinner notwithstanding, Madison played no role in the formation of the 1796 farewell (aside from having, four years before, prepared a draft upon which Washington and Hamilton heavily relied).[33]

If he did not consult Madison in 1796, is it true, as Felix Gilbert hypothesizes, that the president hoped to combine Federalist and Republican viewpoints into a bipartisan address? Gilbert writes that "in giving both Hamilton and Madison a part in the composition of his valedictory," Washington hoped to demonstrate "his conviction that party contrasts did not exclude cooperation in a situation of national interest." The manner in which the chief executive intended to use Madison's draft renders Gilbert's contention highly dubious. The president wanted to quote the 1792 address primarily to demonstrate the author's hypocrisy: had Madison not urged him to remain in office, only to accuse him of lusting for power?[34]

After studying Washington's draft, Hamilton wisely argued that incorporating Madison's 1792 manuscript would produce an awkward and dated farewell. He warned, too, that Washington's claim that the opposition had talked him out of retiring might meet skepticism. Instead, the former treasury secretary volunteered to draw up an entirely new draft, which of course would enable him to put his own imprint on the address. After mature reflection Washington acquiesced in a new version but pointed out that "when the first draft was made, I thought the occasion was fair (as I had latterly been the subject of considerable invective) to say what is there contained of myself."[35]

By casting the president's ideas in more timeless language, Hamilton divorced them somewhat from the context of the Jay Treaty. He based the address's introduction and conclusion—together about one-third of his manuscript—on Madison's 1792 draft. These paragraphs withdrew Washington's name from consideration and explained that the president had wanted to retire after one term but that his advisers had persuaded him to serve again to protect national security. Hamilton wrote the remaining two-thirds (the address's main body) from scratch. Often thought of as a warning against foreign entanglements, this portion actually makes an impassioned plea for the Union's preservation, the admonition against overseas alliances being but one means to achieve this end. Hamilton offered three others as well: Americans must resist political parties (especially sectional ones), guard against constitutional encroachment, and always place national interests first.[36]

The president made insertions and deletions in the draft, including the addition of four new paragraphs to its ending. One of these, expressing the enjoyment he would derive from living as an ordinary citizen "under a free government," Washington based on Madison's 1792 draft. Perhaps the most significant and revealing emendation was the removal of the former treasury secretary's assertion that "the real danger in our system is that the General Government organised as at present will prove too weak rather than too powerful." Despite the break with Madison, in short, Washington had not fully embraced Hamiltonianism. The chief executive worked out a different ghostwriting procedure with Hamilton than he had employed with Madison. Instead of incorporating intended revisions himself, the president returned the manuscript to New York for changes, something he had never done with any of Madison's compositions. After Hamilton reworked the farewell, Washington edited it a final time.[37]

The president adhered to Madison's four-year-old recommendation to combine his retirement announcement and his parting advice into a single message addressed to the American people and published in a newspaper. The finished product appeared in David Claypoole's Philadelphia *American Daily Advertiser.* Washington even followed Madison's advice on timing the address, delivering it to the public on 19 September, almost the exact time of year the younger Virginian had urged in 1792. In the context of 1796, however, releasing the message only a few weeks before the choosing of electors served partisan objectives. Until Washington withdrew, the Republicans could not campaign for a successor, because they would never be foolhardy enough to oppose the incumbent. In an age of slow communications and primitive party organization, the decision not to publish before mid-September dealt the Republicans a heavy blow, denying them time to marshal their strength behind Jefferson. What governed the timing of Washington's Farewell? Perhaps, attempting to remain above party, he withheld his declaration in hopes of eliminating campaigning on both sides, not realizing that the decision played into Federalist hands. More likely, given his view that a Republican victory would repudiate his policies, he timed his Farewell to favor John Adams's election.[38]

Even more than its timing, the valedictory's content helped the Federalists. Couching the warning against foreign entanglements in general terms did not mitigate its impact against the pro-Gallic Republicans. French minister Pierre Auguste Adet's fall 1796 campaigning for Jefferson's election only lent credibility to the charge that the opposition took its orders from Paris. Historian Alexander

DeConde writes that the Farewell was not a "timeless, and unbiased warning to the nation" but "a piece of partisan politics directed specifically against Republicans and Francophiles who had made Washington's last years miserable. . . . It became the opening blast in the presidential campaign, contrived to prevent the election of Thomas Jefferson." The president insisted that his address would be a nonpartisan document that would leave "the field clear for *all*," but its timing and content state otherwise. However much Washington liked to think of himself as being above party, his valedictory proves that he had become a Federalist.[39]

Not surprisingly, Madison viewed the Farewell not as selfless advice to the country but as a partisan manifesto. He condemned its rejection of overseas commitments as both a thinly veiled attack on the Republicans and an attempt permanently to rupture relations with France. The message's "tenor and date" had been carefully arranged to turn the decisive mid-Atlantic electorate against Jefferson. As usual, Madison attributed the president's behavior to the Federalists surrounding him. The address showed that Washington was "compleatly in the snares of the British faction. . . . It has been known that every channel has been latterly opened, that could convey to his mind a rancor against that country [France] and suspicions of all who are thought to sympathise with its revolution. . . . But it was not easy to suppose his mind wrought up to . . . adopt some parts of the performance." Of course having his draft scrapped in favor of Hamilton's added pique to Madison's disgust. If only he had seen Washington's original draft![40]

In 1823 Madison mused that "at some future day it may be an object with the curious to compare" his 1792 manuscript with Hamilton's 1796 version. The most remarkable difference, he guessed, lay in "what is omitted, [rather] than in what is added in the Address as it stands." This comment refers to Hamilton's failure to echo Madison's praise of the Constitution and republican government, which the Virginian interpreted as proof of the author's preference for a British-style monarchy. No doubt the contrast between the drafts struck Madison when he first read the Farewell in 1796, as well as the fact that Washington had not restored to the address any tributes to government of, by, and for the people.[41]

With time, Madison nevertheless came to appreciate both the Farewell and his own significant role in its genesis, even in 1825 urging Jefferson to include it in the University of Virginia's curriculum. It contains "nothing which is not good," he remarked, "unless it be the laudatory reference . . . to the Treaty of 1795 with G. Britain, which ought not to weigh against the sound sentiments characterizing it." Even though Madison took no part in preparing the final Farewell, Felix Gilbert's attribution is nevertheless accurate: "'Washington in collaboration with Madison and Hamilton' might be the most correct formulation of the authorship of this document." Although his contribution did not match Hamilton's, Madison nevertheless deserves some credit for one of America's most celebrated political messages.[42]

When, early in the nineteenth century, a dispute over the Farewell's authorship arose between the political descendants of Washington and Hamilton, Madison claimed credit neither for himself nor for his erstwhile rival. Privately he commented: "It is very inconsiderate in the friends of Genl. Washington to make the merit of the Address a question between him & Col: Hamilton. . . . They ought to claim for him the merit only of cherishing the principles & views addressed to his Country, & for the Address itself the weight given to it by his sanction; leaving the literary merit whatever it be to the friendly pen employed on the occasion." He feared that if Hamilton became known as the author, the Farewell would be viewed "not as the pure legacy of the Father of his Country, as has been all along believed, but as the performance of another held in different estimation." He kept his own 1792 ghost authorship secret so as not to support the allegation that the president turned to Hamilton in 1796. Besides, Madison did not want to break his promise to Washington "forbidding publicity, at least till the lapse of time should wear out the seal on it, & the truth of history should put in a fair claim to such disclosures." Madison guarded Washington's posthumous reputation as carefully as he would watch over Jefferson's.[43]

THE House, recognizing that Madison's special relationship with the president had ended, for the first time in eight years did not name him chairman of the committee to prepare an answer to Washington's final annual message. Even though he did not draft the reply (that duty devolved on the chair), he acquiesced in praise for the "wise, firm, and patriotic" behavior of the administration, as well as expressions of "gratitude and admiration" for Washington's public service. During the floor debate Republican William B. Giles tried to strike out the accolades. Reluctant to be victimized by further confrontations with the president and eager to bury the hatchet with a man he truly admired, Madison did not support this effort.

After the House defeated Giles's maneuver, Madison for the last time joined in carrying the answer to the president. Echoing the representatives' conciliatory tone, Washington promised to employ "all honorable means to preserve peace and to restore . . . harmony and affection between" the United States and France, whose relations had deteriorated after the Jay Treaty. Washington's report on Gallic affairs, delivered in January 1797, reviewed the state of affairs between the two nations since 1793. It included instructions to Monroe's replacement, Charles C. Pinckney, to notify the Directory that America maintained its friendly disposition toward France. Before seeing the message, Madison hoped it would "heal, rather than irritate" wounded relations, but he expected the worst. "I cannot look around at the men who counsel" Washington "or look back at the snares into which he has hitherto been drawn without great apprehensions," he moaned. After reading the "Belligerent" communication, the congressman resumed his lament: "The British party since this overt patronage of their cause, no longer wear the mask. A war with France & an alliance with G. B. enter both into print & conversation; and no doubt can be entertained that a push will be made to screw up the P. to that point before he quits the office." After all that he had witnessed, not even this scenario surprised him, but Madison avoided confrontation, hoping Washington would avert war with France if left unchallenged.[44]

When Washington asked Hamilton about sending an envoy extraordinary to France, the New Yorker replied that fairness required balancing Jay's negotiations in London with the appointment of a bipartisan commission to Paris. Washington's eyes must have bulged when he read Hamilton's Republican candidate: "Mr. Madison will have the confidence of the French & of the opposition. . . . Unless Mr. Madison will go there is scarcely another character that will afford advantage." The suggestion was out of the question! The president would have nothing more to do with his former friend, even if it meant ignoring Hamilton. Besides, after having turned down offers to become secretary of state in 1793 and special envoy to France in 1794, Madison would not, he knew, accept the assignment. Instead, Washington sent no commissioner at all.[45]

The Fourth Congress's last session witnessed Washington's and Madison's last collaborative effort. Although the chief executive had never before needed an intermediary to obtain the younger Virginian's assistance, their friendship had by now so deteriorated that they could cooperate only with the help of a go-between. Rather than the president, federal district commissioner Alexander White lined up Madison's support for the call for a national university in the last annual message. In making his pitch White played upon Madison's continued affection for Washington. "The establishment of a National University . . . is an object which the President has much at heart," White pleaded. The commissioner emphasized that the final message offered the perfect opportunity for success, because Congress would be inclined to grant the "last request of a departing Friend." Aware of the estrangement between the two men, White tiptoed around their troubled relations. He assured Madison that "your Sentiments at large will have great weight . . . with the President were they communicated as yours which I shall do or not as you please." It is possible that in trying to get Washington and Madison to cooperate on behalf of public education, White also hoped to reconcile his two companions.[46]

After meeting with Madison, the district commissioners sent Washington a memorial to be placed before Congress requesting permission to receive contributions for a university. The president conveyed the petition to Madison, either by having a secretary deliver it or possibly by summoning him to a final meeting. If a personal consultation took place, it must have been brief and formal, maybe even strained or awkward. At any rate, Madison presented and defended the memorial to Congress and was appointed to a select committee to consider it. But the House declined to act, most members apparently considering such an institution beyond Congress's means, powers, or responsibilities. One cannot help wondering whether the collaborators would have enjoyed more success had they been on better terms.[47]

Late in December 1796, when Madison received his last invitation to a state dinner at the executive mansion, the final round of celebrations and ceremonies honoring the retiring president commenced. On 22 February, Congress wished the president a happy birthday, and that evening the Madisons probably joined 1,200 others at Rickett's Amphitheatre for the birthnight ball. "Even Democrats forgot for a moment their enmity and seemed to join heartily in the festivity," commented a Federalist. The president's last levee occurred on 28 February, the final drawing room followed three days later, and a public dinner for 240 guests took place on 4 March. On one of these occasions, the two men probably said goodbye for what both knew was the last time. About leaving office, Washington wrote, "Although the prospect of retirement is most grateful to my soul . . . I am not without my regrets at parting with (perhaps never more to meet) the few intimates whom I love." Because the younger Virginian no longer enjoyed membership in that select group, the final leave-taking must have been stiff and discomfiting for both men. The First Family did not offer the Madisons any parting mementos, as they did the Powels, Hamiltons, McHenrys, Wolcotts, Pickerings, and Morrises.[48]

On 4 March 1797 Washington and Madison attended John Adams's presidential inauguration in Congress Hall's House of Representatives chamber. Without speaking a word, the departing executive stole the show. As he entered the room and took a seat on the dais, Madison and the rest of the waiting crowd burst into applause. Amid the flushed faces that packed the floor, Adams noted "scarcely a dry eye but Washington's." Although relieved to see his erstwhile friend finally out of office, Madison's emotions, too, must have welled as the curtain fell on a political career that had dominated American politics for half of his own life. Of course Washington's was not the only tenure that ended that day, as Madison, after four terms, now relinquished his congressional seat. "In retiring from the public service at that juncture," Madison later reminisced, "he had the example of Geo. Washington." It is fitting that these two men departed together, because their collaboration had helped to define and establish the office that Adams now assumed. The ship of state that they helped navigate through dangerous seas could now be turned over to new pilots. By the end of March, both retirees had left the capital for Virginia.[49]

Returning to their native state, the two men immersed themselves in renovating their homes and managing their plantations. Contrary to self-characterizations, however, neither withdrew from politics. Both maintained a steady correspondence with party leaders and carefully followed national affairs. But the similarities end there, because from 1797 to 1799 Washington and Madison were further apart ideologically than ever before.[50]

Madison initially saw the new president as an improvement over his predecessor because he thought Adams would refuse to kowtow to High Federalists like Hamilton. But Madison quickly became alarmed that the new chief would conspire to replace republicanism with monarchy. He feared that Adams would provoke hostilities with France to whip up a war frenzy at home, enabling Congress to raise taxes and standing armies and forbid written and spoken criticisms of the government. Despite his forebodings, Madison remained confident the people would turn the monarchists out of office.[51]

For the former chief executive, it was not Adams and the Federalists who threatened the American Republic but the Republicans. By persuading France that the administration possessed so little popular support that it could be insulted with impunity, the opposition had led the United States to the brink of war. The ex-president accused Madison and his followers of masking their designs behind accusations of Federalist despotism. "The friends of Government who are anxious to maintain its neutrality, and to preserve the Country in peace . . . are charged . . . as being Monarchists, Aristocrats, and infractors of the Constitution; which according to their [the opposition's] Interpretation . . . would be a mere Cypher." Washington asserted that "the Republicans, as they have very erroneously called themselves," are the "curse of this country."[52]

During the summer of 1798, after hearing of France's insulting refusal to treat with American envoys Charles C. Pinckney, John Marshall, and Elbridge Gerry, Congress enacted war preparations, including the enlistment of a 12,000-man

"New Army." In July, Adams nominated and the Senate confirmed Washington as lieutenant general, but unlike in 1787, 1789, and 1792, Madison did not join the chorus of appeals for Washington to resume public office. After insisting on personally choosing his subordinate officers and refusing to take the field until hostilities actually commenced, Washington answered the call. He reached this decision surprisingly quickly, considering how he had anguished over attending the Federal Convention and serving as president. However much he dreaded renewed service, he simply could not sit idly by while Republican traitors (including Madison) tore down a government he had spent twenty years building. Washington publicly endorsed the administration's policies, while privately he called for even "more energetic" defense measures. In officering the army Washington imposed a political litmus test, refusing to recruit Republicans out of fear that they would "create disturbances in the Military, as they have done in the Civil administration of their Country." Ultimately he allied himself with the High Federalists, who opposed Adams's attempt to negotiate a peaceful settlement with France.[53]

Their opposite reactions to James Monroe's *A View of the Conduct of the Executive* illustrate the ideological gulf that divided the former collaborators. After being recalled from France, Monroe, with encouragement from Madison, prepared a defense of his diplomatic conduct that charged the Washington administration with tricking him into misinforming the Directory about Jay's negotiations with Britain. When France became enraged over the deception, the American government had made him the scapegoat, Monroe claimed. Madison expressed pleasure with the vindication and hoped that it would receive wide distribution, especially in the South. But Washington responded with a fit of rage, penciling a point-by-point refutation into the book's margins. He blamed the Directory's negative reaction to the Jay Treaty on Monroe, whom he accused of having pursued a partisan agenda instead of his country's true interests. The ex-president even suspected Republicans (presumably including Madison) of having funneled anti-administration propaganda to Paris via Monroe.[54]

Their responses to the Alien and Sedition Acts also measure how far apart the collaborators had drifted. In 1798 Congress passed laws extending the naturalization period, allowing the deportation of alleged subversive aliens, and making defamation of high federal officials a criminal offense. Madison, who considered these statutes a flagrant violation of the Bill of Rights, hoped the states could keep the federal government within its constitutional bounds. He anonymously wrote resolutions, which Virginia's 1798 General Assembly overwhelmingly adopted, asserting that the laws exceeded congressional authority and urging the states to cooperate in securing their repeal.[55]

Washington, who had no idea that his erstwhile collaborator had written the strictures, voiced disgust with the Old Dominion for approving them. "The Alien and Sedition Laws" have "employed many Pens . . . in the Assembly of this State," he wrote. "They have points to carry, from which no reasoning, no inconsistency of conduct, no absurdity, can divert them." The ex-president believed that the Republican outcry was more demagogic than principled: "The Alien and Sedition Laws, are now the desiderata in the Opposi[t]ion. But any thing else would have done; and something there will always be, for them to torture, and to disturb the public mind with their unfounded and ill favored forebodings."[56]

Washington's reaction to Madison's *Aurora General Advertiser* essays, too, captures his intellectual divergence from his former right-hand man. Early in 1799, after considerable prodding from Jefferson, Madison contributed two anonymous essays to Benjamin Franklin Bache's Philadelphia *Aurora.* In "Political Reflections" he addressed the Federalist charge that the Directory used war as an excuse to introduce tyranny to France. Rather than disputing the accusation, Madison warned that the American executive must not be allowed to follow the French example. Instead of blindly following the administration, Madison urged the citizenry to make sure that it stayed within legal bounds.[57]

Whether Washington read either of Madison's essays cannot be determined, but his attitude toward the *Aurora,* its publisher, and its content suggests that he would have seen red, because few men aroused his ire as much as Bache. In addition to being an extreme Republican partisan, the editor in 1797 had published forged letters purporting to have been written by the commander in chief during the Revolution. "His calumnies are to be exceeded only by his Impudence, and both stand unrivalled," Washington complained. Even worse than his tactics were Bache's apparent motives: "There seems to be no bounds to his attempts to destroy all confidence, that the People might . . . have, in their government; thereby dissolving it, and producing a disunion of the States." Not only did Washington despise Bache, he also deprecated essays like Madison's that paralleled Adams's policies with the French Directory's. "But no conduct is too absurd, or inconsistent for some men to give into," he complained.[58]

Despite the ideological differences illustrated by Monroe's vindication, the Alien and Sedition Acts, and the *Aurora* articles, Madison retained profound admiration and respect for Washington. After observing Adams's first year in office, he compared America's first chief executives:

There never was perhaps a greater contrast between two characters, than between those of the present President & of his predecessor. . . . The one cold, considerate & cautious, the other headlong & kindled into flame by every spark that lights on his passions: the one ever scrutinizing into public opinion, and ready to follow where he could not lead it: the other insulting it by the most adverse sentiments & pursuits: W. a hero in the field, yet overweighing every danger in the Cabinet:—A. without a single pretension to the character of a Soldier, a perfect Quixotte as a Statesman: The former chief Magistrate pursuing peace every where with sincerity, tho' mistaking the means: the latter taking as much pains to get into war, as the former took to keep out of it. The contrast might be pursued into a variety of other particulars.

Madison clung to the notion that his party, not the Federalists, embodied Washington's republican ideals. Madison felt vindicated in 1798 when Republicans attended a celebration in Philadelphia honoring Washington's birthday that Adams's supporters, considering the event an insult to the incumbent, boycotted. He wrote that "the nonattendance of the adamites" should be "presented to the public in such a manner . . . as to satisfy the real friends of Washington, as well as the people generally, of the true principles & views of those who have been the loudest in their hypocritical professions of attachment to him." As late as July 1798, before Washington accepted his military commission, Madison convinced himself that the ex-president did not approve his successor's policies. "There are circumstances which make me believe," he chortled, "that the hotheaded proceedings of Mr. A are not well relished in the cool climate of Mount Vernon." Although the publication of the ex-president's correspondence with Adams shattered Madison's illusions, he possessed too much respect for his former friend to question the decision to take command of the army.[59]

Washington, in contrast, remained bitter. After returning to Mount Vernon, he never again even mentioned Madison's name in his letters or writings, lumping Madison with the "Bachite Republicans" whom he accused of trying to overturn the Constitution. By 1799 he believed that a crisis was at hand. Thanks to the Republicans, the French Directory stood convinced that Americans would not defend their government against an invasion, a reckless course, Washington noted with disgust, in which he thought Virginia led the way. He expected the 1799 general assembly to be especially critical; unless loyal men took seats, the legislature might take even more drastic measures than the Virginia Resolutions. Earlier in his career Washington would have looked to his collaborator to provide the parliamentary leadership he envisioned. But in 1799 he viewed Madison not as the solution but as part of the problem. Instead he appealed to Patrick Henry to redeem the Old Dominion: "When measures are systematically, and pertinaciously pursued, which must eventually dissolve the Union . . . ought characters who are best able to rescue their Country from the pending evil to remain at home?" Henry agreed to enter the assembly but died before taking his seat.[60]

Word that Washington had prevailed upon Henry to stand for the legislature caused Republicans to plead that Madison, too, return to Richmond. "Mr. Henry has certainly declared for the next Assembly, in obedience to the call from General Washington," wrote John Taylor of Caroline. "There will be no member present capable of counterpoising Mr. Henry, unless you will come; and if you do, his defeat at this crisis will certainly happen." Agreeing to run, Madison easily won the election, and then in December 1799 he helped to purge Federalists from state office. For governor, Madison nominated none other than Washington's bête noire, James Monroe. When a Federalist pointed out that to elect the controversial diplomat would insult the former president, Madison disingenuously responded that elevating Monroe would not affront anyone, because no official reason for his recall from Paris had ever been publicized. After Madison defended Monroe's public and private character, the assembly easily elected him governor.[61]

On 12 December, Washington rode to his Mount Vernon farms through a mixture of rain, sleet, and snow. The following morning he awoke with a cold but nevertheless went about his daily routine. "In the evening," recorded Tobias Lear, the

> [news]Papers were brought from the Post Office, and he sat in the Parlour, with Mrs. Washington & myself reading them till about nine o'clock—when Mrs. W . . . left the General & myself reading the papers. He was very cheerful and when he met with anything interesting or entertaining, he wd. read it aloud as well as his hoarseness would permit him. He requested me to read to him the debates of the Virginia Assembly on the election of a Senator and Governor;—and on hearing Mr. Madison's observations respecting Mr. Monroe, he appeared much affected and spoke with some degree of asperity on the subject, which I endeavored to moderate, as I always did on such occasions.

Washington took to bed but awakened during the night with a throat so inflamed that he could barely speak or even breathe. The family hastily summoned doctors who complied with the patient's request to be bled. This treatment proved unavailing; early the next morning George Washington died.[62]

Four days later, when word reached Richmond, Madison informed the legislature: "Death has robbed our country of its most distinguished ornament, and the world of one of its greatest benefactors. George Washington, the Hero of Liberty, the father of his Country, and the friend of man is no more. The General Assembly of his native state were ever the first to render him, living, the honors due to his virtues. They will not be the second, to pay to his memory the trib-ute of their tears." Madison proposed that the delegates wear mourning badges throughout the session, to which the assembly agreed unanimously. Four days later he joined a "grand funeral procession" to the State Capitol to hear the Rev-erend John D. Blair's eulogy. There is no evidence that Madison spoke at this cer-emony, but it is unlikely that anyone present could have addressed Washington's merits and achievements more skillfully.[63]

Madison probably never fully understood that when he publicly questioned the refusal to hand over the Jay Treaty papers, he became the president's enemy. Just as he had initiated everything else in the collaboration, Washington thereupon ini-tiated an end to it. Why was the ex-president unable to forgive this trespass? And why did Madison, who experienced a public humiliation at Washington's hands, come away from the relationship without bitterness? Perhaps this outcome is a re-sult of the men's temperaments and the high degree of friendship they once en-joyed. Washington, ever sensitive to criticism and disloyalty, could not forgive his close colleague for deserting him. Madison, rarely vindictive, always in control of his passions, could not surrender his warm sentiments for his friend. Generational differences, too, help answer this question. Coming of age in the years before the Revolution, Washington viewed politics on a personal rather than an organiza-tional level. He could not reconcile himself to political parties and equated po-litical opposition with unpardonable betrayal. But for Madison, whose apprenticeship came during the ideologically charged 1770s, partisan differences did not interfere with his individual loyalty to Washington.[64]

EPILOGUE

W HY HAS THE Washington-Madison collaboration, the greatest partnership of the American founding, also been the most unheralded? The simplest answer is that Washington and Madison themselves kept it a secret by having one or both partners work behind the scenes. Before 1789 Washington concealed his actions to maintain his disinterested image, while after 1789 Madison, lacking an official administration post, counseled rather unobtrusively. With the exception of a period of months during the ratification campaign, the collaboration never drew public attention. Even at its zenith in 1789 and 1790, only the highest federal officials had an inkling of its existence, and few of them understood its true extent. The only obvious clue to the collaboration that these two men left behind is their private correspondence, which each carefully guarded as long as he lived.

An additional reason that the collaboration has gone unrecognized is that it did not leave behind a body of literature comparable to that produced by the other Revolutionary pairings, one capable of captivating succeeding generations in search of a profound statement or well-turned phrase. The John Adams–Thomas Jefferson association produced not only the Declaration of Independence but also a lively and engaging collection of letters. The James Madison–Alexander Hamilton collaboration contributed the *Federalist,* perhaps the greatest political commentary ever written by Americans. And the Thomas Jefferson–James Madison friendship bequeathed both the Virginia Statute for Religious Freedom and a personal correspondence that has been called "the most extended, the most elevated, the most significant exchange of letters between any two men in the whole sweep of American history."[1] The Washington-Madison collaboration simply did not generate a comparable corpus. But consider what it did accomplish. The collaboration played an indispensable role in putting down a threat to civilian control of the government at Newburgh, in calling the 1787

Federal Convention, in getting Washington to attend the convention, in putting forth the Virginia Plan, in securing the Constitution's ratification, in managing Washington's acceptance of the presidency, in launching the federal government, in obtaining the Bill of Rights, in working out the Compromise of 1790, in getting Washington to accept a second term, and in producing his Farewell Address.

Obviously Madison is not the reason the collaboration has been neglected, because he is recognized as a partner in two of the three other Revolutionary duos. Rather, the problem is Washington. The first president has not only been misunderstood ideologically as a career-long High Federalist, but his political significance has also been misread. Washington has been portrayed as too much of a popular figurehead and as too passive a political leader, when in fact he was the central politician of his age. Why have previous studies of Revolutionary collaborations consistently ignored and therefore marginalized Washington, the central participant in the drama? The answer has to do with his leadership style. Because his governance was in many ways so subtle—he seemed reluctant to assume political office, acted behind the scenes, and often wrote unrevealing letters—Washington himself is partially responsible for many historians' decision to relegate him to the background. Washington's collaboration with Madison casts him in a new light, showing that we must return him to center stage, to which his contemporaries repeatedly called him.

Conversely, Madison's collaboration with Washington shows that the younger Virginian richly deserves the attention and acclaim that historians have lavished on him as the Father of the Constitution. Yet it also shows that Madison was more than a brilliant philosopher and political scientist. He was an equally skilled practical statesman, one as capable of accomplishing great deeds as of thinking great thoughts. In short, Madison was Washington's ideal collaborator in meeting the great challenge posed by American independence: the need to find a republican solution to the problems of republican government.

CONTEMPORARIES saw many similarities between Washington and Madison, a comparison (as Drew McCoy points out) that few Americans today would make.[2] What could the large and vigorous Washington have had in common with the scrawny, bookish Madison? According to Edward Coles, Madison's modesty and shyness "made him appear a little reserved and formal, and had the effect, like similar traits in the character of Gen'l. Washington, to keep applicants and other obtrusive persons from approaching too near, and being too familiar with him." These common characteristics probably are not coincidental; Madison may well have modeled his behavior after his collaborator's. After all, he thought that "what particularly distinguished" Washington "was a modest dignity which at once commanded the highest respect, and inspired the purest attachment." Madison's emulation probably went beyond personality. During his presidency, a time of war, he, like Washington, resisted the temptation for Caesarism, remaining true to republicanism under the most trying of circumstances. Madison's collaboration with Washington thus may have had a profound influence on his career, causing him to imitate consciously what he admired most about Washington.[3]

Madison always retained warm memories of his collaborator. After he himself retired from the presidency, he remarked that Washington's "strength of character lay in his integrity, his love of justice, his fortitude, the soundness of his judgment, and his remarkable prudence." Madison's esteem manifested itself in many ways: in his wife's decision to rescue Washington's portrait from the burning President's House, in the anecdotes and reminiscences he loved to tell his guests, and in the many likenesses of Washington he displayed at Montpelier.[4]

In 1788 and 1792 Madison promised that if death prevented Washington from leaving office voluntarily, he would make sure the public understood the president's intentions. Washington lived to fulfill his retirement pledge, but Madison protected his friend's posthumous reputation in other ways. In the dispute between Washington's and Hamilton's followers over the Farewell Address, Madison kept his own 1792 involvement confidential, fearing that if either he or Hamilton got credit for draftsmanship, it would diminish the document's impact on Americans. Similarly, in 1828 Madison refused Jared Sparks's request to publish his correspondence with Washington: "You will be aware . . . that some of his letters, especially when written in haste, shew specks of inaccuracy which though not derogating at all from the greatness of his character, might disappoint readers abroad accustomed to regard him as a model even in the performances of the pen. It is to be presumed that his correspondence with me . . . has more references to subjects and occasions involving confidential traits, than his correspondence with those less intimate with him."[5] Not only did Madison avoid enhancing his own reputation at Washington's expense, he (unlike John Adams) never became jealous of Washington's fame. Instead he enjoyed the knowledge that he had helped Washington maintain the personal image that was truly indispensable to the creation of the American Republic.

NOTES

Abbreviations

AH   Alexander Hamilton
ER   Edmund Randolph
GW   George Washington
JM   James Madison
TJ   Thomas Jefferson

DLC   Library of Congress
NjP   Princeton University Library
PHi   Historical Society of Pennsylvania
VHi   Virginia Historical Society

DPCUS   *Debates and Proceedings in the Congress of the United States*
DGW   *Diaries of Washington*
DHFFC   *Documentary History of the First Federal Congress*
DHFFE   *Documentary History of the First Federal Elections*
DHROC   *Documentary History of the Ratification of the Constitution*
JHDV   *Journal of the House of Delegates of Virginia*
NDFC   *Notes of Debates in the Federal Convention*
PAH   *Papers of Alexander Hamilton*
PGW-CS   *Papers of George Washington, Confederation Series*
PGW-PS   *Papers of George Washington, Presidential Series*
PGW-RS   *Papers of George Washington, Retirement Series*
PJM   *Papers of James Madison, Congressional Series*
PTJ   *Papers of Thomas Jefferson*
RFC   *Records of the Federal Convention*
WGW   *Writings of George Washington*

Introduction

1. Koch, *Jefferson and Madison;* Banning, *Jefferson and Madison;* Smith, *Republic of Letters.*

2. Peterson, *Adams and Jefferson.* On the JM-AH collaboration, see Banning, *Sacred Fire;* Mathews, *If Men Were Angels;* Sharp, *American Politics in the Early Republic;* Elkins and McKitrick, *Age of Federalism;* Nelson, *Liberty and Property,* 1–21.

3. The following works, for example, ignore the GW-JM collaboration: Freeman et al., *Washington;* Ferling, *Washington;* Miller, *Federalist Era;* Elkins and McKitrick, *Age of Federalism.*

4. Banning, *Sacred Fire,* 13–42.

5. Ibid., 51, 274. Other works on Madison that mention the collaboration include Ketcham, *Madison,* 331, and Rutland, *Madison,* 56–57, 94.

6. The best biographies of GW are Freeman et al., *Washington;* Flexner, *Indispensable Man;* Flexner, *Washington;* and Ferling, *Washington.*

7. Adams, *Jared Sparks* 1:558; Abbot, "An Uncommon Awareness," 7–12. Jared Sparks recorded this description during an interview with JM. For contemporary descriptions of GW, see Chinard, *Washington as the French Knew Him.*

8. The best biographies of JM are Brant, *Madison;* Ketcham, *Madison;* Rutland, *Madison;* and Rakove, *Madison.* Two outstanding monographs with considerable biographical content are McCoy, *Last of the Fathers,* and Banning, *Sacred Fire.*

9. Adair, "Madison's Autobiography," 198–99.

10. Edward Coles to Hugh Blair Grigsby, 23 Dec. 1854, Grigsby Papers, VHi. Contemporary reports of Madison's height range from five feet to five feet seven inches. See, for example, "Edward Coles's Notes on Madison . . . ," June 1828, Coles Papers, NjP.

11. See McCoy, *Last of the Fathers,* and esp. Banning, *Sacred Fire.*

12. See, for example, Charles, *Origins of the American Party System;* McDonald, *Presidency of Washington;* Elkins and McKitrick, *Age of Federalism.*

13. Phelps, *Washington and American Constitutionalism.* Phelps provides much-needed attention to Washington's leadership style and constitutional significance but by overestimating Washington's pessimism about republicanism's viability renders too Hamiltonian an image.

1. Winning Independence

1. Trumbull, "Seige and Capture of York," 332; Baker, "Itinerary of Washington," 15:173–74.

2. Ibid.; *Pennsylvania Packet,* 8 Sept. 1781; Brant, *Madison* 2:162–63; JM to Edmund Pendleton, 3 Sept. 1781, *PJM* 3:247; Jackson, "Washington in Philadelphia," 133–34; Morris Diary, Ferguson et al., *Papers of Morris* 2:172–76.

3. Selby, *Revolution in Virginia,* 1–5; Meade, *Henry,* 44–56; Brant, *Madison* 1:180; Marchione, *Mazzei,* 217.

4. Address to Captain Patrick Henry and the Gentlemen Independents of Hanover, 9 May 1775, JM to William Bradford, 9 May 1775, *PJM* 1:146–47, 144–45; *DGW* 3:323–27; Freeman et al., *Washington* 3:410–15.

5. See Schwartz, *Washington.*

6. Editorial Note, JM to TJ, 16 Mar. 1784, *PJM* 1:214, 8:9; Ammon, *Monroe,* 175; Mayer, *Henry,* 316; Sydnor, *American Revolutionaries,* 63, 86–87.

7. Ketcham, *Madison,* 78; McIlwaine et al., *Journals* 2:64–66; Patrick Henry in Council to the Virginia Delegates in Congress, 20 Jan. 1778, *PJM* 1:219–21.

8. GW to Patrick Henry, 19 Feb. 1778, Patrick Henry to the Speaker of the House of Delegates, 13 May 1778, Henry, *Henry* 3:148–49, 157, 162; Patrick Henry to Thomas Smith, 22 May 1778, McIlwaine et al., *Official Letters,* 278; McIlwaine et al., *Journals* 2:107, 113.

9. Brant, *Madison* 1:334; Meade, *Henry,* 139–43. On Henry's correspondence with GW, see Henry, *Henry* 1:483–85, 3:142–242. On the council's varied activities, see McIlwaine et al., *Journals* 2:64–255.

10. Mayer, *Henry,* 317; Meade, *Henry,* 144; Patrick Henry to Henry Laurens, 18 June 1778, Henry, *Henry* 3:177, 1:560. On the *rage militaire,* see Royster, *Revolutionary People at War,* chap. 1.

11. Malone, *Jefferson* 1:306, 314–22; Peterson, *Jefferson,* 171–72, 184–91.

12. Ketcham, *Madison,* 80; Rakove, *Madison,* 18; Selby, *Revolution in Virginia,* 135–37. On GW's relations with civilian authorities, see Higginbotham, *Washington.*

13. On GW's carefully self-cultivated public image, see Longmore, *Washington,* ix–x.

14. McIlwaine et al., *Journals* 2:117–18; Patrick Henry to GW, 18 Apr. 1778, GW to Patrick Henry, 16 May 1778, Henry, *Henry* 3:156, 167.

15. GW to Benjamin Harrison, 18–30 Dec. 1778, *WGW* 13:462–68; Brant, *Madison* 1:360–63; Rakove, *Beginnings of National Politics,* 216–39.

16. GW to Benjamin Harrison, 18–30 Dec. 1778, *WGW* 13:466–68; Credentials as a Delegate to Continental Congress, 14 Dec. 1779, *PJM* 1:318 and n.1.

17. Credentials as a Delegate to the Continental Congress, 14 Dec. 1779, *PJM* 1:318 n.1. On Henry and Walker, see Tyler, *Encyclopedia.* On Jones, see ibid.; *Dictionary of American Biography;* Ford, *Letters of Jones;* Rutland, *Madison Encyclopedia;* JM to James Monroe, 11 Dec. 1784, James Monroe to JM, 1 Feb. 1785, *PJM* 8:183 n.1, 237. That copies of many of GW's letters to Joseph Jones rest among JM's papers in the DLC suggests that Jones shared them with JM.

18. GW to Benjamin Harrison, 18–30 Dec. 1778, *WGW* 13:464; Brant, *Madison* 1:265–69; "Money," Sept. 1779–Mar. 1780, *PJM* 1:302–10; Adair, "Madison's Autobiography," 200.

19. JM to James Madison, Sr., 8 Dec. 1779, *PJM* 1:315; Brant, *Madison* 1:368–69.

20. JM to TJ, 27 Mar. 1780, *PJM* 2:6; Carp, "Origins of the Nationalist Movement," 369–70; GW to Joseph Jones, 31 May 1780, *WGW* 18:453.

21. JM's copy of GW's 31 May 1780 letter to Jones is in the Madison Papers, DLC. Credentials as a Delegate to the Continental Congress, 14 Dec. 1774, *PJM* 1:318 n.1.

22. Carp, "Origins of the Nationalist Movement"; Banning, *Sacred Fire,* 13–42; Rakove, *Beginnings of National Politics,* 243–74; Henderson, *Party Politics,* 157–217; Ketcham, *Madison,* 120–36.

23. Notes on Debates, 27 Feb. 1783, JM to Joseph Jones, 17 Oct., 12 Dec. 1780, *PJM* 6:298, 2:137, 238–39; Brant, *Madison* 2:121–26.

24. JM to ER, 29 May 1782, *PJM* 4:298; Brant, *Madison* 2:172–76.

25. See, for example, Virginia Delegates to TJ, 17 Apr., 1 May 1781, to Benjamin Harrison, 15 Jan., 1 Oct. 1782, *PJM* 3:75, 99, 4:30, 5:176.

26. William Ellery and JM to the Committee of Congress at Headquarters, 5 May 1780, Board of Admiralty to Nathaniel Shaw, Jr., 9 May 1780, JM to TJ, c. 5 Oct. 1780, *PJM* 2:17, 25, 111; GW to Francis Lewis, 13 May 1780, *WGW* 18:352; Ferling, *Washington,* 319. On the American reaction to Arnold's treason, see Royster, *Revolutionary People,* chap. 6.

27. JM to Edmund Pendleton, 16 Jan. 1781, Virginia Delegates to TJ, 30 Jan. 1781, *PJM* 2:287, 300; GW to the President of Congress, 6 Jan. 1781, to William Livingston, 23 Jan. 1781, Circular to the New England States, 29 Jan. 1781, *WGW* 21:66, 132–33, 156–57. For dates on which GW's letters were read in Congress, see Ford et al., *Journals of the Continental Congress,* or JM's Notes on Debates in *PJM,* vols. 5–7.

28. Notes on Debates, 7, 8 Nov. 1782, Motion on Instructions to GW, 7–8 Nov. 1782, *PJM* 5:251, 255, 248–49; Freeman et al., *Washington* 5:412–14, 419–20, 425; Brant, *Madison* 2:180–82, 188–90.

29. Ketcham, *Madison,* 102; Introduction, *PJM* 4:xv; GW to AH, 22 Apr. 1783, *PAH* 3:334–36.

30. Motion on Impressment of Supplies, 18 May 1781, *PJM* 3:124; Brant, *Madison* 2:115–17, 158; Banning, *Sacred Fire,* 21.

31. JM to Edmund Pendleton, 27 Nov. 1781, to James Madison, Sr., 30 Mar. 1782, Introduction, *PJM* 3:317, 4:127, xv; Ford et al., *Journals of the Continental Congress* 21:1071–85, 1143–44; GW to Nathanael Greene, 11 Nov. 1781, *WGW* 23:347. For a discussion of the terms *unfamiliar, peripheral,* and *noneffective,* see Bott, *Family and Social Network,* 120–21, and Smith, *Inside the Great House,* 175–230, esp. 205.

32. GW to the President of Congress, 30 Jan. 1782, *WGW* 23:471–72; Jackson, "Washington in Philadelphia," 134–36; Freeman et al., *Washington* 5:403–9; Brant, *Madison* 2:16, 167; Flexner, *Washington* 2:472–75; Schwartz, *Washington,* 150–55; Ford et al., *Journals of the Continental Congress* 21:1163, 22:71; Baker, "Itinerary of Washington," 15:291–92.

33. JM to Edmund Pendleton, 13 Nov. 1781, *PJM* 3:302; *JHDV,* Oct. 1781, 43; GW to Lafayette, 4 Jan. 1782, to ER, 8 Jan. 1782, *WGW* 23:431, 435; Bernier, *LaFayette: Hero of Two Worlds,* 134, 138.

34. For the differences between the nationalists, see Banning, *Sacred Fire,* 13–42, 146. For the ultranationalist program, see Ferguson, *Power of the Purse,* 165–66, 120–24; Ferguson, "The Nationalists of 1780–1783," 241–51.

35. Kohn, "Inside History of the Newburgh Conspiracy," 189–95.

36. Ibid., 191–206; Notes on Debates, 13, 24 Jan. 1783, *PJM* 6:31–34, 120–21; Ferguson, *Power of the Purse,* 146–76; AH to GW, 13 Feb. 1783, *PAH* 3:253–55. Nelson and Skeen argue that Gates and his followers were not planning a coup (Nelson, "Horatio Gates at Newburgh," 143–58, and Skeen, "The Newburgh Conspiracy Reconsidered," with "A Rebuttal" by Kohn, 273–98). I have adopted Kohn's interpretation because it explains events at Newburgh more persuasively, especially the anonymous addresses.

37. JM to ER, 28 Jan., 25 Feb. 1783, Notes on Debates, 28 Jan. 1783, *PJM* 6:157, 286, 142; Ferguson, *Power of the Purse,* 158; Kohn, "Inside History," 193.

38. Notes on Debates, 20 Feb. 1783, *PJM* 6:265–66.

39. JM to ER, 25 Feb. 1783, ibid., 286–87; Banning, *Sacred Fire,* 27–33.

40. Introduction, Report on Public Credit, 6 Mar. 1783, Notes on Debates, 4 Apr. 1783, JM to TJ, 22 Apr. 1783, *PJM* 6:xviii–xix, 311–14, 433 n.3, 481; Ferguson, *Power of

the Purse, 165–66; Joseph Jones to GW, 6 May 1783, Ford, *Letters of Jones,* 103; Rakove, *Beginnings of National Politics,* 318–19.

41. Notes on Debates, 17 Mar. 1783, *PJM* 6:349 n.1; GW to the President of Congress, 12 Mar. 1783, *WGW* 26:211 nn.18–19; Kohn, "Inside History," 188, 206–7.

42. GW to AH, 4 Mar. 1783, *PAH* 3:277–79; Joseph Jones to GW, 27 Feb. 1783, Ford, *Letters of Jones,* 99–100; Kohn, "Inside History," 207–14; Notes on Debates, 17 Mar. 1783, *PJM,* 6:349 n.1; GW to the President of Congress, 12 Mar. 1783, to the Officers of the Army, 15 Mar. 1783, *WGW* 26:211–12, 222–27; Ferling, *Washington,* 311.

43. Notes on Debates, 17 Mar. 1783, JM to ER, 18 Mar. 1783, *PJM* 6:348, 356; GW to the President of Congress, 12 Mar. 1783, *WGW* 26:211–12; Kohn, "Inside History," 220; JM to Henry Colman, 25 Aug. 1826, Hunt, *Writings of Madison* 9:251.

44. GW to Congress, 18 Mar. 1783, to Joseph Jones, 18 Mar. 1783, *WGW* 26:229–32, 232–34; JM to ER, 25 Mar. 1783, *PJM* 6:392; Kohn, "Inside History," 212–13. A copy of GW's letter to Jones still remains in the Madison Papers, DLC.

45. Notes on Debates, 21 Apr. 1783, Address to the States, 25 Apr. 1783, *PJM* 6:478 nn.1, 2, 488–94, 495 n.33; Kohn, "Inside History," 211–14.

46. Circular to the States, 8 June 1783, *WGW* 26:483–92.

47. GW to William Gordon, 8 July 1783, ibid., 27:49–51; Banning, *Sacred Fire,* 33–42.

48. GW to AH, 4, 16 Apr. 1783, AH to GW, 3 Mar., 4 Apr. 1783, *PAH* 3:315–16, 329–31, 292–93, 317–21; Kohn, "Inside History," 214–15, 27.

49. Joseph Jones to JM, 8, 14, 28 June 1783, JM to ER, 8 July 1783, *PJM* 7:118–9, 144, 197, 216; Ferguson, *Power of the Purse,* 168–71; Kohn, "Inside History," 215–16.

50. Bowling, *The Creation of Washington, D.C.,* 30–34; Introduction, JM to ER, 13 Oct. 1783, *PJM* 7:xvii–xviii, 378 n.16. On Congress's stint in Princeton, see Sheridan and Murrin, *Congress at Princeton.*

51. Introduction, Joseph Jones to JM, 21 July 1783, Joseph Chew to JM, 6 Nov. 1783, JM to TJ, 20 Sept. 1783, to ER, 8 July 1783 (for dates when JM visited Princeton), *PJM* 7:xvii, 237 n.11, 353, 399, 217 n.2; Ferling, *Washington,* 403; Freeman et al., *Washington* 5:453; Rhode Island Delegates to the Governor of Rhode Island, 8 Sept. 1783, David Howell to the Governor of Rhode Island, 9 Sept. 1783, Burnett, *Letters of Members of the Continental Congress* 7:287–88, 292; Baker, "Itinerary of Washington," 15:410–17; Ketcham, *Madison,* 35; GW to George Clinton, 11 Sept. 1783, *WGW* 27:148.

52. Introduction, *PJM* 7:xli; Trumbull, *Autobiography, Reminiscences, and Letters of Trumbull,* 262–63; Wills, *Cincinnatus,* 14; JM to John Trumbull, 1 Mar. 1835, Rives and Fendall, *Letters and Writings of Madison* 4:376–77.

2. Improving Rivers and Friendships

1. Virginia Delegates to GW, 12 Apr. 1780, GW to JM, 22 Apr. 1783, JM to GW, 29 Apr. 1783, *PJM* 2:13, 6:484–85, 505; James Duane to GW, 29 Jan. 1781, Smith et al., *Letters of Delegates to Congress* 16:635; GW to James McHenry, 24 Apr. 1783, *WGW* 26:357 and n.1.

2. GW to JM, 12 June 1784, *PJM* 8:67–68; GW to Patrick Henry, 12 June 1783, to Richard Henry Lee, 12 June 1783, *WGW* 27:421–23.

3. TJ to JM, 25 May 1784, Bill to Aid Thomas Paine, 28 June 1784, JM to GW, 2 July, 12 Aug. 1784, *PJM* 8:44 n.5, 88–89, 91–92, 98–99; *JHDV,* May 1784, 82, 84–88.

4. *JHDV,* May 1784, 8, 38, 44, 73–74, 80–81; Schwartz, *Washington,* 35; Resolution for Procuring a Statue of GW, 22 June 1784, *PJM* 8:85.

5. *DGW* 4:57–68; GW to Benjamin Harrison, 10 Oct. 1784, to Robert Morris, 1 Feb. 1785, *PGW-CS* 2:89–98, 309–15.

6. Seele, *Beautiful Machine,* 8–12; GW to John Witherspoon, 10 Mar. 1784, Advertisement for Western Lands, 10 Mar. 1784, GW to the Countess of Huntington, 27 Feb. 1785, *PGW-CS* 1:197–200, 201–3, 2:392–94; Adams, "Washington's Interest in Western Lands," 72–74.

7. GW to Benjamin Harrison, 10 Oct. 1784, to James Warren, 7 Oct. 1785, *PGW-CS* 2:89–98, 3:300.

8. GW to Thomas Johnson, 12 Nov. 1786, to Marquis de Lafayette, 25 July 1785, ibid., 4:359–60, 3:153.

9. Bacon-Foster, *Early Chapters,* 8–17; Sanderlin, *Great National Project,* 22–27; *History of the Washington Bicentennial Celebration* 1:124, 156.

10. GW to TJ, 29 Mar. 1784, *PGW-CS* 1:237–40; Nute, "Washington and the Potomac"; Bacon-Foster, *Early Chapters,* 17–30.

11. GW to TJ, 29 Mar. 1784, *PGW-CS* 1:237–40; JM to TJ, 25 Apr. 1784, *PJM* 8:22 n.4.

12. GW to Chevalier de Chastellux, 12 Oct. 1783, *WGW* 27:189–90; TJ to GW, 15 Mar. 1784, GW to TJ, 29 Mar. 1784, *PGW-CS* 1:215–18, 237–40.

13. *DGW* 4:1–71.

14. TJ to JM, 20 Feb., 25 Apr., 8, 25 May 1784, JM to TJ, 16 Mar. 1784, *PJM* 7:424–26, 8:24, 31–32, 43, 9–11.

15. JM to TJ, 20 Aug. 1784, to Marquis de Lafayette, 20 Mar. 1785, ibid., 100–110, 250–54.

16. GW to Henry Lee, 18 June 1786, *PGW-CS* 4:118; JM to Marquis de Lafayette, 20 Mar. 1785, *PJM* 8:250–54. For Madison's views on political economy, see McCoy, *Elusive Republic.*

17. JM to TJ, 9 Jan. 1785, Resolutions Appointing Virginia Members of a Potomac River Commission, 28 June 1784, JM to TJ, 3 July 1784, *PJM* 8:226, 89, 95; *JHDV,* May 1784, 84.

18. GW to Benjamin Harrison, 10 Oct. 1784, to Richard Henry Lee, 14 Dec. 1784, to Robert Morris, 1 Feb. 1785, *PGW-CS* 2:89–98, 181–83, 309–15.

19. Baker, "Washington after the Revolution," 18:404; *JHDV,* Oct. 1784; *Virginia Gazette and Weekly Advertiser,* 20 Nov. 1784; *Pennsylvania Packet, and Daily Advertiser,* 30 Nov., 4 Dec. 1784; Christian, *Richmond,* 23; GW to Officials of the City of Richmond, 15 Nov. 1784, *PGW-CS* 2:135–36. Lafayette had just landed in Richmond after touring the northern states. William Cabell Rives also thought JM wrote this address (Rives, *Life and Times of Madison* 1:612). The *PJM* excludes the address, probably because no proof of JM's authorship exists.

20. GW to JM, 28 Nov. 1784, JM to TJ, 9 Jan. 1785, *PJM* 8:159, 223. For a discussion of effective friendship, see Bott, *Family and Social Network,* 120–21, and Smith, *Great House,* 205.

21. *Virginia Gazette and Weekly Advertiser,* 20 Nov. 1784; Henry Lee to GW, 18 Nov. 1784, *PGW-CS* 2:140 n.2; GW to JM, 28 Nov. 1784, *PJM* 8:159–60. GW chose not to rely on Fairfax County's representatives because they did not plan to attend the session long enough to see the legislation through.

22. GW to JM, 28 Nov. 1784, JM to Richard Henry Lee, 11 Dec. 1784, to TJ, 9 Jan. 1785, *PJM* 8:159–60, 180–81, 223–24.

23. *Pennsylvania Packet, and Daily Advertiser,* 7 Dec. 1784; GW to JM, 28 Nov., 3 Dec. 1784, JM to TJ, 9 Jan. 1785, *PJM* 8:159, 12:478–79, 8:224; *JHDV,* Oct. 1784.

24. Ibid.; GW to Marquis de Lafayette, 23 Dec. 1784, *PGW-CS* 2:228–29; Bacon-Foster, *Early Chapters,* 45–48.

25. GW to JM, 28 Dec. 1784, JM to TJ, 9 Jan. 1785, *PJM* 8:203–5, 224; GW and Horatio Gates to the Virginia Assembly, 28 Dec. 1784, GW to Henry Knox, 5 Jan. 1785, *PGW-CS* 2:235–36, 253.

26. JM to TJ, 9 Jan. 1785, Bill Providing Funds for James River Canal, 18 Dec. 1784, JM to GW, 1, 9 Jan. 1785, *PJM* 8:223–25, 191–94, 208–9, 234–35; *JHDV,* Oct. 1784, 99, 100–109.

27. Hening, *Statutes at Large* 11:510–25, 450–62; GW to JM, 28 Dec. 1784, *PJM* 8:204.

28. Resolutions Authorizing an Interstate Compact on Navigation and Jurisdiction of the Potomac, 28 Dec. 1784, JM to GW, 1, 9 Jan. 1785, *PJM* 8:206–7, 208–9, 234–35; *JHDV,* Oct. 1784, 91, 101–2.

29. Bill for Granting James Rumsey a Patent for Ship Construction, 11 Nov. 1784, JM to TJ, 9 Jan., 27 April 1785, *PJM* 8:131–33, 227, 268; *DGW* 4:67–68; *JHDV,* Oct. 1784, 28; Certificate to James Rumsey, 7 Sept. 1784, *PGW-CS* 2:69; Brant, *Madison* 2:370.

30. Act Giving Canal Company Shares to GW, 4 Jan. 1785, JM to James Madison, Sr., 6 Jan. 1785, to TJ, 9 Jan. 1785, *PJM* 8:215–16, 217, 226; Hening, *Statutes at Large* 11:525–26; *JHDV,* Oct. 1784, 105–8; William Grayson to GW, 10 Mar. 1785, *PGW-CS* 2:420.

31. Rice, "Internal Improvements in Virginia," 45–46.

32. Bacon-Foster, *Early Chapters,* 57–60; Pickell, *New Chapter,* 65–68; Watson, *Men and Times of the Revolution,* 244–46.

33. Bacon-Foster, *Early Chapters,* 68–84; Pickell, *New Chapter,* 60–118; Brown, *Patowmack Canal,* 3–13; Littlefield, "Eighteenth Century Plans," 291–322; Garrettt, "Washington's Patowmack Canal," 719–52.

34. Bacon-Foster, *Early Chapters,* 84–153; Brown, *Potowmack Canal,* 3–13; Sanderlin, *Great National Project,* 35–44; Pickell, *New Chapter,* 114–18; Littlefield, "Eighteenth Century Plans," 291–322; Garrett, "Washington's Potowmack Canal," 719–52; Adams, "Washington's Interest in the Potomac Company," 80–85, and "Origin of the Baltimore and Ohio Railroad," 97–102.

35. Dunaway, *History of the James River and Kanawha Company,* 19–46.

36. Sanderlin, *Great National Project,* 45–60, 282–94; Littlefield, "Eighteenth Century Plans," 291–322; Garrett, "Washington's Potowmack Canal," 719–52; Seele, *Beautiful Machine,* 10.

37. JM to TJ, 9 Jan. 1785, *PJM* 8:226.

38. Memorial and Remonstrance against Religious Assessments, 20 June 1785, ibid., 295–306.

39. George Mason to GW, 2 Oct. 1785, GW to George Mason, 3 Oct. 1785, Rutland, *Papers of Mason* 2:830–32. On GW's religious views, see Boller, *Washington and Religion.* See also chap. 4 below.

40. Mount Vernon Compact, Mar. 1785, Rutland, *Papers of Mason* 2:812–23; ER to JM, 17 July 1785, George Mason to JM, 9 Aug. 1785, *PJM* 8:324–25, 337–39; Morris, "The Mount Vernon Conference," 38–40.

41. George Mason to JM, 7 Dec. 1785, JM to James Monroe, 30 Dec. 1785, to TJ, 3 Oct. 1785, *PJM* 8:434–36, 466–67, 375; *JHDV,* Oct. 1785, 114, 117–19; Hening, *Statutes at Large* 12:50–55; *DGW* 4:189, 205–6.

42. Edward Coles to William Cabell Rives, 19 June 1857, Coles Papers; GW to JM, 22 Oct. 1785, Noah Webster to JM, 30 June 1792, *PJM* 8:380, 14:335–36.

43. Hallam, "Houdon's *Washington* in Richmond," 73–74; Lossing, *Washington's Mount Vernon,* 77. On whether JM witnessed Houdon take GW's life mask, see Seymour, "Houdon's *Washington* at Mount Vernon," 151–52, esp. n.25. Seymour judiciously concludes that the issue cannot be determined for sure. Gilbert Chinard believes that the impression was made before JM arrived (Chinard, *Houdon in America,* xviii). Charles Henry Hart and Edward Biddle insist that Houdon cast the mold in JM's presence (Hart and Biddle, *Memoirs of the Life and Works of Houdon,* 200–201). TJ described Houdon's method of making a life mask as "most revolting." Houdon required his subject to "lie down and have your face plaistered over with gypsum" (TJ to Wilson Cary Nicholas, 15 Mar. 1818, Jefferson Papers, DLC). See also TJ to JM, 18 Oct. 1825, Smith, *Republic of Letters* 3:1942–43.

44. TJ to JM, 8 Feb. 1786, *PJM* 8:487; Hallam, "Houdon's *Washington* in Richmond," 77; *George Wahington: Jean Antoine Houdon, Sculptor,* 21–22.

45. GW to JM, 30 Nov. 1785, *PJM* 8:430; Hansen, "Our Eyes Behold Each Other," in Nardi, *Men's Friendships,* esp. 53–54.

46. GW to JM, 22 Oct. 1785, *PJM* 8:380.

47. For an explanation of this terminology, see Bott, *Family and Social Network,* 120–21, and Smith, *Great House,* 175–230, esp. 205. Like Bott, I have equated written with oral communication, since geographical separation forced JM and GW to write to one another instead of meeting face-to-face. I have added political favors to Smith's definition of intimacy ("mutual aid in sickness and economic concerns"). Although GW and JM exchanged financial advice and expressed concern over one another's health, their mutual aid was primarily political.

48. GW to Thomas Hutchins, 20 Aug. 1786, *PGW-CS* 4:222; JM to GW, 18 Mar. 1787, GW to JM, 31 Mar. 1787, *PJM* 9:314, 344.

49. Royster, *Light Horse Harry Lee,* 73–75; Henry Lee to JM, 29 Aug., 19 Nov. 1788, GW to JM, 17 Nov. 1788, JM to GW, 5 Nov. 1788, Remarks on the Situation at Great Falls, 14 Jan. 1789, *PJM* 11:321–22, 356, 349–50, 334, 421–23. In 1786 JM requested GW's advice on land speculation in upstate New York, where he was considering a joint purchase with James Monroe. After GW pronounced the proposed investment a smart one, JM bought the land and later resold it for nearly twice what he had paid (JM to TJ, 12 Aug. 1786, ibid., 9:97; Ketcham, *Madison,* 146–47).

50. JM to Henry Lee, 30 Nov. 1788, 13 Apr. 1790, Henry Lee to JM, 8 Dec. 1788, Remarks on the Situation at Great Falls, 14 Jan. 1789, *PJM* 9:371–72, 13:148, 9:387, 421–23; Henry Lee to TJ, 6 Mar. 1789, TJ to Henry Lee, 11 Sept. 1789, *PTJ* 14:619–21, 15:415–16; Henry Lee to GW, 9, 14 Feb. 1789, GW to Henry Lee, 13 Feb. 1789, to TJ, 13 Feb. 1789, *PGW-PS* 1:286, 303–4, 302, 299; Royster, *Light Horse Harry Lee,* 75–77.

51. Stewart, "Chesapeake and Ohio Canal," 6; GW to Benjamin Harrison, 22 Jan. 1785, *PGW-CS* 2:282–84; JM to TJ, 27 Apr. 1785, *PJM* 8:267. On how GW gained power by giving it up, see Wills, *Cincinnatus,* 3, 23.

52. JM to GW, 20 Oct. 1785, GW to JM, 29 Oct. 1785, *PJM* 8:380, 388; GW to

William Grayson, 22 Jan. 1785, to Benjamin Harrison, 22 Jan. 1785, to TJ, 25 Feb. 1785, to Patrick Henry, 27 Feb. 1785, *PGW-CS* 2:280–81, 282–84, 381–82, 391–92.

53. GW to Patrick Henry, 29 Oct. 1785, *PGW-CS* 3:326–27; GW to JM, 29 Oct. 1785, Amendments to the Act Conveying Canal Shares to GW, 16 Nov. 1785, *PJM* 8:388, 420–22; *JHDV,* Oct. 1785, 31–32, 39–40, 43; Hening, *Statutes at Large* 12:42–44.

54. JM to GW, 20 Oct. 1785, GW to JM, 29 Oct. 1785, JM to TJ, 22 Jan. 1785, *PJM* 8:380, 388, 474; Last Will and Testament, 9 July 1799, *WGW* 37:278–81.

55. JM to TJ, 12 Aug. 1786, *PJM* 9:93–95.

3. Framing and Ratifying the Constitution

1. Resolutions to Strengthen Powers of Congress, 19 May 1784, Bill Granting Congress Limited Power to Regulate Commerce, 5 June 1784, Resolution Authorizing a Commission to Examine Trade Regulations, 21 Jan. 1786, JM to TJ, to James Monroe, 22 Jan. 1786, ER to JM, 1 Mar. 1786, *PJM* 8:38–39, 57, 470–71, 476–77, 482–83, 495; *JHDV,* Oct. 1785, 32, 153; *NDFC,* 9.

2. JM to GW, 9 Dec. 1785, to James Monroe, 19 Mar. 1786, Daniel Carroll to JM, 13 Mar. 1786, *PJM* 8:439, 505, 496; *NDFC,* 9.

3. JM to TJ, 18 Mar. 1786, to James Monroe, 14 Mar., 13 May 1786, *PJM* 8:503, 498, 9:55.

4. James Monroe to JM, 31 May 1786, JM to James Monroe, 21 June 1786, to TJ, 12 Aug. 1786, ibid., 68–69, 82–83, 96–97.

5. GW to Henry Lee, 5 Apr. 1786, to Marquis de Lafayette, 10 May 1786, to John Jay, 18 May, 15 Aug. 1786, *PGW-CS* 4:4,42, 55–56, 213; GW to JM, 30 Nov. 1785, *PJM* 8:429. For variations in GW's optimism, compare, for example, GW to William Grayson, 26 July 1786, with GW to Marquis de Chastellux, 18 Aug. 1786, *PGW-CS* 4:485–86, 523–24.

6. Morris, *Forging of the Union,* 252–57.

7. *DGW* 5:56–57; James Monroe to JM, 7 Oct. 1786, Editorial Note, JM to GW, 1 Nov. 1786, Bill Providing for Delegates to the Convention of 1787, 6 Nov. 1786, Resolutions Reaffirming American Rights to Navigate the Mississippi, 29 Nov. 1786, *PJM* 9:143, 147, 156, 163–64, 181–83.

8. JM to GW, 8 Nov. 1786, *PJM* 9:166.

9. David Stuart to GW, 25 Dec. 1786, *PGW-CS* 4:477. On Stuart, see Rose, "Dr. David Stuart"; JM to GW, 1, 8 Nov., 7, 24 Dec. 1786, *PJM* 9:155–56, 166–67, 199–200, 224–25.

10. GW to JM, 18 Nov. 1786, *PJM* 9:170–71.

11. GW to JM, 16 Dec. 1786, ibid., 215–16. On the Society of the Cincinnati, see Wills, *Cincinnatus,* 138–48.

12. Resolution to Select Commissioners to a Federal Convention, 30 Nov. 1786, JM to GW, 7 Dec. 1787, *PJM* 9:187, 199; *JHDV,* Oct. 1786, 21, 28, 68, 85–86; Hening, *Statutes at Large* 12:256–57.

13. GW to JM, 16 Dec. 1786, JM to GW, 24 Dec. 1786, *PJM* 9:215–16, 224; Stuart to GW, 19 Dec. 1786, GW to ER, 21 Dec. 1786, *PGW-CS* 4:468–69, 471–72.

14. JM to James Madison, Sr., 12 Dec. 1786, James Monroe to JM, 6 Feb. 1787, JM to TJ, 19 Mar. 1787, *PJM* 9:206, 256, 318; *DGW* 5:98–99.

15. GW to ER, 9 Apr. 1787, *PGW-CS* 5:135–36. See also Wills, *Cincinnatus,* 4, 153.

16. GW to ER, 28 Mar., , 9 Apr. 1787, to John Jay, 10 Mar. 1787, to Henry Knox, 8 Mar. 1787, *PGW-CS* 5:112–14, 135–36, 79–80, 74–75; Wills, *Cincinnatus,* 155–58.

17. GW to James Mercer, 15 Mar. 1787, *PGW-CS* 5:88. See also Marshall, *Washington* 4:129–47; JM to Edward Everett, 3 June 1827, *RFC* 3:476; Wills, *Cincinnatus,* 156. Many historians have judged GW harshly for his hesitancy to attend the convention. See, for example, Freeman et al., *Washington* 6:84–86. My interpretation follows Garry Wills's argument that GW acted with justifiable caution. See Wills, *Cincinnatus,* 151–72.

18. JM to GW, 21 Feb. 1787, Notes on Debates, 21 Feb. 1787, GW to JM, 31 Mar. 1787, *PJM* 9:286, 290–91, 342.

19. JM to TJ, 19 Mar., 23 Apr. 1787, to ER, 15 Apr. 1787, Resolution to Transfer Negotiations with Spain to Madrid, 18 Apr. 1787, Notes on Debates, 25, 26 Apr. 1787, ibid., 319, 400, 380, 388, 404–6, 407.

20. ER to JM, 1, 7 Mar. 1787, ibid., 301, 303; GW to Robert Morris, 5 May 1787, *PGW-CS* 5:171; Morris, *Forging of the Union,* 262–66. The best source on Shays's Rebellion is Szatmary, *Shays' Rebellion.*

21. Henry Knox to GW, 23 Oct., 17 Dec. 1786, Henry Lee to GW, 17 Oct. 1786, GW to David Stuart, 6 Dec. 1786, to Henry Knox, 26 Dec. 1786, 3 Feb. 1787, to David Humphreys, 26 Dec. 1786, *PGW-CS* 4:299–302, 460–62, 295, 446, 481–83, 5:7–9, 4:478–80; Banning, *Sacred Fire,* 105; GW to JM, 5 Nov. 1786, 31 Mar. 1787, *PJM* 9:161, 342–43.

22. GW to David Humphreys, 26 Dec. 1786, to John Jay, 10 Mar. 1787, *PGW-CS* 4:478–80, 5:79–80.

23. GW to Henry Knox, 8 Mar. 1787, ibid., 5:74–75.

24. GW to David Humphreys, 26 Dec. 1786, 8 Mar. 1787, to Henry Knox, 25 Feb. 1787, to John Jay, 10 Mar. 1787, to James Mercer, 15 Mar. 1787, JM to GW, 18 Mar. 1787, ibid., 4:479, 5:72–73, 52–53, 80, 92–94. Knox advised GW to go to Philadelphia, but Humphreys strongly urged him to stay home (Knox to GW, 19 Mar. 1787, Humphreys to GW, 24 Mar. 1787, ibid., 5:96–97, 103).

25. JM to GW, 21 Feb. 1787, to ER, 25 Feb. 1787, *PJM* 285, 299; Reardon, *Randolph,* 94; ER to GW, 11 Mar. 1787, GW to ER, 28 Mar. 1787, to JM, 31 Mar. 1787, *PGW-CS* 5:83–84, 112–14, 114–17.

26. ER to GW, 2 Apr. 1787, *PGW-CS* 5:121–22; ER to Virginia Delegates, 4 Apr. 1787, JM to ER, 15 Apr. 1787, *PJM* 9:366, 378; Wills, *Cincinnatus,* 162.

27. David Humphreys to GW, 24 Mar. 1787, *PGW-CS,* 5:103. JM erroneously credited AH with doing more than he to persuade GW (JM to Noah Webster, 12 Oct. 1804, Hunt, *Writings of Madison* 7:166).

28. JM to ER, 25 Feb. 1787, to Edmund Pendleton, 24 Feb., 22 Apr. 1787, *PJM* 9:299, 295, 395; Banning, *Sacred Fire,* 104–5.

29. GW to Theodorick Bland, 18 Nov. 1786, *PGW-CS* 4:377–78.

30. GW to Robert Morris, 5 May 1787, ibid., 5:171; JM to ER, 15 Apr. 1787, to TJ, 15 May 1787, *PJM* 9:379, 415; Ketcham, *Madison,* 190–93; Baker, "Washington after the Revolution," 17:176; *DGW* 5:155.

31. GW to JM, 31 Mar. 1781, *PJM* 9:342–44; GW to David Stuart, 1 July 1787, to Marquis de Lafayette, 15 Aug. 1787, *PGW-CS* 5:240, 296. On GW's wish to see the states weakened, see Higginbotham, "George Washington's Contributions to Constitutionalism," in Higginbotham, *War and Society in Revolutionary America,* 193–213. On the state

constitutions and their weaknesses, see Wood, *Creation of the American Republic,* chaps. 4–6.

32. GW to John Jay, 15 Aug. 1786, to Henry Knox, 3 Feb. 1787, *PGW-CS* 4:213, 5:9; GW to JM, 31 Mar. 1787, *PJM* 9:343.

33. Banning, *Sacred Fire,* 71–75; Rakove, *Madison,* 19–43; Notes on Ancient and Modern Confederacies, Apr.–June 1786, Vices of the Political System of the United States, Apr. 1787, *PJM* 9:3–24, 345–58.

34. JM to GW, 16 Apr. 1787, source note to Notes on Ancient and Modern Confederacies, *PJM* 9:382–87, 22; Notes on the Sentiment and on the Government of John Jay, Henry Knox, and James Madison, [c. April 1787], *PGW-CS* 5:164–66. Banning convincingly argues that with the exception of the congressional veto, JM was less interested in increasing Congress's powers than in making the general government strictly national in structure. Moreover, Banning suggests that JM did not come to favor a wholly national central government acting directly on the people until after the convention opened (*Sacred Fire,* 113–21, 139–49).

35. Banning, *Sacred Fire,* 128–29, 146.

36. JM to James Madison, Sr., 27 May 1787, *PJM* 10:10; GW to Arthur Lee, 20 May 1787, *PGW-CS* 5:191; George Mason to George Mason, Jr., 20 May 1787, Rutland, *Papers of Mason* 3:880; *NDFC,* 16–17.

37. JM to ER, 8 Apr. 1787, *PJM* 9:369–70; *NDFC,* 30–33.

38. *NDFC,* 17–18, 23–24; GW to Henry Knox, 31 May 1787, *PGW-CS* 5:209–10.

39. *NDFC,* 27–116; JM to John Tyler, n.d., *RFC,* 3:525.

40. *NDFC,* 75–78, 82–87, 115–17. I have concluded that GW favored the lower house's popular election based on his 17 Sept. 1787 speech.

41. Ibid., 118–21.

42. Ibid., 121–245.

43. Ibid., 224, 254, 293–95; GW to AH, 10 July 1787, *PAH* 4:225.

44. *NDFC,* 297–306; Holcombe, "Role of Washington in the Framing of the Constitution," 317–34; "Genuine Information," William Steele to Jonathan D. Steele, Sept. 1825, *RFC* 3:190, 471–72; James Monroe to TJ, 27 July 1787, GW to TJ, 31 Aug. 1788, *PTJ* 11:631, 13:556. Freeman believes GW did not attend the meeting (*Washington* 6:101 n.134).

45. *NDFC,* 297–306; Banning, *Sacred Fire,* 117–18. Based on GW's desire to weaken the states, I believe that he supported the congressional negative. In an 8 June vote on that subject, JM wrote, "Genl. W. not consulted" (*NDFC,* 92). Freeman speculates that GW's colleagues spared him from revealing just how strong he wanted the central government to be (*Washington* 6:97). JM, Blair, and McClurg supported the veto, while Mason and ER opposed. Under these circumstances the fact that GW was not asked to take a stand indicates that he favored the veto: because one more yes vote would not have changed the outcome, it could be dispensed with. Had he opposed the veto, on the other hand, he would have been consulted because his vote would have changed the entire delegation's position. These circumstances suggest that whenever possible, GW's allies kept him above the fray. Remaining noncontroversial protected his nonpartisan image, making him more effective at winning behind-the-scenes concessions.

46. *NDFC,* 297–306, 501–2, 628–30, 645; *DGW* 5:176; JM to TJ, 6 Sept. 1787, *PJM* 10:164; GW to Henry Knox, 19 Aug. 1787, *PGW-CS* 5:297. After the Great Compromise,

JM also advocated the executive's popular election, presidential instead of senatorial appointment of judges, greater executive treaty-making authority, and limiting the Senate's impeachment power (*NDFC*, 317, 327, 343–44, 520, 605). I do not agree with Irving Brant or Ralph Ketcham that JM retreated from nationalism after the Great Compromise (Brant, *Fourth President*, 170–80; Ketcham, *Madison*, 215). Instead, my interpretation follows Banning, *Sacred Fire*, 158.

47. *NDFC*, 616–52.

48. Ibid., 655, 659; Editorial Note, *PJM* 10:8; Secretary of State: Convention Papers Received from GW, 19 Mar. 1796, *RFC* 3:370–71. I disagree with Glenn Phelps's claim that Washington suggested the change strictly to boost the Constitution's ratification chances, not because he wanted to make the document more republican (*Washington and American Constitutionalism,* 100–101).

49. William Steele to Jonathan D. Steele, Sept. 1825, *RFC* 3:467. Not surprisingly, GW praised James Wilson for being "as able, candid, & honest a member as any in Convention" (GW to David Stuart, 17 Oct. 1787, *PGW-CS* 5:379). For AH's doubts about republicanism, see his 26 June speech, *NDFC*, 196.

50. *NDFC*, 196, 75, 263–64, 327, 375–76, 438, 111.

51. Ibid., 449. JM feared that allowing the House to originate appropriations, a concession he judged useless to the large states, would become a quid pro quo for state equality in the Senate.

52. Ibid., 650–52. This technique reveals two other occasions when GW and JM voted alike and one instance in which they voted differently. On 16 Aug. both opposed allowing Congress to print paper money, and on 15 Sept. they supported the finished Constitution. On 7 Sept. they divided over whether to add a council of state to the executive, with JM favoring and GW opposing (ibid., 471, 652, 601).

53. James McClurg to JM, 5 Aug. 1787, *PJM* 10:135.

54. Joseph Jones to JM, 13 Sept. 1787, ibid., 167.

55. See also William Lewis to Thomas Lee Shippen, 11 Oct. 1787, *PTJ* 12:229–31.

56. Freeman argues that GW's contribution to the convention was limited to his presence. Holcombe goes much further, claiming that GW played an indispensable role as a behind-the-scenes compromiser (Freeman, *Washington* 6:113; Holcombe, "Role of Washington," 332–34).

57. *NDFC*, 18; *DGW* 5:185; William Pierce's character sketches of delegates to the Federal Convention, John Quincy Adams Memoirs, 19 Nov. 1818, *RFC* 3:94–95, 426. The delegates also served on committees before and after convention sessions. Even sickness could not keep JM from attending (JM to TJ, 6 Sept. 1787, James McClurg to JM, 5 Sept. 1787, *PJM* 10:163, 162).

58. GW to Bushrod Washington, 9 Nov. 1787, *PGW* 5:424.

59. William Pierce's character sketches of delegates to the Federal Convention, *RFC* 3:94.

60. GW to Annis Boudinot Stockton, 30 June 1787, to Richard Peters, 4 Mar. 1788, *PGW-CS* 5:238, 6:142; *NDFC*, 17; Benjamin Franklin to Thomas Jordan, 18 May 1787, *RFC* 3:21; *DGW* 5:157, 160–61, 166, 173–74, 176, 180, 185; Ketcham, *Madison,* 216; JM to James Madison, Sr., 12 Aug. 1787, *PJM* 10:146.

61. GW to Sir Edward Newenham, 29 Aug. 1788, *PGW-CS* 6:488.

62. Leibiger, "Madison and Amendments to the Constitution"; JM to TJ, 6 Sept., 24 Oct. 1787, *PJM* 10:163–64, 209–14.

63. *Federalist* Nos. 14, 37–58, 62–63, *PJM* 10:284–88, 359ff. On JM's rapid acceptance of a partly national, partly federal government, see Banning, *Sacred Fire,* 166–233.

64. GW to Marquis de Lafayette, 7 Feb., 28 Apr. 1788, to John Cowper, 25 May 1788, to Francis Adrian Ven Der Kemp, 28 May 1788, to TJ, 31 Aug. 1788, *PGW-CS* 6:95–96, 242–46, 289–90, 300–301, 493–94; JM to Edward Everett, 3 June 1827, *RFC* 3:476.

65. GW to Henry Knox, 15 Oct. 1787, to Marquis de Lafayette, 7 Feb. 1788, *PGW-CS* 6:95, 5:375; JM to TJ, 24 Oct. 1787, *Federalist* No. 38, *PJM* 10:207–8, 369.

66. GW to Marquis de Lafayette, 7 Feb. 1788, to Charles Pettit, 16 Aug. 1788, *PGW-CS* 6:95–97, 447; JM to GW, 14 Dec. 1787, to Edmund Pendleton, 21 Feb. 1788, *PJM* 10:327, 532.

67. JM to Ambrose Madison, 11 Oct. 1787, to TJ, 9 Dec. 1787, 22 Apr. 1788, *PJM* 10:192, 312, 11:28; GW to Henry Knox, 15 Oct. 1787, to ER, 8 Jan. 1788, *PGW-CS* 5:375–76, 6:17.

68. *Federalist* Nos. 20, 45, 46, General Defense of the Constitution, 6 June 1788, Weaknesses of the Confederation, 7 June 1788, Power to Levy Direct Taxes, 11 June 1788, Power to Levy Direct Taxes, 11 June 1788 [speeches before Virginia convention], *PJM* 10:323, 429, 439, 11:84–88, 93, 114, 117; GW to Bushrod Washington, 10 Nov. 1787, *PGW-CS* 5:422–23. On the Federalist persuasion, see Wood, *Creation of the American Republic,* chaps. 12–13; on the Antifederalist mentality, see Storing, *What the Antifederalists Were For.*

69. GW to James Wilson, 4 Apr. 1788, to Benjamin Lincoln, 2 Apr. 1788, *PGW-CS* 6:199, 188; JM to TJ, 9 Dec. 1787, to GW, 3 Mar. 1788, *PJM* 10:312, 556; "Objections to this Constitution of Government" [c. 16 Sept. 1787], Rutland, *Papers of Mason* 3:991–93.

70. GW to JM, 10 Oct. 1787, JM to GW, 18 Oct. 1787, to Edmund Pendleton, 28 Oct. 1788, George Nicholas to JM, 5 Apr. 1788, JM to George Nicholas, 8 Apr. 1788, *PJM* 10:190, 196, 224, 11:9, 13; GW to Henry Knox, 15 Oct. 1787, to Bushrod Washington, 10 Nov. 1787, to James Wilson, 4 Apr. 1788, to Benjamin Lincoln, 2 Apr. 1788, *PGW-CS* 5:375–76, 421, 6:199–200, 188.

71. GW to Benjamin Lincoln, 28 Feb. 1788, to Rufus King, 29 Feb. 1788, *PGW-CS* 6:134, 133; Zagarri, *David Humphreys' "Life of General Washington,"* 35, 43; JM to William Short, 24 Oct. 1787, *PJM* 10:221.

72. JM to ER, 7 Oct. 1787, to Ambrose Madison, 11 Oct. 1787, to GW, 18 Nov. 1787, Editorial Note, *PJM* 10:186, 192, 254, 259–63; GW to Jonathan Trumbull, Jr., 5 Feb. 1788, to David Humphreys, 10 Oct. 1787, *PGW-CS* 6:93, 5:365.

73. JM to GW, 18 Nov. 1787, to ER, 2 Dec. 1787, to TJ, 11 Aug. 1788, Joseph Jones to JM, 18 Dec. 1787, Reverend James Madison to JM, 9 Feb. 1788, *PJM* 10:254, 290, 330, 487, 11:226–27; GW to AH, 30 Oct. 1787, 13 Aug. 1788, to Henry Knox, 5 Feb. 1788, *PGW-CS* 5:396, 6:444, 88. Knox answered GW that "the publication signed *Publius* is attributed to the joint efforts of Mr Jay, Mr Maddison and Colo. Hamilton" (Knox to GW, 10 Mar. 1788, ibid., 6:150).

74. GW to David Stuart, 30 Nov. 1787, *PGW-CS* 5:467; JM to GW, 20 Nov., 7 Dec. 1787, *PJM* 10:283, 295. Davis's *Chronicle* printed essays 1–3 in Dec. 1787. The following Old Dominion papers also ran some of the pieces: *Norfolk and Portsmouth Journal,* one;

Virgina Gazette and Independent Chronicle (Richmond), two; and the *Virginia Gazette* (Winchester), one. In 1788 John M'Lean published a two-volume edition of the *Federalist* in New York, Norfolk, and Richmond. Volume 1 (nos. 1–36) appeared in Virginia in April. Volume 2 (nos. 37–85) came out in June (Editorial Note, *DHROC* 8:180–83; Crane, "Publius in the Provinces," 590).

75. GW to JM, 7 Dec. 1787, 5 Feb. 1788, *PJM* 10:296, 469; GW to Chevalier de La Luzerne, 7 Feb. 1788, *PGW-CS* 6:99; GW to AH, 28 Aug. 1788, *PAH* 5:206–8. On the differences between JM's and AH's *Federalist* essays, see Banning, *Sacred Fire,* 195–233.

76. JM to GW, 30 Sept., 14, 18, 28 Oct., 18, 20 [30] Nov., 7, 14, 20, 26 Dec. 1787, 14, 20, 25, 28 Jan., 1, 3, 8, 11, 15 Feb. 1788, *PJM* 10:179–81, 194–95, 196–97, 225–26, 253–54, 283–84, 295, 327, 333–34, 345–46, 372, 399, 419–20, 437–38, 455, 464–65, 481–82, 498–99, 510. On the ratification campaign, see Rutland, *Ordeal of the Constitution.*

77. JM to GW, 20 Dec. 1787, GW to JM, 10 Jan. 1788, *PJM* 10:334, 358; GW on the Constitution, 27 Dec. 1787–20 Feb. 1788, *DHROC* 8:276–81; GW to Benjamin Lincoln, 11 Feb. 1788, *PGW-CS* 6:107.

78. GW to JM, 10, 22 Oct., 5 Nov., 7 Dec. 1787, 10 Jan., 5 Feb., 2 Mar. 1788, Rufus King to JM, 6 Jan. 1788, JM to Rufus King, 23 Jan. 1788, to Tench Coxe, 30 Jan. 1788, *PJM* 10:189–90, 203–4, 242–43, 296–98, 257–58, 468–69, 553, 351, 409, 445. For the Virginia Assembly's actions, see The General Assembly Calls a State Convention, 25–31 Oct. 1787, and The General Assembly Adopts an Act for Paying the State Convention Delegates, 30 Nov.–27 Dec. 1787, *DHROC* 8:110–20, 183–93.

79. JM to Edmund Pendleton, 20 Sept. 1787, GW to JM, 10 Oct. 1787, 5 Feb., 2 Mar. 1788, JM to GW, 20 Feb. 1788, to Ambrose Madison, 8 Nov. 1787, *PJM* 10:171, 190, 469, 553, 526–27, 244; Tobias Lear to John Langdon, 3 Apr. 1788, *DHROC* 9:699; Tobias Lear to John Langdon, 31 Jan. 1789, Brighton, *Checkered Career,* 57; GW to Marquis de Lafayette, 28 Apr. [–1 May] 1788, *PGW-CS* 6:243.

80. JM to Eliza House Trist, 25 Mar. 1788, to TJ, 19 Feb. 1788, to GW, 3 Mar. 1788, *PJM* 11:5, 10:519, 556; *DGW* 5:287; Tobias Lear to William Prescott, Jr., 4 Mar. 1788, *DHROC* 8:456; Zagarri, *Humphreys' "Life of General Washington,"* 44; GW to Caleb Gibbs, 28 Feb. 1788, *PGW-CS* 6:131–32.

81. Joseph Spencer to JM, 28 Feb. 1788, JM to Eliza House Trist, 25 Mar. 1788, George Nicholas to JM, 5 Apr. 1788, JM to George Nicholas, 8 Apr. 1788, to ER, 10 Apr. 1788, *PJM* 10:540–42, 11:5, 9, 12, 19; *DGW* 5:287; Butterfield, "Elder John Leland," 188–92.

82. George Nicholas to JM, 5 Apr. 1788, JM to GW, 10 Apr. 1788, to James McHenry [c. 10 Apr. 1788], to Daniel Carroll [c. 10 Apr. 1788], to Charles Pinckney? [c. 10 Apr. 1788], GW to JM, 2 May 1788, *PJM* 11:8–9, 20, 21, 33; GW to Thomas Johnson, 20 Apr. 1788, to James McHenry, 27 Apr. 1788, *PGW-CS* 6:217–18, 234–35; Thomas Johnson to GW, 10 Oct. 1788, *PGW-PS* 1:42.

83. JM to ER, 10 Jan. 1788, *PJM* 10:355; TJ to William Carmichael, 15 Dec. 1787, Landholder VI, *Connecticut Courant,* 10 Dec. 1787, *Virginia Herald,* 21 Feb. 1788, *Philadelphia Independent Gazetteer,* 12 Oct. 1787, Kaminski et al., *DHROC* 8:241, 230, 400, 55; GW to William Persse, 2 Mar. 1789, *PGW-PS* 1:356.

84. Virginia ratification convention proceedings, 25 June 1788, *DHROC* 10:1538–42, 1550–58; Banning, *Sacred Fire,* 234–64.

85. JM to GW, 4, 13, 18, 23, 25, 28 June 1788, GW to JM, 8 June 1788, *PJM* 11:77, 134, 152–53, 168, 178, 183, 100.

86. GW to Jonathan Trumbull, Jr., 8 June 1788, to John Jay, 8 June 1788, to Henry Knox, 17 June 1788, to Charles Cotesworth Pinckney, 28 June 1788, *PGW-CS* 6:325, 319, 333, 361.

87. Bushrod Washington to GW, 7 June 1788, *Pennsylvania Mercury,* 26 June 1788, *Massachusetts Centinel,* 25 June 1788, *DHROC* 10:1581, 1688, 1684.

88. Virginia ratification convention proceedings, 9, 12 June 1788, ibid., 9:1051–52, 1033–34, 1210–11, 1223; James Monroe to TJ, 12 July 1788, *PJM* 10:1705.

89. GW to JM, 23 June 1788, *PJM* 11:170.

90. TJ to JM, 8 Oct. 1787, JM to TJ, 19 Feb. 1788, ibid., 188, 519; *DGW* 5:357; GW to Gouverneur Morris, 28 Nov. 1788, *PGW-PS* 1:135.

91. JM to GW, 27 July 1788, *PJM* 11:209; GW to Jonathan Trumbull, Jr., 20 July 1788, *PGW-CS* 6:390.

4. Washington's "Prime Minister"

1. JM to GW, 11, 24 Aug. 1788, GW to JM, 17 Aug., 23 Sept. 1788, JM to Edmund Pendleton, 20 Oct. 1788, *PJM* 11:230, 240, 234, 261–62, 307; New York Circular Letter, 28 July 1788, Elliot, *Debates in the Several State Conventions* 2:413–14.

2. Henry Lee to GW, 13 Sept. 1788, GW to Henry Lee, 22 Sept. 1788, *PGW-CS* 6:511, 529; Virginia Calls a Second Constitutional Convention, *DHROC* 10:1761–68; GW to JM, 23 Sept. 1788, JM to ER, 17 Oct., 2, 23 Nov. 1788, Edward Carrington to JM, 22 Oct. 1788, JM to GW, 21 Oct. 1788, *PJM* 11:305, 329, 360, 305–6, 309–10. Lance Banning argues that JM equivocated about running for the Senate, hoping to be drafted. If so, then JM emulated, albeit with decidedly disappointing results, a practice his collaborator had mastered.

3. Charles Lee to GW, 29 Oct. 1788, GW to David Stuart, 10 Nov., 2 Dec. 1788, *PGW-PS* 1:82–83, 102, 147; Edward Carrington to JM, 9 Nov. 1788, JM to ER, 23 Nov. 1788, GW to JM, 18 Nov. 1788, *PJM* 11:336, 362, 351.

4. George Lee Turberville to JM, 13 Nov. 1788, *PJM* 11:343–44; *DHFFE* 2:293–96; Ammon, *Monroe,* 75–76; GW to David Stuart, 2 Dec. 1788, *PGW-PS* 1:148.

5. Henry Lee to JM, 19 Nov. 1788, AH to JM, 23 Nov. 1788, *PJM* 11:357, 367; David Humphreys to TJ, 29 Nov. 1788, *DHFFE* 4:100; Ingersoll, "Notes of a Visit to Montpelier."

6. Edward Carrington to JM, 14 Nov. 1788, Hardin Burnley to JM, 16 Dec. 1788, JM to GW, 14 Jan., 6 Apr. 1789, GW to JM, 22 Mar. 1789, *PJM* 11:346, 398–99, 418, 12:26, 50; *DGW* 5:436–37; Gouverneur Morris to GW, 28 Nov. 1788, *PGW-PS* 1:138. On the Mount Vernon family, see Thane, *Potomac Squire.*

7. JM to George Eve, 2 Jan. 1789, to Thomas Mann Randolph, 13 Jan. 1789, to a Resident of Spotsylvania County, 27 Jan. 1789, to GW, 14 Jan. 1789, Edward Stevens to JM, 31 Jan. 1789, GW to JM, 16 Feb. 1789, *PJM* 11:404–5, 415–17, 428–29, 418, 438 nn.1, 2, 446; Leibiger, "Madison and Amendments."

8. AH to GW, 13 Aug., Sept. 1788, GW to AH, 28 Aug., 3 Oct. 1788, *PAH* 5:201–2,

220–23, 207–8, 222–24; Benjamin Lincoln to GW, 24 Sept. 1788, Thomas Johnson to GW, 10 Oct. 1788, Gouverneur Morris to GW, 6 Dec. 1788, GW to Benjamin Lincoln, 26 Oct. 1788, to Gouverneur Morris, 28 Nov. 1788, to Jonathan Trumbull, Jr., 4 Dec. 1788, to Lewis Morris, 13 Dec. 1788, to William Gordon, 23 Dec. 1788, *PGW-PS* 1:6–7, 42, 165–66, 71–73, 136, 159, 178, 200.

9. JM to TJ, 8 Oct. 1788, Memorandum on a Discussion of the President's Retirement, 5 May 1792, *PJM* 11:276, 14:300–301.

10. Zagarri, *Humphreys' "Life of General Washington,"* 44–54. Although Humphreys dated his talks with GW in July 1788, the events he describes actually took place in June. See *DGW* 5:339–40; David Humphreys to TJ, 29 Nov. 1789, *DHFFE* 4:101.

11. Zagarri, *Humphreys' "Life of General Washington,"* 44–54. As late as 29 Nov. 1788, Humphreys was unsure about his employer's course (David Humphreys to TJ, 29 Nov. 1788, *DHFFE* 4:101).

12. Memorandum on a Discussion of the President's Retirement, 5 May 1792, *PJM* 14:300–301.

13. GW to Nathaniel Gorham, 21 July 1788, *PGW-CS* 6:373n; GW to Henry Knox, 1 Apr. 1789, *PGW-PS* 2:2.

14. JM to TJ, 17 Oct. 1788, to GW, 5 Nov. 1788, AH to JM, 25 Nov. 1788, *PJM* 11:296–97, 334, 366; AH to James Wilson, 25 Jan. 1789, *DHFFE* 4:148; GW to Benjamin Lincoln, 26 Oct. 1788, *PGW-PS* 1:72–73; Zagarri, *Humphreys' "Life of General Washington,"* 51.

15. GW to JM, 2, c. 30 Jan., 16 Feb. 1789, JM to GW, 14 Jan., 16 Feb. 1789, *PJM* 11:409 and n.1, 437–38, 446, 417; Jared Sparks to JM, 22 May 1827, Adams, *Life and Writings of Sparks* 2:211.

16. GW to JM, 16 Feb. 1789, *PJM* 11:446; Undelivered First Inaugural Address: Fragments, *PGW-PS* 2:152–73; JM to Jared Sparks, 30 May 1827, Adams, *Life and Writings of Sparks* 2:211–13.

17. GW to Henry Lee, 14 Feb. 1789, to Battaile Muse, 19 Feb. 1789, *PGW-PS* 2:304, 323; JM Chronology, *PJM* 12:xxvi. The wording of GW's subsequent requests for replies to the House and Senate also point to JM's authorship of the inaugural. See GW to JM, 5, 17 May 1789, ibid., 131–32, 166.

Assessments of JM's role in preparing the address vary. *PJM* designates it a JM document even though no autograph draft survives (ibid., 120–21). Ralph Ketcham finds the evidence that JM ghostwrote the speech conclusive (Ketcham, "Two New Letters," 54–60). *PGW* more cautiously concludes that GW "may well have asked his [JM's] assistance" and emphasizes that the president "made his own alterations" (*PGW-PS* 2:153–54). An observation by Humphreys is instructive: "Those who pretend that everything published in his [GW's] name was written by himself and those who desire to have it believed that he was incapable of being the author of many of those interesting compositions, were equally erroneous in their opinions" (Zagarri, *Humphreys' "Life of General Washington,"* 52).

18. First Inaugural Address, 30 Apr. 1789, *PGW-PS* 2:173–77; GW to James McHenry, 31 July 1788, to Benjamin Lincoln, 28 Aug. 1788, to TJ, 31 Aug. 1788, *WGW* 30:29, 63, 83. The retention of a strong endorsement of amendments is further indication that JM ghostwrote the inaugural.

19. Harry Innes to GW, 18 Dec. 1788, *PGW-PS* 1:187–89; JM to GW, 8 Mar. 1789, *PJM* 12:5–6 n.3.

20. JM to GW, 5 Mar., 6 Apr. 1789, GW to JM, 30 Mar. 1789, JM to Edmund Pendleton, 19 Apr. 1789, *PJM* 12:3, 49, 41–42, 89; *DHFF* 1:4, 7–9, 16–17, 3:9–11, 19, 23; Bickford and Bowling, *Birth of the Nation,* 9; Harrison, "Washington in New York in 1789," 852, 857; Hoffman, "President Washington's Cherry Street Residence," 88–102. GW's letter makes it clear that he had discussed housing with JM, and their only opportunity to do so had been at Mount Vernon in Feb. 1789. On Charles Thomson, see Bowling, "Good-By 'Charle.'"

21. *DGW* 5:445–47. On GW's trip to New York, see Bowen, *History of the Centennial Celebration,* 1–36; Freeman et al., *Washington* 6:141–84; Baker, "Washington after the Revolution," 19:329–39; *PGW-PS* 2:59–115; *DHFFE* 4:245–50; Cogswell, "Washington's Reception as President," 244.

22. Baker, "Washington after the Revolution," 19:336–37; *DHFFC* 3:32–33; Bickford and Bowling, *Birth of the Nation,* 9. On GW's inauguration, see Bowen, *History of the Centennial Celebration,* 40–58; Freeman et al., *Washington* 6:185–98; *DHFFE* 4:263–74; Griswold, *The Republican Court,* 121–22; Tobias Lear Diary, Sparks, *Writings of Washington* 10:463; Lamb, "Inauguration of Washington, 1789," 452–53; Bowling and Veit, *Maclay Diary,* 9.

23. Tobias Lear Diary, Sparks, *Writings of Washington* 10:463; Bowen, *History of the Centennial Celebration,* 49; Bowling and Veit, *Maclay Diary,* 13; Ames, *Works of Fisher Ames* 1:34.

24. Bowling and Veit, *Maclay Diary,* 18; Bowen, *History of the Centennial Celebration,* 46, 49, 50. A speech of seventy-three pages would have taken three hours to deliver.

25. Rachal, *Journal and Letters of Col. John May,* 124; Baker, "Washington after the Revolution," 19:429–33.

26. Freeman et al., *Washington* 6:183; GW to William Heath, 9 May 1789, *PGW-PS* 2:238.

27. Bickford and Bowling, *Birth of the Nation,* 1, 3, 5. The following paragraphs focus on the First Congress's first session, but they occasionally draw examples from the second and third sessions.

28. GW to Catherine Sawbridge Macaulay Graham, 9 Jan. 1790, *PGW-PS* 4:552.

29. *DHFFC* 3:43, 45–47; Lear Diary, Sparks, *Writings of Washington* 10:464; Editorial Note, GW to JM, 5, 17 May 1789, Reply of the President to the House of Representatives, 8 May 1789, Reply of the President to the Senate, 18 May 1789, *PJM* 12:120–21, 131–32, 166, 141–42, 166–67.

30. GW to JM, 5 Aug. 1789, *PJM* 12:325; *DHFFC* 3:138.

31. Conferences with a Committee of the United States Senate, 8, 10 Aug. 1789, *PGW-PS* 3:400–403, 408–9; GW to JM, 9 Aug. 1789, *PJM* 12:328; *DHFFC* 2:29–30. On GW's relations with the Senate, see Swanstrom, *United States Senate,* esp. chaps. 7 and 8.

32. TJ to GW, 24 Apr. 1790, GW to JM, 27 Apr. 1790, *PGW-PS* 5:342–46 and n.1, 349; *DGW* 6:68. GW also consulted TJ, John Adams, and John Jay. See ibid.

33. GW to John Adams, 10 May 1789, John Adams to GW, 17 May 1789, AH to GW, 5 May 1789, *PGW-PS* 2:245–46, 312–14, 211–14. John Jay and Robert R. Livingston

were also consulted, but no record of their replies remains (GW to Jay, 11 May 1789, Livingston to GW, 2 May 1789, ibid., 270, 192–96; GW to JM, 12 May 1789, *PJM* 12:157).

34. White, *Federalists*, 109; Proctor, "After Dinner Anecdotes," 257–58. See also Adair, "Madison's Autobiography," 203; Notes on Levees and Assumption, 16 Feb. 1793, *PTJ* 25:208.

35. Bowling and Veit, *Maclay Diary*, 136–37, 342; TJ to JM, 9 June 1793, *PJM* 15:27; *DGW* 6:53. During the First Congress's second session (Jan.–July 1790), the only session that GW kept a full record of his dinner guests, JM dined with the First Family on Jan. 28, Mar. 11, 25, and July 8 (ibid., 23, 45, 53, 89).

36. James Tilton to GW, 25 Apr. 1789, GW to Edward Stevens, 21 Mar. 1789, to Samuel Vaughan, 21 Mar. 1789, *PGW-PS* 2:128, 1:422, 426; Fleet, "Madison's 'Detached Memoranda,'" 541. The first four volumes of *PGW-PS* are filled with letters from office seekers. AH, John Jay, and John Adams also assisted GW. On GW's appointment policies, see White, *Federalists*.

37. JM to TJ, 30 June 1789, ER to JM, 19, 23 July 1789, GW to JM, 9 Aug., c. 8, c. 23 Sept. 1789, *PJM* 12:271–72, 298–99, 306, 328, 390, 420; GW to Edmund Pendleton, 28 Sept. 1789, *PGW-PS* 4:104–5.

38. GW to JM, c. 23 Sept. 1789, Tobias Lear to JM, 7 Feb. 1790, JM to Tobias Lear, 7 Feb. 1790, *PJM* 12:420, 13:29, 29–30; GW to James McHenry, 30 Nov. 1789, *PGW-PS* 4:342.

39. *DGW* 5:456; JM to ER, 17 June 1789, GW to JM, c. 8 Sept. 1789, *PJM* 12:229, 390. Lee received no appointment.

40. Arthur Lee to Tench Coxe, 15 Sept. 1789, Coxe Papers, PHi (I would like to thank Kenneth R. Bowling for directing me to this letter); Tench Coxe to JM, 17, 28 Sept. 1789, *PJM* 12:404–8, 424.

41. ER to JM, 19, 23 July 1789, Edward Carrington to JM, 9 Sept., 20 Dec. 1789, John Dawson to JM, 13 Sept. 1789, JM to TJ, 24 July 1791, Pinckney to JM, 6 Aug. 1791, *PJM* 12:298–99, 306, 391–92, 462–63, 401, 53, 14:66–68; Edward Carrington to GW, 11 May 1789, *PGW-PS* 2:266. Although Henry Lee and Henry Knox also pushed Carrington, neither mentioned the specific office the applicant desired. Carrington thus correctly attributed his appointment as federal marshal primarily to JM (ibid., 3:100). For examples of letters to JM now located in the Washington Papers, DLC, see Henry Lee to JM, 25 Jan. 1790, James Callaway to JM, 12 Mar. 1790.

42. ER to JM, 10, 15 Mar., 27 Apr., 20 May 1790, JM to ER, 6, 19 May 1790, *PJM* 13:96, 107–8, 180, 224, 189, 222; Reardon, *Randolph*, 192–93.

43. JM to TJ, 30 June 1789, *PJM* 12:271–72; Bowling and Veit, *Maclay Diary*, 121.

44. *DHFFC* 2:50; GW to TJ, 13 Oct. 1789, *PGW-PS* 4:174; JM to TJ, 17 May, 8 Oct. 1789, TJ to JM, 28 Aug. 1789, *PJM* 12:185, 433, 364–65.

45. JM to TJ, 8 Oct. 1789, to Henry Lee, 4 Oct. 1789, JM Chronology, *PJM* 12:433, 427, xxiv; TJ to GW, 15 Dec. 1789, *PTJ* 16:34–35.

46. JM Chronology, JM to GW, 4 Jan. 1790, to TJ, 8 Oct. 1789, 24 Jan. 1790, *PJM* 12:xxiv, 467, 433, 13:4; Peterson, *Jefferson*, 392–93.

47. GW to TJ, 21 Jan. 1790, TJ to GW, 14 Feb. 1790, *PTJ* 16:116–18, 184; JM to GW, 4 Jan. 1790, to TJ, 24 Jan., c. 11 Feb. 1790, TJ to JM, 14 Feb. 1790, JM to GW, 28 Feb. 1790, *PJM* 12:467, 13:4, 32, 41–42, 70.

48. Peterson, *Jefferson*, 394–95; Gouverneur Morris to AH, 24 Oct. 1792, *PAH* 12:617.

49. GW's Queries concerning Negotiations with Spain, c. 25 July 1789, Memorandum for GW, c. 8 Oct. 1789, *PJM* 12:310–11, 433–34.

50. GW to David Stuart, 26 July 1789, *PGW-PS* 3:321; *DGW* 6:14–16.

51. Title for the President [speech before Congress], 11 May 1789, *PJM* 12:155; GW to David Stuart, 26 July 1789, *PGW-PS* 3:323. The best source on the titles controversy is James H. Hutson, "John Adams' Title Campaign." For a discussion of hidden-hand leadership, see Greenstein, *Hidden-Hand Presidency,* 58–65. Although this is a twentieth-century term, I believe that it accurately describes GW's leadership style.

52. *DHFFC* 3:32, 45, 55–56, 1:24, 40–41, 45; John Adams to Mercy Warren, 8 Aug. 1807, "Correspondence between John Adams and Mercy Warren," 4:438; Bowling and Veit, *Maclay Diary,* 40.

53. JM to TJ, 9, 23 May 1789, Title for the President [speech before Congress], 11 May 1789, *PJM* 12:143, 183, 155; GW to David Stuart, 26 July 1789, *PGW-PS* 3:323.

54. Tonnage Duties, 21 Apr., 4 May 1789, Import Duties, 25 Apr. 1789 [speeches before Congress], *PJM* 12:97–100, 125–30, 109–13; Fisher Ames to George Richards Minot, 2 July 1789, Ames, *Works of Ames* 1:57–60. On JM and commercial discrimination, see McCoy, *Elusive Republic,* chap. 6.

55. Robert Dick to GW, 28 Mar. 1789, GW to JM, 11 May 1789, to David Stuart, 26 July 1789, *PGW-PS* 1:454–57, 2:270–71, 3:323–24; JM to James Madison, Sr., 5 July 1789, *PJM* 12:279. JM described GW as "so much disappointed" at discrimination's defeat that "he would not have signed the Bill, but for the expectation given him that the Senate would provide for the object in some other mode deemed more eligible" (Fleet, "Madison's 'Detached Memoranda,'" 542). See also Adair, "Madison's Autobiography," 205.

56. Navigation and Trade [speech before Congress], 25 June 1790, Address of the President to Congress, 8 Dec. 1790, *PJM* 13:256, 313; *DPCUS,* 1st Cong., 3d sess., 2015, 2022; *American State Papers, Foreign Relations* 1:128, 300–304.

57. Leibiger, "Madison and Amendments," 460–68; Banning, *Sacred Fire,* 288.

58. JM to Richard Peters, 19 Aug. 1787, GW to JM, c. 31 May 1789, *PJM* 12:346, 191.

59. Boller, *Washington and Religion,* 123.

60. Ibid., 45–65, 43; Proctor, "After-Dinner Anecdotes," 263.

61. Samuel Johnston to JM, 22 May, 8 July 1789, JM to Samuel Johnston, 21, 22 June 1789, JM to GW, 20 Nov. 1789, *PJM* 12:178, 284–85, 249, 256, 453; GW to the Governor and Council of North Carolina, 19 June 1789, The Governor and Council of North Carolina to GW, 10 May 1789, *PGW-PS* 3:47–48, 48–49.

62. Bowling and Veit, *Maclay Diary,* 97; Amendments to the Constitution [speech before Congress], 8 June 1789, Removal Power of the President [speech before Congress], 16 June 1789, *PJM* 12:202, 225–26.

63. *DGW* 5:456; William Loughton Smith to Edward Rutledge, 9–[15] Aug. 1789, Rodgers, "Letters of William Loughton Smith," 14–15. Although Smith uses the word *cabinet,* GW had not yet begun having group meetings with department heads. Smith's use of the term suggests that JM did indeed play the role of prime minister.

5. Friendship Tested

1. GW to the House of Representatives, 8 May 1789, 13 Dec. 1790, 29 Oct. 1791, to the Senate, 18 May 1789, 13 Dec. 1790, Address of the President to Congress, 8 Dec.

1790, GW to JM, c. 23 Sept. 1789, *PJM* 12:141–42, 13:322, 14:89, 12:166–67, 13:322, 311–15, 12:420. JM visited Mount Vernon once in 1790 and once in 1791 but never went there again (JM Chronology, ibid., 13:xxvii, 14:xxviii). "Cabinet" is used loosely here to describe the department heads collectively. Formal cabinet meetings began late in 1791.

2. TJ to GW, 1 Apr., 12 July 1790, *PGW-PS* 5:301, 6:58–61; TJ to GW, 16 May 1792, *PTJ* 23:518–19; TJ to JM, 18 Aug. 1791, *PJM* 14:71. See, for example, AH to JM, 24 Nov. 1790, TJ to JM, 1 Jan. 1791, ibid., 13:306, 341.

3. Nelson, *Liberty and Property,* xi–xv, 1–65; Elkins and McKitrick, *Age of Federalism,* 106–23; Cooke, *Hamilton,* 73–84.

4. Report Relative to a Provision for the Support of Public Credit, 9 Jan. 1790, *PAH* 6:51–168; Nelson, *Liberty and Property,* 49; Bickford and Bowling, *Birth of the Nation,* 61–66; Elkins and McKitrick, *Age of Federalism,* 137.

5. Assumption of the State Debts [speech before Congress], 1 Mar. 1790, JM to Henry Lee, 13 Apr. 1790, *PJM* 13:75, 148. For a review of the literature on the Country persuasion in Britain and America, see Elkins and McKitrick, *Age of Federalism,* 13–29.

6. Republican Distribution of Citizens [published in the *National Gazette*], 3 Mar. 1792, *PJM* 14:246. See also McCoy, *Elusive Republic;* Breen, *Tobacco Culture.*

7. Elkins and McKitrick, *Age of Federalism,* 92–114. For a review of the literature on the Court persuasion in Britain and America, see ibid., 13–29.

8. Discrimination between Present and Original Holders of the Public Debt [speeches before Congress], 11, 18 Feb. 1790, *PJM* 13:34–38, 47–59. Having opposed discrimination in the Confederation Congress, JM favored it in 1790 because of "outrageous specula-tions" and fraudulent transactions that subsequently occurred at the expense of the uninformed (Adair, "Madison's Autobiography," 204–5). JM did not yet know that GW opposed discrimination.

9. Elkins and McKitrick, *Age of Federalism,* 116–18; GW to David Stuart, 28 Mar. 1790, *PGW-PS* 5:287.

10. Elkins and McKitrick, *Age of Federalism,* 133; Breen, *Tobacco Culture,* 124–59; GW to David Stuart, 28 Mar. 1790, to Beverly Randolph, 24 Aug. 1790, *PGW-PS* 5:286–88, 6:320–21; GW to Theodorick Bland, 15 Aug. 1786, to Marquis de Lafayette, 15 Aug. 1786, *PGW-CS* 4:210–11, 214–16; GW to Marquis de LaFayette, 28 July 1791, *WGW* 31:324; In-gersoll, "Notes of a Visit to Mr. Madison."

11. Ferling, *First of Men,* 418–20; First Inaugural Address, *PGW-PS* 2:156–57 n.10.

12. JM to ER, 21 Mar. 1790, *PJM* 13:110; Proctor, "After-Dinner Anecdotes," 263.

13. Elkins and McKitrick, *Age of Federalism,* 118–19; GW to David Stuart, 15 June 1790, *PGW-PS* 5:523–27; Assumption of State Debts [speeches before Congress], 24 Feb., 1 Mar., 22 Apr. 1790, JM to TJ, 8 Mar. 1790, *PJM* 13:62–63, 75, 163–74, 95. As with dis-crimination, JM had favored assumption while in the Confederation Congress.

14. Assumption of the State Debts [speech before Congress], 22 Apr. 1790, *PJM* 13:167–68; Banning, *Jeffersonian Persuasion,* 48.

15. Bowling, *Creation of Washington,* 162–73.

16. Ibid., 128–29, 174–85; Fisher Ames to Thomas Dwight, 11 June 1790, Ames, *Works of Ames* 1:80; Bowling and Veit, *Maclay Diary,* 302.

17. "Explanations of the 3. volumes bound in marbled paper," 4 Feb. 1818, Ford, *Works of Jefferson* 1:175; TJ's Account of the Bargain on the Assumption and Residence Bills [1792?], *PTJ* 17:205–7; Bowling, *Creation of Washington,* 184–85.

18. Bowling, *Creation of Washington,* 106–26, 182; Bowling, *Creating the Federal City,* 39–60, 72–73; Bowling and Veit, *Maclay Diary,* 308.

19. Bowling, *Creation of Washington,* 185–86, 205; Sweig, "Capital on the Potomac," 94. Alexander White, who represented Virginia's upriver counties, may have been kept in the dark about the promises to Lee and the Carrolls (Sweig, "Capital on the Potomac," 90).

20. Bowling, *Creation of Washington,* 186–201; Location of the Capital [speech before Congress], 6 July 1790, *PJM* 12:265; JM's Concurring Opinion, [14 July 1790], *PTJ* 17:199–200; Bowling and Bickford, *Birth of the Nation,* 71.

21. Bowling, *Creating the Federal City,* 78; GW to Marquis de La Luzerne, 10 Aug. 1790, *PGW-PS* 6:229; JM to James Monroe, 17 Apr. 1790, *PJM* 13:151.

22. Report on a National Bank, 13 Dec. 1790, *PAH* 7:236–342; Nelson, *Liberty and Property,* 22–36.

23. Bowling, "Bank Bill," 59–71.

24. The Bank Bill [speeches before Congress], 2, 8 Feb. 1791, *PJM* 13:372–82, 383–87.

25. JM to Edmund Pendleton, 13 Feb. 1791, ibid., 390; Elkins and McKitrick, *Age of Federalism,* 234. Kenneth Bowling argues that JM used constitutional objections as a "smoke screen" to hide his fear that the bank would prevent removal to the Potomac. See Bowling, *Creation of Washington,* 216, and Bowling, "Bank Bill," 59–71. My interpretation sides with Banning, *Sacred Fire,* 325–33.

26. Bowling, *Creation of Washington,* 217; Opinion on the Constitutionality of the Bill for Establishing a National Bank, 15 Feb. 1791, *PTJ* 19:280, source note; Fleet, "Madison's 'Detached Memoranda,'" 542; Bowling, "Bank Bill," 67. See also TJ to Elijah Griffin, 15 May 1825, Jefferson Papers.

27. Draft Veto of the Bank Bill, 21 Feb. 1791, *PJM* 13:395; Opinion on the Constitutionality of an Act to Establish a Bank, 23 Feb. 1791, *PAH* 8:63–134. The public did not yet know the authorship of the individual *Federalist* essays. See Editorial Note, *PJM* 10:259–63.

28. Bowling, *Creation of Washington,* 212–19; Bowling, *Creating the Federal City,* 66, 68.

29. GW to Edmund Pendleton, 23 Sept. 1793, *WGW* 33:96. These comments probably refer to the bank bill, because GW wrote them in response to Pendleton's complaints against AH's program (Pendleton to GW, 11 Sept. 1793, Mays, *Letters and Papers of Pendleton* 2:613–15).

30. JM to TJ, 1 May 1791, *PJM* 14:16; Randall, *Jefferson* 1:631. See also Fleet, "Madison's 'Detached Memoranda,'" 543; Procter, "After-Dinner Anecdotes," 257.

31. Bowling and Veit, *Maclay Diary,* 368; Bowling, *Creation of Washington,* 209; Bowling, *Creating the Federal City,* 65; JM to TJ, 8 Aug. 1791, Notes on William Loughton Smith's *Politics and Views,* [c. 4 Nov. 1792], *PJM* 14:69, 400; Randall, *Jefferson* 1:631; GW to Gouverneur Morris, 28 July 1791, *WGW* 31:329.

32. Report on the Subject of Manufactures, 5 Dec. 1791, *PAH* 10:230–340; Nelson, *Liberty and Property,* 37–51; Elkins and McKitrick, *Age of Federalism,* 107–9, 258–63; JM to Henry Lee, 1 Jan. 1792, Bounty Payments for Cod Fisheries [speech before Congress], 6 Feb. 1792, *PJM* 14:180, 220–24.

33. GW to Beverly Randolph, 22 Nov. 1789, *WGW* 30:462–63 (*PGW-PS* does not print this letter in full: see 3:195n); To the United States Senate and House of Representatives, 8 Jan. 1790, ibid., 4:543–48; GW to AH, 14 Oct. 1791, *PAH* 9:384.

34. Bounty Payments for Cod Fisheries [speech before Congress], 6 Feb. 1792, *PJM* 14:220–24; Elkins and McKitrick, *Age of Federalism,* 270–82.

6. Founding Washington, D.C.

1. Bowling, *Creation of Washington,* ix–xi, 1–13.
2. GW to George Clinton, 11 Sept. 1783, to Arthur Young, 5 Dec. 1791, *WGW* 27:148, 31:438; Location of the Capital [speeches before Congress], 3 Sept. 1789, 6 July 1790, *PJM* 12:369–81, 13:264–67; GW to Richard Henry Lee, 8 Feb. 1785, to William Grayson, 22 June 1785, *PGW-CS* 2:332–33, 3:69; In 1790 the center of population actually lay southwest of the Susquehanna River, but at the time Americans thought it lay northeast of that waterway (Bowling, *Creation of Washington,* 8).
3. JM to GW, 24 Aug. 1788, *PJM* 11:241; Bowling, *Creation of Washington,* 4, 113–14, 213–14; McCoy, "Virginia Port Bill," 288–303. On GW and Alexandria, see Netherton et al., *Fairfax County, Virginia,* 83–149; Sweig, "Capital on the Potomac," 76–77.
4. Bowling and Veit, *Maclay Diary,* 227; GW to TJ, 29 Mar. 1784, *PGW-CS* 1:239; GW to Arthur Young, 5 Dec. 1791, *WGW* 31:438; McCoy, *Elusive Republic;* Bowling, *Creation of Washington,* x–xi, 24.
5. JM to TJ, 17 July 1783, William Grayson to JM, 21 Aug. 1785, *PJM* 7:230, 8:349; Bowling, *Creation of Washington,* 50–57; GW to George Clinton, 11 Sept. 1783, *WGW* 27:148; GW to William Grayson, 22 June 1785, *PGW-CS* 3:69.
6. *RFC* 2:325; General Defense of the Constitution [speech before Virginia Convention], 6 June 1788, *PJM* 11:81.
7. JM to GW, 11, 24 Aug. 1788, *PJM* 11:229–30, 240–42.
8. JM to GW, 14 Sept. 1788, GW to JM, 3, 17 Aug., 23 Sept. 1788, ibid., 254, 219, 234, 261; Bowling, *Creation of Washington,* 88–97.
9. JM Chronology, JM to Edmund Pendleton, 14 Sept. 1789, *PJM* 11:xxvi, 12:402–3; Bowling, *Creation of Washington,* 88–97, 105.
10. Location of the Capital [speeches before Congress], 3, 4 Sept. 1789, *PJM* 12:369–81; Bowling, *Creation of Washington,* 142–60; David Stuart to GW, 12 Sept. 1789, *PGW-PS* 4:28.
11. JM to Henry Lee, 4 Oct. 1789, to GW, 20 Nov. 1789, *PJM* 12:425–27, 452–53; Bowling, *Creation of Washington,* 162–63.
12. Daniel Carroll to JM, 4 Oct. 1789, *PJM* 12:428; Bowling, *Creation of Washington,* 163–66; Sweig, "Capital on the Potomac," 85–86, 95–104.
13. JM to Henry Lee, 4 Oct. 1789, *PJM* 12:425–27; *JHDV,* Oct. 1789, 115, 129; Hening, *Statutes at Large* 13:43–44; Bowling, *Creation of Washington,* 125–26; Sweig, "Capital on the Potomac," 80–81.
14. JM to GW, 20 Nov. 1789, *PJM* 12:452–53.
15. Bowling, *Creation of Washington,* 208; Editorial Note, *PJM* 14:1. On TJ and the founding of Washington, D.C., see Malone, *Jefferson* 2:371–87; Editorial Note, *PTJ* 20:3–72; Young, *Washington Community,* 1–10. While Young's general thesis that GW, JM, and TJ designed the seat of government to comport with the Constitution is sound, no evidence supports his specific argument that GW distributed the government's three branches spatially to accord with the separation of powers. Rather, placing the Capitol and the Presidential Palace over a mile apart served the practical purpose of dividing the

coveted buildings between rival landholder interests. See Bowling, *Creation of Washington,* 224.

16. Memorandum on the Residence Act, c. 29 Aug. 1790, *PJM* 13:294–96; Commission Appointing Commissioners for the Permanent Seat of Government, 22 Jan. 1791, *WGW* 31:200.

17. TJ's Report to GW on Meeting Held at Georgetown, 14 Sept. 1790, TJ to GW, 17 Sept. 1790, *PTJ* 17:461–63, 466–67. On the GW-Mason estrangement, see Henriques, "Uneven Friendship." GW's fears about Mason's intentions were justified; Mason may have secretly supported Representative Elbridge Gerry's campaign against the 1790 Residence Act. See Sweig, "Capital on the Potomac," 93–94 n.39.

18. GW to Congress and Proclamation, 24 Jan. 1791, *WGW* 31:201–4. On GW's Potomac tour, see Bowling, *Creation of Washington,* 210–11; Bryan, *History of the National Capital* 1:108–15.

19. *DGW* 6:103–5, 164–65; Scisco, "Site for the 'Federal City,'" 123–47; TJ to JM, 26 Aug. 1791, *PJM* 14:74; TJ to D.C. Commissioners, 28 Aug. 1791, Queries for D. C. Commissioners, 28 Aug. 1791, TJ to GW, 8 Sept. 1791, *PTJ* 22:88–89, 89–91, 136. Kenneth R. Bowling points out to me that by 1791 L'Enfant had anglicized his first name.

20. Bryan, *History of the National Capital* 1:159–60; Third Annual Address to Congress, 25 Oct. 1791, *WGW* 31:400; Young, *Washington Community,* 19–20.

21. GW to D.C. Commissioners, 17 Jan. 1792, *WGW* 31:461–2; GW to TJ, 11 Feb., 13 Jan. 1792, *PTJ* 23:109, 41. See also GW to TJ, 9 Mar. 1793, ibid., 25:345.

22. Bowling, *Creation of Washington,* 220–21; Bryan, *History of the National Capital* 1:155–73; GW to the D.C. Commissioners, 1, 18 Dec. 1791, to Peter Charles L'Enfant, 2, 13 Dec. 1791, *WGW* 31:432–33, 445–48, 434–35, 442–44; Malone, *Jefferson* 2:381.

23. TJ to GW, 1 Dec. 1791, GW to TJ, 15, 26 Feb., 14 Mar. 1792, TJ to Peter Charles L'Enfant, 22, 27 Feb. 1792, Peter Charles L'Enfant to TJ, 26 Feb. 1792, TJ to George Walker, 1 Mar. 1792, *PTJ* 22:367, 23:120, 160, 283–84, 141, 161, 150–58, 188; Daniel Carroll to JM, 25, 29 Nov., 12, 21 Dec. 1791, GW to JM, 19 Feb. 1792, *PJM* 14:129, 130–31, 147, 174, 234.

24. GW to JM, 14 Oct. 1793, JM to GW, 24 Oct. 1793, *PJM* 15:126–28, 129–31. In 1793 GW also asked JM what compensation would be necessary to retain competent commissioners (GW to TJ, 9 Mar. 1793, Opinion on Compensation to the D.C. Commissioners, 11 Mar. 1793, *PTJ* 25:345, 360–61).

25. *RFC* 2:325, 616; Pangle and Pangle, *Learning of Liberty,* 149–51; Bryan, *History of the National Capital* 1:251–54; Last Will and Testament, 9 July 1799, First Annual Address to Congress, 8 Jan. 1790, GW to ER, 15 Dec. 1794, to the D.C. Commissioners, 28 Jan. 1795, to Robert Brooke, 16 Mar. 1795, Eighth Annual Address to Congress, 7 Dec. 1796, *WGW* 30:493–94, 35:59, 106–8, 149–51, 316–17: National University [speech before Congress], 26 Dec. 1796, *PJM* 16:436–38.

26. TJ to GW, 23 Feb. 1795, Jefferson Papers; GW to TJ, 15 Mar. 1795, *WGW* 34:147–48; TJ to JM, 23 Feb. 1795, JM to TJ, 23 Mar. 1795, *PJM* 15:479, 493.

27. Bryan, *History of the National Capital* 1:264–70; GW to Congress, 8 Jan. 1796, *WGW,* 34:420; Loan for the City of Washington [speech before Congress], 22 Feb. 1796, JM to TJ, 6 Mar., 4 Apr. 1796, *PJM* 16:231, 247, 286.

28. Postal Road Survey [speech before Congress], 5 Feb. 1796, *PJM* 16:213; Bowling, *Creation of Washington,* 239, 242.

29. Elkins and McKitrick, *Age of Federalism,* 163–93. TJ, too, is a father of the national capital. Unlike GW and JM, however, from 1785 to 1789 he was not involved in the Potomac campaign because of his public service in France.

7. Four More Years

1. GW to JM, 20 May 1792, *PJM* 14:311; Notes of a Conversation with GW, 10 July 1792, *PTJ* 24:210–11. Although he did not use the word *cabinet,* GW by November 1791 regularly called his department heads together to advise him on policy (Freeman et al., *Washington* 6:334–35 and n.72; White, *Federalists,* 38–41; Reardon, *Randolph,* 207).

2. Memorandum on a Discussion of the President's Retirement, 5 May 1792, *PJM* 14:302; Notes of a Conversation with GW, 10 July 1792, *PTJ* 24:210–11. See Cunningham's discussion of terminology in *Jeffersonian Republicans,* vii–ix. Sharp describes these groupings as "proto-parties," united more by ideology than organization (*American Politics in the Early Republic,* 8–10, 33–34).

3. Marsh, "Jefferson-Madison Vacation," 70–72; Cunningham, *Jeffersonian Republicans,* 11–12; Elkins and McKitrick, *Age of Federalism,* 240–42; Peterson, *Jefferson,* 437–43; TJ to GW, 5, 20 June 1791, to JM, 18 Aug. 1791, *PTJ* 20:466–67, 558, 22:48–49.

4. Marsh, "Freneau and Madison," 189–94; Lewis Leary, *That Rascal Freneau,* 186–97; Cunningham, *Jeffersonian Republicans,* 14–19.

5. *National Gazette* Essays, 19 Nov. 1791–20 Dec. 1792, *PJM* 14:110ff.; Elkins and McKitrick, *Age of Federalism,* 262–70; Leary, *That Rascal Freneau,* 197–246; Marsh, *Freneau's Published Prose:,* 62–94; JM to Henry Lee, 18 Dec. 1791, *PJM* 14:154.

6. An American No. II, 11 Aug. 1792, *PAH* 12:189. That GW read the *National Gazette* is clear from his frequent references to it, quoted by TJ in Notes of Conversations with GW, 10 July 1792, 7 Feb., 23 May, 2 Aug. 1793, *PTJ* 24:210–11, 25:155, 26:101–2, 602–3.

7. GW to Tobias Lear, 14 Oct. 1791, *WGW* 31:387; GW to AH, 17 Oct. 1791, *PAH* 9:403; JM to James Madison, Sr., 30 Oct. 1791, *PJM* 14:90.

8. Cunningham, *Jeffersonian Republicans,* 22, 270–71; Preface, JM to James Madison, Sr., 15 Mar. 1792, to Edmund Pendleton, 25 Mar. 1792, *PJM* 14:xix–xxii, 253, 263.

9. Reardon, *Randolph,* 207–9; Memoranda of Consultations with the President, 11 Mar.–9 Apr. 1792, *PTJ* 23:264; GW to the House of Representatives, 5 Apr. 1792, *WGW* 32:16–17; JM to Henry Lee, 15 Apr. 1792, *PJM* 14:288; *DPCUS,* 2d Cong., 1st sess., 120, 541, 548–50. On the Apportionment Bill, see Opinion on Apportionment Bill, 4 Apr. 1792, *PTJ* 22:370–76, Freeman et al., *Washington* 6:343–48, and esp. Currie, *Constitution in Congress.* Currie argues that GW signed a less equitable and constitutionally inferior bill than the one he vetoed, because the successful bill denied states like Delaware (with a population of 58,000) a second representative. The 1:30,000 ratio, Currie points out, should have applied not to individual states but to Congress as a whole.

10. AH to Edward Carrington, 26 May 1792, *PAH* 11:426–45.

11. Notes of a Conversation with GW, 10 July 1792, *PTJ* 24:210–11. On Madison's belief in a conspiracy against republicanism, see "The Union. Who Are Its Real Friends?" 31 Mar. 1792, and JM's attitude toward GW's approval of the bank bill in JM to TJ, 1 May 1791, *PJM* 14:274–75, 16.

12. GW to JM, 19 Feb. 1792, Memorandum on a Discussion of the President's Retirement, 5 May 1792, *PJM* 14:234, 299–304.

13. Memorandum on a Discussion of the President's Retirement, 5 May 1792, ibid., 299–304.

14. GW to JM, 20 May 1792, ibid., 310–12.

15. JM to GW, 20 June 1792, ibid., 319–24.

16. TJ to JM, 1, 4 June 1792, JM Chronology, ibid., 313, 314–15, xxix; TJ to GW, 23 May 1792, *PTJ* 23:535–40. After sending this letter, TJ requested and JM sent a list of congressmen suspected of having been corrupted by treasury policies in case GW demanded specifics (TJ to JM, 4 June 1792, JM to TJ, 12 June 1792, *PJM* 14:314–15, 318).

17. Notes of a Conversation with GW, 10 July 1792, *PTJ* 24:210–11; TJ to JM, 11 July 1792, *PJM* 14:342.

18. GW to AH, 29 July 1792, AH to GW, 18 Aug. 1792, *PAH* 12:129–34, 228–58; Freeman et al., *Washington* 6:366. The president attributed the accusations to his "quandom friend" George Mason.

19. An American and T.L. essays, AH to Edward Carrington, 26 May 1792, Gouverneur Morris to AH, 24 Oct. 1792, An American No. II, 11 Aug. 1792, *PAH* 12:157ff., 11:426–45, 12:617, 189. In a draft of An American No. 1, AH identified JM by name but deleted it before publication (ibid., 158 and n.8). Contemporaries immediately recognized JM as the "friend" to whom AH referred; see ER to JM, 12 Aug. 1792, Henry Lee to JM, 10 Sept. 1792, *PJM* 14:349, 363. AH surely exaggerated his shock at the rupture with Madison, because the differences between the two had become obvious during the writing of the *Federalist* essays. See Banning, *Sacred Fire,* 195–233, 396–402.

20. Smith, *Politics and Views,* 17, 18, 22–23; Ketcham, *Madison,* 333.

21. James Monroe to JM, 18 Sept. 1792, For *Dunlap's American Daily Advertiser,* 22 Sept., 20 Oct. 1792, TJ to JM, 1, 17 Oct. 1792, JM to TJ, 9, 23 Oct. 1792, *PJM* 14:367, 368–70, 387–92, 375, 386, 377, 392; Brant, *Madison* 3:362.

22. GW to TJ, 23 Aug. 1792, TJ to GW, 9 Sept. 1792, *PTJ* 24:315–18, 354–59; GW to AH, 26 Aug. 1792, AH to GW, 9 Sept. 1792, *PAH* 12:276–77, 347–50; GW to Henry Lee, 20 Jan. 1793, *WGW* 32:310.

23. Freeman et al., *Washington* 6:379, 383–84; Flexner, *Indispensable Man,* 265–74; TJ to JM, 1 Oct. 1792, *PJM,* 14:374; Elkins and McKitrick, *Age of Federalism,* 292; In 1796 GW followed JM's advice of four years earlier by issuing his Farewell Address in mid-September.

24. Twohig, *Journal of the Proceedings of the President,* 53–54. The Federalists, like the Republicans, favored GW's reelection for partisan purposes. See AH to GW, 30 July 1792, *PAH* 12:137–39. Early in October, JM learned from TJ that GW still "declares himself quite undecided about retiring," especially "if strong motives against it exist. He thinks if he declares a month before the day of election [by the Electoral College] it will be sufficient: consequently that he may make his declaration even after the meeting of Congress." Knowing that GW would not withhold such an important announcement to the last minute, JM correctly attributed the president's statement to wishful thinking. TJ's use of the words "declares himself" also cast doubt on the assertion (TJ to JM, 1 Oct. 1792, *PJM* 14:374). JM's 11 Oct. 1792 letter to James Monroe assumes that GW would serve another term (ibid., 382).

25. Elkins and McKitrick, *Age of Federalism,* 295–302; Risjord, *Chesapeake Politics,* 422; Notes on the Giles Resolutions, 2 Mar. 1793, *PTJ* 25:311; Flexner, *Washington* 3:384–85. For an excellent analysis, see Sheridan, "Thomas Jefferson and the Giles Resolutions," 589–608.

26. Resolutions Censuring the Secretary of the Treasury [speech before Congress], 1 Mar. 1793, JM to TJ, 12 Apr. 1793, *PJM* 14:459–60, 15:7; Elkins and McKitrick, *Age of Federalism*, 295–302; Cooke, *Hamilton*, 125–26.

27. Leary, *That Rascal Freneau*, 220–23, 236.

28. GW to JM, 20 May 1792, 14 Oct. 1793, *PJM* 14:312, 15:127; GW to the Secretaries of the Treasury and War, 27 Feb. 1793, *WGW* 32:361. JM had, at GW's request, helped write the 1790 and 1791 annual messages. GW appears to have written his brief second inaugural address himself (Notes of a Conversation with GW, 1 Oct. 1792, *PTJ* 24:433–35). On GW as a "president above party," see Ketcham, *Presidents above Party,* 89–93. On GW's attempt to pursue a middle course and ER's role in helping to identify it, see Reardon, *Randolph,* 189, 207, 220–22, 231, 238, 248–49. Reardon concludes that ER supplanted JM as GW's right-hand man: "Randolph . . . unequivocally supported and sustained the cautious statesmanship of the President and helped him steer a middle course that would avoid the dangerous shoals of partisan diplomacy. By August of 1793 Randolph had become Washington's most trusted advisor, a position he had earned through his uncompromising loyalty to the President and his policies" (ibid., 238).

8. "Neutrality"

1. GW to Catherine Macaulay Graham, 9 Jan. 1790, to Marquis de La Luzerne, 29 Apr. 1790, *PGW-PS* 4:553, 5:358–60; JM to Edmund Pendleton, 4 Mar. 1790, *PJM* 13:86–87. See also Sears, *Washington and the French Revolution,* chaps. 1–5. Lafayette described the present as "a tribute which I owe as a son to my adopted father, as an aide-de-camp to my general, as a missionary of liberty to its patriarch" (Lafayette to GW, 17 Mar. 1790, *PGW-PS* 5:242). Lafayette, twenty-five years the president's junior (JM was nineteen years younger than the president), enjoyed a more emotional—even filial— relationship with GW that the congressman never experienced.

2. GW to Marquis de La Luzerne, 29 Apr. 1790, GW to Comte de Rochambeau, 10 Aug. 1790, *PGW-PS* 5:360, 6:231; GW to Marquis de Lafayette, 10 June 1792, *WGW* 32:54; JM to ER, 21 Mar. 1790, to Hubbard Taylor, 11 Oct. 1791, Resolution on the French Constitution [speech before Congress], 10 Mar. 1792, *PJM* 13:110, 14:78–79, 250–52; Memoranda of Consultations with the President, 12 Mar. 1792, *PTJ* 23:260–61; *DPCUS,* 2d Cong., 1st sess., 457.

3. JM to George Nicholas, 15 Mar. 1793, *PJM* 14:472; Sears, *Washington and the French Revolution,* chap. 6; GW to TJ, 20 Oct. 1792, *PTJ* 24:505. See also Memoranda of Consultations with the President, 12 Mar. 1792, Notes of a Meeting on Edmond Charles Genet, 20 Aug. 1793, ibid., 23:260–61, 26:730–32. If the two men did not exchange their views directly, then JM would have heard the president's opinions through TJ, who thought Gouverneur Morris made GW pessimistic about French affairs (Memoranda of Consultations with the President, 12 Mar. 1792, ibid., 23:260–61). GW knew JM's position from congressional speeches in the newspapers. See, for example, Resolution on the French Constitution, 10 Mar. 1792, and Repayment of Bank Loan, 26 Dec. 1792, *PJM* 14:250–52, 430–32.

4. Elkins and McKitrick, *Age of Federalism,* 336–39. GW originally entitled his pronouncement "A Proclamation" (illustration following page 25:400 in *PTJ*). Tobias Lear, however, called it a "Proclamation of Neutrality" (Twohig, *Journal of the Proceedings of the President,* 117–18).

5. JM to TJ, 13, 19, 29 June 1793, *PJM* 15:29, 33, 38.

6. TJ to JM, 11 Aug. 1793, ibid., 58. For examples of TJ's misleading accounts of cabinet meetings, see his letters to JM during May, June, and July 1793, ibid., 15ff.

7. Leary, *That Rascal Freneau,* 233–36; JM to TJ, 29 June 1793, TJ to JM, 9 June 1793, *PJM* 15:38, 27; Notes on James Cole Montflorence and on Federalist Intrigues, 18 July 1793, *PTJ* 26:522–23. Elkins and McKitrick suggest that Freneau and Veritas "may well have been one and the same" (*Age of Federalism,* 360).

8. Notes of Conversations with GW, 23 May, 2 Aug. 1793, *PTJ* 26:102, 601–3; Timothy Dwight to Oliver Wolcott, 1793, Gibbs, *Memoirs of the Administrations of Washington and Adams* 1:107.

9. Pacificus I–VII, 29 June–27 July 1793, *PAH* 15:33ff.; TJ to JM, 19 June, 7 July 1793, *PJM* 15:33, 43.

10. JM to TJ, 18, 22, 30 July 1793, *PJM* 15:44–45, 46–47, 48–49.

11. TJ to JM, 3, 11 Aug. 1793, JM to TJ, 30 July, 12, 20, 22 Aug. 1793, ibid., 50, 54–55, 48, 59–60, 62, 63.

12. Helvidius I, 24 Aug. 1793, ibid., 66–73. GW probably would not have recognized whose *Federalist* essays JM quoted (see chap. 5, note 27 above).

13. Helvidius I–V, 24 Aug.–18 Sept. 1793, ibid., 66ff.; Ketcham, *Madison,* 346–48.

14. JM to TJ, 8 May 1793, *PJM* 15:12. On the Genet mission, see Ammon, *Genet Mission,* and Sheridan, "Recall of Edmond Charles Genet."

15. TJ to JM, 11 Aug. 1793, JM to TJ, 16 Sept. 1793, *PJM* 15:57, 113. All five Helvidius essays address Pacificus I (Fleet, "Madison's 'Detached Memoranda,'" 567–68).

16. GW to the Merchants and Traders of the City of Philadelphia, 17 May 1793, to Alexander White, 23 Nov. 1793, *WGW* 32:460, 33:155–56. TJ recorded that the author of Pacificus "is universally known" (TJ to JM, 3 Aug. 1793, *PJM* 15:50).

17. Notes of Cabinet Meetings, 18, 21 Nov. 1793, *PTJ* 27:400, 411–12; Fifth Annual Address to Congress, 3 Dec. 1793, *WGW* 33:164. See also Memorandum of Matters to Be Communicated to Congress, Nov. 1793, ibid., 160; House of Representatives to the President, 6 Dec. 1793, *PJM* 15:160; Fisher Ames to George Richards Minot, 6 Dec. 1793, Ames, *Works of Ames* 1:132; William Loughton Smith to Edward Rutledge, 6 Dec. 1793, Rodgers, "Letters of William Loughton Smith," 50. ER drafted the address's passages on the proclamation (Readon, *Randolph,* 245–46).

18. JM to Archibald Stuart, 1 Sept. 1793, to TJ, 2 Sept. 1793, *PJM* 15:87–88, 92; Ammon, *Genet Mission,* 132–46.

19. Resolutions on Franco-American Relations, 27 Aug. 1793, *PJM* 15:76–80; Elkins and McKitrick, *Age of Federalism,* 364–65; Caroline Resolves concerning Relations with France, 10 Sept. 1793, Edmund Pendleton to GW, 11 Sept. 1793, Mays, *Letters and Papers of Pendleton* 2:608–12, 613–15; GW to Edmund Pendleton, 23 Sept. 1793, *WGW* 33:91–92; *Independent Chronicle* (Boston), 17 Oct. 1793.

20. GW to JM, 14 Oct. 1793, JM to GW, 24 Oct. 1793, John Beckley to JM, 20 Nov. 1793, *PJM* 15:126–28, 129–31, 140–41.

21. Malone, *Jefferson* 3:8–10; Notes of a Conversation with GW, 6 Aug. 1793, *PTJ* 26:627–30. TJ stayed in office to the end of 1793.

22. JM to TJ, 2 Sept. 1793, *PJM* 15:94. TJ enclosed an account of his conversation with GW in his 11 Aug. 1793 letter to JM (ibid., 58).

23. JM to TJ, 2 Sept. 1793, ibid., 94; Henry Lee to JM, 3 Mar. 1834, Hunt, *Writings of Madison* 9:532–33.

24. TJ to JM, 19 May, 9 June 1793, *PJM* 15:19, 26–27.

25. JM to TJ, 2 Sept. 1793, ibid., 93; Notes of a Conversation with GW, 6 Aug. 1793, *PTJ* 26:627–30.

26. TJ to JM, 11 Aug. 1793, *PJM* 15:57; Reardon, *Randolph,* 189, 250–51; Fleet, "Madison's 'Detached Memoranda,'" 541.

27. Report on Commerce, 16 Dec. 1793, *PTJ* 27:532–79; Commercial Discrimination [speeches before Congress], 3 Jan.–5 Feb. 1794, *PJM* 15:167ff.; Elkins and McKitrick, *Age of Federalism,* 375–88.

28. GW to Congress, 5 Dec. 1793, 24 Feb. 1794, to the Senate, 26 Feb. 1794, to Richard Henry Lee, 15 Apr. 1794, *WGW* 33:171–72, 281, 282 n.8, 331; *American State Papers, Foreign Relations* 1:141–246, 325–26.

29. Elkins and McKitrick, *Age of Federalism,* 389; Resolution on Nonintercourse with Great Britain, 18 Apr. 1794, *PJM* 15:312–13; GW to the Senate, 16 Apr. 1794, *WGW* 33:332–3; *DPCUS,* 3d Cong., 1st sess., 602–3, 605, 90.

30. GW to ER, 15 Apr. 1794, to Tobias Lear, 6 May 1794, *WGW* 33:329–30, 356–57; Reardon, *Randolph,* 262–63, 266–69; JM to TJ, 14 Apr. 1794, *PJM* 15:307; AH to GW, 14 Apr. 1794, *PAH* 16:261–79. Sensing their advantage in the president's councils, Federalist senators Oliver Ellsworth, Rufus King, and Caleb Strong pressed GW to name a special envoy to Britain (King, *Life and Correspondence of King* 1:517–18). By naming Jay, GW set a precedent for executive initiative in diplomatic crises (Elkins and McKitrick, *Age of Federalism,* 388–89).

31. JM to TJ, 14, 28 Apr., 11 May 1794, *PJM* 15:307, 316, 327–28.

32. Military Establishment [speech before Congress], 30 May 1794, JM to TJ, 14 Mar., 25 May, 1 June 1794, ibid., 284, 339–40, 337, 340; Oliver Ellsworth to Oliver Wolcott, Sr., 16 Apr. 1794, Gibbs, *Memoirs of the Administrations of Washington and Adams* 1:135.

33. James Monroe to TJ, 26, 27 May 1794, Hamilton, *Writings of Monroe* 1:298, 300; Brown, *Autobiography of Monroe,* 57–58; Ammon, *Monroe,* 112–14. JM also recommended Aaron Burr. It is unclear whether GW offered the envoyship to JM in person or through ER.

34. JM to TJ, 26 May 1794, *PJM* 15:338.

9. Domestic Order and Disorder

1. JM to TJ, 2 Mar. 1794, *PJM* 15:270. GW last used "My Dear Sir" on 14 Oct. 1793. Beginning 10 Jan. 1794, he opened his letters with "Dear Sir" (ibid., 126, 175).

2. TJ to JM, 29 June 1793, GW to JM, 10 Jan., 8 Feb. 1794, ibid., 15:41, 175, 254; GW to Sir John Sinclair, 20 July 1794, *WGW* 33:438–40. In addition to JM, GW consulted TJ, John Adams, and Pennsylvania assemblyman Richard Peters about Sinclair's suggestion. On GW's interest in farming, see the many letters he wrote to his Mount Vernon managers in *WGW,* vols. 30–35. On JM's growing affinity for agriculture, see Ketcham, *Madison,* 372–75.

3. McCoy, *Last of the Fathers,* 253–322; Ketcham, *Madison,* 12–13, 148–49, 224–25, 315–16, 374–75, 551–52, 625–30. On GW and slavery, see Flexner, *Washington* 4:112–25, 432–48. On JM and slavery, see "James Madison's Attitude toward the Negro." JM's secretary and close friend Edward Coles claimed that in lieu of freeing his slaves in his will,

JM bequeathed them to his wife with the understanding that she would emancipate them upon her death. If Coles is correct, then Dolley Madison reneged on her promise (Coles to Hugh Blair Grigsby, 23 Dec. 1854, Grigsby Papers; Coles to Nelly C. Willis, 10 Dec. 1855, Coles Papers).

4. Brant, *Madison* 3:406; Catharine Coles to Dolley Payne Todd, 1 June 1794, *PJM* 15:342. On Dolley Payne Todd Madison and her courtship, see Brant, *Madison* 3:401–14; Ketcham, *Madison*, 376–83; Moore, *Madisons*, 1–20; Anthony, *Dolly Madison*, 1–54, 79–97; Arnett, *Mrs. James Madison*, 1–69; Sifton, "'What a Dread Prospect,'" 182–88.

5. On Harewood, see Wayland, *Washingtons and Their Homes*, 129–49. Samuel Washington (1734–1781) was GW's oldest full brother. Charles Town was named after the president's youngest full brother. On George Steptoe Washington (1773–1809), the son of Samuel Washington and his fourth wife, Anne Steptoe Allerton Washington, see *DGW* 4:93.

6. Cutts, *Memoirs and Letters of Dolley Madison*, 15–16. Lucia Cutts was Anna Payne Cutts's granddaughter. Brant considers this story "dubious" but admits that it "fits the facts" (*Madison* 3:408). Other writers place more faith in the anecdote. See Ketcham, *Madison*, 379–80; Anthony, *Dolly Madison*, 83–84; Arnett, *Mrs. Madison*, 59–60; Moore, *Madisons*, 11. On Martha Washington's maternal instincts, see Flexner, *Washington* 4:433.

7. William W. Wilkins to Dolley Payne Todd, 22 Aug. 1794, Dolley Payne Todd to Eliza Collins Lee, 16 Sept. 1794, *PJM* 15:352, 357; Anthony, *Dolly Madison*, 84–89; Arnett, *Mrs. James Madison*, 60; Moore, *Madisons*, 11–17. On the Washingtons' brief engagement, see Higginbotham, "Washington and Revolutionary Asceticism," in Hofstra, *Washington and the Virginia Backcountry*. On "marriage trauma," see Cott, *Bonds of Womanhood*, 74–83.

8. JM to Dolley Payne Todd, 18 Aug. 1794, to James Madison, Sr., 5 Oct. 1794, *PJM* 15:351, 361–62; Wayland, *Washingtons and Their Homes*, 129–49; *DGW* 4:11, 13. The Hites later erected their home Belle Grove on the site of Old Hall.

9. GW to Marquis de Chastellux, 25 Apr. 1788, *PGW–CS* 6:228; GW to Henry Lee, 21 July 1793, *WGW* 33:24. Don Higginbotham writes that GW "possessed healthy attitudes about romantic love and marriage," and "that he prized domestic felicity above all other pleasures and rewards" (Higginbotham, "Washington and Revolutionary Asceticism," in Hofstra, *Washington and the Virginia Backcountry*, 234–35).

10. Henry Lee to JM, 23 Sept. 1794, *PJM* 15:359; Arnett, *Mrs. James Madison*, 62.

11. JM to James Madison, Sr., 5 Oct. 1794, *PJM* 15:361; *DGW* 6:191.

12. JM to Edmund Pendleton, 2 Jan. 1791, *PJM* 13:344. The excise did not pass without considerable localist opposition. For a legislative history, see Slaughter, *Whiskey Rebellion*, 95–106.

13. Slaughter, *Whiskey Rebellion*, 95, 109–24, 158–89.

14. GW to David Humphreys, 20 July 1791, to AH, 7 Sept. 1792, *WGW* 31:319, 32:143. On GW's southern tour, see *DGW* 6:96–163; Slaughter, *Whiskey Rebellion*, 143–57. For how GW's attitudes toward the West shaped his response to the Whiskey Rebellion, see ibid., 75–90. On GW's legal suit against his Washington County, Pennsylvania, tenants, see *PGW-CS* 2:338–58.

15. Elkins and McKitrick, *Age of Federalism*, 451–61.

16. Ibid., 485; Slaughter, *Whiskey Rebellion*, 154–57, 163–68; GW to Henry Lee, 26 Aug. 1794, *WGW* 33:475–76.

17. Third Annual Address to Congress, 25 Oct. 1791, Proclamation, 15 Sept. 1792, Fourth Annual Address to Congress, 6 Nov. 1792, *WGW* 31:399–400, 32:150–51, 208–9; GW to AH, 17 Sept. 1792, *PAH* 12:391–92; Slaughter, *Whiskey Rebellion,* 144–51.

18. Notes on William Loughton Smith's *Politics and Views,* c. 4 Nov. 1792, Address of the House of Representatives to the President, 9 Nov. 1792, JM to Edmund Pendleton, 16 Nov. 1792, *PJM* 14:399, 403–4, 408–9.

19. Sydnor, *Gentlemen Freeholders,* chap. 7.

20. Slaughter, *Whiskey Rebellion,* 175–89.

21. GW to Charles Mynn Thurston, 10 Aug. 1794, *WGW* 33:465; Flexner, *Washington* 4:166–71; Kohn, "Washington Administration's Decision to Crush the Whiskey Rebellion," 567–84; Slaughter, *Whiskey Rebellion,* 151–52, 168, 205–21; Elkins and McKitrick, *Age of Federalism,* 478–83.

22. JM to Hubbard Taylor, 15 Nov. 1794, to TJ, 16 Nov. 1794, to James Monroe, 4 Dec. 1794, *PJM* 15:378, 379, 406.

23. George Nicholas to JM, 29 Nov. 1794, TJ to JM, 30 Oct., 28 Dec. 1794, ibid., 393–94, 366, 426–27.

24. ER to GW, 11, 21 Oct. 1794, Conway, *Omitted Chapters,* 194–95, 230; GW to ER, 16 Oct. 1794, *WGW* 34:3.

25. GW to Thornton Fleming et al., 30 Jan. 1793, *WGW* 32:321; ER to GW, 21 Oct. 1794, Conway, *Omitted Chapters,* 230.

26. Editorial Note, Republican Society of South Carolina to JM, 12 Mar. 1794, *PJM* 15:153, 279–80; Fisher Ames to Thomas Dwight, 29 Nov. 1794, Ames, *Works of Ames* 1:153–54; Cobbett, *Porcupine's Works* 2:45.

27. GW to ER, 16 Oct. 1794, to John Jay, 1–5 Nov. 1794, Sixth Annual Address to Congress, 19 Nov. 1794, *WGW* 34:3–4, 17–18, 28–35; Freeman et al., *Washington* 7:220; Flexner, *Washington* 4:192.

28. JM to James Monroe, 4 Dec. 1794, to TJ, 30 Nov. 1794, Address of the House of Representatives to the President, 21 Nov. 1794, *PJM* 15:406, 396, 386–87.

29. JM to TJ, 30 Nov., 21 Dec. 1794, to James Monroe, 4 Dec. 1794, House Address to the President [speech before Congress], 27 Nov. 1794, ibid., 396–97, 419, 406, 390–91; *DPCUS,* 3d Cong., 2d sess., 793–94, 796; Elkins and McKitrick, *Age of Federalism,* 484–88.

30. JM to TJ, 30 Nov. 1794, to James Monroe, 4 Dec. 1794, *PJM* 15:397, 406; *DPCUS,* 3d Cong., 2d sess., 950; Baldwin, *Whiskey Rebels,* 260–62.

31. *Political Observations,* 20 Apr. 1795, *PJM* 15:522.

32. Notes of a Meeting on Edmond Charles Genet, 2 Aug. 1793, *PTJ* 26:601–3; Flexner, *Washington* 4:191. Far from dissuading the president, ER recommended the verbal assault on the societies (ER to GW, 11 Oct. 1794, Conway, *Omitted Chapters,* 195).

33. Fleet, "Madison's 'Detached Memoranda,'" 561–62; Proclamation, 1 Jan. 1795, Richardson, *Messages and Papers* 1:171–72.

34. JM to TJ, 23 Mar. 1795, GW to JM, 6 Dec. 1795, Bartholomew Dandridge, Jr., to JM, 31 Mar. 1795, *PJM* 15:493, 16:140 and n.1, 15:505; GW to Sir John Sinclair, 31 Dec. 1795, 20 Feb. 1796, *WGW* 34:412–13, 468–69.

10. Estrangement and Farewell

1. GW to the Senators, 3 Mar. 1795, *WGW* 131; JM to TJ, 23 Mar. 1795, to James Monroe, 26 Mar. 1795, *PJM* 15:493, 496; Daniel, *Vindication of Edmund Randolph,* 18; Elkins and McKitrick, *Age of Federalism,* 406–14.

2. Freeman et al., *Washington* 7:256 and n.102; Combs, *Jay Treaty,* 161–62.

3. JM to James Monroe, 4 Dec. 1794, to TJ, 11 Jan., 15 Feb. 1794, to Robert R. Livingston, 8 Feb. 1795, Pierce Butler to JM, 12, 17, 24, 26 June 1795, to Robert R. Livingston, 10 Aug. 1795, to Henry Tazewell, 25 Sept. 1795, *PJM* 15:405, 441, 473, 468–69, 16:14–16, 23, 24, 24–25, 47, 94.

4. Petition to the General Assembly of the Commonwealth of Virginia, 12 Oct. 1795, *PJM* 16:102. For a discussion of JM's ideal political economy, see McCoy, *Elusive Republic.*

5. JM to Henry Tazewell, 25 Sept. 1795, Robert R. Livingston to JM, 6 July 1795, JM to Robert R. Livingston, 10 Aug. 1795, *PJM* 16:94, 34–35, 48.

6. Freeman et al., *Washington* 7:260–62 and nn.130–33; GW to AH, 3, 13, 14, 29 July 1795, Remarks on the Jay Treaty, 9–11 July 1795, *PAH* 18:398–400, 461–63, 466–67, 524–25, 404–54 (esp. 451–54). AH resigned as secretary of the treasury in Jan. 1795.

7. GW to ER, 22 July 1795, *WGW* 34:244; Freeman et al., *Washington* 7:285 and n.95, 279 and n.75; Dispatch Number 10, 31 Oct. 1794, Reardon, *Randolph,* 371–80; Flexner, *Washington* 4:222–36. On ER's resignation, see Reardon, *Randolph,* 284–334; Brant, "Randolph, Not Guilty!" 180–98; Tachau, "Washington and the Reputation of Randolph," 15–34.

8. ER to JM, 1 Nov. 1795, JM to James Monroe, 26 Jan. 1796, *PJM* 16:117, 204; Ferling, *Washington,* 462. Reardon finds JM's analysis "perceptive" (*Randolph,* 333). Tachau suggests that JM was "probably . . . secure enough to have attempted a reconciliation between the president and his former secretary of state" but was "not moved to do so" ("Washington and the Reputation of Randolph," 33). I maintain that by 1795 JM neither gave GW unsolicited advice nor interfered with his business. Besides, ER was almost definitely beyond reclamation in the executive's eyes.

9. Daniel, *Vindication of Randolph,* 45; GW to AH, 29 Oct. 1795, AH to GW, 5 Nov. 1795, *PAH* 19:356–58, 395–97; JM to TJ, 7 Feb. 1796, *PJM* 16:215; Flexner, *Washington* 4:248–51; GW to Timothy Pickering, 27 July 1795, *WGW* 34:251. "The offer of the Secretaryship of State to P. Henry is a circumstance which I should not have believed without the most unquestionable testimony," JM exclaimed (JM to TJ, 6 Dec. 1795, *PJM* 16:139).

10. GW to Gouverneur Morris, 22 Dec. 1795, 4 Mar. 1796, to ER, 29, 31 July 1795, to Henry Knox, 20 Sept. 1795, to the Boston Selectmen, 28 July 1795, to John Adams, 20 Aug. 1795, *WGW* 34:403, 483, 256, 266, 311, 252–54 and n.66, 280; JM to James Monroe, 20 Dec. 1795, Joseph Jones to JM, 17 Feb. 1796, TJ to JM, 27 Mar. 1796, *PJM* 16:169, 225, 281.

11. The Defense, 22 July 1795–9 Jan. 1796, GW to AH, 29 July 1795, *PAH* 18:475ff., 524–25; Editorial Note, Petition to the General Assembly of the Commonwealth of Virginia, 12 Oct. 1795, *PJM* 16:62–69, 95–104; *JHDV,* Nov. 1795, 28; Farnham, "Virginia Amendments of 1795," 75–88. Rufus King contributed ten additional essays to the series.

12. GW to AH, 29 Oct., 16 Nov. 1795, *PAH* 19:359, 431; Seventh Annual Address, 8 Dec. 1795, *WGW* 34:386–93; James Monroe to JM, 29 Oct. 1795, George Nicholas to

JM, 6 Nov. 1795, James Jackson to JM, 17 Nov. 1795, Robert Simons to JM, c. 1 Feb. 1796, JM to TJ, 13, 27 Dec. 1795, to James Monroe, 20 Dec. 1795, Address of the House of Representatives to the President, c. 14 Dec. 1795, *PJM* 16:115, 120, 129, 210, 163, 173, 169, 164–66; *DPCUS,* 4th Cong., 1st sess., 144–48. Of the House's 105 members, Fisher Ames counted 56 Republicans and 49 Federalists (Ames to Thomas Dwight, 30 Dec. 1795, Ames, *Works of Ames* 1:180).

13. Flexner, *Washington* 4:261–64; GW to AH, 29 Oct. 1795, AH to GW, 19 Nov. 1795, *PAH* 19:354–55, 452–53; GW to JM, 22 Jan., 6 Mar. 1796, *PJM* 16:200–201, 252; *DPCUS,* 4th Cong., 1st sess., 423, 798, 1202; *American State Papers, Miscellaneous* 1:149.

14. JM to Edmund Pendleton, 7 Feb. 1796, to TJ, 13, 27 Dec. 1795, Editorial Note, JM to James Monroe, 20 Dec. 1795, 26 Feb. 1796, to James Madison, Sr., 17 Jan. 1796, *PJM* 16:217, 163, 173, 143, 170, 233, 191; *DPCUS,* 4th Cong., 1st sess., 455.

15. Freeman et al., *Washington* 7:347–48; Combs, *Jay Treaty,* 174–75; Editorial Note, Jay's Treaty [speech before Congress], 7 Mar. 1796, *PJM* 16:144–45, 254; Fleet, "Madison's 'Detached Memoranda,'" 544–45.

16. Jay's Treaty [speech before Congress], 10 Mar. 1796, JM to TJ, 4 Apr. 1796, *PJM* 16:255–63, 286; *DPCUS,* 4th Cong., 1st sess., 426–44.

17. GW to Oliver Wolcott, Jr., 1 Mar. 1796, to the House of Representatives, 30 Mar. 1796, *WGW* 34:482, 35:2–5; AH to GW, 7, 29 Mar. 1796, GW to AH, 31 Mar. 1796, *PAH* 20:68–69, 85–103, 103–5. For the vote cited by GW, see *RFC* 2:382–83. GW and JM almost definitely sided with the majority on this vote, but the latter subsequently advocated legislative sanction for some treaties.

18. Fisher Ames to George Richards Minot, 2 Apr. 1796, Ames, *Works of Ames* 1:191; JM to TJ, 8 Nov. 1795, *PJM* 16:121; Ketcham, *Madison,* 361–62.

19. JM to TJ, 4, 11 Apr. 1796, to James Monroe, 18 Apr. 1796, *PJM* 286, 308, 333.

20. JM to TJ, 4 Apr. 1796, ibid., 286; John Beckley to James Monroe, 2 Apr. 1796, Beckley Papers, VHi; *DPCUS,* 4th Cong., 1st sess., 771–72. The caucus was the first of its kind ever held.

21. Fleet, "Madison's 'Detached Memoranda,'" 543–45; JM to TJ, 11 Apr. 1796, Jay's Treaty [speech before Congress], 6 Apr. 1796, *PJM* 16:308, 290–301. JM's 2 Feb. 1791 speech referred to the Federal Convention's decision not to include the granting of charters of incorporation among Congress's enumerated powers. See ibid., 13:34, and *RFC* 2:325, 615–16.

22. JM to TJ, 11 Apr. 1796, *PJM* 16:308.

23. *RFC* 2:394; Memoranda of Consultations with the President, 9 Apr. 1792, *PTJ* 23:263.

24. JM to James Madison, Sr., 11 Apr. 1796, Jay's Treaty [speech before Congress], 15 Apr. 1796, *PJM* 16:310, 313–25.

25. Elkins and McKitrick, *Age of Federalism,* 431–49; Kurtz, *Presidency of John Adams,* 59–77; JM to TJ, 23 Apr., 9 May 1796, to James Monroe, 18 Apr. 1796, to James Madison, Sr., 25 Apr. 1796, *PJM* 16:335, 352, 333, 338. The admonition to "follow where Washington leads" appeared in a Boston circular letter and was reprinted in the 7 May 1796 *Philadelphia Gazette* (ibid., 352 n.1).

26. Ketcham, *Madison,* 365; Editorial Note, JM to TJ, 1, 22 May 1796, to James Monroe, 14 May 1796, *PJM* 16:149, 343, 364, 357. JM's prestige remained undiminished in Virginia. In November 1796 he received assurances that he would be unanimously elected governor if he chose to run (ibid., 414).

27. GW to Edward Carrington, 1 May 1796, *WGW* 35:32.

28. For a study of public opinion during the Federalist Era, see Buel, *Securing the Revolution.*

29. Marshall, *Washington* 5:206–7.

30. GW to Charles Carroll, 1 May 1796, *WGW* 35:30. In May and December 1796, JM attended state dinners at the executive mansion (*PJM* 16:355, 430). JM's visits to Mount Vernon ended in 1791.

31. GW to Thomas Pinckney, 22 May 1796, *WGW* 35:62; AH to GW, 10 May 1796, GW to AH, 15 May 1796, *PAH* 20:173, 174–75.

32. GW to AH, 15 May 1796, *PAH* 20:174–78; Farewell Address [First Draft], 15 May 1796, *WGW* 35:51–61.

33. GW to JM, 12 May 1796, *PJM* 16:355. On JM's supposed participation in the preparation of the draft GW sent AH, see Paltsits, *Washington's Farewell Address,* 30, 241–43; Freeman et al., *Washington* 7:381 and n.288; Gilbert, *To the Farewell Address,* 125, 168.

34. Gilbert, *To the Farewell Address,* 124.

35. AH to GW, 30 July 1796, GW to AH, 25 Aug. 1796, *PAH* 20:265, 308.

36. Ibid.; Draft of GW's Farewell Address, 30 July 1796, ibid., 265–88. For a fuller discussion of AH's use of JM's draft, see ibid., 169–70.

37. Draft of GW's Farewell Address, 30 July, GW to AH, 25 Aug., 1 Sept. 1796, AH to GW, 5 Sept. 1796, ibid., 265–88, 307–9, 311–14, 317–18; Farewell Address, 19 Sept. 1796, *WGW* 35:214–38.

38. AH had suggested "that the declaration of your intention should be suspended as long as possible & suffer me to add that you should *really hold the thing undecided to the last moment*" since it would force the parties to "electioneer conditionally" (AH to GW, 5 July 1796, *PAH* 20:247).

39. DeConde, "Washington's Farewell," 641–58; GW to AH, 26 June 1796, *PAH* 20:239. My interpretation of GW's behavior follows Hofstadter, *Idea of a Party System,* 96–99; Charles, *Origins of the American Party System,* 44; and DeConde, *Entangling Alliance,* 469. Elkins and McKitrick hesitate to call GW a Federalist partisan (see *Age of Federalism,* 495).

40. JM to James Monroe, 29 Sept. 1796, *PJM* 16:403–4.

41. JM to TJ, 27 June 1823, Hunt, *Writings of Madison* 9:138.

42. JM to TJ, 8 Feb. 1825, Rives and Fendall, *Letters and Writings of Madison* 3:482; Gilbert, *To the Farewell Address,* 169. Arthur Markowitz judiciously concludes that the valedictory was "a product of the combined pens of Washington, Hamilton, and to a lesser extent Madison, with the President serving as the editor-in-chief" ("Washington's Farewell," 189).

43. JM to TJ, 27 June 1823, Hunt, *Writings of Madison* 9:137–39. On JM's defense of TJ's legacy, see Koch, *Jefferson and Madison,* 260–90. AH's authorship did not become public knowledge until 1859 (Flexner, *Washington* 4:306).

44. Eighth Annual Address to Congress, 7 Dec. 1796, GW to Congress, 19 Jan. 1797, *WGW* 35:318–19, 369–70; JM to TJ, 10, 19, 25 Dec. 1796, 15, 29 Jan., 5 Feb. 1797, *PJM* 16:425, 433, 435, 456, 476, 483–84; Address of the House of Representatives to GW, 15 Dec. 1796, Reply of the President, 16 Dec. 1796, Richardson, *Messages and Papers* 1:199–201, 201–2; *DPCUS,* 4th Cong., 2d sess., 1591, 1598, 1611–12, 1666–68.

45. GW to AH, 22 Jan. 1797, AH to GW, 25–31 Jan. 1797, *PAH* 20:476–77, 480–81. Six weeks later JM refused John Adams's offer to become a special envoy to France (The Anas, 2 Mar. 1797, Ford, *Writings of Jefferson* 1:335).

46. Alexander White to JM, 26 Sept. 1796, *PJM* 16:401–2.

47. Alexander White to JM, 2 Dec. 1796, National University [speech before Congress], 26 Dec. 1796, ibid., 421, 437; *DPCUS,* 4th Cong., 2d Sess., 1601, 1695, 1697–1702; *Journal of the House of Representatives* 2:613.

48. GW to JM, 16 Dec. 1796, *PJM* 16:430; Griswold, *Republican Court,* 416; GW to Henry Knox, 2 Mar. 1797, *WGW* 35:409; Freeman et al., *Washington* 7:432, 434 and nn.167–68, 444.

49. Baker, "Washington after the Revolution," 21:192 n.1; Adair, "James Madison's Autobiography," 203.

50. GW to James McHenry, 3 Apr. 1797, to James Anderson, 7 Apr. 1797, *PGW-RS* 1:71, 79–81; JM to James Monroe, 11 Dec. 1798, *PJM* 17:184.

51. JM to James Monroe, 29 Sept. 1796, 17 Dec. 1797, to TJ, 19 Dec. 1796, 22 Jan. 1797, 21 Jan., 13, 20 May, 29 Dec. 1798, Political Reflections, 23 Feb. 1799, *PJM* 16:404, 17:61–62, 16:433, 471, 17:69, 130, 134, 191, 237–43.

52. GW to Charles Cotesworth Pinckney, 4 Dec. 1797, *PGW-RS* 1:502–3; GW to John Adams, 4 July 1798, to William Vans Murray, 10 Aug. 1798, to Lafayette, 25 Dec. 1798, to Bushrod Washington, 5 May 1799, to Charles Carroll, 2 Aug. 1798, to William Heth, 5 Aug. 1798, *WGW* 36:313–14, 406, 37:66, 201, 36:384, 389.

53. GW to Henry Knox, 9 Aug. 1798, to James McHenry, 5 July, 15 Oct. 1798, 17 Nov. 1799, to John Adams, 13 July 1798, to Charles Carroll, 2 Aug. 1798, *WGW* 36:398, 318–20, 491, 37:428–29, 36:327–29, 384. On Congress's war measures, see Kohn, *Eagle and Sword,* 224–29; GW to AH, 27 Oct. 1799, *PAH* 23:568–70.

54. James Monroe, *View of the Conduct of the Executive;* JM to TJ, 21 Jan. 1798, James Monroe to JM, 5 July, 1 Aug., 1 Sept. 1796, 24 Sept. 1797, *PJM* 17:69, 16:374–77, 387–89, 392–94, 17:48–49; GW to AH, 8 May 1796, *PAH* 20:162–63; Remarks on James Monroe's *View of the Conduct of the Executive,* Mar. 1798, *WGW* 35:39, 36:194–237. "Poor Washington into what hands has he fallen," wrote Monroe in his letter of 1 Sept. For an assessment of Monroe's diplomacy, see Elkins and McKitrick, *Age of Federalism,* 498–513.

55. Virginia Resolutions, 21 Dec. 1798, *PJM* 17:185–90. On the Alien and Sedition Acts, see Smith, *Freedom's Fetters.* On the Virginia Resolutions, see Koch and Ammon, "Virginia and Kentucky Resolutions," 145–76.

56. GW to William Vans Murray, 26 Dec. 1798, to John Marshall, 30 Dec. 1798, to Bushrod Washington, 31 Dec. 1798, *WGW* 37:72, 76, 81.

57. Editorial Note, Political Reflections, 23 Feb. 1798, *PJM* 17:211–14, 237–43.

58. Freeman et al., *Washington* 7:435–36; GW to Jeremiah Wadsworth, 6 Mar. 1797, to Timothy Pickering, 11 Dec. 1797, *PGW-RS* 1:117, 515; GW to Timothy Pickering, 4 Aug. 1799, *WGW* 37:323.

59. JM to TJ, 18 Feb., 12 Mar., 20 May, 3, 10 June 1798, *PJM* 17:82, 90, 134, 142, 150; Kurtz, *Presidency of Adams,* 294. On 4 July 1798 JM composed a holiday toast to "G. W. the Hero of liberty" (Toasts for an American Dinner, 4 July 1798, PJM 17:161).

60. GW to James McHenry, 27 July 1798, to Patrick Henry, 15 Jan. 1799, *WGW* 36:368, 37:87–90; Mayer, *Son of Thunder,* 471–72.

61. John Taylor to JM, 4 Mar. 1799 (Taylor quoted a letter from Creed Taylor), Elec-

tion of James Monroe [speech before General Assembly], 6 Dec. 1799, *PJM* 17:245–46, 286–87; Beeman, *Old Dominion,* 211–13.

62. Lear, *Letters and Recollections,* 129–32. About TJ's 1802 visit to Mount Vernon, Martha Washington assured John Cotton Smith "that, next to the loss of her husband, it was the most painful occurrence of her life" (Smith, *Correspondence and Miscellanies,* 224–25). A visit from JM would probably have evoked the same sentiment.

63. Death of GW [speech before General Assembly], 18 Dec. 1799, *PJM* 17:295; *Virginia Gazette, and General Advertiser,* 24 Dec. 1799.

64. On JM's temperament, see McCoy, *Last of the Fathers,* chap. 1. GW never absolved those who crossed him. Others, including Horatio Gates, Charles Lee, George Mason, and ER, suffered JM's fate.

Epilogue

1. Julian Boyd, quoted in Smith, *Republic of Letters* 1:xvii.

2. Drew McCoy writes that "the linking of Madison to Washington, quite common in the postwar years [War of 1812] . . . [is] almost inconceivable today." He adds that "so many of the character traits ascribed to the decidedly uncharismatic Washington by his adoring contemporaries—diffidence, modesty, self-restraint, patience, steadiness, and perseverance, for instance—were also especially applicable to Madison's character and behavior, and were therefore central to his countrymen's veneration of him" (*Last of the Fathers,* 16 and n.17).

3. Edward Coles to Hugh Blair Grigsby, 23 Dec. 1854, Grigsby Papers; Fleet, "Madison's 'Detached Memoranda,'" 541.

4. Fleet, "Madison's 'Detached Memoranda,'" 540–41; Ingersoll, "Notes of a Visit to Madison"; Martineau, *Retrospect of Western Travel* 2:11; Moffatt and Carriere, "A Frenchman Visits Norfolk," 202.

5. JM to Jared Sparks, 5 Jan. 1828, Hunt, *Writings of Madison* 9:297.

SELECTED BIBLIOGRAPHY

Manuscript Collections

Historical Society of Pennsylvania
    Tench Coxe Papers
Library of Congress
    Thomas Jefferson Papers
    James Madison Papers
    George Washington Papers
Princeton University
    Edward Coles Papers
Virginia Historical Society
    John Beckley Papers
    Hugh Blair Grigsby Papers

Newspapers

Independent Chronicle (Boston)
Pennsylvania Packet (Philadelphia)
Pennsylvania Packet, and Daily Advertiser (Philadelphia)
Virginia Gazette, and General Advertiser (Richmond)
Virginia Gazette and Weekly Advertiser (Richmond)
Washington Globe

Printed Primary Sources

Abbot, W. W., et al., eds. *The Papers of George Washington.* Confederation Series. 6 vols. Charlottesville, Va., 1992–97.
——. *The Papers of George Washington.* Presidential Series. 6 vols. to date. Charlottesville, Va., 1987—.
Adair, Douglass, ed. "James Madison's Autobiography," *William and Mary Quarterly,* 3d ser., 2 (1945): 191–209.

Adams, John, and Mercy Warren. "The Correspondence between John Adams and Mercy Warren," *Collections of the Massachusetts Historical Society,* 5th ser., 4 (1878): 317–511.

American State Papers: Documents, Legislative and Executive, of the Congress of the United States . . . . 38 vols. Washington, D.C., 1832–61.

Ames, Seth, ed. *The Works of Fisher Ames.* 2 vols. Boston, 1854.

Bowling, Kenneth R., and Helen Veit, eds. *The Diary of William Maclay.* Baltimore, 1988.

Boyd, Julian S., et al., eds. *The Papers of Thomas Jefferson.* 27 vols. to date. Princeton, N.J., 1950—.

Brown, Stuart Gerry, ed. *The Autobiography of James Monroe.* Syracuse, N.Y., 1959.

Burnett, Edmund C., ed. *Letters of Members of the Continental Congress.* 8 vols. Washington, D.C., 1921–36.

Chinard, Gilbert, ed. *Washington as the French Knew Him.* Princeton, N.J., 1940.

Cobbett, William. *Porcupine's Works.* 12 vols. London, 1801.

Cogswell, James Lloyd. "Washington's Reception as President at New York," *Historical Magazine* 4 (1860): 244.

Cutts, Lucia Beverly. *Memoirs and Letters of Dolley Madison . . . Edited by Her Grand-Niece.* Boston, 1886.

Daniel, P. V., ed. *A Vindication of Edmund Randolph, Written by Himself and Published in 1795.* Richmond, 1855.

The Debates and Proceedings in the Congress of the United States . . . . 42 vols. Washington, D.C., 1834–56.

De Pauw, Linda Grant, et al., eds. *Documentary History of the First Federal Congress.* 14 vols. to date. Baltimore, 1972—.

Elliot, Jonathan, ed. *The Debates in the Several State Conventions, on the Adoption of the Federal Constitution . . . .* 5 vols. Washington, D.C., 1861.

Farrand, Max, ed. *The Records of the Federal Convention of 1787.* 1937 rev. ed. in 4 vols. Rept. New Haven 1974.

Ferguson, E. James, et al., eds. *The Papers of Robert Morris, 1781–1784.* 7 vols. to date. Pittsburgh, 1973—.

Fitzpatrick, John C., ed. *The Writings of George Washington, from the Original Manuscript Sources, 1745–1799.* 39 vols. Washington, D.C., 1931–44.

Fleet, Elizabeth, ed. "Madison's 'Detached Memoranda,'" *William and Mary Quarterly,* 3d ser., 3 (1946): 534–68.

Ford, Paul Leicester, ed. *The Writings of Thomas Jefferson.* Federal Ed. 12 vols. New York, 1904–5.

Ford, Worthington Chauncey, et al., eds. *The Journals of the Continental Congress.* 34 vols. Washington, D.C., 1904–37.

——, ed. *The Letters of Joseph Jones of Virginia, 1777–1787.* Washington, D.C., 1889.

Gibbs, George, ed. *Memoirs of the Administrations of Washington and John Adams . . . .* 2 vols. New York, 1846.

Hamilton, Stanislaus Murray, ed. *The Writings of James Monroe . . . .* 7 vols. New York, 1898–1903.

Hening, William Waller, ed. *The Statutes at Large; Being a Collection of all the Laws of Virginia . . . .* 13 vols. Richmond and Philadelphia, 1819–23.

Henry, William Wirt. *Patrick Henry: Life, Correspondence, and Speeches.* 3 vols. New York, 1891.

Hunt, Gaillard, ed. *The Writings of James Madison.* 9 vols. New York, 1900–1910.

Hutchinson, William T., et al., eds. *The Papers of James Madison.* Congressional Series. 17 vols. Chicago and Charlottesville, Va., 1962–91.

Ingersoll, Charles Jared. "Notes of a Visit to Mr. Madison," *Washington Globe,* Aug. 1836.

Jackson, Donald, and Dorothy Twohig, eds. *The Diaries of George Washington.* 6 vols. Charlottesville, Va., 1976–79.

Jensen, Merrill, et al., eds. *The Documentary History of the First Federal Elections.* 4 vols. Madison, Wis., 1976–89.

Journal of the House of Delegates of the Commonwealth of Virginia . . . . Oct. 1781, May 1784, Oct. 1784, Oct. 1785, Oct. 1786, Oct. 1788, Oct. 1789, Nov. 1795. Richmond, 1828.

Journal of the House of Representatives. 9 vols. Washington, D.C., 1826.

Kaminski, John, et al., eds. *The Documentary History of the Ratification of the Constitution.* 14 vols to date. Madison, Wis., 1976—.

King, Charles R., ed. *The Life and Correspondence of Rufus King.* 6 vols. New York, 1894–1900.

Koch, Adrienne, ed. *Notes of Debates in the Federal Convention of 1787 Reported by James Madison.* Athens, Ohio, 1966.

Lear, Tobias. *Letters and Recollections of George Washington . . . .* New York, 1906.

McIlwaine, H. R., et al., eds. *Journals of the Council of State of Virginia.* 5 vols. Richmond, 1931–82.

——. *Official Letters of the Governors of the State of Virginia,* vol. 1, *Letters of Patrick Henry.* Richmond, 1926.

Marchione, Margherita, ed. (Eugene Scalia, trans.). *Philip Mazzei: My Life and Wanderings.* Morristown, N.J., 1980.

Martineau, Harriet. *Retrospect of Western Travel.* 3 vols. London, 1838.

Mays, David John, ed. *The Letters and Papers of Edmund Pendleton.* 2 vols. Charlottesville, Va., 1967.

Moffatt, L. G., and J. M. Carriere, eds. "A Frenchman Visits Norfolk, Fredericksburg, and Orange County, 1816," pt. 2, *Virginia Magazine of History and Biography* 53 (1945): 197–214.

Monroe, James. *A View of the Conduct of the Executive, in the Foreign Affairs of the United States . . . .* Philadelphia, 1797.

Nute, Grace L., ed. "Washington and the Potomac: Manuscripts of the Minnesota Historical Society," pt. 1, *American Historical Review* 28 (1922–23): 503–18.

Proctor, "CC," ed. "After-Dinner Anecdotes of James Madison: Excerpts from Jared Sparks' Journal for 1829–31," *Virginia Magazine of History and Biography* 60 (1952): 255–65.

Rachal, William M. E., ed. *Journal and Letters of Col. John May.* Cincinnati, 1973.

Richardson, James D., ed. *Messages and Papers of the Presidents.* 20 vols. New York, 1897–1916.

[Rives, William Cabell, and Philip R. Fendall, eds.] *Letters and Other Writings of James Madison.* 4 vols. New York, 1865.

Rodgers, George C., ed. "Letters of William Loughton Smith to Edward Rutledge," *South Carolina Historical Magazine* 69 (1968): 1–25.

Rutland, Robert A., ed. *The Papers of George Mason.* 3 vols. Chapel Hill, N.C., 1970.

Sheridan, Eugene R., and Murrin, John M., eds. *Congress at Princeton: Being the Letters of Charles Thomson to Hannah Thomson, June–October, 1783.* Princeton, N.J., 1985.

Sifton, Paul G., ed. "'What a Dread Prospect . . .': Dolley Madison's Plague Year," *Pennsylvania Magazine of History and Biography* 87 (1963): 182–88.

Smith, James Morton, ed. *The Republic of Letters: The Correspondence between James Madison and Thomas Jefferson, 1776–1826.* 3 vols. New York, 1995.

Smith, John Cotton. *The Correspondence and Miscellanies . . . .* New York, 1847.

Smith, Paul H., et al., eds. *Letters of Delegates to Congress, 1774–1789.* 25 vols. to date. Washington, D.C., 1976—.

Smith, William Loughton. *The Politics and Views of a Certain Party Displayed.* N.p., 1792.

Sparks, Jared, ed. *The Writings of George Washington.* 12 vols. Boston, 1837.

Syrett, Harold C., et al., eds. *The Papers of Alexander Hamilton.* 27 vols. New York, 1961–87.

Trumbull, John. *Autobiography, Reminiscences, and Letters of John Trumbull.* New York, 1841.

Trumbull, Jonathan. "Minutes and Occurrences respecting the Siege and Capture of York," *Proceedings of the Massachusetts Historical Society* 14 (1875–76): 331–38.

Twohig, Dorothy, ed. *The Journal of the Proceedings of the President, 1793–1797.* Charlottesville, Va., 1981.

——, et al., eds. *The Papers of George Washington.* Retirement Series. 2 vols. to date, Charlottesville, Va., 1998—.

Watson, Winslow C., ed. *Men and Times of the Revolution, or, Memoirs of Elkanah Watson.* New York, 1856.

Zagarri, Rosemarie, ed. *David Humphreys' "Life of General Washington," with George Washington's "Remarks."* Athens, Ga., 1991.

Secondary Sources

Abbot, W. W. "An Uncommon Awareness of Self: The Papers of George Washington," *Prologue* 21 (1989): 7–12.

Adams, Herbert B. *The Life and Writings of Jared Sparks.* 2 vols. Boston, 1893.

——. "Origin of the Baltimore and Ohio Railroad," *Johns Hopkins Studies in Historical and Political Science,* ser. 3, no. 1, 97–102.

——. "Washington's Interest in the Potomac Company," *Johns Hopkins Studies in Historical and Political Science,* ser. 3, no. 1, 79–91.

——. "Washington's Interest in Western Lands," *Johns Hopkins University Studies in Historical and Political Science,* ser. 3, no. 1, 55–77.

Ammon, Harry. *The Genet Mission.* New York, 1973.

——. *James Monroe: The Quest for National Identity.* New York, 1971.

Anthony, Katherine. *Dolly Madison: Her Life and Times.* Garden City, N.J., 1949.

Arnett, Ethel Stephens. *Mrs. James Madison: The Incomparable Dolley.* Greensboro, N.C., 1972.

Bacon-Foster, Cora. *Early Chapters in the Development of the Patomac Route to the West.* Rept. New York, 1971.

Baker, William S. "Itinerary of General Washington from June 15, 1775, to December 23, 1783," *Pennsylvania Magazine of History and Biography* 14 (1890): 111–42, 253–80, 335–63, 15 (1891): 41–87, 143–90, 291–320, 394–428.

——. "Washington after the Revolution, 1784–1799," *Pennsylvania Magazine of History and Biography* 18 (1894): 389–418, 19 (1895): 22–50, 170–96, 307–39, 428–59, 20 (1896): 41–76, 176–203, 334–69, 473–503, 21 (1897): 20–50, 185–215, 273–98.

Baldwin, Leland D. *Whiskey Rebels: The Story of a Frontier Uprising.* Pittsburgh, 1939.

Banning, Lance. *Jefferson and Madison: Three Conversations from the Founding.* Madison, Wis., 1995.

——. *The Jeffersonian Persuasion: Evolution of a Party Ideology.* Ithaca, N.Y., 1978.

——. *The Sacred Fire of Liberty: James Madison and the Founding of the Federal Republic.* Ithaca, N.Y., 1995.

Beeman, Richard R. *The Old Dominion and the New Nation.* Lexington, Ky., 1972.

Bernier, Olivier. *LaFayette: Hero of Two Worlds.* New York, 1983.

Bickford, Charlene Bangs, and Kenneth R. Bowling. *Birth of the Nation: The First Federal Congress, 1789–1791.* Madison, Wis., 1989.

Boller, Paul F., Jr. *George Washington and Religion.* Dallas, 1963.

Bott, Elizabeth. *Family and Social Network: Roles, Norms, and Extended Relationships in Ordinary Urban Families.* 2d ed. New York, 1971.

Bowen, Clarence Winthrop. *The History of the Centennial Celebration of the Inauguration of George Washington as First President of the United States.* New York, 1892.

Bowling, Kenneth R. "The Bank Bill, the Capital City, and President Washington," *Capitol Studies* 1 (1972): 59–71.

——. *Creating the Federal City, 1774–1800: Potomac Fever.* Washington, D.C., 1988.

——. *The Creation of Washington, D.C.: The Idea and Location of the American Capital.* Fairfax, Va., 1991.

——. "'Good-by Charle': The Lee-Adams Interest and the Demise of Charles Thomson, Secretary of Congress, 1774–1789," *Pennsylvania Magazine of History and Biography* 100 (1976): 314–35.

Brant, Irving. "Edmund Randolph, Not Guilty!" *William and Mary Quarterly,* 3d ser., 7 (1950): 180–98.

——. *The Fourth President: A Life of James Madison.* London, 1970.

——. *James Madison.* 6 vols. Indianapolis and New York, 1941–61.

Breen, T. H. *Tobacco Culture: The Mentality of the Great Tidewater Planters on the Eve of the Revolution.* Princeton, N.J., 1985.

Brighton, Ray. *The Checkered Career of Tobias Lear.* Portsmouth, N.H., 1985.

Brown, Alexander Crosby. *The Patowmack Canal: America's Greatest Eighteenth Century Engineering Achievement.* Alexandria, Va., n.d.

Bryan, Wilhelmus Bogart. *A History of the National Capital.* 2 vols. New York, 1914.

Buell, Richard, Jr. *Securing the Revolution: Ideology in American Politics, 1789–1815.* Ithaca, N.Y., 1972.

Butterfield, L. H. "Elder John Leland: Jeffersonian Itinerant," *Proceedings of the American Antiquarian Society* 62 (1952): 154–242.

Carp, E. Wayne. "Origins of the Nationalist Movement of 1780–1783: Congressional Administration and the Continental Army," *Pennsylvania Magazine of History and Biography* 107 (1983): 363–92.

——. *To Starve the Army at Pleasure: Continental Army Administration and American Political Culture, 1775–1783.* Chapel Hill, N.C., 1984.

Charles, Joseph. *The Origins of the American Party System: Three Essays.* Chapel Hill, N.C., 1956.

Chinard, Gilbert. *Houdon in America.* Baltimore, 1930.

Christian, W. Asbury. *Richmond: Her Past and Present.* Richmond, 1912.

Combs, Jerald A. *The Jay Treaty: Political Battleground of the Founding Fathers.* Berkeley, Calif., 1970.

Conway, Moncure Daniel. *Omitted Chapters of History Disclosed in the Life and Papers of Edmund Randolph . . . .* New York, 1888.

Cooke, Jacob. *Alexander Hamilton.* New York, 1982.

Cott, Nancy. *The Bonds of Womanhood: "Women's Sphere" in New England, 1780–1835.* New Haven, 1977.

Crane, Elaine F. "Publius in the Provinces: Where Was *The Federalist* Reprinted outside New York City?" *William and Mary Quarterly,* 3d ser., 21 (1964): 589–92.

Cunningham, Noble. *The Jeffersonian Republicans: The Formation of Party Organization, 1789–1801.* Chapel Hill, N.C., 1957.

Currie, David. *The Constitution in Congress: The Federalist Period, 1789–1801.* Chicago, 1997.

DeConde, Alexander. *Entangling Alliance: Politics and Diplomacy under George Washington.* Durham, N.C., 1969.

——. "Washington's Farewell, the French Alliance, and the Election of 1796," *Mississippi Valley Historical Review* 43 (1957): 641–58.

Dunaway, Wayland Fuller. *History of the James River and Kanawha Company.* New York, 1922.

Elkins, Stanley, and Eric McKitrick. *The Age of Federalism: The Early American Republic, 1788–1800.* New York, 1993.

Farnham, Thomas J. "The Virginia Amendments of 1795: An Episode in the Opposition to Jay's Treaty," *Virginia Magazine of History and Biography* 75 (1967): 75–88.

Ferguson, E. James. *The Power of the Purse: A History of American Public Finance, 1776–1790.* Chapel Hill, N.C., 1961.

Ferling, John E. *The First of Men: A Life of George Washington.* Knoxville, Tenn., 1988.

Flexner, James Thomas. *George Washington.* 4 vols. Boston, 1965–72.

——. *Washington: The Indispensable Man.* New York, 1974.

Freeman, Douglas Southall, et al. *George Washington: A Biography.* 7 vols. New York, 1948–57.

Garrett, Wilbur E. "George Washington's Patowmack Canal," *National Geographic* 171 (1987): 716–53.

George Washington: Jean Antoine Houdon, Sculptor. Providence, 1931.

Gilbert, Felix. *To the Farewell Address: Ideas of Early American Foreign Policy.* Princeton, N.J., 1961.

Greenstein, Fred I. *The Hidden-Hand Presidency: Eisenhower as Leader.* New York, 1982.

Griswold, Rufus. *The Republican Court; or, American Society in the Days of Washington.* New York, 1867.

Hallam, John. "Houdon's *Washington* in Richmond: Some New Observations," *American Art Journal* 10 (1987): 7380.

Harrison, Constance Cary. "Washington in New York in 1789," *Century Magazine* 37 (1889): 850–59.

Hart, Charles Henry, and Edward Biddle. *Memoirs of the Life and Works of Jean Antoine Houdon.* Philadelphia, 1911.

Henderson, James H. *Party Politics in the Continental Congress.* New York, 1974.

Higginbotham, Don. *George Washington and the American Military Tradition.* Athens, Ga., 1985.

——. *War and Society in Revolutionary America: The Wider Dimensions of Conflict.* Columbia, S.C., 1988.

History of the George Washington Bicentennial Celebration. 5 vols. Washington, D.C., 1932.

Hoffman, Henry B. "President Washington's Cherry Street Residence," *New-York Historical Society Quarterly Bulletin* 23 (1939): 88–102.

Hofstadter, Richard. *The Idea of a Party System: The Rise of Legitimate Opposition in the United States.* Berkeley, Calif., 1969.

Hofstra, Warren, ed. *George Washington and the Virginia Backcountry.* Madison, Wis., 1998.

Holcombe, Arthur. "The Role of Washington in the Framing of the Constitution," *Huntington Library Quarterly* 4 (1956): 317–34.

Hutson, James H. "John Adams' Title Campaign," *New England Quarterly* 41 (1968): 30–39.

Jackson, Joseph. "Washington in Philadelphia," *Pennsylvania Magazine of History and Biography* 56 (1932): 110–55.

"James Madison's Attitude toward the Negro," *Journal of Negro History* 6 (1921): 74–112.

Ketcham, Ralph. *James Madison: A Biography.* New York, 1971.

——. *Presidents above Party: The First American Presidency, 1789–1829.* Chapel Hill, N.C., 1984.

——. "Two New Letters," *Manuscripts* 11 (1959): 54–60.

Koch, Adrienne. *Jefferson and Madison: The Great Collaboration.* New York, 1950.

Koch, Adrienne, and Harry Ammon. "The Virginia and Kentucky Resolutions: An Episode in Jefferson's and Madison's Defense of Civil Liberties," *William and Mary Quarterly,* 3d ser., 5 (1948): 145–76.

Kohn, Richard H. *Eagle and Sword: The Federalists and the Creation of the Military Establishment in America, 1783–1802.* New York, 1975.

——. "The Inside History of the Newburgh Conspiracy: America and the Coup d'Etat," *William and Mary Quarterly,* 3d ser., 27 (1970): 187–220.

——. "The Washington Administration's Decision to Crush the Whiskey Rebellion," *Journal of American History* 59 (1972): 567–84.

Kurtz, Stephen. *The Presidency of John Adams: The Collapse of Federalism, 1795–1800.* Philadelphia, 1957.

Lamb, Martha J. "The Inauguration of Washington, 1789," *Magazine of American History* 20 (1888): 433–60.

Leary, Lewis. *That Rascal Freneau: A Study in Literary Failure.* New Brunswick, N.J., 1941.

Leibiger, Stuart. "James Madison and Amendments to the Constitution, 1787–1789: 'Parchment Barriers,'" *Journal of Southern History* 59 (1993): 441–68.

Littlefield, Douglas R. "Eighteenth Century Plans to Clear the Potomac River: Technology, Expertise, and Labor in a Developing Nation," *Virginia Magazine of History and Biography* 93 (1985): 291–322.

Longmore, Paul. *The Invention of George Washington.* Berkeley, Calif., 1988.

Lossing, Benjamin. *George Washington's Mount Vernon.* New York, 1870.

McCoy, Drew R. *The Elusive Republic: Political Economy in Jeffersonian America.* Chapel Hill, N.C., 1980.

——. *The Last of The Fathers: James Madison and the Republican Legacy.* Cambridge, 1989.

——. "The Virginia Port Bill of 1784," *Virginia Magazine of History and Biography* 83 (1975): 288–303.

McDonald, Forrest. *The Presidency of George Washington.* Lawrence, Kans., 1974.

Malone, Dumas. *Jefferson and His Time.* 6 vols. Boston, 1948–81.

Markowitz, Arthur. "Washington's Farewell and the Historians: A Critical Review," *Pennsylvania Magazine of History and Biography* 94 (1970): 173–91.

Marsh, Philip. *Freneau's Published Prose: A Bibliography.* Metuchen, N.J., 1970.

——. "The Jefferson-Madison Vacation," *Pennsylvania Magazine of History and Biography* 71 (1947): 70–72.

——. "Philip Freneau and James Madison," *Proceedings of the New Jersey Historical Society* 65 (1947): 189–94.

Marshall, John. *George Washington.* 5 vols. Rept. New York, 1980.

Matthews, Richard K. *If Men Were Angels: James Madison and the Heartless Empire of Reason.* Lawrence, Kans., 1995.

Mayer, Henry. *A Son of Thunder: Patrick Henry and the American Republic.* New York, 1986.

Meade, Robert. *Patrick Henry: Practical Revolutionary.* New York, 1969.

Miller, John C. *The Federalist Era, 1789–1801.* New York, 1960.

Moore, Virginia. *The Madisons: A Biography.* New York, 1979.

Morris, Richard B. *The Forging of the Union, 1781–1789.* New York, 1987.

——. "The Mount Vernon Conference: First Step toward Philadelphia," *This Constitution* 6 (1985): 38–40.

Nardi, Peter M., ed. *Men's Friendships.* Newbury Park, Calif., 1992.

Nelson, John R., Jr. *Liberty and Property: Political Economy and Policymaking in the New Nation, 1789–1812.* Baltimore, 1987.

Nelson, Paul D. "Horatio Gates at Newburgh, 1783: A Misunderstood Role," *William and Mary Quarterly,* 3d ser., 29 (1972): 143–58.

Netherton, Nan, et al. *Fairfax County, Virginia: A History.* Fairfax, Va., 1978.

Paltsits, Victor Hugo. *Washington's Farewell Address.* New York, 1935.

Pangle, Thomas L., and Lorraine Smith Pangle. *The Learning of Liberty: The Educational Ideas of the American Founders.* Lawrence, Kans., 1993.

Peterson, Merrill. *Adams and Jefferson: A Revolutionary Dialogue.* Athens, Ga., 1976.

——. *Thomas Jefferson and the New Nation.* New York, 1970.

Peterson, Svend. *A Statistical History of the American Presidential Elections.* New York, 1968.

Phelps, Glenn. *George Washington and American Constitutionalism*. Lawrence, Kans., 1993.

Pickell, John. *A New Chapter in the Early Life of Washington in Connection with the Narrative History of the Potomac Company*. New York, 1856.

Rakove, Jack. *The Beginnings of National Politics: An Interpretive History of the Continental Congress*. New York, 1974.

———. *James Madison and the Creation of the American Republic*. Glenview, Ill., 1990.

Randall, Henry S. *The Life of Thomas Jefferson*. 3 vols. New York, 1858.

Reardon, John J. *Edmund Randolph: A Biography*. New York, 1974.

Rice, Philip Morrison. "Internal Improvements in Virginia, 1775–1860." Ph.D. diss., University of North Carolina at Chapel Hill, 1948.

Risjord, Norman K. *Chesapeake Politics, 1781–1800*. New York, 1978.

Rives, William Cabell. *The Life and Times of James Madison*. 3 vols. Boston, 1859–68.

Rose, Ruth. "Dr. David Stuart: Friend and Confidant of George Washington," *Northern Virginia Heritage* 10 (1988): 9–14.

Royster, Charles. *Light Horse Harry Lee and the Legacy of the American Revolution*. Cambridge, 1981.

———. *A Revolutionary People at War: The Continental Army and American Character, 1775–1783*. Chapel Hill, N.C., 1979.

Rutland, Robert A. *James Madison: The Founding Father*. New York, 1987.

———. *The Ordeal of the Constitution: The Antifederalists and the Ratification Struggle of 1787–1788*. Norman, Okla., 1965.

———, ed. *The James Madison Encyclopedia*. New York, 1995.

Sanderlin, Walter S. *The Great National Project: A History of the Chesapeake and Ohio Canal*. Baltimore, 1946.

Schwartz, Barry. *George Washington: The Making of an American Symbol*. New York, 1987.

Scisco, Louis Dow. "A Site for the 'Federal City': The Original Proprietors and Their Negotiations with Washington," *Records of the Columbia Historical Society of Washington, D.C.*, 1957–59, 123–47.

Sears, Louis Martin. *George Washington and the French Revolution*. Detroit, 1960.

Seele, John. *Beautiful Machine: Rivers and the Republican Plan, 1755–1815*. New York, 1991.

Selby, John. *The Revolution in Virginia, 1775–1783*. Williamsburg, Va., 1988.

Seymour, Charles, Jr. "Houdon's *Washington* at Mount Vernon Re-Examined," *Gazette des Beaux-Arts*, 6th ser., 33 (1948): 137–58.

Sharp, James Roger. *American Politics in the Early Republic: The New Nation in Crisis*. New Haven, 1993.

Sheridan, Eugene R. "The Recall of Edmond Charles Genet," *Diplomatic History* 18 (1994): 463–88.

———. "Thomas Jefferson and the Giles Resolutions," *William and Mary Quarterly*, 3d ser., 49 (1992): 589–608.

Skeen, C. Edward. "The Newburgh Conspiracy Reconsidered," *William and Mary Quarterly*, 3d ser., 31 (1974): 273–98.

Slaughter, Thomas. *The Whiskey Rebellion: Frontier Epilogue to the American Revolution*. New York, 1986.

Smith, Daniel Blake. *Inside the Great House: Planter Family Life in Eighteenth-Century Chesapeake Society.* Ithaca, N.Y., 1980.

Smith, James Morton. *Freedom's Fetters: The Alien and Sedition Acts and American Civil Liberties.* Ithaca, N.Y., 1966.

Stewart, Andrew. "Chesapeake and Ohio Canal," Report No. 228, *Reports of Committees,* 19th Congress, First Session.

Storing, Herbert. *What the Antifederalists Were For.* Chicago, 1981.

Swanstrom, Roy. *The United States Senate, 1787–1801.* Washington, D.C., 1988.

Sweig, Donald."A Capital on the Potomac: A 1789 Broadside and Alexandria's Attempts to Capture the Cherished Prize," *Virginia Magazine of History and Biography* 87 (1979): 74–104.

Sydnor, Charles S. *American Revolutionaries in the Making.* New York, 1965.

Szatmary, David P. *Shays' Rebellion: The Making of an Agrarian Insurrection.* Amherst, Mass., 1980.

Tachau, Mary K. Bonsteel. "George Washington and the Reputation of Edmund Randolph," *Journal of American History* 73 (1986): 15–34.

Thane, Elswyth. *Potomac Squire.* New York, 1963.

Wayland, John W. *The Washingtons and Their Homes.* Staunton, Va., 1944.

White, Leonard D. *The Federalists: A Study in Administrative History.* New York, 1956.

Wills, Garry. *Cincinnatus: George Washington and the Enlightenment.* Garden City, N.J., 1984.

Wood, Gordon. *The Creation of the American Republic, 1776–1787.,* Chapel Hill, N.C., 1969.

Young, James Sterling. *The Washington Community, 1800–1828.* New York, 1966.

INDEX

Italicized page numbers refer to illustrations.
Abbreviations: AH = Alexander Hamilton, TJ = Thomas Jefferson, JM = James Madison, ER = Edmund Randolph, GW = George Washington.

Abbot, W. W., 6
Adams, John, 106, 111, 112, 144, 159, 165, 180, 212, 220, 225, 243, 244, 254, 260; collaboration with TJ, 1, 223; as vice president, 103, 109; and titles controversy, 118–19; inauguration of as president, 216–17; JM on, 217, 219–20; and deteriorating relations with France, 217–18
Adet, Pierre August, 212
Agriculture, 182–83, 254
Alexandria, Va., 13, 35, 40, 41, 94, 105, 132, 136, 144–47
Alien Act, 218–19
American Daily Advertiser, 212
Ames, Fisher, 108, 131, 175, 192, 204, 258
Anacostia River, 132, 146
Anglican Church, 48
Annapolis, Md., 31–32, 42–43, 59
Annapolis Convention, 50, 59–61, 64, 142
Anthony, Katherine, 185
Antifederalism, 86–100, 119, 120–22, 135, 141, 157, 159, 206
Appalachian Mountains, 187, 191
Apportionment Bill, 156, 159, 167, 250
Armstrong, John, Jr., 27
Arnold, Benedict, 21

Articles of Confederation, 20, 22, 30, 50, 51, 60, 64–66, 72, 87, 95
Asgill, Charles, 21–22
Aurora General Advertiser, 219

Bache, Benjamin Franklin, 219–20
Ballendine, John, 38
Balmain, Alexander, 185
Baltimore, Md., 38, 42–43, 101, 105, 141
Baltimore and Ohio Railroad, 47
Bank of England, 134
Bank of the United States, 133–38, 166, 247
Banning, Lance, 2, 3, 9, 19–20, 73, 77, 237, 241, 247
Baptists, 122
Barbados, 4
Bastille, 169
Bath, Va., 44
Beaumarchais, Pierre Augustin Caron de, 23
Belle Grove, 255
Belmont (Philadelphia), 83
Berkeley County, Va., 184
Biddle, Edward, 234
Blackburn, Thomas, 42–43
Blair, John, 62, 70, 74, 77, 78, 80, 93, 237
Blair John D., 222
Blount, Thomas, 205–7
Boller, Paul F., Jr., 121
Boston, Mass., 176, 201, 258
Botetourt County, Va., 47
Bott, Elizabeth, 234
Boudinot, Elias, 106